Commentary on Thomas Aquinas's Virtue Ethics

Although St. Thomas Aquinas famously claimed that his *Summa Theologiae* was written for "beginners," contemporary readers find it unusually difficult. Now, amid a surge of interest in virtue ethics, J. Budziszewski clarifies and analyzes the text's challenging arguments about the moral, intellectual, and spiritual virtues, with a spotlight on the virtue of justice. In what might be the first contemporary commentary on Aquinas's virtue ethics, he juxtaposes the original text with paraphrase and detailed discussion, guiding us through its complex arguments and classical rhetorical figures. Keeping an eye on contemporary philosophical issues, he contextualizes one of the greatest virtue theorists in history and brings Aquinas into the interdisciplinary debates of today. His brisk and clear style illuminates the most crucial of Aquinas's writings on moral character and guides us through the labyrinth of this difficult but pivotal work.

J. Budziszewski is Professor of Government and Philosophy at the University of Texas at Austin, where he also teaches courses in religious studies and in the law school. His work includes numerous books as well as a blog, *The Underground Thomist*. Budziszewski thinks and writes chiefly about classical natural law, conscience and self-deception, moral character, family and sexuality, religion and public life, authentic versus counterfeit toleration and liberty, and the state of our common culture.

Commentary on Thomas Aquinas's Virtue Ethics

J. BUDZISZEWSKI

University of Texas at Austin

CAMBRIDGE
UNIVERSITY PRESS

CAMBRIDGE
UNIVERSITY PRESS

University Printing House, Cambridge CB2 8BS, United Kingdom

One Liberty Plaza, 20th Floor, New York, NY 10006, USA

477 Williamstown Road, Port Melbourne, VIC 3207, Australia

4843/24, 2nd Floor, Ansari Road, Daryaganj, Delhi - 110002, India

79 Anson Road, #06-04/06, Singapore 079906

Cambridge University Press is part of the University of Cambridge.

It furthers the University's mission by disseminating knowledge in the pursuit of education, learning, and research at the highest international levels of excellence.

www.cambridge.org
Information on this title: www.cambridge.org/9781107165786
DOI: 10.1017/9781316694138

First published 2017

A catalogue record for this publication is available from the British Library.

ISBN 978-1-107-16578-6 Hardback

Analytical Contents

St. Thomas investigates whether the traditional understanding of virtue,
derived from St. Augustine of Hippo via Peter Lombard, is correct. He
considers six possible objections, concerning whether virtue is a good
quality, whether it is a quality of the mind, whether it enables us to live
rightly, whether it is possible for it to be employed badly, and whether it is
brought about in us by God. To solve the problem, he works out the formal,
material, final, and efficient causes of virtue.

Can a person who lacks intellectual virtue still possess moral virtues such as
fortitude, temperance, and justice? For a variety of reasons, at first it seems
that this is possible. For example, common observation suggests that some
people who do not reason well are morally virtuous. However, Thomas
shows that although not all intellectual virtues are necessary for moral
virtue, the intellectual virtues of prudence and understanding are necessary
for moral virtue.

The previous chapter asked whether a person who lacks intellectual
virtue can still possess moral virtue; conversely, this chapter asks whether
a person who lacks moral virtue can still possess intellectual virtue.

St. Thomas considers a variety of reasons for thinking that this may be possible, having to do with moral development, with the similarity between moral deeds and craftsmanship, and with the common observation that some people who lack moral virtue seem to advise themselves well. He concludes, however, that although other intellectual virtues can exist without moral virtue, the intellectual virtue of prudence does require moral virtue. Taking this chapter together with the previous one, we see that neither complete moral virtue nor complete intellectual virtue is possible without the other.

According to a widely held view, all moral virtues pivot or depend on four pivotal or paramount virtues – prudence, justice, temperance, and fortitude – sometimes called "cardinal" virtues after the Latin word for a hinge. If true, this fact would provide a much more powerful way of understanding the virtues than had been offered by the influential philosopher Aristotle – who, after helpfully suggesting that each moral virtue is a "mean" between opposite extremes, had presented a diffuse list of twelve "means" without explaining why he listed just these twelve and not others. Responding to various objections, St. Thomas presents compelling reasons for thinking that the four virtues called cardinal surpass the other moral virtues and are, in a certain sense, their heads. The first is prudence, or practical wisdom, the bridge between the moral and intellectual virtues, which brings the power of moral reasoning to its full and proper development. The other three are fortitude, or courage; temperance, or restraint; and justice, or fairness. All of the other "acquired" virtues are associated in some way with these four (as we will find later that all of the "infused" virtues are associated in some way with faith, hope, and charity).

Some have suggested that although it is correct to think that all of the acquired moral virtues depend on a smaller number of cardinal virtues, nevertheless certain other virtues besides prudence, fortitude, temperance, and justice should also be called cardinal. Magnanimity has been proposed because it spurs great acts of every virtue; humility, because it gives firmness to every virtue; and patience, because it is through patience that the acts of every other virtue are fully carried out. Without in any way disparaging magnanimity, humility, or patience, St. Thomas argues that the fourfold list of cardinal virtues should be left as it stands. Not only are these four concerned with matters of paramount importance, but every other moral virtue turns out to depend on them. In particular, magnanimity and patience turn out to be aspects of the cardinal virtue of fortitude, and humility turns out to be an aspect of the cardinal virtue of temperance.

Besides the four cardinal virtues, the classical tradition had identified three
"theological" or spiritual virtues: Faith, hope, and charity or love. The
suggestion that we may need spiritual virtues over and above the ordinary
qualities of good character is ridiculous to the secular sort of mind. Do such
virtues exist? In one sense, it may seem obvious that they exist, but care
is needed because the popular culture gives each of these terms different
meanings than what the tradition intends. Confidence that my friend will
not betray me is not the spiritual virtue of faith; optimism that I will get a
raise in salary is not the spiritual virtue of hope; giving money to worthy
causes is not the definition of charity; and even though the merely natural
loves are good, the love called charity is different from the love of a man
and a woman, the love of a mother for her child, or the love of two friends.
St. Thomas shows that in their correct meanings, the three theological
virtues are genuine, and that they bear the same relation to the virtues
infused by Divine grace that the cardinal virtues bear to the virtues acquired
by human effort.

Is virtue implanted in the constitution of human beings – does it in some
sense belong to us just because we possess a human nature? The query
sounds very modern: Many secular people believe that we are naturally
good, and corrupted only by some disorder of social life which might
perhaps be corrected by social engineering. According to Christianity, the
human condition is much more complex, for although we were endowed by
the Creator with a good nature, this good gift is presently in bad condition.
A further complication is that although the term "natural" is sometimes
used for things we do without having to learn them, it is also used for things
we must learn in order to reach our full and appropriate development. In
the former sense, it is "natural" to breathe; in the latter sense, it is "natural"
to make friends. St. Thomas responds to the query not just theologically but
also philosophically, considering what it means for something to be true of
us "by nature," reviewing the history of the problem from the pre-Socratic
philosopher Anaxagoras to his own time, and finally disentangling the
senses in which virtue can and cannot be called natural to human beings.

According to the tradition, the "acquired" virtues are brought about in us
by practicing the acts which correspond to them until they become habitual.
Is this true? Up to this point in his discussion, St. Thomas has assumed the
habituation hypothesis to be correct; in the present chapter, he scrutinizes
it to find out whether it really is. He takes up and discusses various reasons
for thinking that it is false, for example the theological argument that

apart from Divine grace humans can do nothing to become virtuous, and the metaphysical argument that a cause (in this case repeated acts) cannot be more perfect than its effect (in this case complete virtue). His solution depends on a distinction between virtues which are directed to the good as measured by the rule of human reason, and virtues which are directed to the good as measured by the Divine law. The former can be brought about by habituation; the latter can be brought about in us only by the work of God Himself.

Can we pick and choose among the virtues – is it possible to possess some of them without the others? The classical tradition supposes that this is impossible; if you are defective in any virtue, then to some degree you will be defective in each of them, so that if you are serious about cultivating any of them you must cultivate all of them. Yet today, we often view the virtues as disconnected, saying things like "He may be a crooked businessman, but he's good to his mom," "Even a bad man can be a good statesman," and "There is honor among thieves." St. Thomas takes very seriously the reasons for thinking that the classical view is false, for example, the everyday observation that a man may perform the acts of one virtue without performing the acts of another. Ultimately, however, Thomas defeats the objections by distinguishing between fully developed virtues, and merely incipient or incomplete virtues. The former really are mutually dependent and interconnected; the latter are not. He shows that this conclusion can be reached in two different ways, depending on the precise method adopted for distinguishing among the cardinal virtues.

Capital vices are those from which other vices arise; they are like leaders and directors of all the other vices. Just as we must practice all of the virtues to be fully developed in any of them, so we cannot let one vice into the house without opening the door wide to its brothers. The question in this chapter, however, is not so much whether certain vices should be considered capital, but which vices they are. The tradition had viewed seven vices as capital: Vainglory, envy, anger, sloth, covetousness, gluttony, and lust. Various reasons can be offered for thinking either that this list is defective, some obvious (for example that since there are four cardinal virtues, there must be four capital vices), some not so obvious (for example that although gluttony and lust concern pleasure, and sloth and envy concern sadness, the list should also include vices pertaining to the other chief passions, hope and fear). By means of a subtle and multifaceted analysis of the psychology of sin as a distortion of the natural desire for happiness, St. Thomas defends the traditional enumeration, comparing the seven capital vices to seven generals with pride as their queen.

Is mercy a virtue? At first it may seem that it is not. In the first place, pity,
like anger, can impede deliberation. In the second place, the virtue of justice
involves punishment, but mercy involves remission of punishment. Besides,
even if the acts of mercy are meritorious, it might be argued that they are
merely effects of another virtue, so that mercy is not a virtue in itself. In
careful response to these objections, St. Thomas shows that the virtue of
mercy is as genuine as the virtue of justice. Although unregulated passion
may indeed impede deliberation, the virtue of mercy is neither unregulated
nor a passion. Moreover, far from being an impediment to justice, mercy
may actually serve the purposes of justice, provided that certain conditions
are met. Finally, mercy is not merely an effect of charity, but a distinct virtue
subordinate to charity, for it concerns a particular mode in which the acts of
charity are carried out.

According to a long tradition, justice is "a constant and perpetual will to
give to each person his right." In our day the expression "right" is most
often used to signify a liberty to do something, for example the right
to bear arms, to speak freely, or to worship according to conscience. In
the classical definition of justice, however, the term is used in a much
broader sense: A person's "right" is whatever is his, whatever he deserves,
whatever is properly due to him. The present chapter's query is whether
this time-honored definition suitably expresses the essence of justice. St.
Thomas considers six objections, each of which targets some element in
the definition. Objections 1 and 2 deny that justice "a will"; Objection
3 denies that it is "perpetual"; Objection 4, that it is both "perpetual"
and "constant," as though these words signified different qualities; and
Objections 5 and 6, that it "renders to each one his right."

Before I can render someone what is due to him, I have to know what is
due to him. So the act of giving him his right seems to presuppose a prior
act of judging what his right is. Then is judgment itself the characteristic act
of justice? So it would seem, yet this answer lays us open to difficulties. For
example, if judging is an act of the intellect, wouldn't it be the characteristic
act of an intellectual rather than a moral virtue? And isn't some kind of
judgment required by every virtue, not only by judgment? On the other
hand, judgment seems to be what judges do. Where then does this leave the
rest of us – is no one just but the judge? To complicate matters still further,

it might even be said that judgment belongs neither to the ordinary person nor to the judge, for St. Paul says that judgment, in some sense, is the act of "the spiritual man." We see then that what might at first appear to be a fatuous question – "Is judgment the characteristic act of justice?" – turns out to be a stumper. St. Thomas unravels the difficulties.

Human law appoints certain persons judges, but is it really right for any mere human to stand in judgment? The Objectors think that the answer should be "No"; in their view, human judgment is condemned both by natural and Divine law. In the relativistic ambiance of our own times as well, "judgmentalism" has been judged and found wanting. Yet there is a certain difficulty with antijudgmentalism, for if no one may judge others, then how is it that we may deliver an unfavorable judgment upon those who do judge others? Could it be that we have passed judgment upon judgment too quickly – or perhaps that only certain kinds of judgment are illicit? If so, which kinds? St. Thomas investigates the various senses in which human beings may and may not "judge."

The act of judgment is the means by which justice is actualized, and justice is in turn connected with all the rest of the virtues. Normally, we should do as the written law directs, but earlier in the *Summa* St. Thomas has considered exceptions: (1) Under certain conditions custom can abolish written law. (2) Under certain conditions one may disobey so-called unjust laws, and may even be obligated to disobey them. (3) When cases arise which the written law was not intended to cover, those who have the authority to make the law may also suspend it. (4) In emergencies, when such cases arise but there is no time to consult authority, the citizens themselves may set aside the words of the law and follow its intention instead. Here, though, St. Thomas is not thinking of either lawmakers or ordinary citizens. Must judges follow the written law? And must they do as its very words direct, or may they sometimes set aside the words and follow its intention instead? This inquiry is not just about constitutional rules or judicial role definitions. Taken in its broadest sense it concerns how such matters are related to human moral character.

Is justice destroyed when judgment is usurped – when a person is judged by someone who has no public authority to do so? Usurpation of judgment is judging a case without jurisdiction, seizing the power of judgment from the person to whom it belongs. However, in the present chapter St. Thomas is not asking whether it is unjust for a judge to make the sorts of judgments which properly belong to, say, the legislature; he has already established that this is wrong, because the judge must render judgment according to the law.

Rather he is asking whether it is unjust for someone else to make the sorts of judgments which properly belong to the judge himself. The usurper, the "someone else," might be another judge who has no jurisdiction in the case, or it might be someone who is not a judge at all. St. Thomas defends the traditional view that the usurpation of judgment is a violation of justice – that judging without proper jurisdiction always destroys justice – even if the usurper renders the correct judgment.

Although the many aspects of justice may be called "parts" of justice, they are not all "parts" in the same sense. The present chapter is about the "potential" parts of justice, meaning the secondary virtues which in some way resemble justice or are associated with it. Before St. Thomas, the thinkers who had investigated the potential parts of justice had enumerated them in a bewildering variety of ways. In the present Article, he defends the sixfold classification of Marcus Tullius Cicero against the sevenfold classification of Macrobius, the ninefold classification of Pseudo-Andronicus, the fivefold classification of "certain others" whom he does not name, and a single suggestion drawn from Aristotle. Characteristically, he does not simply discard the thoughts of all these others; whenever he comes upon a worthy insight, he works out what the writer was getting at and finds room for it in a subtler scheme to which the present chapter is merely an introduction.

The notion of some people that virtue ethics is a way of doing ethics without rules would strike St. Thomas as very strange, for the acts to which the virtues predispose us are things which we ought to do; he always connects virtues with precepts, dispositions of character with authoritative rules. In the present chapter he is concerned with the famous set of authoritative rules known as the Ten Commandments. Although they are part of Divine law, Thomas thinks they are also precepts of natural law, upheld by reason. The great question of the chapter – whether they are precepts of justice – should be taken not in the sense "Do they have anything to do with justice?" but in the sense "Is justice is their main concern?" For according to the classical tradition, the Divine law addresses all of the virtues, not only justice – yet in some sense the Ten Commandments specialize in the virtue of justice. What Thomas investigates is whether this view of their special concern is correct.

Acknowledgments

I would like to thank D. H. Williams, with whom I corresponded about a sentence in his translation of St. Hilary of Poitiers's *Commentary on Matthew*, and my friend Arlen Nydam, for chatting with me about other Latin matters. External reviewers generously gave time and insight to the manuscript, and the University of Texas granted me the boon of a semester free of teaching for its completion. I am grateful to students for questions, to friends for solidarity, and to students who became friends for double blessing. To God, I owe life in the two greatest senses; to my parents, in two more; to my wife, Sandra, in two more still. For whatever is wrong in these pages, the fault is mine alone.

Ante Studium
(Before Study)

Ineffable Creator, Who out of the treasures of Your wisdom appointed treble hierarchies of Angels and set them in admirable order high above the heavens; Who disposed the diverse portions of the universe in such elegant array; Who are the true Fountain of Light and Wisdom, and the all-exceeding Source: Be pleased to cast a beam of Your radiance upon the darkness of my mind, and dispel from me the double darkness of sin and ignorance in which I have been born.

You Who make eloquent the tongues of little children, instruct my tongue and pour upon my lips the grace of Your benediction. Grant me penetration to understand, capacity to retain, method and ease in learning, subtlety in interpretation, and copious grace of expression.

Order the beginning, direct the progress, and perfect the conclusion of my work, You Who are true God and Man, Who live and reign forever and ever. Amen.

– Thomas Aquinas

Introduction

The wise say that the best thing is not to read many books but to read a few great books truly well. This is a bit overstated, for a number of books are worth reading. But the best reason for reading them is to develop the discernment by which we can recognize the few great ones when at last we come upon them.

One of these few is the *Summa Theologiae* of Thomas Aquinas, and one of the great themes of that work is virtue, or character – moral, intellectual, and spiritual. This volume is a commentary on selected texts from the theory of virtue therein presented. Although the commentary is entirely self-contained, it also complements and extends my previous *Commentary on Thomas Aquinas's Treatise on Law*, along with its online partner volume, the *Companion to the Commentary*,[1] for one of the great questions in virtue ethics is how moral virtues are related to laws, moral rules, and the activity of judging.

THE BACKGROUND AND SIGNIFICANCE OF THE TOPIC

The topic of virtue has always been central to the aspiration of the humane studies to investigate what it means to live well. During the last generation, however, questions about character have taken fire. Spurred by a variety of thinkers, including G. E. M. Anscombe,[2] Peter Geach,[3] and Alasdair

---

[1] Both books published by Cambridge University Press in 2014. Elsewhere in this book, I refer to them by their titles alone. The *Companion* is available online at no cost, both at the Resources link of the Cambridge catalog page for the *Commentary* and at my website, www
.undergroundthomist.org/sites/default/files/related-documents/Companion-to-the-
Commentary-FINAL.pdf.

[2] G. E. M. Anscombe, "Modern Moral Philosophy," *Philosophy* 33, no. 124 (1958): 1–16. This work is widely credited with having originated the renaissance of virtue ethics.

[3] Peter Geach, *The Virtues* (Cambridge: Cambridge University Press, 1977).

MacIntyre,[4] inquiry into the virtues has surged in a variety of fields – at first primarily in philosophy and theology but more recently in law, social science, and across the disciplines. To mention but a single example, one of the new approaches in jurisprudence focuses on the qualities of moral and intellectual character necessary to be a good judge.[5] I call this approach new because it is new for us, but it actually revives a very old approach, taken, for example, by the authors of the US Constitution.

Although some writers turn to the topic of moral character as though no one had ever done so before, the rise of interest in the virtues has naturally generated an increase of interest in Thomas Aquinas, one of the greatest – I would say the greatest – theorists of virtue in history. However, no contemporary commentary on Aquinas's virtue ethics exists, a problem which is acute because Aquinas is an exceptionally difficult thinker. Even in his *Summa Theologiae*, which he famously said was for "beginners," the style, terminology, philosophical and theological background, and mode of argument are opaque to most persons today. This is true not only for students and general readers but even for most scholars trained in the modern fashion. Without the assistance of a commentary that illuminates the text not only in the context of Aquinas's own theoretical milieu but with a sensitivity to contemporary philosophy and social science, many of the most interesting of the themes and questions of this great body of work are overlooked or else grossly misunderstood.

WHY NOT JUST BE VIRTUE PLURALISTS?

Unless we hope eventually to find the true answers to our questions, there is no point in asking about virtue or anything else. I expect this claim to meet criticism.[6] We are told that it is illiberal to seek the "true" answers to fundamental questions because an infinity of reasonable views can be held about them, all of them conflicting. There are too many philosophies, too many religions, too many sacred texts. Often this Babel of discordant voices is presented as something new. It isn't. After all, the Tower of Babel is a very ancient tale, and just as many voices, sects, and doctrines quarreled in premodern times as today. Nor were the thinkers of those times deaf to all the racket. St. Augustine of Hippo contended with Gnostics, Platonists, Jews, Stoics, and Epicureans, among others; Maimonides wrote a *Guide for the Perplexed*; Thomas Aquinas cast his *Summa Theologiae* in the form of disputed questions. Babel is not a modern revolution but the enduring condition of the fallen human race.

---

[4] Alasdair MacIntyre, *After Virtue*, 2nd ed. (Notre Dame, IN: University of Notre Dame Press, 1984).
[5] See, e.g., Timothy Cantu, "Virtue Jurisprudence and the American Constitution," *Notre Dame Law Review* 88, no. 3 (2013): 1521–1542.
[6] The next few paragraphs are adapted from J. Budziszewski, *The Revenge of Conscience: Politics and the Fall of Man*, rev. ed. (Eugene, OR: Wipf and Stock, 2010).

What is really new is the *manner* in which some of us respond to Babel. The classical way, which is St. Thomas's way, is both *apologetical* and *noetic*. I mean by calling it apologetical, after the Greek word for a speech in defense, that he stakes a claim and defends it; he makes some one voice in the Babel his own, then takes on his opponents by arguing the issues on their merits. And I mean by calling his way noetic, after the Greek word for knowledge or understanding, that his arguments appeal to shared knowledge rather than shared ignorance. For a classical reasoner does not take the Babel around him quite at face value. If I seem completely ignorant of a basic moral precept, he will say that the reason is less likely to be that I really do not know it than that I am trying not to think about it. Moreover, he will regard an age like ours as exceptional even for this broken world. Before too long, any culture in deep denial must come to its senses or collapse, for the consequences of denying first principles are cumulative and inescapable.

By contrast, a fashionable contemporary way of responding to Babel is both *anti-noetic* and *anti-apologetical*. The virtue pluralists – so we may call them – are anti-noetic because they do take the Babel around them at face value, or at least they claim to. Their arguments appeal to shared ignorance rather than shared knowledge. So far as we know, they say, an enormous variety of religions and philosophies are equally in the dark and equally in the light. Although they may well agree that our age is exceptional rather than typical, they see this fact not as an omen of corruption but as a portent of an impending forward leap – a sign that our old philosophies have exhausted themselves and we need to try something new.

What is the something new? This is where being anti-apologetical comes in. The virtue pluralist denies the need to make one voice in the Babel his own and denies that he is doing so; he refuses to stake out a position, then argue its claims on their merits. By adopting a posture of neutrality among competing goals and aspirations, of equal concern and respect for every view of virtue, he tries to escape the futility of interminable arguments and carve out a new moral sphere in which people of every point of view can get along: sodomists with socialists, pickpockets with Platonists, hedonists with Hasidim. Thus, for example, he does not object to St. Thomas's doctrine of the virtues as a *mistaken* point of view; disputing its claims would be too crude. Rather, he objects to it as a *point of view* – just one more of the pullulating things down there among the Platonists and pickpockets. Virtue pluralism floats chastely above them, out-topping knowledge by the sheer determination not to need to know.[7]

Alas for the virtue pluralist, this doesn't work. Virtue pluralism does not really float above all of the contrasting views of the virtues. It only seems to. For

---

[7] The most influential example of this sort of thinking is John Rawls, *Political Liberalism* (New York: Columbia University Press, 1993, 2005).

example, is there a way to have equal concern and respect for the opinions of the virtues held by both the terrorist and the persons he aims to blow up? Either he gets his way, or they get away. Is there a way to have equal concern and respect for both monogamous and polygamous marriages? Legal arrangements that allow both monogamy and polygamy are in fact polygamous. Rather than floating above the contrasting views about virtue and tolerating them all, virtue pluralism smuggles a particular view of the virtues into law and popular culture without having to argue for it – *just by pretending that it is not a point of view*. This clever authoritarianism rules with a rod of iron, enforcing its judgments by complaining about judgmentalism.

I have embarked on this book in the conviction that virtue pluralism is a sham and that the classical way of investigating the virtues is correct. The riot of unreasonable views about the virtues does not require us to suspend judgment; rather, the pretense of suspending judgment makes the riot of unreasonable views seem reasonable. The reasonable response to the riot is not to suspend judgment but to learn to judge more reasonably. We must not be ashamed of seeking the truth of things, and we should seek it with all our minds and hearts.

We will tolerate those who disagree with us – I do not of course mean terrorists or rapists – but we will do so not because of what we don't know but because of what we do know. For it is with good reason that we believe that God, by His nature, does not desire an unwilling obedience and that faith, by its nature, cannot be coerced.

THE PRINCIPLE OF SELECTION

To include *all* of St. Thomas's writings about virtue in the commentary would be impossible, because even without commentary, they take up hundreds of pages; with commentary, they would take up thousands. However, there is no need to include everything, for with proper commentary on the most essential texts, the reader is able to navigate the deep waters of the omitted writings by himself. For this reason, I am focusing on the celebrated *Summa Theologiae* and have selected just eighteen of its "Articles"[8] or chapters about virtue for inclusion and discussion in this book.

Some of these eighteen I have chosen because they lay the theoretical groundwork for understanding moral character. These are considered in Part I. With the exception of the Article on the capital vices, which is taken from the *Treatise on Vice and Sin*, all of these are from the section of the *Summa* called the *Treatise on Habits*. Others I have chosen because they apply and extend the analysis of virtue in general to the specific virtue of justice, especially in relation to law. These are considered in Part II. With the exception of the Article

---

[8] From Latin *articulus*, meaning "part," originally the part of a limb between the joints.

on mercy, which is taken from the *Treatise on Charity*, all of these are from the *Treatise on Justice*.

Where helpful and appropriate, I have also referred to other parts of the *Summa*, to other works of St. Thomas, to works mentioned by St. Thomas, to various other works, and to my two previous books on the *Treatise on Law*.

HOW THIS COMMENTARY IS COMPOSED

One cannot carefully read Thomas Aquinas without being changed, and one must be in very sorry shape for this change to be for anything but the better. Although he is a difficult writer, I do not think one must be an expert to study him. In fact, sometimes the experts make him still harder. As one scholar remarks, "his commentators will readily obscure his meaning, in explaining some point of their own; for true illumination, we must go to the master. Fortunately, we still have his works to explain what his commentators are driving at! It is quite a relief to return to him after cutting our way through their entanglements."[9]

I do not want to be that obscuring kind of expert, and that is one of the reasons I have written this commentary as I have – in readily the classical, line-by-line format in which one can *always* go back to the master, indeed, in which his words cannot be avoided. All of his text is there. Even when lengthy, my remarks are strictly subordinate, for each of my own words is chained to his.

At the opening of each Article, I begin with an English version of the text itself, using the celebrated Blackfriars translation, which is in the public domain and is considered the gold standard. In a parallel column, I provide a paraphrase of the text, which renders the argument more readable but is composed with careful attention to the meaning of the Latin original. After the paraphrase, I offer line-by-line (in a few cases, even phrase-by-phrase) analysis, which takes up difficulties as they arise and goes far beyond the paraphrase. My intention is to make the arguments accessible and cogent to scholars, to students, and even to serious general readers.

In a few conspicuous cases, when I think the Blackfriars translation is misleading, I call attention to the fact. In most cases, though, my small emendations are silent. For example, the Blackfriars translation renders the words of 1 Corinthians 2:15 in the Vulgate, *diffunditur in cordibus nostris*, as "poured forth in our hearts," which follows the Douay-Rheims version (DRA), but I have preferred "diffused in our hearts," which is more literal. On the other hand, sometimes my paraphrase is very free; I may even add to the text or re-arrange it. This sort of thing is unacceptable in a translation but welcome in a paraphrase, and since the book provides both paraphrase and translation, the

---

[9] A. G. Sertillanges, *Thomas Aquinas* (Manchester, NH: Sophia Institute Press, 1910, 2011), Chapter 7.

reader may enjoy the benefits of both. A reviewer of my previous commentary suggested adding yet another parallel column, showing the original Latin. I would love to. However, this would add significantly to the length and cost of the book without a sufficient benefit, since the Latin text is readily available online.[10]

This may be a suitable place to insert my standard disclaimer. Where pronouns are concerned, I generally follow the traditional English convention – the one everyone followed, before politically motivated linguistic bullying became fashionable – according to which such terms as "he" and "him" are already "inclusive." Unless the context clearly indicates the masculine, they have always been used to refer to a person of either sex. Readers who choose differently may write differently; I ask only that they extend the same courtesy to me. In the meantime, since my language includes masculine, feminine, neuter, and inclusive pronouns, any rational being who feels excluded has only him-, her-, or itself to blame.

Some may think I do not spend enough time quarreling with critics of St. Thomas. My conviction is that before we enter these quarrels, we had better make sure we understand him. If we do understand him, many of the criticisms fall away like dead leaves. It is not that an intelligent person cannot disagree with the Angelic Doctor. Not even those who work in his tradition agree with him about everything. But the first step in identifying a real disagreement is to take a thinker seriously enough to be persuaded if he is, in fact, correct.

HOW ST. THOMAS WRITES

Readers encountering St. Thomas for the first time – sometimes the second and the third times – are likely to meet obstacles of three kinds. First is the genre in which the *Summa* is written; second is its rhetorical figures; and finally is its attitude and style.

The literary genre in which the *Summa* is composed is the formal disputation, which resembles a debate with a built-in review of the literature. Disputation is an extremely concise way of presenting and analyzing the state of a question that is under consideration. It puts all of the competing views in the clearest possible confrontation, so that one can pull up one's sleeves and solve the problem. The same format is always followed: first is the *utrum*, the "whether," always in the form of a yes-or-no question, usually one to which the traditional answer is yes. In second place are the principal objections to a "Yes" answer, set forth in a list. These might also be called the difficulties. Third comes the *sed contra*, the "on the contrary" or "on the other hand," a restatement of the traditional view. Fourth is the *respondeo*, or "I answer that," also called the *solutio*, or solution, expressing the author's own view. Finally,

---

[10] For example, at www.corpusthomisticum.org/iopera.html.

the author makes use of the solution to reply to the objections, resolving each difficulty in turn.

At first it seems that St. Thomas's style is plain and unornamented. Actually this impression is mistaken, for he uses quite a few figures of speech. However, he does not always use the *same ones* we do – his rhetorical profile is more classical than modern. For example, he makes less use of metaphor, which is one of our own favorite figures. On the other hand, he makes far greater use of metonymy, the figure in which a part of something stands for the whole thing, a figure we use so seldom that we often fail to recognize it when we meet it. This sort of failure can be deadly to understanding, not only concerning his own works but concerning a great deal of ancient, medieval, and biblical literature, for if we take a metonymical statement literally, we will view it as having a much narrower meaning than it really does. For example, when St. Thomas characterizes temperance in terms of withstanding the temptation of sexual pleasure, we will mistakenly think that it has nothing to do with other pleasures, although his real meaning is that this particular pleasure is its greatest and most characteristic challenge. Similarly, when the Decalogue prohibits bearing false witness, we will erroneously suppose that other kinds of lying are permitted, although actually the commandment refers to the most dreadful kind of lying to signify the evil of all lying. We might complain, "Why don't the authors of these texts *tell* when they are using metonymy?" That would be like expecting a contemporary writer to tell us when he is using a simile: we are expected to know. Eventually some enterprising scholar will provide a comprehensive study of St. Thomas's rhetorical figures. In this book I content myself with calling attention to a few of them as we go along.

As to St. Thomas's attitude and style: I venture to say that if other books hamper readers because of their faults, the *Summa* detains them in large part because of its virtues. Perhaps the most common hindrances are St. Thomas's supposed dryness and lack of warmth, his view of intellectual authority, his view of faith and reason, his view of how to study reality, and his apparent failure to consider the objections that some people of our day find most cogent. In the introduction to my previous *Commentary on St. Thomas's Treatise on Law*, I discussed these obstacles at some length, but here, adapting those remarks, I will say only a few words about each.

St. Thomas's prose is like climbing to the top of a great height, which is wonderful and exhilarating if you survive it. Some love the heights; others don't. It may seem dry at the top of the mountain. Thomistic prose is clean, terse, minimalist. It epitomizes Mark Twain's rule "eschew surplusage." It is like the Platonic ideal of concision come to earth. This makes it essential that we read as precisely as St. Thomas writes and take the time to unpack his succinct definitions.

Most people also find his style cold, as we find mathematics cold. But mathematicians don't find their field cold; although they certainly find it austere, they also find it heady, exhilarating, and, above all, beautiful. It sets their pulses pounding, or, if not their pulses, something in the intellect that feels much the same. Why don't the rest of us see what they see, feel what they feel, pound as they pound? Sometimes, perhaps, we do. Many of us can remember moments in our mathematical training when our minds leaped and our hearts caught, because suddenly it all came together and *had to be just that way*. The better we understood the math, the more often we experienced those moments; the more often we experienced them, the greater was our desire to understand. As it is when mathematicians are doing math, so it is when St. Thomas is doing philosophy and theology. If we find his writing cold, we find it so in large part because it is difficult and demanding. There is a warming cure for that: study.

A different sort of obstacle lies in St. Thomas's view of intellectual author- ity – or at least what we take his view of it to be. Often my students are an- noyed by the mere fact that he quotes so much from other thinkers. So little does our style of intellectual training cherish humility – and so thoroughly has it been drummed it into us that the so-called argument from authority is a fallacy – that we tend to confuse humility with fallacy. A popular bumper sticker commands, "Question authority!" There ought to be one that coun- sels, "Choose among authorities wisely." There is nothing wrong with asking a geologist about the chemical composition of limestone, since I can't possibly have firsthand knowledge of everything, and he knows more about limestone than I do. Careful use of authority serves the ends of reason, provided that one has reasonable assurance of the supposed authority's honesty, reliability, and qualifications; the question asked concerns his own field of expertise; one con- siders not just his answers but the reasons he gives for them; and, if authorities differ, one consults the other ones too. This is exactly how St. Thomas does consult authority. Notice too that not all *reference* to authority is *deference* to authority. Although humility requires that we consider what other respected thinkers have thought, it does not require that we accept their reasoning if we find something wrong with it. One must separate the wheat from the chaff, and this is exactly what St. Thomas tries to do. It is just that before discarding the chaff, we had better make sure it is really chaff.

If anything about an author annoys modern readers more than quoting from thinkers of antiquity, it is quoting from the Bible. The notion that faith and reason are opposites has become a reflex with many of us. As one of my un- dergraduates protested recently, "But isn't all this just a religious argument?" At least she recognized that there was an argument! My graduate students are often even more thoroughly indoctrinated in the nostrums of the academy than my undergraduates; only with the greatest difficulty am I able to get some of them to recognize that St. Thomas offers arguments at all. Like the citizens of Oceana, George Orwell's fictional dystopia, they have been conditioned in such a way as to find certain lines of reasoning impossible to recognize as lines of reasoning. Confronted with them, they can only say "fallacy of argument from religious authority," which is their way of saying "crimethink."

This conditioned response has a history. Early in the modern era, many thinkers began to mistrust faith, viewing it as "blind" and an enemy of reason. Their watchword was "reason alone." One of the difficulties of this stance is that reason cannot test its own reliability, any more than soapstone can test its own hardness. Any conclusion *accomplished by reasoning* that the conclusions of reasoning can be trusted would be circular, because it would take for granted the very thing that it was trying to prove. Perhaps it is not surprising that the descendants of these thinkers began to mistrust reason itself, holding that the mind is locked in its own mazes, unable to penetrate external reality. "How can we know anything?" we complain. When it turns to someone like St. Thomas, the complaint becomes especially bitter: "Who is *he* to think he can know anything?"

St. Thomas certainly thinks it is *possible* for the mind to become locked in its own mazes. This is a permanent liability of our fallen state. Yet he takes an extraordinarily high view of the power of both reason and Christian faith to illuminate reality, and he views them not as enemies but as friends. To be sure, he does not think they are the same thing. Although there may be rational grounds for trust in God, and rational grounds for believing that biblical revelation about God is authentic (and he thinks that there are), one must still take that step of believing. Obviously, my reasons are not the same as trust; faith surpasses reason. Even so, they are reasons *for* trust; though faith surpasses reason, it is not irrational. In fact, not only does reason come to the cleansing aid of faith but also faith enables reason to reach further, to ask better questions, to become in every way more fully what it is meant to be.

The final obstacle is that moderns tend to view St. Thomas's approach to the study of reality as naive, unsophisticated, and obsolete, because it sets *things* before *knowledge*. He approaches all kinds of *things* this way – material objects, volitions, qualities, whatever they may be – for no matter what we are studying, we have to know something before we can investigate how we know it. But in the modern era, we reverse this procedure. Before studying what there is to know, we insist on a critique of our ability to know anything at all.

This shift, called the *epistemological turn,* has had a variety of bad results. First comes extreme skepticism, along with contempt for tradition and common sense. Of course even the skeptic has to assume that *something* is true; otherwise, he has no way to decide what to do and how to live – the rational springs of action lose their springiness, and he is left with nothing but his prejudices. In practice, then, extreme skepticism turns into its opposite, extreme conventionalism. For the supposed skeptic doesn't really reject prejudice; he unquestioningly accepts every prejudice that has learned to put on skeptical airs. Another way to say this is that someone who has made the epistemological turn has not really turned aside from the study of *things*. He continues to practice it, but he does so ineptly, because he does not pay attention to what he is doing.

At first it seems modest and reasonable to proceed "critically," to scrutinize the instrument of knowledge before relying on the things that we supposedly know. For how often we have been misled by things that seem obvious but turn out not to be true! A straight stick inserted halfway into water may look bent, but this is a mere trick of the light, produced by the diffraction of light. Shouldn't we guard against such errors? Certainly, but there is something fishy about the illusion of the bent stick. Yes, it is really an illusion. But how did we find that out? How did we discover this weakness in our powers of knowing things? *By knowing something*: By finding out that the stick was straight after all.

How could we have thought that the instrument of knowledge could test itself before it had any actual knowledge to test itself against? "Test before you buy" is a good rule for reason to apply to things other than reason but not a good rule for reason to apply to itself; it isn't as though there were another sort of product on the shelf. First try to know something, *then* go ahead and criticize the power of knowing. You will find out the weaknesses of the reasoning power only in the act of using it. That is how St. Thomas proceeds.

A NOTE ON CITATIONS

Because I also supply many cross-references, it may be helpful to explain how the sections of the *Summa Theologiae* are cited. In the body of the text, I spell out the citations, but in the footnotes, I use abbreviations. First, the part is indicated: "I" for the First Part of the *Summa*, "I-II" for the First Part of the Second Part, "II-II" for the Second Part of the Second Part, "III" for the Third Part, and "Supp." for the Supplement. "Q." followed by a numeral identifies the Question; the numbering of questions begins anew in each part. "Art." followed by a numeral identifies the Article. Citations are further specified by the abbreviation "Obj.," with a numeral, for an objection or the Latin preposition "ad," with a numeral, for a reply to an objection. If a citation specifies neither an objection, a reply to an objection, nor the *sed contra*, then it refers either to the whole Article or, if one is quoting from it, to the *respondeo*. For example, "S.T., II-II, Q. 60, Art. 1, ad 2" means "*Summa Theologiae*, Second Part of the Second Part, Question 60, Article 1, Reply to Objection 2," but "S.T., I-II, Q. 58, Art. 5" refers either to Article 5 in its entirety or to the "I answer that" part of Article 5.

Several other systems of citation are also widely used. The First Part, or *Prima Pars*, is sometimes designated 1, 1a, or Ia; the First Part of the Second Part, or *Prima Secundae Partis*, is sometimes designated 1-2, 1a-2ae, or Ia-IIae; the Second Part of the Second Part, or *Secunda Secundae Partis*, is sometimes designated 2-2, 2a-2ae, or IIa-IIae; and the Third Part, or *Tertia Pars*, is sometimes designated 3, 3a, or IIIa. In an abbreviation like "1a-2ae," the "a" and "ae" are endings of the words *Prima* and *Secundae*. I should also mention that the body of an Article is also sometimes called the *corpus*, abbreviated *cor.*

I am writing for scholars too, but for the convenience of beginners, in quoting from works other than the *Summa*, such as the writings of Aristotle, I try to use reliable editions that are in the public domain and are available on the internet. Sometimes this is impossible or inconvenient. The specialists, of course, will have their own favorite translations. When I provide quotations from the Bible, I most often use either the Douay-Rheims American version (DRA), which is an American English translation of the Latin Vulgate that St. Thomas used, and which is also employed by the Dominican Fathers, or the Revised Standard Version, Catholic Edition (RSV-CE), which is sometimes more clear and often more beautiful. Which translation I am using is always indicated in footnotes. When the chapter and verse divisions of the Douay-Rheims differ from those of more recent translations, I indicate this fact in the notes as well.

PART I

MORAL CHARACTER IN GENERAL

The definition of happiness some give – "Happy is the man who has all he desires," or "whose every wish is fulfilled" – is a good and adequate definition if taken in one sense, but inadequate if taken in another. For if we take it to mean "Happy is the man who has all that he naturally desires," then it is true, because nothing satisfies his natural desire except the complete good – that is what happiness is. But if we take it to mean "Happy is the man who has all that his mind believes to be desirable" then it is false. For to have certain things that man desires belongs not to happiness but to unhappiness; the possession of such things hinders him from having the complete good that he naturally desires, just as the mind sometimes accepts things as true that are a hindrance to the knowledge of truth. This is why Augustine added to the definition of happiness that the man "desires nothing amiss." The first part of the definition, "Happy is the man who has all that he desires," suffices only if understood in this way.

– Thomas Aquinas[1]

[1] I-II, Q. 5, Art. 8, ad 3, slightly paraphrased.

I-II, QUESTION 55, ARTICLE 4

Whether Virtue Is Suitably Defined?

TEXT	PARAPHRASE
[1] *Whether virtue is suitably defined?*	Is the traditional definition of virtue fitting?

"Virtue is a good quality of the mind that enables us to live in an upright way and cannot be employed badly – one which God brings about in us, without us." St. Thomas respectfully begins with this widely accepted definition because it would be arrogant to dismiss the result of generations of inquiry without examination. The ultimate source of the view which it encapsulates is St. Augustine of Hippo, but Augustine did not use precisely this wording. His more diffuse remarks had been condensed into a formula by Peter Lombard,[2] and the formula was then further sharpened by the Lombard's disciples.

Although St. Thomas begins with the tradition, he does not rest with it – he goes on to consider whether the received definition is actually correct. The first two Objections protest calling virtue a *good* quality. The third protests calling it a quality *of the mind*. The fourth objects to the phrase that it *enables us to live rightly* and the fifth to the phrase that it *cannot be employed badly*. Finally, the sixth protests the statement that *God brings it about in us, without us.*

Although, in the end, St. Thomas accepts the definition, he does not accept it quite in the sense in which some of his predecessors did. In particular, Peter Lombard had presented it as a definition of *all* virtue, but St. Thomas does not agree. As stated, St. Thomas thinks it characterizes only infused virtue – the spiritual dispositions poured into us as an undeserved gift of divine grace.

---

[2] Peter Lombard, *Sentences*, II, Distinction 27, Chapter 1: *Virtus est, ut ait Augustinus, bona qualitas mentis, qua recte vivitur et qua nullus male utitur, quam Deus solus in homine operatur* (Virtue, says Augustine, is a good quality of the mind that enables us to live in an upright way, that nobody uses badly, and that God alone works in man).

3

However, he points out later that with a single slight modification, the definition can be made to apply to acquired virtue as well – to the dispositions we develop by practice and habituation. Once that change is made, the definition becomes fully universal.

For the moment, St. Thomas treats the distinction between infused and acquired virtues as a given, but later in the *Summa*, he explains, explores, and defends it. At the right time in this book we will give it more attention.

Objection 1. [1] *It would seem that the definition, usually given, of virtue, is not suitable, to wit:* "Virtue is a good quality of the mind, by which we live righteously, of which no one can make bad use, which God works in us, without us." [2] *For virtue is man's goodness, since virtue it is that makes its subject good.* [3] *But goodness does not seem to be good, as neither is whiteness white. It is therefore unsuitable to describe virtue as a "good quality."*	Objection 1. Apparently the definition customarily assigned to virtue is unfitting: the one that says "Virtue is a good quality of the mind that enables us to live in an upright way and cannot be employed badly – one which God brings about in us, without us." For since virtue is the very quality of something that *makes* it good, a man's virtue and his goodness are the very same thing. Hence, to call his virtue good is to call his goodness good. But to call goodness good is absurd, like calling whiteness white. So to call a virtuous quality a "good" quality is inappropriate.

[1] The Objector reminds us of the entire definition in order to attack its first element.

[2] Virtue "makes" man good in the sense that if he has virtue he is good, and if he doesn't, he isn't.

[3] Snow is white, but whiteness itself has no color, because it is not matter; the number six is even, but evenness itself is not even, because it is not a number. The Objector argues that in the same way, a virtuous man is good, but goodness itself is not good. But if goodness cannot be called good, then virtue – which is the same thing – cannot be called good either.

Objection 2. [1] *Further, no difference is more common than its genus; since it is that which divides the genus.* [2] *But good is more common than quality, since it is convertible with being. Therefore "good" should not be put in the definition of virtue, as a difference of quality.*	Objection 2. Moreover, the traditional definition places virtue in the genus of quality, since it is a quality of the mind. Now we classify the things in a genus into species by considering the differences among them, and in the case of virtue, the difference we are considering is a quality some minds have and others lack. Very well, what quality is it? A *good* quality, we are told. But goodness is much too broad a criterion to distinguish among members of a genus, because being and goodness are equivalent: *everything* that has being is good in *some* respect.

[1] Suppose one marine biologist divides the genus of water-dwellers according to the kind of water in which they dwell, and another divides them according to their skin color. Notice that the former biologist has chosen a difference which *inheres* in the genus of water-dwellers; only water-dwellers can be distinguished according the kind of water in which they dwell. If we want our definitions to correspond to the essential forms of things, this is the way to proceed. But the latter biologist has chosen a difference that does *not* inhere in the genus of water-dwellers, for color might be used to distinguish many things far beyond the genus – a fish might be red or blue, but so might a parrot or a snake. This kind of definition is not necessarily bad – in fact, for certain special purposes, it may be quite useful – but it does not correspond to the essential forms of things.

Now since we are trying to find out the essential form of virtue, and since we agree that virtue belongs to the genus of qualities, we should be considering differences that *inhere* in the genus of qualities and that therefore do not apply beyond it. However, the Objector protests that "good" is not a difference of this kind. It would be bad enough that besides good and bad qualities there are also good and bad meals, good and bad men, and so forth. But it is even worse than that, for in a certain sense, good is universal – as we are about to see.

[2] Goodness and essential being are co-extensive. Their "convertibility" is well expressed by St. Augustine when he writes, "Yet all things should rightly be praised in virtue of the fact that they are! For they are good merely in virtue of the fact that they are."[3] Even a bad person is good *just insofar as he is a person*; even a bad song is good *just insofar as it is a song*. To forestall a possible objection, we must add that what St. Augustine means by "things" is not all things but only the sorts of things that classical philosophers call substances, or natures. For example, he would say that the body is good, but he would not say that sickness is good; sickness is not a nature but a privation or deficiency in the proper order of a nature. It is not a *something* but rather a *something wrong* or a *something missing*.

| Objection 3. [1] Further, as Augustine says (De Trin. xii, 3): "When we come across anything that is not common to us and the beasts of the field, it is something appertaining to the mind." [2] But there are virtues even of the irrational parts; as the Philosopher says (Ethic. iii, 10). Every virtue, therefore, is not a good quality "of the mind." | Objection 3. Still further, Augustine points out that differences of mind are what distinguish us from irrational creatures such as beasts. But the distinguishing quality of virtue cannot lie in minds, because, as Aristotle, the preeminent philosopher, points out in the third book of the Nicomachean Ethics, even our irrational powers can have virtues. Thus, not all virtues are good qualities of the mind. |

---

[3] Augustine of Hippo, *Augustine: On the Free Choice of the Will, On Grace and Free Choice, and Other Writings*, trans. Peter King (Cambridge: Cambridge University Press, 2010), Book 3, Chapter 7, Section 21.

[1] One must take the quotation marks which are so often inserted into the Blackfriars translation with a grain of salt, because St. Thomas is usually paraphrasing rather than quoting. What he probably has in mind is the place where St. Augustine says, "But that of our own which thus has to do with the handling of corporeal and temporal things, is indeed rational, in that it is not common to us with the beasts; but it is drawn, as it were, out of that rational substance of our mind, by which we depend upon and cleave to the intelligible and unchangeable truth, and which is deputed to handle and direct the inferior things."[4]

[2] The term "soul" refers to the pattern, or formal principle, the presence or absence of which makes the difference between a human corpse and an embodied human life. In the passage cited, Aristotle observes that temperance and fortitude are virtues of the irrational "parts" or powers of the soul, reminding us of his earlier remark that temperance is chiefly concerned with the regulation of pleasures. The Objector's point is that if even something irrational, such as the appetitive power of the soul, can either have or lack virtue, then virtue has nothing essential to do with rationality.

By the way, in calling the powers of the soul "parts," St. Thomas does not mean that the soul can be disassembled into components which can then be built back up, otherwise the essential unity of the soul would be in question. He distinguishes among several senses in which something can be called a part of something else. The integral parts of a principal thing really are components – they are the distinct elements that must concur for its perfection or completion. In this sense the wall, roof, and foundations are parts of a house. The subjective parts of a principal thing are its species or kinds. In this sense *ox*, *lion*, and *dog* are subjective parts of the genus animal. The potential parts of a principal thing are various things connected with it, directed to certain secondary acts or matters, which do not have its whole power. Only in the last sense are the appetitive power and the reasoning power "parts" of the soul.[5]

St. Thomas calls Aristotle "the Philosopher" not because Aristotle is the only philosopher but because he is the greatest one. Employing similar metonymical expressions, he calls St. Paul "the Apostle," St. Augustine of Hippo "the Theologian," Peter Lombard "the Master," Averroes "the Commentator," and each of the jurisconsults quoted in Justinian's *Digest* "the Jurist," and with equal respect calls Moses Maimonides "Rabbi Moses." We should not suppose from his respectful manner of referring to Aristotle that St. Thomas always agrees with him; where necessary, he corrects him, and even where he does agree with him, he often reworks and extends his argument, making it clearer, more precise, and more capacious. For instance, as we see later, he reorganizes

---

4 Augustine of Hippo, *On the Trinity*, trans. Arthur West Haddan (public domain), Book 12, Chapter 3, available at http://newadvent.org/fathers/1301.htm.

5 II-II, Q. 48, Art. 1. We consider the idea of the potential parts of a principal virtue more closely in II-II, Q. 80, Art. 1, in connection with the principal virtue of justice.

Aristotle's own diffuse classification of the virtues according to a more powerful fourfold scheme and adds a whole new level to it by considering not only
the acquired but also the infused dispositions of character, along with their
corresponding effects.

Objection 4. [1] *Further, righteousness seems to belong to justice; whence the righteous are called just.* [2] *But justice is a species of virtue. It is therefore unsuitable to put "righteous" in the definition of virtue, when we say that virtue is that "by which we live righteously."*	**Objection 4.** Still further, rightness seems to concern justice, which is why the same people are called both right and just. But justice is not the whole of virtue; it is one virtue among others. Thus, to include rightness in the definition of *all* virtue – as we do when we say that virtue is that "which enables us to live rightly" – is inappropriate.

[1] The Latin term St. Thomas uses is *rectitude*, from which we derive the
English word of the same spelling, meaning straightness or uprightness as contrasted with crookedness. It is derived from the verb *rego*, which means to
guide, govern, or regulate. We use uprightness as a synonym for justice in English, too, but in English we lack the overtones of guidance (which is too bad).

[2] The Objector argues that if rectitude is a synonym for the specific virtue
of justice, then it is incorrect to say that it refers to virtue in general.

Objection 5. [1] *Further, whoever is proud of a thing, makes bad use of it. But many are proud of virtue,* [2] *for Augustine says in his Rule, that "pride lies in wait for good works in order to slay them."* [3] *It is untrue, therefore, "that no one can make bad use of virtue."*	**Objection 5.** Besides, pride is a vice, so anyone who is proud of something is employing the thing wrongly. But as Augustine reminds us in his *Rule*, many are proud of virtue: "Pride lies in ambush even for good deeds so that it can destroy them." So they *are* using virtue badly; so virtue *can* be used badly.

[1] The Objector's counterexample depends on the fact that the Latin
term *usus* is much broader than the English term "use." In many cases where
Latin speaks of using something, in English we would speak instead of exercising it, enjoying it, or having some other involvement with it. So, although
an English-speaking reader might mount the same protest, he would probably come up with a different counterexample – perhaps that the virtue of
fortitude can be employed for robbing banks, or that the virtue of friendship
can be exercised by helping a companion conceal an act of dishonesty.

[2] The influential *Rule of the Servants of God*, composed by St. Augustine,
is not a detailed set of ordinances but an explanation of the principles for the
regulation of a community of persons consecrated to the monastic life. He remarks in Chapter 1, Section 7 that although every other kind of sin lies in the
evil deeds themselves, pride lurks in wait (*insidiatur*) even for good deeds, so
that they are ruined and lost.

[3] The Objector reasons that since it is possible to be proud of virtue's works, virtue can indeed be put to bad use.

Objection 6. [1] *Further, man is justified by virtue.* [2] *But Augustine commenting on John 14:12:*[6] *"He shall do greater things than these," says [Tract. lxxii[7] in Joan.: Serm. xv de Verb. Ap. 11]:* [3] *"He who created thee without thee, will not justify thee without thee."* [4] *It is therefore unsuitable to say that "God works virtue in us, without us."*	Objection 6. Still further, virtue is what makes a man just, what puts him in the right. But in a comment on Christ's remark to His disciples in the Gospel of John that he who believes in him "will do greater things than these," Augustine remarks, "He who created you without you, will not justify you without you." Thus, to say that God brings about virtue in us "without us" is unfitting.

[1] In the broadest sense, to be justified is to be *made* just or upright, and what accomplishes this is virtue. Protestant readers should take note that neither the Objector nor St. Thomas himself is claiming that this can take place without the supernatural grace of God. We return to this point in the Reply.

[2] The RSV-CE translates the verse, "he who believes in me will also do the works that I do; and greater works than these will he do, because I go to the Father." In his *Tractate 72 on the Gospel of John*, Chapter 1, St. Augustine takes it as his springboard for a broader discussion of the relation between what man does and what God does.

[3] St. Augustine makes remarks like this in several places. The version of the remark most closely matching St. Thomas's paraphrase is in Sermon 169, Chapter 11, where St. Augustine says *qui ergo fecit te sine te, non te iustificat sine te,* "therefore He who made you without you, will not justify you without you," using the word "made" *(fecit)* instead of St. Thomas's "created" *(creavit)*, which is more precise. Although *Tractate 27 on the Gospel of John* does not contain the remark exactly, it strongly suggests it, for at one point St. Augustine comments that without us, God made us, and a little later he remarks that the grace of Christ works in us, though not without us.

[4] The Objector takes the idea that God brings about virtue in us *without us* to mean that He brings it about without any involvement on our part whatsoever. As we will see in the Reply to the Objection, St. Thomas considers this interpretation mistaken.

On the contrary, We have the authority of Augustine from whose words this definition is gathered, and principally in De Libero Arbitrio ii, 19.	On the other hand, the traditional definition comes to us by the authority of St. Augustine himself, for it is drawn together from his own words, especially in the second book of *On Freedom of the Will.*

---

[6] Correcting the Blackfriars citation, which gives the verse as John 15:11 instead of John 14:12.

[7] Correcting the Blackfriars citation, which gives the tractate as xxvii (27) instead of lxxii (72).

"Virtue is a good quality of the mind, by which we live righteously) of which no one can make bad use, which God works in us, without us."

The "on the other hand" section of a disputation is not the writer's own view but a restatement of the traditional view which has just been challenged. Here St. Thomas simply points out the traditional source from which the definition is derived – St. Augustine's remarkably wide-ranging dialogue *On Freedom of the Will*, which St. Thomas quotes often. Following are some of the remarks from the dialogue St. Thomas may have in mind (not all of them, however, from Book 2).

- "With respect to chastity, well, seeing that it is a virtue, who would doubt that it is located in the mind itself?"[8]
- "Hence if it is precisely by a good will that we embrace and take delight in this will, and put it ahead of all the things that we are unable to retain just by willing to do so, then, as the argument has shown, our mind will possess those very virtues whose possession is the same thing as living rightly and honorably. The upshot is that anyone who wills to live rightly and honorably, if he wills himself to will this instead of transient goods, acquires so great a possession with such ease that having what he willed is nothing other for him than willing it."[9]
- "Consider justice, which no one uses for evil. Justice is counted among the highest goods there are in human beings – as well as all the virtues of the mind, upon which the right and worthwhile life is grounded. For no one uses prudence or courage or moderateness for evil. Right reason prevails in all of them, as it does in justice itself (which you mentioned). Without it they could not be virtues. And no one can use right reason for evil."[10]
- "No one uses the virtues for evil, but the other goods – namely, the intermediate and small goods – can be used not only for good but also for evil. Hence no one uses virtue for evil, because the task of virtue is the good use of things that we can also fail to use for good."[11]
- "Instead, you conform your mind to those unchangeable rules and beacons of the virtues, which live uncorruptibly in the truth itself and in the wisdom that is common, to which the person furnished with virtues whom you put forward as a model for your emulation has conformed and directed his mind."[12]
- "Thus if every good were taken away, what will be left is not something, but instead absolutely nothing. Yet every good is from God. Therefore, there is no nature that is not from God."[13]
- "But since we cannot rise of our own accord as we fell of it, let us hold on with firm faith to the right hand of God stretched out to us from above,

[8] Augustine of Hippo, *Augustine*, Book 1, Chapter 5, Section 12.
[9] Ibid., Book 1, Chapter 13, Section 29.   [10] Ibid., Book 2, Chapter 18, Section 50.
[11] Ibid., Book 2, Chapter 19, Section 50.   [12] Ibid., Book 2, Chapter 19, Section 52.
[13] Ibid., Book 2, Chapter 20, Section 54.

namely our Lord Jesus Christ; let us await Him with resolute hope and desire Him with burning charity [love]."[14]

- "These are not mediocre goods: that the soul by its very nature takes precedence over any material body; that the soul has the ability, with the help of its Creator, to cultivate itself and by religious efforts it can acquire and possess all the virtues through which it may be freed from the torments of trouble and the blindness of ignorance."[15]

I answer that, [1] *This definition comprises perfectly the whole essential notion of virtue.* [2] *For the perfect essential notion of anything is gathered from all its causes. Now the above definition comprises all the causes of virtue.* [3] *For the formal cause of virtue, as of everything, is gathered from its genus and difference, when it is defined as "a good quality": for "quality" is the genus of virtue, and the difference, "good."* [4] *But the definition would be more suitable if for "quality" we substitute "habit," which is the proximate genus.* [5] *Now virtue has no matter "out of which" it is formed, as neither has any other accident; but it has matter "about which" it is concerned, and matter "in which" it exists, namely, the subject.* [6] *The matter about which virtue is concerned is its object, and this could not be included in the above definition, because the object fixes the virtue to a certain species, and here we are giving the definition of virtue in general.* [7] *And so for material cause we have the subject, which is mentioned when we say that virtue is a good quality "of the mind."*	**Here is my response.** The traditional definition completely encompasses the entire rational meaning of virtue – all that the concept includes, without leaving anything out. For the complete rational idea of each thing is drawn together from all four of its causes – formal, material, final, and efficient – and the definition of virtue in question *does* collect all four of its causes. The *formal* cause of each thing, including virtue, is grasped from the genus to which it belongs and the difference which distinguishes it from other elements in that genus. This is done when virtue is defined as a "good quality," for virtue belongs to the genus of quality and differs from other qualities because it is a good one. It would have been still better to define it as a good *habit*, because habit, or disposition, is the *kind* of quality that it is, but "quality" will do. The *material* cause of a thing is its matter, which may be taken in three senses: the matter *of* which it is composed, the matter *to* which it pertains, or the matter *in* which it exists. Now virtue is not composed *of* anything – it is an "accident" or nonessential property of something else (a mind), and no accident is composed of anything. So matter in the first sense could not have been included in its definition. Virtue does have matter *to* which it pertains – its object, that to which it is directed – but this could not have been included in the definition either, because we are speaking of virtue in general, and the object of virtue depends on what kind of virtue we are talking about. That leaves matter in the third sense, the thing *in* which virtue exists, which is the

[14] Ibid., Book 2, Chapter 20, Section 54.   [15] Ibid., Book 3, Chapter 20, Section 56.

material cause of virtue – subject (the mind), formal cause = good quality

[8] *The end of virtue, since it is anoperative habit, is operation.* [9] *But it must be observed that some operative habits are always referred to evil, as vicious habits: others are sometimes referred to good, sometimes to evil; for instance, opinion is referred both to the true and to the untrue: whereas virtue is a habit which is always referred to good: and so the distinction of virtue from those habits which are always referred to evil, is expressed in the words "by which we live righteously":* [10] *and its distinction from those habits which are sometimes directed unto good, sometimes unto evil, in the words, "of which no one makes bad use."* [11] *Lastly, God is the efficient cause of infused virtue, to which this definition applies; and this is expressed in the words "which God works in us without us."* [12] *If we omit this phrase, the remainder of the definition will apply to all virtues in general, whether acquired or infused.*

mind – thus, quite properly, the definition states that virtue is a good quality *of the mind.* The *final* cause of a thing is its end or purpose. Virtue is a habit or disposition concerning things that are done; so its end or purpose is operation. But we must say more than this about its final cause, because some operative dispositions always tend toward evil (in particular, the vices tend toward evil), and others may tend either toward either good or evil (for example, opinions – intellectual dispositions to believe something – may be either true or false) – but virtue always tends toward good. The definitional phrase "which enables us to live rightly" distinguishes virtue from the first kind of operative habit, and the definitional phrase "which cannot be employed wrongly" distinguishes it from the second.

The *efficient* cause of a thing is the force, means, or agency by which it comes into being. Since the definition in question concerns only "infused" virtue, the agency that infuses it into us is God. This is fittingly made clear by saying that God brings it about "in us, without us." If we wish to make the definition more general, so that it applies not only to infused virtues but also to virtues acquired by habituation, then this phrase may be omitted.

[1] Though usually St. Thomas employs words sparingly, here he permits himself a redundancy in order to emphasize that the traditional definition contains everything it should: both "perfect" (*perfecte*) and "whole" (*totam*) convey the idea of completeness. The term that the Blackfriars translate as "essential notion" and that I render as "rational meaning" is the very broad term *rationem.*

[2] St. Thomas borrows the fourfold classification of the causes of a thing from Aristotle, *Metaphysics*, Book 5, Chapter 2. The word "cause" broadly means that which explains what it is. The pattern or functional organization of a thing is its formal cause, or form. The constituents or elements of which it is composed, or to which it is essentially related, are its material cause, or matter – matter being anything that can receive a form. The purpose for the sake of which it exists is its final cause, or end; we may add that the meanings of the term "purpose" as applied to purposes in things, purposes in minds, and purposes in the mind of God are not identical but analogical. Finally, the force, means, or agency by which something comes into being is its efficient cause, or

power. For example, the matter of the heart is muscle; its form is a functional arrangement of interlocking chambers; its power is embryogenesis; and its end is pumping blood. Aristotle explains in his own way:

"Cause" means (1) that from which, as immanent material, a thing comes into being, e.g. the bronze is the cause of the statue and the silver of the saucer, and so are the classes which include these. (2) The form or pattern, i.e. the definition of the essence, and the classes which include this (e.g. the ratio 2:1 and number in general are causes of the octave), and the parts included in the definition. (3) That from which the change or the resting from change first begins; e.g. the adviser is a cause of the action, and the father a cause of the child, and in general the maker a cause of the thing made and the change-producing of the changing. (4) The end, i.e. that for the sake of which a thing is; e.g. health is the cause of walking. For "Why does one walk?" we say; "that one may be healthy"; and in speaking thus we think we have given the cause. The same is true of all the means that intervene before the end, when something else has put the process in motion, as e.g. thinning or purging or drugs or instruments intervene before health is reached; for all these are for the sake of the end, though they differ from one another in that some are instruments and others are actions.[16]

[3] An illustration of the general point is that the genus of man is "animal," his difference from other animals is "rational," and so his form is "rational animal." In the same way, the genus of virtue is "quality," its difference from other qualities is "good," and so its form is "good quality."

[4] St. Thomas points out that a virtue is not any kind of quality but the kind of quality called *habitus*. This Latin term is much broader than its English cognate, "habit," which we tend to use for things we do without thinking about them. By contrast, a *habitus* can be any kind of dispositional quality whatsoever, whether natural, acquired, or infused – even a tendency concerning *how or what* we think.[17]

[5] Since virtue is not composed of anything, one might be inclined to say that it has no matter. However, it is essentially related to certain matter, and this is the matter that we call its material cause. One way in which a virtue may be essentially related to matter is that this matter is its *object*. The object of generosity, for example, is the giving of things to others.

[6] However, different virtues have different objects. For example, the object of temperance is not the same as the object of fortitude. So no particular object of virtue is properly included in the definition of virtue in general.

[7] Another way in which a virtue may be essentially related to matter is that this matter is its *subject* – that *in which* the virtue inheres. In what then does virtue inhere? It inheres in the mind. Therefore, the mind is its material

---

[16] Aristotle, *Metaphysics*, trans. W. D. Ross (public domain), Book 5, Chapter 2.

[17] Occasionally English speakers do use the term "habit" in the broader sense. For example, in Robert Louis Stevenson's story "The Suicide Club," one of the characters says, "I am in the habit of looking not so much to the nature of a gift as to the spirit in which it is offered" (public domain).

cause. To contemporary readers, it may seem strange to describe mind as material, but the puzzle is easily dispelled when we remember that by matter he means anything that can receive a form. He is not using the term "matter" as we do when we say that the brain is material but thinking is nonmaterial but rather as we do when we say that the matter of thinking is thoughts.

[8] Despite the impression conveyed by this phrasing, St. Thomas is not reasoning circularly. He is merely reminding us of something we all already know – that virtue concerns things that we do. Philosophy *always and necessarily* begins with common opinion. Though not everything in common opinion is true, there is always some grain of truth in it, or it could never seem plausible in the first place. The philosopher's task is to separate that grain from the chaff – to sift, purify, rectify, elevate, and ennoble it. If it tried to tell us things we haven't a clue about, then how could we know whether its claims were true?

[9] The awkward verb "referred" is not in the Latin; for example, the clause translated "are always referred to evil" means merely "are always to evil" (or "always tend toward evil" (my paraphrase). Of course in a particular case a vice might produce the right act by chance; for example, a coward might flee from a particular danger from which a man of fortitude or courage would also have withdrawn. However, fortitude is the disposition which always directs us to do the right thing *in the right way* and *for the right reasons*, whereas cowardice either does the right thing accidentally or fails to do it at all.

[10] To contemporary readers, the claim that it is impossible to put virtue to bad purposes may seem preposterous, but see the Reply to Objection 5.

[11] St. Thomas can assume that his readers are already familiar with the distinction between acquired and infused virtues, because even though they are only beginning their formal study of theology, they have already been catechized. For contemporary readers, of course, this is not necessarily the case. He returns to the distinction in more detail later, but for present purposes it is sufficient to understand that unlike the acquired virtues, the infused virtues are a pure gift of grace.

[12] Thus the *general* definition of virtue becomes simply "Virtue is a good quality of the mind that enables us to live in an upright way and cannot be employed badly."

Reply to Objection 1. [1] *That which is first seized by the intellect is being: wherefore everything that we apprehend we consider as being,* [2] *and consequently as one, and as good, which are convertible with being. Wherefore we say that essence is being and is one and is good; and that oneness is*	Reply to Objection 1. The sheer being of things enters the intellect before anything else does. For this reason, to everything our minds grasp we attribute being – and we also attribute to it unity and goodness, because these three things are equivalent. This is why we use the same terms for them. For essence, or being as such, we use the words "being," "one," and "good"; for unity as such, the same three terms; and for goodness as such, again the same three terms.

> being and one and good: and in like manner goodness.
>
> [3] *But this is not the case with specific forms, as whiteness and health; for everything that we apprehend, is not apprehended with the notion of white and healthy.* [4] *We must, however, observe that, as accidents and non-subsistent forms are called beings, not as if they themselves had being, but because things are by them; so also are they called good or one, not by some distinct goodness or oneness, but because by them something is good or one.* [5] *So also is virtue called good, because by it something is good.*

> Now we do not speak this way about *specific* forms, such as whiteness and health, for we do not attribute whiteness and health to everything we grasp, as we attribute being to everything we grasp. Yet sometimes we do speak in a similar way, for we call the nonessential properties of things (such as whiteness) beings, and we call the nonsubsistent forms of things (such as health) beings. This way of speaking does not imply that such things have a particular kind of being in themselves, but only that other things have being *by means* of them. In the same way, we sometimes describe such things as good, or as one, not because they have a particular kind of goodness or unity in themselves, but merely because through them, other things have goodness or unity.
>
> It is in *this* sense that virtue is called good – simply in the sense that some good thing is good *because of it.*

[1] The mind thinks, "What's that?" grasping that something *is*. Only afterward does it think, "Oh, it's a dog," grasping what *kind* of thing it is. The mind's recognition of being is implicit in its recognition of everything else.

[2] Essential being is "convertible with" – equivalent to – not only goodness, but also unity. Not only is each nature *good* merely because it is, but also each nature is the *one* thing it is merely because it is.

[3] What we have just said about being does not hold for specific forms. Our minds recognize being in everything they grasp, but they do not recognize, say, whiteness or health in everything they grasp, because not everything is white or healthy.

[4] Two things must be elucidated here: The meaning of *accident*, and the meaning of *nonsubsistent*. In philosophical terminology, the former is something which depends on the existence of something else. Some accidents pertain to a thing's essence – for example, the accident of man's ability to find something funny arises from his essential rationality. Others accidents – for example, the accident of Fred's brown hair – do not depend on a thing's essence. Virtue itself does not belong to man essentially, but the potentiality for virtue does belong to him essentially.

In turn, a nonsubsistent thing is something that exists and acts, not in itself, but in something else; for example, a man's virtue does not exist and act in itself, but in his mind. When we call a nonsubsistent thing a "being," "good," and "one," we do not mean it has being in itself, is good in itself, and has its own essential unity, but only that it makes the thing which has it the one good being that it is.

[5] Thus, to call a man's virtue "good" is merely to say it is what makes him good, so the Objector's protest does not apply. Contemporary readers may wonder why St. Thomas didn't just say so and leave it at that. Do we really need all of that information about accidents and nonsubsistent beings? Maybe not – but the whole reason the Objector goes wrong is that he knows just enough about metaphysics to be confused about it. The only way to unconfuse him is to teach him a little bit more.

Reply to Objection 2.	Reply to Objection 2.
[1] *Good, which is put in the definition of virtue, is not good in general which is convertible with being, and which extends further than quality, but the good as fixed by reason,* [2] *with regard to which Dionysius says (Div. Nom. iv) "that the good of the soul is to be in accord with reason."*	Reply to Objection 2. The Objection would be valid if in describing virtue as a "good" quality the definition were referring to goodness in general – for goodness in general really is equivalent to being in general, and really does exceed any particular quality. But the word "good" in the definitional phrase "good quality" refers not to goodness in general, but only to good reasoning. Pseudo-Dionysius makes the same point when he remarks in *On the Divine Names* that the good of the soul (as distinguished from other goods) is to be in conformity with reason.

[1] St. Thomas's point is that although every nature is good just because it is, the specific meaning of goodness is different for each kind of good thing – something the Objector overlooks. True, all these meanings of good are analogous. Nevertheless, a good man is not good in the same sense as a good racehorse; similarly, a good racehorse is not good in the same sense as a good meal. In defining virtue, we are speaking merely of the virtue of a good human being, so Objection 2 loses its point.

Contemporary analytical philosophers express much the same point that St. Thomas is making by distinguishing between predicative and attributive adjectives. A predicative adjective such as "red" means the same thing no matter what kind of thing we are talking about – for example, the redness of a rocket and the redness of a racecar are the same thing. But the meaning of an attributive adjective such as "fast" depends on what kind of thing we are talking about – a rocket which traveled only at the speed of a fast racecar would not be considered a fast rocket.

[2] St. Thomas is not quoting *On the Divine Names* but paraphrasing it. The author, a Christian neo-Platonist enormously influential in medieval times who wrote under the pseudonym "Dionysius the Areopagite," explains in Chapter 4, Section 32 of the work that "In the case of a devil evil lies in being contrary to spiritual goodness; in the soul it lies in being contrary to reason; in the body it lies in being contrary to nature."[18]

---

[18] I have modernized the language by changing "lieth" to "lies" and "the being" to "being." See also Chapter 4, Section 4, where Pseudo-Dionysius writes "after the Good all things do yearn – those

| Reply to Objection 3. [1] *Virtue cannot be in the irrational part of the soul, except in so far as this participates in the reason (Ethic. i, 13).* [2] *And therefore reason, or the mind, is the proper subject of virtue.* | Reply to Objection 3. True, we do describe certain virtues as being virtues of the nonrational parts of the soul. But this is a figure of speech; as Aristotle explains in the first book of his *Nicomachean Ethics*, we speak this way only to the degree to which the nonrational parts *share* in reason by submitting to its rule. Strictly speaking, virtue lies only in the reasoning power itself. |

[1] In his *Nicomachean Ethics*, Book 1, Aristotle explains that the various irrational or powers of the soul do not all have the same relation to the power of reason. The sheer power to take in nutrition and grow has no connection with reason at all. On the other hand, even though the appetitive or desiring power is also something different from reason, it can share or participate in reason simply in the sense of submitting to it. As St. Thomas remarks concerning a related passage, in Book 3, "that part of the soul is called irrational which is designed by nature both to conform to, and to obey reason.... Such is the sensitive appetite to which the passions of the soul belong. Hence all the virtues dealing with the passions must be placed in the sensitive appetite."[19]

[2] Our own era has been tremendously influenced by the diametrically opposite view of David Hume, who writes in 1739 that "Reason is, and ought only to be the slave of the passions, and can never pretend to any other office than to serve and obey them." But Hume is cheating; he defines all impulses affecting the will as passions, then says only passions can affect the will.[20]

| Reply to Objection 4. [1] *Justice has a righteousness of its own by which it puts those outward things right which come into human use, and are the proper matter of justice, as we shall show further on (60, 2; II-II, 58, 8).* [2] *But the righteousness which denotes order to a due end and to the Divine law, which is the rule of the human will, as stated above (Question 19, Article 4), is common to all virtues.* | Reply to Objection 4. We may speak of rectitude, or rightness, in two senses. The rectitude distinctive to justice sets the external things which are at man's disposal in proper order. But the rectitude which regulates human will, putting it in order with respect to its proper ends and to the Divine law, is common to all the virtues. The latter will be explained more fully later on; the former was explained earlier in the *Summa*. |

that have mind and reason seeking It by knowledge, those that have perception seeking It by perception, those that have no perception seeking It by the natural movement of their vital instinct, and those that are without life and have mere existence seeking It by their aptitude for that bare participation whence this mere existence is theirs." *Dionysius the Areopagite: On the Divine Names and the Mystical Theology*, trans. C. E. Rolt (public domain), available on the internet at www.ccel.org/ccel/rolt/dionysius.i.html.

[19] Thomas Aquinas, *Commentary on Aristotle's Nicomachean Ethics*, Book 3, Lecture 19, trans. C. J. Litzinger, rev. ed. (Notre Dame, IN: Dumb Ox Books, 1993), p. 196. Available online at www.dhspriory.org/thomas/english/Ethics.htm.

[20] David Hume, *A Treatise of Human Nature*, Book 2, Chapter 3, Section 3 (public domain).

[1] St. Thomas explains later that in certain matters, the rectitude of what one person does depends on whether it is commensurate with someone else. For example, paying the grocer a certain amount of money is just if that is what I owe him, but unjust if it falls short. "Particular" justice – justice in the sense of one virtue among others, rather than as a synonym for virtue in general – is the virtue which regulates such operations.

[2] God has ordained that not only in particular justice, but in all matters, human will is to be regulated by the reflection of the Divine Reason in human reason. Each virtue has its own part to play in such regulation – justice in one way, but the other virtues in other ways. As St. Thomas writes,

> Wherever a number of causes are subordinate to one another, the effect depends more on the first than on the second cause: since the second cause acts only in virtue of the first. Now it is from the eternal law, which is the Divine Reason, that human reason is the rule of the human will, from which the human derives its goodness. Hence it is written (Psalm 4:6–7): "Many say: Who showeth us good things? The light of Thy countenance, O Lord, is signed upon us": as though to say: "The light of our reason is able to show us good things, and guide our will, in so far as it is the light of your countenance, that is, derived from it."[21] It is therefore evident that the goodness of the human will depends on the eternal law much more than on human reason: and when human reason fails we must have recourse to the Eternal Reason.[22]

Reply to Objection 5. One can make bad use of a virtue objectively, for instance by having evil thoughts about a virtue, e.g. by hating it, or by being proud of it: but one cannot make bad use of virtue as principle of action, so that an act of virtue be evil.	Objection 5. One can employ a virtue badly *as an object*, for example by thinking evil thoughts about it – say, by hating or taking pride in it. But one cannot employ a virtue badly as a root or principle of how affairs should be conducted, so that even something evil is an act of virtue.

St. Thomas plays on the fact that the Latin word *usus* can be either a noun or a verb: One can "use" a virtue badly as an object, but a virtue cannot serve as the *principle* of bad "use." To use something as an object is to do something concerning it. So another example of using virtue badly as an object might be taking advantage of someone else's virtue – for instance, cowards might shove all the risks of defending the community onto the courageous. But the *principio* or "principle" of an action is its starting point, the root from which it springs – and the principle of action of these cowards is their cowardice.

---

[21] For clarity, I have rephrased Blackfriars' "in so far as it is the light (i.e. derived from) Thy countenance," in the light of the Latin, *inquantum est lumen vultus tui, idest a vultu tuo derivatum.*
[22] I-II, Q. 19, Art. 4.

Someone might say that a virtue *can* be used badly as a principle of action. For example, a bank robber must be able to stir himself up to acts which expose him to danger, and persons of fortitude or courage must be able to do that too. But here the resemblance ends, for part of the meaning of fortitude is grasping *for what reasons* something is to be done, and the bank robber lacks such wisdom. His rule is not the defense of true goods, but simply getting what he wants. We might express this point by saying that the bank robber is not exercising fortitude, but only bravery. In much the same way, we might say that a man who helps his companion conceal an act of dishonesty is exercising not true friendship, but only attachment. Although he is certainly trying to further a personal relationship, friendship in the highest sense aims at a partnership in a truly good life.

Reply to Objection 6. [1] *Infused virtue is caused in us by God without any action on our part, but not without our consent. This is the sense of the words, "which God works in us without us."* [2] *As to those things which are done by us, God causes them in us, yet not without action on our part, for He works in every will and in every nature.*	Reply to Objection 6. The meaning of the words "which God brings about in us without us" is that infused virtue is poured into us by God, rather than generated in us by our own efforts – not that He pours it into us without our consent. To be sure, even the things which we do in connection with His grace are brought about by God with our cooperation, for He works *within* every will and nature (rather than violently acting on it from without).

[1] How is it possible for God to instill the infused virtues into us "without any action on our part" and yet with our consent? Isn't consent *something that we do?* As we are about to see, St. Thomas agrees; I suggest that the Blackfriars translation "without any action on our part" is a little too strong. What St. Thomas actually writes is that God causes infused virtue in us without our *agentibus* – we are not the ones who generate, initiate, drive, or conduct the act.

[2] Even concerning the infused virtues, which are caused in us by God, there are "things which are done by us." The fact that we cannot generate them in ourselves by our own will and nature does not mean that our power and will in receiving them are disengaged. If that were the case, then they would not be "our" virtues at all; God would be pulling us with strings, operating us by remote control, like servomechanisms. Rather God works *in and through* the nature and will of those whom He redeems. He works through our will insofar as we consent; he works through our nature because He has created us with the "obediential" potentiality to *receive* from Him what we cannot do for ourselves (III, Question 11, Article 1). For example, in the case of the infused virtue of faith, *it is really we who believe*, but we are enabled to do so through

His work in us. If it were not for His grace, we could not even cooperate with His grace; yet we really do cooperate with His grace.

Actually, St. Thomas holds that we need the help of God even concerning the acquired virtues, which we develop by means of discipline and habituation – though in their case God's help is needed in a different way. We return to this point in the commentary on I-II, Question 62, Article 1.

Whether There Can Be Moral without Intellectual Virtue?

TEXT	PARAPHRASE
Whether there can be moral without intellectual virtue?	Can a person who lacks intellectual virtue have moral virtue?

Moral virtues are dispositions concerning choice, dispositions which incline us to seek the right action between excess and deficiency in every sphere of conduct. This right action is called the "mean." For example, the moral virtue of fortitude, which may also be called courage or firmness, inclines us to keep our fear under control so that we can attain the mean between cowardice and rashness. Just because it does regulate fear, it also regulates daring, "which attacks the objects of fear in the hope of obtaining some good."[1] If we habitually give in too much to fear we are cowards; if we habitually give in too much to daring we are rash; but if we habitually strike the mean then we have fortitude.

Intellectual virtues are dispositions which bring about "right reason"—which put the power of reasoning in proper order, which is much more than following the rules of logic. So the question is whether the moral virtues can attain the mean that they seek even if our power of reasoning has not been set in right order by the intellectual virtues.

It is important to realize that right reason is not the same as being smart; we are not asking the elitist question, "Can a person be good without being clever and well-educated?" Right reason is more like reasoning straight instead of crooked. So we might also phrase the question, "Can a person habitually do the right thing even if his thinking is askew?"

---

[1] II-II, Q. 141, Art. 3.

Objection 1. [1] *It would seem that moral [virtue] can be without intellectual virtue. Because moral virtue, as Cicero says (De Invent. Rhet. ii) is "a habit like a second nature in accord with reason."* [2] *Now though nature may be in accord with some sovereign reason that moves it, there is no need for that reason to be united to nature in the same subject, as is evident of natural things devoid of knowledge.* [3] *Therefore in a man there may be a moral virtue like a second nature, inclining him to consent to his reason, without his reason being perfected by an intellectual virtue.*	**Objection 1.** Apparently moral virtue *can* exist in a person who lacks intellectual virtue. True, Marcus Tullius Cicero declares that moral virtue is a habit which works as though it were natural and which is in agreement with reason. But as we see in things that have no cognition whatsoever, the "reason" by which natural things are guided need not be intrinsic to their natures; it is sufficient for a superior reason to put them into action. So it is quite possible that a man may have a moral virtue which works as though it were natural, and inclines him to do what reason requires, even though his own power of reason has not been put in complete and proper order by intellectual virtue.

[1] A variety of more or less synonymous phrases are used in the *Summa* to convey the interesting idea that although the disposition to act virtuously is not innate in human nature, it completes or fulfills our nature and resembles our natural dispositions. Although the term "second nature" *(secundam naturam)* is used in some places for the idea, the expression actually used here is "in the mode or manner of virtue *(in modum naturae),* which is borrowed from Marcus Tullius Cicero.[2] Among the other expressions the *Summa* uses from time to time for second nature are *quodammodo ... naturam* ("in a certain way natural"), *assimilari naturae* ("in simulation of nature"), and *connaturaliter* ("with, or according to, nature").

A massive source of confusion among human beings is that through habituation, not only virtues but also vices can come to seem like "second nature." However, only virtues are truly "in the manner of nature," because only virtues promote the rational unfolding of our human potentiality. Vices thwart it.

[2] Consider a doe nursing her calf, or a dog assisting his owner to herd sheep. The action of the doe is in accord with the reason of God, who implanted its natural inclinations by means of creation; the action of the dog is in accord with the reason of both God, who implanted its natural inclinations, and the shepherd, who adapted these inclinations to his ends by teaching it to herd. Although each creature acts in accord with some reason superior to it, neither possesses rationality in itself. The doe is merely following its nature. The dog is following both its nature and the "second nature" acquired by training.

---

[2] The Objector is quoting Cicero's *De Inventione* ("On [Rhetorical] Invention"), Book 2, Section 159. The Latin text may be found online at http://scrineum.unipv.it/wight/invs2.htm#2.159.

[3] The Objector reasons that if, by either nature or second nature, even a creature devoid of reason can do what reason would approve, so much more can a man whose reasoning is merely imperfect.

Objection 2. [1] *Further, by means of intellectual virtue man obtains perfect use of reason.* [2] *But it happens at times that men are virtuous and acceptable to God, without being vigorous in the use of reason. Therefore it seems that moral virtue can be without intellectual [virtue].*	**Objection 2.** Moreover, although it is true that completely well-ordered reasoning requires intellectual virtue, nevertheless it can happen that men who do not reason well are virtuous and pleasing to God. Apparently, then, moral virtue really can thrive without intellectual virtue.

[1] Although the expression "perfect use of reason" is literally correct, it is a little misleading because the Latin term *perfectum* has different overtones than its English cognate. I have tried to convey this by paraphrasing *rationis usum perfectum* as "completely well-ordered reasoning."

[2] The Objector suggests that some good people are not very bright. (One might add that there are some forms of stupidity which one must be highly intelligent and educated to commit, but that is another story.)

Objection 3. [1] *Further moral virtue makes us inclined to do good works.* [2] *But some, without depending on the judgment of reason, have a natural inclination to do good works.* [3] *Therefore moral virtues can be without intellectual virtues.*	**Objection 3.** Still further, although moral virtue brings about the inclination to do good deeds, some people have a natural inclination to do such deeds, even without exercising rational judgment. This shows that moral virtues can exist without intellectual virtues.

[1] As we saw in our discussion of I-II, Question 55, Article 4, the inclination to do the right thing is not something that virtue merely chances to bring about sometimes; it belongs to the *essence* of virtue, to what it *is*, and so to its proper definition.

[2] St. Thomas writes earlier in the Summa that something can be said to be natural to a person in either of two senses: It may pertain to his species nature (to the tendencies all humans have by virtue of their essence), or it may pertain to his individual nature (to the tendencies which belong to him in particular).[3] The Objector is speaking of individual nature. His point is that just as some people seem to be born with a musical or a humorous bent of character, so some seem to find it easier than others do to act virtuously, even apart from how they have been brought up. They spontaneously act with such qualities as kindness, honesty, and generosity.

[3] I-II, Q. 63, Art. 1.

The expression "individual nature" is merely a way of speaking, one which is easy to misunderstand. A person with a very good or very bad "individual nature" does not have a different species nature than other humans; otherwise he would belong to a different species and be subject to a different natural law! As St. Thomas makes clear in other places, what he really has is an especially good or bad *disposition* of the nature he shares with everyone else. We might say that his nature is in a healthy or unhealthy condition.

[3] The Objector argues that since some persons incline toward virtuous deeds without even having to think about them, moral virtue must be independent of intellectual virtue.

On the contrary, Gregory says (Moral. xxii) that "the other virtues, unless we do prudently what we desire to do, cannot be real virtues." But prudence is an intellectual virtue, as stated above (Question 57, Article 5). Therefore moral virtues cannot be without intellectual virtues.	**On the other hand,** we have the authority of Gregory the Great, who says in his *Morals,* a commentary on the book of Job, that unless they are guided by prudence, the rest of the virtues are not genuine. But as we have discussed earlier, prudence is an intellectual virtue. It follows that moral virtue without intellectual virtue is impossible.

St. Thomas is paraphrasing St. Gregory's remark, "And so one virtue without another is either none at all or but imperfect.... For neither is it real prudence which has not justice, temperance, fortitude, nor perfect temperance which has not fortitude, justice, and prudence, nor complete fortitude which is not prudent, temperate, and just, nor genuine justice which has not prudence, fortitude, and temperance."[4]

Why does St. Gregory mention just four virtues? Because these are the "cardinal" or paramount virtues, as St. Thomas will explain in I-II, Question 61, Articles 2 and 3. Notice, by the way, that St. Gregory is saying more than that the moral virtues depend on prudence. Actually he maintains that *each* of the virtues – whether moral or intellectual – requires the support of the *all* of the others. St. Thomas returns to this doctrine, called the unity or interconnectedness of the virtues, in I-II, Question 65, Article 1, which we take up later.

I answer that, [1] *Moral virtue can be without some of the intellectual virtues, viz. wisdom, science, and art; but not without understanding and prudence.* [2] *Moral virtue cannot be without*	**Here is my response.** Not every intellectual virtue is necessary for moral virtue. For example, moral virtue does not require the intellectual virtue of wisdom, which concerns the knowledge of first principles, science, which concerns the knowledge of demonstrations from principles, or art,

[4] *Morals on the Book of Job by St. Gregory the Great,* trans. John Henry Parker, J. G. F. Rivingon, and J. Rivington (public domain), Book 22, Chapter 2, available on the internet at www.lectionarycentral.com/GregoryMoraliaIndex.html.

prudence, because it is a habit of choosing, i.e. making us choose well. [3] Now in order that a choice be good, two things are required. First, that the intention be directed to a due end; and this is done by moral virtue, which inclines the appetitive faculty to the good that is in accord with reason, which is a due end. [4] Secondly, that man take rightly those things which have reference to the end: [5] and this he cannot do unless his reason counsel, judge and command aright, which is the function of prudence and the virtues annexed to it, as stated above (57, A5, 6). Wherefore there can be no moral virtue without prudence: [6] and consequently neither can there be without understanding. For it is by the virtue of understanding that we know self-evident principles both in speculative and in practical matters. [7] Consequently just as right reason in speculative matters, in so far as it proceeds from naturally known principles, presupposes the understanding of those principles, so also does prudence, which is the right reason about things to be done.

which concerns the technique of making things. However, moral virtue does require the intellectual virtues of prudence and of understanding, and is impossible without them.

The reason why moral virtue cannot exist without prudence is that prudence is the disposition by which we make good choices. To make this matter clear, however, notice that two different conditions must be satisfied for a choice to be good.

The first of these conditions concerns moral virtue, for the intention of the chooser must be directed toward the proper end. Moral virtue brings this about by making him desire what is rationally fitting; this is what it means for the end to be proper. So far there is no connection with intellectual virtue.

But the second condition does concern intellectual virtue, for the chooser must also grasp those things which the end requires, something he cannot do unless reason advises, judges, and directs him the right way. As explained earlier in the *Summa*, reason will not function the right way without prudence, along with the subordinate intellectual virtues which prudence employs.

It follows that moral virtue is impossible without prudence – and for the same reason, it is impossible without understanding. Understanding is the virtue that completes or "perfects" the natural disposition of the mind to grasp the naturally known starting points of both theory and practice. Without these starting points, right reason could never get going or make progress in things to be known – and without prudence, which is right reason in practice, it would be equally crippled concerning things to be done.

[1] Each of the terms "science," "wisdom," "prudence," "art," and "understanding" presents difficulties because its contemporary English meaning is so different from the meanings of the Latin term translated. However, since these are the terms used by almost all English-speaking scholars, I have retained them lest even greater confusions result.[5]

[5] The following discussion is indebted to I-II, Q. 57, esp. Arts. 2 and 3.

Today we tend to use the term "science" for a social practice devoted to finding out how natural processes work in order to manipulate them. St. Thomas uses the term *scientia* not for a social practice, but for an intellectual virtue, one aimed not at manipulation, but at knowledge. Specifically, it is the intellectual virtue involved in deriving and retaining conclusions from principles. So in this sense, not only are physics and chemistry sciences, but so are mathematics, ethics, and theology.

The intellectual virtue St. Thomas calls *sapientia*, here rendered "wisdom," may be viewed as a kind of *scientia*, because it too concerns deriving conclusions from principles. However, its subject matter is distinctive, because what it investigates is the highest causes of things. In themselves, first causes are the first and most important objects of knowledge – the most knowable of all, so to speak. But such are the limitations of our finite minds that we arrive at the knowledge of them not at the beginning of our inquiry but at the very end, as its apex or culmination.

It is particularly easy to misapprehend what St. Thomas means by the intellectual virtue of *prudentia*, "prudence," because under the influence of Immanuel Kant, English speakers tend to draw a sharp distinction between the moral and the "merely prudential" – a distinction which *assumes, without investigation,* that moral and intellectual virtues are unrelated. By prudence, however, St. Thomas means *recta ratio agibilium,* "right reason in practice," reason applied to the right ordering of acts which achieve ends. Whether and in what way prudence is related to moral virtue can now be investigated.

The intellectual virtue St. Thomas calls *ars,* "art" in the sense of craftsmanship, is *recta ratio factibilium,* reason applied to the right ordering of productive activities. It is something like prudence, except it is not about things to be done, but things to be made. The crafts of the carpenter and ironsmith are art. The craft of the so-called "rocket scientist" also turns out to be an art (rather than a science), although, like any art, it may employ findings of the sciences.

It will be more convenient to discuss the intellectual virtue of *intellectus,* "understanding," a few paragraphs below.

[2] Both moral virtue, and the intellectual virtue of prudence, have something to do with choosing well, but they do not have the *same thing* to do with choosing well. St. Thomas is about the explain the difference.

[3] The first prerequisite for choosing well is that the chooser's appetites or desires must be regulated so that they are docile to the guidance of reason instead of going off on their own. For example, fear and anger are disciplined by the moral virtue of fortitude or courage, and both the urge to give in to all pleasure and the urge to deny all pleasure are disciplined by the moral virtue of temperance. In contemporary English, it may seem strange to call all of these impulses appetites. However, St. Thomas uses the expression "appetite" for several different kinds of stirrings. I may be stirred up to pursue what seems

good, such as the dinner on my plate; such are the passions of the concupiscible appetite. On the other hand, I may be stirred up to resist what hinders the
good or threatens it with harm, such as the dog who steals dinner from my
plate; such are the passions of the irascible appetite. Sometimes, the passions
of the irascible appetite *counteract* the passions of the concupiscible appetite
(I, Question 81, Article 2). For example, I may be angry with myself for enjoying a pleasure in which I should not have indulged. As we see later, in a certain
way this makes fortitude and temperance allies.

St. Thomas's distinction among the among the rational, irascible, and concupiscible "parts" of the soul reminds many readers of the tripartite view of
the soul famously advanced in Plato's *Republic*. However, the two accounts
have several important differences. One difference is that although Plato would
agree that what St. Thomas calls "concupiscibility" is appetite, he thinks of
irascibility as something altogether different – as a kind of "spiritedness." As
we have seen, however, for St. Thomas the concupiscible and irascible powers
both pertain to appetite, but not to the same kind. The concupiscible power
concerns the appetite for the "delectable" good, for the sort of good which is
desired for its own sake. By contrast, the irascible power concerns the appetite
for the "arduous" good, for the good of *overcoming obstacles* to the delectable
good.

Another reason is that for Plato, these powers are what are called "integral" parts of the soul: They are parts in the same way that walls, roof, and
floor are parts of a house. For St. Thomas, by contrast, they are what are
called "potential" parts, abilities that deal with certain secondary matters
but lack the power of the whole. Why does this matter? Because if they are
integral parts, then a human being lacks substantial unity. He is not a single
thing with a single nature; each of his parts has its own "nature," and Plato's
hope of harmony among them is futile. But if they are potential parts, then
a human being does possess substantial unity; he is a single subsistent thing
with a single nature, and although his powers can be distinguished, they are
not truly separate things. Rather they are aspects of a single thing, the soul,
the underlying unity of which is shown by their relation to the soul's master
power, which is reason.

If reason is truly sovereign, then one might ask how it is ever possible for the
irascible and concupiscible appetites to defy reason. The answer lies in how reason exercises its sovereignty. Borrowing an analogy from Aristotle, St. Thomas
says reason commands the lower powers not by a "despotic sovereignty," the
way slaves are commanded by their master, but by a "royal and political sovereignty," the way free men are ruled by their governor. Even though they are
subject to his rule, they "have in some respects a will of their own," so that they
can resist his commands.[6]

---

[6] See I, Q. 81, Art. 3, ad 2; I-II, Q. 17, Art. 7; and I-II, Q. 56, Art. 4, ad 3. The quotation is from
I-II, Q. 9, Art. 2, ad 3.

euboli a
g nome
synesis

[4] It is one thing for appetite to be docile to right reason *so that* it can be guided to the mean; it is another thing for right reason *to guide it to the mean*, to show the chooser what must be done. Moral virtue accomplishes the first thing, but prudence accomplishes the second.

[5] As we have just seen, prudence guides the moral virtues by *finding* the mean between excess and deficiency at which each of them disposes us to aim, and then *commanding* the appropriate act. However, because command is a complex intellectual power, dependent on several subordinate powers, so also prudence is a complex intellectual virtue, employing several subordinate virtues. Each of these subordinate virtues puts just one of these subordinate powers into right order. The subordinate virtue called *euboulia* causes us to employ good "counsel," in other words to deliberate well – for prudence is what enables us to give good advice, and here prudence itself is viewed as an advisor. The virtues of *gnome* and *synesis* both involve good judgment, but *synesis* causes us to judge well in particular practical matters according to the common rules of thumb, while *gnome* causes us to judge well according to higher, universal principles when the common rules of thumb are insufficient.[7] St. Thomas borrows these Greek terms from Aristotle, since there are no good equivalents in Latin (there aren't in English either). *Synesis*, by the way, should not be confused with *synderesis*, which we will discuss shortly.

[6] The intellectual virtue of *intellectus*, "understanding," is the intellectual virtue which perfects our natural recognition of first principles – the starting points of reasoning, which are known in themselves rather than by drawing inferences from other things we know. A good example is the principle of noncontradiction. Our minds habitually rely on such principles, even if they do not formulate them explicitly. A point which St. Thomas's phrasing does not always make clear – and which is often overlooked – is that not one but two different "habits" or dispositions of the mind are involved here. For on one hand, the mind is naturally endowed with a disposition to know first principles – this comes with being human, and everyone has it. But on the other hand, the intellectual virtue of "understanding" is an *acquired* disposition which perfects or completes the natural disposition. Not everyone has understanding, because it must be developed by intellectual discipline. So it is that although even the child, who has only the natural *habitus* of first principles, relies on the fact that the door is either closed or not closed, St. Thomas, who has the additional, acquired *habitus* of first principles, is able to recognize what the child merely presupposes: That nothing can both *be* and *not be* in the same sense at the same time. As he explains I-II, Question 57, Article 2, "What is known in itself, is as a 'principle,' and is at once understood by the intellect: wherefore the habit that perfects the intellect for the consideration

---

[7] II-II, Q. 51, Arts. 1 and 3. Technically, these are *potential parts* of prudence. For the concept of potential parts, see the previous discussion of I-II, Q. 55, Art. 4, as well as the later discussion of II-II, Q. 80, Art. 1.

of such truth is called 'understanding,' which is the habit of principles [*habitus principiorum*]."

[7] By "speculative" or theoretical reasoning, St. Thomas means not wild guessing or sheer imagination, as in the expression "speculative fiction," but disciplined intellectual inquiry like that which we encounter in the *Summa* itself. Because reasoning may be either theoretical or practical – because it may concern either what is the case or what is to be done – its starting points are twofold also. On the one hand the mind has a natural tendency or *habitus* to know the first starting points of speculative reason, for example the principle of noncontradiction, and on the other hand it has a natural tendency or *habitus* to know the first starting points of practical reason, for example the principle that what a thing naturally seeks after is its good.[8] Here, St. Thomas is treating both of these "habits" as aspects of *intellectus* or understanding, though in other places he distinguishes the habit of the knowledge of the first principles of *practical* reason by the term *synderesis*. The concept of *synderesis* is one of the links between his doctrine of the virtues and his doctrine of natural law.[9]

First principles are known naturally. No one in his right mind asks for a proof of them; they are what we use to prove everything else. The point St. Thomas is making here is that just as *scientia* cannot get started or make progress except by relying on the first principles of speculative reason, so prudence cannot get started or make progress without relying on the first principles of practical reason. As he explains in II-II, Question 47, Article 6, ad 3, "prudence is more excellent than the moral virtues, and moves them: yet *synderesis* moves prudence, just as the understanding of [speculative] principles moves science."[10]

Reply to Objection 1. [1] The inclination of nature in things devoid of reason is without choice: wherefore such an inclination does not of necessity require reason. [2] But the inclination of moral virtue is with choice: and consequently in order that it may be perfect it requires that reason be perfected by intellectual virtue.	Reply to Objection 1. Because the natural inclinations of irrational beings work independently of choice, they have no necessary dependence on reason. However, the kind of inclination that is brought about moral virtue works *through* choice, so its fulfillment requires that reason be brought to its full and appropriate development by intellectual virtue.

[1] Strictly speaking, the hungry wolf does not *choose* whether to attack the buck. Choice is the execution of what results from deliberation, and the

---

[8] I-II, Q. 94, Art. 2. The perceptive form of the first principle of practical reason is "good is to be done and pursued, and evil avoided."

[9] I have discussed *synderesis* at greater length in the *Commentary on Thomas Aquinas's Treatise on Law* (New York: Cambridge University Press, 2014).

[10] Compare II-II, Q. 47, Art. 6; see also Thomas Aquinas, *De Veritate* ("On Truth"), Q. 16, Art. 1.

wolf does not deliberate. It may seem that he does, because if conflicting sense impressions, memories, and instincts come into play, he may hesitate. But a wolf which hesitates is not deliberating any more than a rock which teeters on the edge of a cliff is deliberating.

[2] Although humans experience inclinations, with us it is different than with the other animals. As rational beings, we are drawn to what is good not only through the senses, but through the power to conceive universal principles such as *what is good* and to draw conclusions from them. In fact, our minds *pass judgment* on the promptings of sensual appetite; unlike the wolf, in order to act we must *know what to do*.[11] True, reason can be overcome by strong passion, or placed in a subordinate role so that it only thinks of excuses for doing what passion directs. But in such a case, the person is not acting in a distinctly human way.

The genuine exercise of reason also presupposes freedom:

Man has free-will: otherwise counsels, exhortations, commands, prohibitions, rewards, and punishments would be in vain. In order to make this evident, we must observe that some things act without judgment; as a stone moves downwards; and in like manner all things which lack knowledge. And some act from judgment, but not a free judgment; as brute animals. For the sheep, seeing the wolf, judges it a thing to be shunned, from a natural and not a free judgment, because it judges, not from reason, but from natural instinct. And the same thing is to be said of any judgment of brute animals. But man acts from judgment, because by his apprehensive power he judges that something should be avoided or sought. But because this judgment, in the case of some particular act, is not from a natural instinct, but from some act of comparison in the reason, therefore he acts from free judgment and retains the power of being inclined to various things. For reason in contingent matters may follow opposite courses, as we see in dialectic syllogisms and rhetorical arguments. Now particular operations are contingent, and therefore in such matters the judgment of reason may follow opposite courses, and is not determinate to one. And forasmuch as man is rational is it necessary that man have a free-will.[12]

One might say that the proof of human free will is the very fact that we deliberate. To be sure, the acts of other creatures may be indeterminate just in the sense that it is not immediately clear which impetus is stronger; thus an animal subject to conflicting influences may hesitate, and even a rock may wobble before toppling. But in the case of a rational mind which might go either this way or that, what settles the matter is not a mere impetus, but a judgment.

Not everything about us is subject to free will. For example, I cannot will *not to have* the inclinations which characterize human nature. Even so, I can choose what to do about them.

---

[11] St. Thomas would say that the wolf is not exercising a rational power by which it forms ideas of things, but merely an "estimative" power by which it forms impressions of things. See I-II, Q. 6, Art. 2.

[12] I, Q. 83, Art. 1. The objections and replies in this Article are especially interesting.

Reply to Objection 2. [1] A man may be virtuous without having full use of reason as to everything, provided he have it with regard to those things which have to be done virtuously. In this way all virtuous men have full use of reason. [2] Hence those who seem to be simple, through lack of worldly cunning, may possibly be prudent, according to Matthew 10:16: "Be ye therefore prudent [Douay: 'wise'] as serpents, and simple as doves."	Reply to Objection 2. A virtuous man does not have to be able to reason well about all things, but only about the matters which demand the application of his virtue. All virtuous men reason well in this sense. It follows that those who seem simple-minded because they are devoid of worldly craftiness may well be prudent in their own spheres. This point is reflected in Christ's exhortation to "be as prudent as serpents and simple as doves."

[1] For example, a man who reasons well about the well-being of his family, but who does not reason well about the partnership of associations which make up a political community, might be a virtuous father, but he would not be a virtuous ruler or legislator.

[2] "Be as prudent as serpents and simple as doves" is a literal translation of the Vulgate, the Latin version of the Bible. Contemporary English translations often blunt the point of the paradox, by rendering *simplices*, "simple," as "innocent."

Reply to Objection 3. [1] *The natural inclination to a good of virtue is a kind of beginning of virtue,* [2] *but is not perfect virtue. For the stronger this inclination is, the more perilous may it prove to be, unless it be accompanied by right reason, which rectifies the choice of fitting means towards the due end.* [3] *Thus if a running horse be blind, the faster it runs the more heavily will it fall, and the more grievously will it be hurt.* [4] *And consequently, although moral virtue be not right reason, as Socrates held,* [5] *yet not only is it "according to right reason," in so far as it inclines man to that which is, according to right reason, as the Platonists maintained;*[13] *but also it needs to be "joined with right reason," as Aristotle declares (Ethic. vi, 13).*	Reply to Objection 3. Although the natural inclination to any of those goods to which virtue inclines us gives us a push toward virtue, it is not complete virtue. In fact, the stronger such an inclination is, the more dangerous it may be – unless it is conjoined with right reason, which keeps the choice of means on the right path so that it is appropriate to its proper end. It is just the same way with a blind horse: The faster it runs, the harder it falls and hurts itself. And so, even if moral virtue is not the *same* as right reason (as Socrates maintained), nevertheless, not only does it *incline in the same way* as right reason (as the Platonists maintained), but it must even be *directed by* right reason (as Aristotle maintained).

[13] Although the Blackfriars translators suggest comparison with Plato, *Meno*, Section 41, the position of Socrates in Plato's *Meno* concerning the relation of virtue to practical wisdom is not clearly settled.

[1] Each of the moral virtues directs us to a particular good. St. Thomas calls the bare natural inclination to such a good, *apart from the guidance of reason*, "a sort of inchoate virtue," *quaedam inchoatio virtutis*. In other places he calls it the "seed of virtue," *seminalia virtutum*.[14] Translators often use such expressions as "the nursery of virtue."

[2] For example, although the bare, spontaneous inclination to give to others may protect a person from the vice of miserliness, and so give a push to the development of true generosity, it also exposes him to the opposite vice of prodigality. Rather than exercising judgment about which gifts would be appropriate, he may give merely because it makes him feel good. He is all too likely to give the wrong things, to give too much, or to give to the wrong people. At times he may even give things to persons who will be hurt by his gifts. By being too freehanded, he may also render himself unable to fulfill his duties to those who have just claims on him. The point is not to deny that generosity is a real moral virtue, but to point out that the true and fully developed virtue of generosity finds the mean between excess and deficiency. A mere spontaneous inclination to give to others has the potentiality to become a very good thing, but the better an imperfect thing is, the more damage can result from its misuse. *Corruptio optimi pessima est*: "The corruption of the best is the worst."

[3] The analogy of the blind horse is drawn from Aristotle, *Nicomachean Ethics*, Book 6, Chapter 13. In itself, the horse's strength and swiftness are good, but unless they are directed by vision, calamity may result. Virtue *as such* cannot be misused; but the dispositions which are the seeds of virtue are often misused.

[4] In the dialogue *Protagoras*, Socrates seems to equate virtue with knowledge, although in the dialogue *Meno*, he raises the difficulty that if virtue is no more than knowledge, then it ought to be teachable like geometry, and it seems that it isn't. St. Thomas's view resolves the paradox, for moral virtue involves not just knowledge, but the rectification of appetite with the guidance of right reason.

[5] Here St. Thomas is agreeing with Aristotle. Following is how a recent English translation renders the Latin version of Aristotle's text used by St. Thomas:

In this, Socrates was correct in one respect and wrong in another. He erroneously held that all virtues are species of prudence, but correctly stated that virtue cannot be without prudence. An indication of this is that at the present time all men, in defining virtue, place it in the genus of habit and state to what matters it extends and that it is according to right reason. But right reason is that which is according to prudence. Therefore they all seem to guess in some manner that virtue is the kind of habit that is in accord with prudence. But we must go a little further, for virtue is not merely in conformity

---

[14] See I-II, Q. 51, Art. 1, I-II, Q. 63, Art. 1, and I-II, Q. 67, Art. 1, ad 3. Compare Thomas Aquinas, *De Veritate* ("On Truth"), Q. 16, Art. 1, where he says the natural knowledge of first principles is "a kind of seed of all knowledge," *quasi quoddam seminarium totius cognitionis*.

with reason, but a habit accompanied by reason. But right reason in such matters is prudence. Socrates then was of the opinion that virtues *are* kinds of reason because he thought they were species of knowledge. But we maintain they are *accompanied* by reason. Therefore it is obvious from the discussion how it is not possible for a man to be good in the strict sense without prudence, nor to be prudent without moral virtue.[15]

In large part, what St. Thomas has done in this Article is explain *how* the conclusion, which Aristotle calls obvious from the discussion, is obvious from the discussion – something Aristotle himself does not quite spell out.

---

[15] Thomas Aquinas, *Commentary on Aristotle's Nicomachean Ethics*, Book 6, Lecture 11, trans. C. J. Litzinger, rev. ed. (Notre Dame, IN: Dumb Ox Books, 1993), p. 402. Available online at www.dhspriory.org/thomas/english/Ethics.htm.

Whether There Can Be Intellectual without Moral Virtue?

TEXT	PARAPHRASE
Whether there can be intellectual without moral virtue?	Can a person who lacks moral virtue have intellectual virtue?

Can a person possess both intellectual and moral virtue? Yes, there exist persons who are both wise and good. Can a person lack both intellectual and moral virtue? Yes, the world abounds in fools and reprobates. Can a person have moral but not intellectual virtue? As we learned in the previous Article, this is impossible because moral virtue requires the guidance of prudence. Can a person have intellectual but not moral virtue – can he have prudence, without such qualities as temperance, justice, or fortitude? This is what we are about to investigate.

The answer makes a great deal of difference to a host of other things. For example, every time a new scandal in the world of government, industry, commerce, education, or finance explodes into the headlines, the call goes up that schools of business, law, and public administration should give more attention to teaching ethics. One common approach to teaching ethics is teaching *theories* of ethics. Another is to pose moral quandaries and encourage students to discuss what they would do if they found themselves caught in them. Such classroom approaches share an assumption that becoming ethical is a purely intellectual endeavor, like learning algebra.

However, *if it is really true* that moral and intellectual virtue depend on each other, that neither can exist without the other, then such approaches are desperately mistaken. To one who lacks virtue, the learning of ethical theories and the discussion of ethical quandaries provides nothing more than an occasion for rehearsing his excuses and sharpening his empty cleverness. A book about the virtues, even one as good as Thomas Aquinas's, can be most helpful to someone who is already on the road to virtue, but it will be almost useless to someone who isn't – except in those few cases when someone bumps up against his conscience, as in the case of the young man who told me that the ancient book he was reading was "making him realize that he hadn't led a virtuous life."

The best way to improve the odds of getting virtuous people in positions of influence is to encourage virtue in everyone, raising all in good habits from earliest childhood, confirming them in these habits by sound laws, providing explanations little by little as their minds become able to reflect on experience and receive the form of prudence – explanations which do not substitute for these laboriously acquired dispositions, but which purify, ennoble, and direct them, helping their bearers to piece together why what they were taught is actually right.

Objection 1. [1] *It would seem that there can be intellectual without moral virtue. Because perfection of what precedes does not depend on the perfection of what follows.* [2] *Now reason precedes and moves the sensitive appetite.* [3] *Therefore intellectual virtue, which is a perfection of the reason, does not depend on moral virtue, which is a perfection of the appetitive faculty; and can be without it.*	Objection 1. Seemingly it *is* possible for intellectual virtue to exist in a person without moral virtue. Why? Because reason comes into operation before sensitive appetite does, and brings it into action – but the complete development of what comes first in a sequence does not depend on the complete development of what comes later. From these facts, two things follow. The first is that intellectual virtue, which puts reason in complete order, does not depend on moral virtue, which puts appetite in complete order. The second is that it can exist without it.

[1] First one builds the foundation, then one builds the house. To complete the house, one must complete the foundation, but to complete the foundation it is not necessary to complete the house.

[2] The sense in which reason comes before appetite is that reason recognizes that something is desirable. With irrational animals, desire follows instinct and sense perception alone; with us, something more is involved.

[3] In itself, reason is only a power or capacity; intellectual virtue is what makes reason work well and fittingly. In itself, appetite is also just a power; moral virtue is what makes us desire the right things and keeps us from desiring the wrong ones. So the Objector is claiming that since the former comes first and the latter comes afterward, a person could have the former without the latter; even a scoundrel, he thinks, could be prudent.

Objection 2. [1] *Further, morals are the matter of prudence, even as things makeable are the matter of art.*	Objection 2. Moreover, just as the matter with which art or craftsmanship concerns itself is products (what is to be fashioned), so the matter with which prudence concerns itself is "morals"

[2] *Now art can be without its proper matter, as a smith without iron.* **[3]** *Therefore prudence can be without the moral virtue,* **[4]** *although of all the intellectual virtues, it seems most akin to the moral virtues.*	or deeds (what is to be done for the sake of an end). But craftsmanship can exist without its proper matter; we see this from the fact that a man can be an ironsmith even if he lacks iron to make into things. Pursuing the analogy, it seems that prudence can exist without morality. This is true even though of all the intellectual virtues, it does seem to have the greatest connection with morality.

[1] As we saw in I-II, Question 55, Article 4, one of the senses of "matter" is that to which something pertains. Now the matter to which prudence pertains to is *moralia*, which means what is to be done – in other words, "morals," or moral acts. But the matter to which art or craftsmanship pertains to is *factibilia*, which means what is to be made – in other words, products, such as fences and houses.

[2] Readers may think the Objector has forgotten what he was talking about; instead of speaking of a smith, shouldn't he be speaking of smithcraft, and instead of speaking of iron, shouldn't he be speaking of the things he wants to make out of iron? So far, however, his statement is not incorrect, but merely allusive. Smithcraft is what *makes* a man a smith, so here the Objector is using metonymy, the figure of speech in which a thing is called by the name of something which is associated with it. Iron is the matter *of the matter* of smithcraft, what the things to be made *are made from*, so in that case the Objector is using ellipsis.

[3] Since this is the conclusion, the Objector could have stopped here.

[4] Interestingly, the Objector follows his conclusion with a concession: Though he insists that prudence *can* exist without moral virtue, he seems to agree that this is uncommon, for he remarks that of all the intellectual virtues it is the one "most closely conjoined" (*maxime … coniuncta*) with morals.

Objection 3. **[1]** *Further, prudence is "a virtue whereby we are of good counsel" (Ethic. vi, 5).*[1] **[2]** *Now many are of good counsel without having the moral virtues. Therefore prudence can be without a moral virtue.*	**Objection 3.** Still further, as Aristotle points out in the sixth book of his *Nicomachean Ethics*, prudence is the virtue that enables the power of reason to advise us well. But many who lack the moral virtues advise themselves well. Plainly, then, a man can have prudence even if he lacks moral virtue.

[1] To be of good counsel is to be the kind of person who deliberates well – the kind who can give good advice both to others and to himself, by his own power of reasoning. In the passage in the *Nicomachean Ethics* to which the

---

[1] St. Thomas refers only to Book 6. The reference in the Blackfriars translation to Chapter 9 seems to be incorrect.

Objector refers, Aristotle remarks that a man of good counsel is able to see what is good not only for a particular aspect of life, such as health or strength, but for life as a whole.

[2] The Objector's point is that even a dishonest man may advise himself not to steal, even an intemperate man may advise himself not to indulge in a certain pleasure, and even a coward may advise himself to stand firm. He just doesn't *take* his good advice.

On the contrary, [1] *To wish to do evil is directly opposed to moral virtue; and yet it is not opposed to anything that can be without moral virtue.* [2] *Now it is contrary to prudence "to sin willingly" (Ethic. vi, 5). Therefore prudence cannot be without moral virtue.*	**On the other hand**, although the wish or will to do evil is directly opposed to moral virtue, it does not oppose things which can exist without moral virtue. But as Aristotle argues, prudence is opposed to voluntary sin. It follows that prudence cannot exist without moral virtue.

[1] The flow of the argument in the *sed contra* is a little hard to follow. However, bearing in mind that if one thing directly opposes another, then each of them excludes the other, it can be reorganized as follows:

1. An evil will does not set itself against things which can exist without moral virtue.
2. But an evil will does set itself against prudence.
3. Therefore prudence is not one of those things which can exist without moral virtue.

[2] What Aristotle says is that in art or craftsmanship, someone who makes a mistake on purpose is more acceptable – but that in practical wisdom and moral virtue, it is just the reverse, for the person who sins without meaning to sin is more acceptable. In his *Commentary on Aristotle's Nicomachean Ethics*, St. Thomas elaborates as follows:

Obviously, if a man deliberately makes a mistake in art, he is considered a better artist than if he does not do this of his own will, because then he would seem to act out of ignorance of his art. This is evident in those who deliberately make grammatical errors in their speech. But in the case of prudence a man who willingly sins is less commended than one who sins against his will; the same is true of the moral virtues. This is true because for prudence there is required a rectitude of the appetitive faculty concerning the ends, in order that its principles be preserved. Thus it is clear that prudence is not an art consisting, as it were, only in the truth of reason, but a virtue requiring rectitude of the appetitive faculty after the manner of the moral virtues.[2]

---

[2] Thomas Aquinas, *Commentary on Aristotle's Nicomachean Ethics*, Book 6, Lecture 4, trans. C. J. Litzinger, rev. ed. (Notre Dame, IN: Dumb Ox Books, 1993), p. 372. Available online at www.dhspriory.org/thomas/english/Ethics.htm.

I answer that, [1] *Other intellectual virtues can, but prudence cannot, be without moral virtue. The reason for this is that prudence is the right reason about things to be done* [2] *(and this, not merely in general, but also in particular); [3] about which things actions are.* [4] *Now right reason demands principles from which reason proceeds to argue. And when reason argues about particular cases, it needs not only universal but also particular principles.* [5] *As to universal principles of action, man is rightly disposed by the natural understanding of principles, whereby he understands that he should do no evil; or again by some practical science.* [6] *But this is not enough in order that man may reason aright about particular cases. For it happens sometimes that the aforesaid universal principle, known by means of understanding or science, is destroyed in a particular case by a passion:* [7] *thus to one who is swayed by concupiscence, when he is overcome thereby, the object of his desire seems good, although it is opposed to the universal judgment of his reason.* [8] *Consequently, as by the habit of natural understanding or of science, man is made to be rightly disposed in regard to the universal principles of action; so, in order that he be rightly disposed with regard to the particular principles of action, viz. the ends, he needs to be perfected by certain habits, whereby it becomes connatural, as it were, to man to judge aright to the end.* [9] *This is done by moral virtue: for the virtuous man judges aright of the end of virtue,* [10] *because "such a*

Here is my response. Although other intellectual virtues can exist without moral virtue, prudence cannot exist without moral virtue. The reason for this is that prudence concerns not only right reason about what is to be done in general, but right reason about what is to be done in particular matters (matters in which the end to be sought resides at least partly in the activity itself, rather than in some product or result that it achieves). Why? Because all reasoning requires "principles" or starting points – and reasoning about particulars requires not only universal but particular principles.

Now concerning universal principles of conduct, we are sufficiently guided by natural understanding (by which, for example, we recognize that we must never commit evil) along with "science" (by which we recognize the implications of the principle). But for the proper guidance of our reasoning about particulars, these do not suffice. Why not? Because sometimes, in particular cases, these universal principles are twisted aside by passions. For example, concupiscence overmasters us so that something which is contrary to the universal judgment of reason seems good to us anyway.

And so, just as a man's reasoning is brought into proper order concerning universal principles by natural "understanding," or by the disposition we have called "science," so it must also be brought into proper order concerning particular principles – which are ends or purposes – by certain other dispositions, dispositions which make it connatural or "second nature" for him to judge rightly concerning ends. And what are these dispositions? They are the moral virtues. Just as Aristotle remarks in the third book of the *Nicomachean Ethics*, a virtuous man is one who makes good judgments concerning the end to which virtue has already directed him – *he is precisely the*

man is, such does the end seem to him" (*Ethic. iii, 5*). Consequently the right reason about things to be done, *viz.* prudence, requires man to have moral virtue.	sort of man to whom good ends actually seem good. It follows that right reason in action – that is prudence – requires a man to have moral virtue.

[1] Prudence is about operations. The intellectual virtue of art or craftsmanship is also about operations, but unlike prudence, it concerns not things to be done, but things to be made.

[2] Every moral act is *some kind* of moral act. No one ever performs a "moral act in general"; what one performs is always an act of, say, fortitude or justice.

[3] In my paraphrase, the wordy formulation "matters in which the end to be sought resides at least partly in the activity itself rather than in some product or result that it achieves" elaborates what St. Thomas means by "actions." We see here the error of so-called consequentialist theories of ethics, such as utilitarianism, which think the only point of moral conduct is what results. In effect, consequentialism abolishes the difference between prudence and craftsmanship. By doing so it also denies the possibility of intrinsically evil acts – acts that are wrong no matter what comes of them.

[4] To begin reasoning about what morality requires, it is not enough to know the first principle of practical reason, that good is what all things seek, or to know the first precept of natural law to which it corresponds, that good is to be done and pursued and evil is to be avoided.[3] One must also grasp what courage is, or what justice is, or whatever the virtue in question is.

[5] We have discussed this point previously. Some things are naturally known in themselves, other things are known by drawing inferences. The habit or disposition by which the mind knows the former sort of thing is understanding, and the habit or disposition by which it arrives at the latter sort of thing is science. Why doesn't St. Thomas simply say that we know certain things naturally, rather than saying that we have a habit of knowing them? Because the knowledge in question is not always "actual" – the mind is not always thinking about it. Even so, it is always there in potentiality – the mind has a dispositional tendency to be aware of it, which persists even despite the efforts we sometimes make to distract ourselves and not think about it. Contemporary thinkers try to get at knowledge which is potential but not actual by imagining that we have two minds, one "conscious," one "unconscious." St. Thomas's theory is superior, because it recognizes that despite the subtlety of its operations and the multiplicity of its powers, the mind is not two things but one.

[6] Although *corrumpitur*, the word St. Thomas uses, can certainly mean "destroyed," here it is better translated "corrupted," "seduced," or "perverted" (thus my paraphrase, "twisted aside"). The dispositional tendency to be

---

[3] I-II, Q. 94, Art. 2.

aware of the universal principle continues to exist, but passion so dominates the mind that either the knowledge remains latent, or it is not applied correctly to the case at hand. For example, even in the mind of the murderer there lies the knowledge that deliberately taking innocent human life is wrong. But he may act without thinking, or he may think something like "That piece of excrement? Human? Ha!"

A "passion," by the way, is simply a "movement," or change, of the sensitive appetite.[4] It is not necessarily a hot emotion, like boiling-blood rage. Etymologically, the term is related to the word "passive," for in the broadest sense, a passion is not something we cause to happen, but something that happens to us because of something else. In this sense, even a condition such as intoxication can be called a passion.

[7] No one can do what seems to him bad at the time. The problem is that something evil may seem good at the time. Reason whispers, "Sleeping with that woman wouldn't be good – she's not my wife." But concupiscence says, "You fool, just think of her soft, warm arms," and concupiscence is louder. To be sure, no evil can seem good unless it is good *in some respect*. So even here the problem isn't that a woman's soft, warm arms aren't good as such. The problem is that these particular soft, warm arms aren't good *for him*.

[8] This is the second time we have encountered the concept of connaturality or "second nature." I have offered a more complete discussion of St. Thomas's treatment of the idea in another book.[5]

[9] The end or purpose of justice is just acts, the end or purpose of temperance is temperate acts, and so on. But each of these virtues is a department of being reasonable, for the end of virtue *as such* is to live according to reason. This is because reason is our highest and most distinctive power, the one which lifts us from mere animal to rational animal, the one which makes us human. It isn't that we don't share inclinations with the subrational animals, such as preservation and the procreation of young; we do. But the subrational animals are pulled only by the cords of instinct, whereas we demand to know the rational meaning and purpose of it all. Unless our activities conform to this meaning and purpose, they are wrong, and we are thwarted and unfulfilled.

[10] The morally virtuous man is the one to whom the things that are really good *actually seem good*. What brings about this condition of his appetites is moral virtue. The point of St. Thomas's reference to Aristotle is his observation that although the means to the end can be a matter of deliberation (and so also a matter of prudence), the ends themselves cannot be, "For a doctor does not deliberate whether he shall heal, nor an orator whether he shall persuade,

---

[4] See I-II, Q. 58, Art. 9.
[5] "The Natural, the Connatural, and the Unnatural," in J. Budziszewski, *The Line through the Heart: Natural Law as Fact, Theory, and Sign of Contradiction* (Wilmington, DE: Intercollegiate Studies Institute Books, 2009). An earlier version of the chapter is available online at http://undergroundthomist.org/articles.

nor a statesman whether he shall produce law and order, nor does anyone else deliberate about his end. They assume the end and consider how and by what means it is to be attained … if we are to be always deliberating, we shall have to go on to infinity."[6] In alluding to this passage, St. Thomas does not mean to imply that any end one might pursue would be equally right. On the contrary, persons of virtue have good ends, persons of vice have bad ones. Virtue inclines us to fitting ends; deliberation, taking these ends for granted, finds fitting means.

Reply to Objection 1. [1] *Reason, as apprehending the end, precedes the appetite for the end: but appetite for the end precedes the reason, as arguing about the choice of the means, which is the concern of prudence.* [2] *Even so, in speculative matters the understanding of principles is the foundation on which the syllogism of the reason is based.*	Reply to Objection 1. Reason does precede the desire for the end in the sense that reason must first *grasp* the end to be desired. But the desire for the end precedes reason in the sense that prudence must know what the end is before it can choose means for achieving it. We see something similar even in purely theoretical reasoning, because there too, the understanding of principles comes before reason's construction of a syllogism.

[1] The aspect of reason called understanding *precedes* desire for the end in the sense that reason recognizes the end as truly desirable. This does not require moral virtue. But the aspect of reason which is prudence *is preceded by* desire for the end in the sense that only one who actually does desire the end deliberates about the means to be chosen to achieve it. This does require moral virtue.

[2] In the case of a theoretical syllogism, the premises and the conclusion are all propositions – things to be affirmed. For example, from the propositions "All men are mortal" and "Socrates is a man" follows the affirmation "Socrates is mortal." In the case of what St. Thomas calls a practical syllogism, however, the result is not a proposition, but a decision or judgment – something to be done – which is followed by a choice. For example, from the proposition "Health is good," which supposes the appropriateness of pursuing it, and the proposition "Moderation in eating promotes health," which tells how to accomplish it, a man who possesses the virtue of temperance arrives at the decision "I will practice moderation in eating," which he carries into execution. Plainly, the *decision* to practice moderation because it is good is not the same as the *proposition* that it would be good to practice moderation; the former is an act of the will. However, this act of the will holds the same place in a practical syllogism that the concluding proposition holds in an ordinary syllogism.[7]

---

[6] Aristotle, *Nicomachean Ethics*, trans. W. D. Ross (public domain), Book 3, Chapters 3 and 5; my quotation is from the former.

[7] See I-II, Q. 13, Art. 1, ad 2; Q. 76, Art. 1; Q. 90, Art. 1; and Q. 90, Art. 4.

Reply to Objection 2. [1] *It does not depend on the disposition of our appetite whether we judge well or ill of the principles of art, as it does, when we judge of the end which is the principle in moral matters: in the former case our judgment depends on reason alone.* [2] *Hence art does not require a virtue perfecting the appetite, as prudence does.*	Reply to Objection 2. An artisan makes judgments about how to make something which is to be made, and a man concerned with action makes judgments about how to do something which is to be done. So far, the two processes seem similar, but here the analogy ends. For the question of whether a craftsman has judged well or badly does not depend on the state of his will; it is purely a question of rational technique. By contrast, the question of whether a man has judged well or badly does depend at least partly on the state of his will. So even though craftsmanship does not require the rectification of the appetites by moral virtue, prudence does.

[1] When we say that a craftsman is making skillful judgments, we are not commenting on what he desires to make but only on how well he makes it. But when we say that a man is making good moral judgments, we are commenting not only on how cleverly he gets what he wants but also on whether he wants the right things. To put it another way, someone could be a *good craftsman* but not a good man, but nobody could be a *good man* but not a good man.

[2] So although craftsmanship *as such* does not require the help of moral virtue, prudence does – but of course the craftsman, like everyone, should be a good man as well.

Reply to Objection 3. [1] *Prudence not only helps us to be of good counsel, but also to judge and command well.* [2] *This is not possible unless the impediment of the passions, destroying the judgment and command of prudence, be removed; and this is done by moral virtue.*	Reply to Objection 3. Yes, prudence involves giving ourselves good advice ("I should do this!") – but it also involves good acts of judgment and self-direction. ("That's good!" "Now I do it!") Since these acts are corrupted by passion, complete prudence is impossible unless the impediment is removed – which is accomplished by moral virtue.

[1] The literal meaning of the term St. Thomas uses for command is "precept," or direction. Later in the *Summa*, in the section on law, he remarks that in the broad sense of the term "precept," every law is a kind of precept.[8] The ends of the virtues are in fact natural laws.

[2] Whatever understanding recognizes as good, appetite desires; whatever appetite desires, prudence seeks means to achieve. The point is not that this is how things always work, but that this is the proper order of things, which

[8] I-II, Q. 92, Art. 2, ad 1.

excessively strong passions tend to destroy, but moral virtue – by setting appetite in right order – tends to preserve. Elsewhere in the *Summa* St. Thomas discusses the manifold difficulties which result from the fact that ever since our first parents rebelled against their Maker, the governance of appetite by reason has been disordered.[9]

---

[9] See I-II, QQ. 81–83, 85.

Whether There Are Four Cardinal Virtues?

TEXT	PARAPHRASE
Whether there are four cardinal virtues?	Is the traditional view correct in holding that all moral virtues depend on four pivotal or paramount virtues?

From St. Thomas's frequent mention of Aristotle it would be easy to get the mistaken impression that the two thinkers agree about everything. This is far from the case, and with the present Article we come to one of the chief differences between St. Thomas's theory of virtue and Aristotle's. The analysis Aristotle offers in the *Nicomachean Ethics*, so promising in its starting points, peters out in a diffuse list of twelve "means" of assorted kinds; we are left wondering why he lists just these virtues and not others. Although at various points he does relate his scheme of the virtues to Aristotle's,[1] St. Thomas takes sides with a more powerful and suggestive tradition which holds that although there are a great many moral virtues – certainly far more than twelve – four of them surpass all the others, and are in a certain sense their heads. The first of these is prudence, or practical wisdom, the bridge between the moral and intellectual virtues, which brings the power of moral reasoning to its full and proper development. The other three are fortitude, or courage; temperance, or restraint; and justice, or fairness. All of the other acquired virtues are associated in some way with these four (as we will find later that all of the infused virtues are associated in some way with faith, hope, and charity or love).

The two most common expressions for such virtues among medieval thinkers – "principal virtues" and "cardinal virtues" – had been coined centuries earlier by St. Ambrose of Milan. To call a virtue "principal" is merely to convey its importance. In view of the many meanings of the Latin root *cardo*, however, to call a virtue "cardinal" is to say much more: It evokes the images of a hinge on

---

[1] For example in II-II, Q. 30, Art. 3, taken up later in this book.

which lesser virtues pivot, an axis on which they turn, a point from which they are surveyed, a boundary in which they are contained, and a tenon-and-mortise joint by which they are connected.[2] Each of these images is precise.

Although the idea of all moral virtues depending on four chief moral virtues is properly traced to the Greeks and Romans, especially Plato, Marcus Tullius Cicero, and the Stoics, it is biblical too. To moderns, skeptical of allegory, St. Ambrose might seem to exaggerate its biblical pedigree when he compares the four cardinal virtues with the four rivers of Paradise (*On Paradise*, Book 3, Chapters 14–18), the four ages of salvation history (*On Paradise*, Book 3, Chapters 19–22), the four allegorical creatures in the book of the prophet Ezekiel (*On Virginity*, Book 18, Chapters 114–115), the four wings of these creatures (*On Abraham*, Book 2, Chapter 8, Section 54), the four beatitudes mentioned in the Gospel of Matthew but not in the Gospel of Luke (*Commentary on Luke*, Book 5, Chapters 65–68), and the four good horses drawing the chariot of the soul (*On Isaac, or the Soul*, Book 8, Chapter 65). The most interesting feature of his discussion – and the one which most clearly sets it apart from the conceptions of the pagan writers from whom he borrows – is the way he correlates them with spiritual graces, especially knowledge of God, trust in God, love of God and neighbor, and poverty of spirit.[3]

However, the Old Testament puts the praise of the cardinal virtues in the mouth of Lady Wisdom herself. St. Thomas is particularly fond of the following passage from the book of Wisdom, and quotes it often. He mentions just the final, italicized verse alone at least six times in the *Summa* alone, most often in the *sed contra*, the part of an Article which restates the traditional view:[4]

[Wisdom] reaches mightily from one end of the earth to the other, and she orders all things well. I loved her and sought her from my youth, and I desired to take her for my bride, and I became enamored of her beauty. She glorifies her noble birth by living with God, and the Lord of all loves her. For she is an initiate in the knowledge of God, and an associate in his works. If riches are a desirable possession in life, what is richer than wisdom who effects all things? And if understanding is effective, who more than she is fashioner of what exists? *And if any one loves righteousness, her labors are virtues; for she teaches self-control and prudence, justice and courage; nothing in life is more profitable for men than these.*[5]

---

[2] St. Ambrose first uses the expression "cardinal virtues" in his funeral oration for his brother, *On the Death of Satyrus*, Book 1, Section 57, available on the internet at www.newadvent.org/fathers/3403.htm.

[3] See István P. Bejczy, *The Cardinal Virtues in the Middle Ages: A Study in Moral Thought from the Fourth to the Fourteenth Century* (Leiden, Netherlands: Brill, 2011), pp. 12–17.

[4] I-II, Q. 57, Art. 5, *sed contra*, and Q. 63, Art. 3, *sed contra*; II-II, Q. 47, Art. 5, *sed contra*, Q. 149, Art. 1, Obj. 2, and Q. 23, Art. 7, *sed contra*; and III, Q. 89, Art. 1, *sed contra*.

[5] Wisdom 8:1–7 (RSV-CE), emphasis added. The book of Wisdom, also known as the Wisdom of Solomon, is not to be confused with the book of the Wisdom of Jesus son of Sirach, also known as Ecclesiasticus or Sirach.

Since a host of lesser virtues depends on each of the cardinal virtues, we must take care not to view them narrowly. Consider for example the "parts" of temperance. Since the most difficult and characteristic act of temperance is to regulate the pleasures of touch, this is the act which St. Thomas most often mentions, and so one might easily think that temperance concerns nothing else. On the contrary, it concerns many things, in a number of ways. The *integral* parts of a chief virtue are the conditions which the virtue requires: Thus the integral parts of temperance are attraction to the beauty of temperance, and aversion to the disgrace opposed to temperance. The *subjective* parts of a chief virtue are its species or kinds, each of which has its own subject matter. Thus although temperance in general is concerned with pleasures, its subjective parts include abstinence, which concerns the pleasures of food; sobriety, which concerns the pleasures of drink; chastity, which concerns the pleasures of the procreative act; and purity, which concerns the pleasures incidental to the act, for example the pleasures of kissing and fondling. The *potential* parts of a chief virtue are secondary virtues, which achieve the mean not in the most difficult matter (in this case pleasures of touch), but in less difficult matters. Thus concerning the interior processes of the soul, the potential parts of temperance include continence, humility, and mildness; concerning bodily movements and actions, its potential part is modesty, taken in a broad sense which encompasses discernment of what to do and not do, proper order in our deeds, perseverance, decorum, and gravity; and concerning external things, its potential parts include contentment and simplicity.[6]

Objection 1. [1] *It would seem that there are not four cardinal virtues. For prudence is the directing principle of the other moral virtues, as is clear from what has been said above (Question 58, Article 4).* [2] *But that which directs other things ranks before them. Therefore prudence alone is a principal virtue.*	Objection 1. Apparently the number of cardinal virtues is less than four. We have already seen that prudence guides and regulates the other moral virtues. Surely a virtue which guides and regulates the other virtues is greater in stature than the ones which is guides and regulates. It follows that prudence is the one truly paramount virtue, and all other moral virtues are subordinate to it.

[1] As we saw in the discussion of I-II, Question 58, Article 4, good moral choice depends on two things. In the first place our intention must be directed toward the proper end; the ordinary moral virtues bring this about by making us desire what is rationally fitting. But in the second place we must grasp those things which the end requires, which is impossible without the counsel, judgment, and direction of prudence.

[6] II-II, Q. 143, Art. 1. For the concept of potential parts, see the previous discussion of I-II, Q. 55, Art. 4, as well as the later discussion of II-II, Q. 80, Art. 1.

[2] In Latin, the Objector says that which directs is "principal" or chief. This may at first seem tautological, as though he were saying that the leading thing is the leading thing. Actually he is saying that the thing which is in the leading position in the sense of bringing into order is also in the leading position in the sense of being most important.

| Objection 2. [1] *Further, the principal virtues are, in a way, moral virtues. Now we are directed to moral works both by the practical reason, and by a right appetite, as stated in Ethic. vi, 2.* [2] *Therefore there are only two cardinal virtues.* | Objection 2. Another reason for thinking that there are fewer than four principal virtues is that such virtues concern the domain of morality. But as Aristotle explains in his *Nicomachean Ethics*, the activity of the moral virtues is set in order by just two things: practical reason and right appetite. From this observation it would seem to follow that there are just two cardinal virtues. |

[1] In *Nicomachean Ethics*, Book 6, Chapter 2, Aristotle argues that although three powers of the soul (the senses, reason, and appetite) seem to be involved in the soul's apprehension of truth, its distinctively human actions are originated by just two of these (appetite and reason). Therefore, "both the reasoning must be true and the desire right, if the choice is to be good, and the latter must pursue just what the former asserts."[7]

Aristotle's proof that action is originated by reason and appetite alone is that although the other animals have senses, they do not share in action. We might pursue this argument a little further, for at first it seems odd; don't animals "do things," as we do? Yes, they do things – but no, they don't do them as we do. For by "action," Aristotle means *rational* action, *our* kind of action, of which they are incapable. As St. Thomas explains in his *Commentary* on the work, "dumb animals have senses but do not have social action because they are not masters of their own action; they do not operate from themselves but are moved by natural instinct."[8] We may further add that although some animals have social instincts, only humans are social in the sense intended here, because only humans are partners in a life which aspires to be shaped by recognized truth. This is why ethics has significance for human beings alone.

[2] The Objector's point is that simply that if the *sine qua non* of good choice is that the reasoning is true and the desire is right, then it would seem that there are exactly two cardinal virtues, true reasoning and right desire. So whereas the first Objector suggested that the number of cardinal virtues is not four but only one, the present one suggests that the number is not four but only two.

---

[7] Aristotle, *Nicomachean Ethics*, trans. W. D. Ross (public domain), Book 6, Chapter 2.

[8] Thomas Aquinas, *Commentary on Aristotle's Nicomachean Ethics*, Book 6, Lecture 2, trans. C. J. Litzinger, rev. ed. (Notre Dame, IN: Dumb Ox Books, 1993), p. 359. Available online at www.dhspriory.org/thomas/english/Ethics.htm.

Objection 3. Further, even among the other virtues one ranks higher than another. But in order that a virtue be principal, it needs not to rank above all the others, but above some. Therefore it seems that there are many more principal virtues.	Objection 3. Still further, even among the virtues which are not traditionally called principal, one may be paramount to some of the others. But for a virtue to be described as paramount, it does not have to be more important than all of the others, but only more important than some of them. It seems, then, that virtues of this sort should also be called principal virtues. Viewing the matter this way, the number of principal virtues is far greater than four.

If we picture all the moral virtues as a branching tree, then the Objector does not deny that four great boughs are bigger and more impressive than all the rest. His claim is merely that a lot of other big branches grow from the tree too. They may not be as impressive as the four great ones, but they are certainly more impressive than the twigs. So if the criterion of a cardinal virtue is merely that it is more impressive than some of the other moral virtues, then surely there are more cardinal virtues than four! Each of the other Objectors suggested that the traditional list of cardinal virtues is too long; only this one suggests that it is too short.

On the contrary, Gregory says (Moral. ii): "The entire structure of good works is built on four virtues."	On the other hand, we have the authority of Gregory the Great, who says in the second book of his work *Morals on the Book of Job* that from just four virtues rises the whole framework of moral effort.

In the Old Testament book of Job, a good man is assailed by a series of catastrophes, one after the other. Raiders steal his oxen and asses and slay his servants; fire from heaven consumes his sheep and shepherds; another group of marauders steal his camels and their attendants; finally, a great wind strikes the four corners of his house, causing it to collapse and kill his sons and daughters.

Following the example of the Fathers of the Church, medieval theologians interpreted such passages not only in the literal sense, but also in several figurative senses. In the *typological* sense, an earlier event is taken as foreshadowing a later one. In the *anagogical* sense, a visible reality is taken as disclosing a spiritual reality that cannot be seen. In the *tropological* sense, the literal events are taken as expressing moral truths. Explaining the collapse of the four corners of the house tropologically, St. Gregory writes as follows:

But this house stands by four corners for this reason, that the firm fabric of our mind is upheld by Prudence, Temperance, Fortitude, Justice. This house is grounded on four corners, in that the whole structure of good practice is raised in these four virtues. And hence do four rivers of Paradise water the earth. For while the heart is watered with these four virtues, it is cooled from all the heat of carnal desires. Yet sometimes when idleness steals on the mind, prudence waxes cold; for when it is weary and turns slothful, it neglects to forecast coming events. Sometimes while some delight is

literal, typological, anagogical, tropological
senses of interpretation.

stealing on the mind, our temperance decays. For in whatever degree we are led to take delight in the things of this life, we are the less temperate to forbear in things forbidden. Sometimes fear works its way into the heart and confounds the powers of our fortitude, and we prove the less able to encounter adversity, the more excessively we love some things that we dread to part with. And sometimes self-love invades the mind, makes it swerve by a secret declension from the straight line of justice: and in the degree that it refuses to refer itself wholly to its Maker, it goes contrary to the claims of justice. Thus 'a strong wind smites the four corners of the house,' in that strong temptation, by hidden impulses, shakes the four virtues; and the corners being smitten, the house is as it were uprooted; in that when the virtues are beaten, the con-science is brought to trouble.[9]

Whether or not St. Gregory is right in thinking that the four corners of Job's house *represent* four chief virtues, he is obviously an exponent of the theory of four chief virtues.

I answer that, [1] *Things may be numbered either in respect of their formal principles,* [2] *or according to the subjects in which they are: and either way we find that there are four cardinal virtues.*	Here is my response. We can enumerate things according to either their formal principles or their subjects. No matter which method we use, we discover the same four.
[3] *For the formal principle of the virtue of which we speak now* [4] *is good as defined by reason;* [5] *which good is considered in two ways. First, as existing in the very act of reason: and thus we have one principal virtue, called "Prudence."* [6] *Secondly, according as the reason puts its order into something else;* [7] *either into operations, and then we have "Justice";* [8] *or into passions, and then we need two virtues. For the need of putting the order of reason into the passions is due to their thwarting reason: and this occurs in two ways.* [9] *First, by the passions inciting to something against reason, and then the passions need a curb, which we call "Temperance."* [10] *Secondly, by the passions withdrawing us from following the dictate of reason, e.g.*	The formal principle of moral virtue as such is the rational good. But the rational good can be considered from two points of view. First, with respect to the very activity in which reasoning consists; this gives us one principal virtue, which is called prudence. Second, with respect to the activity of bringing something else into rational order, which gives us three more. One of these three is the virtue called justice, which puts our external deeds, as acts of the will, into rational order. To put our passions into rational order, however, there must be two virtues, because passions may contradict reason in two different ways. On one hand, passion may launch itself against something which reason opposes. The virtue which resists such demands is called temperance. On the other, passion may draw back from something which reason commands,

[9] *Morals on the Book of Job by St. Gregory the Great*, trans. John Henry Parker, J. G. F. Rivin-gon, and J. Rivington (public domain), Book 2, Chapter 76, available on the internet at www. lectionarycentral.com/GregoryMoraliaIndex.html.

through fear of danger or toil: and then man needs to be strengthened for that which reason dictates, lest he turn back; and to this end there is "Fortitude." [11] *In like manner, we find the same number if we consider the subjects of virtue. For there are four subjects of the virtue we speak of now:* [12] *viz. the power which is rational in its essence, and this is perfected by "Prudence";* [13] *and that which is rational by participation,* [14] *and is threefold, the will, subject of "Justice,"* [15] *the concupiscible faculty, subject of "Temperance,"* [16] *and the irascible faculty, subject of "Fortitude."*	for example through fear of danger or hard work. The virtue which hardens reason to stay in the fight is called fortitude. If instead we consider the number of subjects in which the cardinal virtues reside, we find the same number of subjects, and thus the same number of cardinal virtues. One subject is the very power of reason, which is perfected by prudence. The other three are the powers which are can be brought to participate in reason. Justice perfects the power of volition or will; temperance, the "concupiscible" or desiring power; and fortitude, the "irascible" or ardent power.

[1] The formal principle of a virtue is the pattern from which its activity arises. The form is a *cause* of virtue in the sense that without it, the virtue would not be.

[2] The subject of a moral virtue is the power in which it resides. If we were to ask "What is the subject of physical strength – in what does it reside?" the answer would be "its subject is the power of muscular contraction," for muscular contraction is the power in which physical strength is found, the power which such strength brings into full development. Here, of course, we are asking not about the subject of physical strength, but about the subject of moral strength.

[3] In its broadest sense, the term "virtue" may be used for any kind of excellence, but the virtue "of which we speak now" is moral excellence.

[4] The phrase "the good as defined by reason" is a coinage of the Blackfriars translation, but St. Thomas is thinking of more than correct definition. In Latin, what he says is that the formal principle of moral virtue is the "rational good" (*rationis bonum*), which means the ordering of all goods according to the good of reason itself. Reason must put both its own activity and all lower goods into order; consequently it must put both its own activity and the activity of the powers which deal with these lower goods in order. If we are asked why reason is good in the first place, the answer is that this most excellent thing is what we are made for, the distinctive privilege which sets us apart from the subrational creatures; the employment of reason is our highest natural inclination, apart from which we cannot be fulfilled.

We must understand that to when St. Thomas calls reason the human good, he is not speaking only of the ordinary operations of reason, such as discerning what is good to eat, or even of its middling operations, such as discerning the distance to the great galaxy in the constellation Andromeda, or the relation of the hypotenuse to the other two sides. The Supreme Good of reason is found in the knowledge of God Himself, which is perfected in the intellectual vision of the blessed in heaven. As St. Paul says, "For now we see in a mirror dimly, but then face to face. Now I know in part; then I shall understand fully, even as I have been fully understood."[10] A rational creature is one which God has made in His image – ultimately, with His help, for communion with Himself.

[5] The act of reason is good in itself, but if reason is disordered, then for its own sake it must be put into order. Prudence is the virtue which does this with respect to what is to be done. In turn, "speculative" or theoretical reason is the virtue which does so with respect to what is to be known, but here we are concerned only with practical reason.

[6] Even something which is not intrinsically rational can share, or participate, in reason, insofar as it is put into the order which reason demands.

[7] Operations are things that we do or perform – works, deeds, or activities, such as transactions. An example of bringing an operation into rational order is making sure that the amount of money I pay to the baker is proportionate to the amount of bread he gives to me.

[8] As we saw in I-II, Question 58, Article 5, a passion is not necessarily a strong emotion (although it can be); listlessness, for example, is a passion – something which happens to us, or comes over us, because of something else, such as sickness – even though its mark may seem to be not feeling any strong emotion. As we all recognize from experience, the passions often behave as though they had their own opinion of what ought to be done, at variance with the command of reason.

[9] Suppose the passion of concupiscence incited me to sleep with a woman who was not my wife – an action which would be unreasonable, because it would undermine not only the proper conditions for raising children, but also the loving unity between me and my procreative partner. The virtue of temperance would have to step in and hold me back.

[10] In the classical understanding, though *fortitudo* is concerned especially with the danger of death (especially death risked for the sake of the common good, as in war), it regulates not only the fear of danger but also fear of toil. Although the English word "fortitude" still suggests this connection, the English word "courage" tends to be applied more narrowly to the fear of danger alone. Even so, the similarity between these two exercises of fortitude is easy to see. Suppose, through fear of toil or difficulty, I draw back from hard work or from a trying conversation with someone I have wronged, or through fear of bodily harm, I hesitate to defend myself from an attacker or to interpose myself between my children and a vicious dog. In all such cases, the virtue of fortitude must arouse and strengthen me to the performance of the actions which reason commands.

---

[10] 1 Corinthians 13:12 (RSV-CE).

[11] Moral virtue has four subjects, because there are four powers of the soul in which it may reside. It may seem as though this paragraph merely repeats in different language what the former paragraph has already said. There is, to be sure, a certain correspondence between the two paragraphs, but they are making different points. For the former paragraph considers moral virtue according to *what is being done* – practical reason is carrying out its work of bringing about rational order in four different ways. However, the present paragraph considers moral virtue according to *what it is being done to* – reason is bringing about rational order in four different powers of the soul.

[12] Prudence resides in – and perfects – the power of practical reason itself.

[13] The other three virtues reside in – and perfect – the appetitive powers of the soul, powers which, though not rational in themselves, may share in rationality just in the sense that they accept reason's rule.

[14] St. Thomas defines the will as rational appetite – appetite in the sense that it desires something, rational in the sense that it carries the command of reason into execution – for the will properly seeks not just what seems good to the senses, but what the mind recognizes as truly good. The reason why justice cannot be located in the sensitive appetite, as temperance and fortitude are, is that it considers the *relations* between one man and another – so that we give each person neither more nor less than what is "due" to him, neither more or less than he deserves – and the consideration of relations is an act of the intellect:

Now the appetite is twofold; namely, the will which is in the reason and the sensitive appetite which follows on sensitive apprehension, and is divided into the irascible and the concupiscible.... Again the act of rendering his due to each man cannot proceed from the sensitive appetite, because sensitive apprehension does not go so far as to be able to consider the relation of one thing to another; but this is proper to the reason. Therefore justice cannot be in the irascible or concupiscible as its subject, but only in the will.[11]

[15] The concupiscible faculty is the power of desiring the "delectable" good; for example, hunger and sexual desire are movements of the concupiscible faculty. This power is called "concupiscible" because it can fall prey to concupiscence, to desire which is inordinate, or improperly directed. The virtue which keeps this from happening is temperance – the settled and disciplined disposition of desiring what should be desired, but refraining from what should not be desired.

[16] The irascible faculty is the power of desiring the "arduous" good; for example, being stirred up to stand firm against contempt, or to defend an endangered friend against attack, are movements of the irascible faculty. Fortitude is the virtue which gives us not just the spirit for the fight, but the *ordinate*

---

[11] See II-II, Q. 58, Art. 4.

spirit for the fight: Not only are we just as stirred up as we need to be, but we are also just as cautious as we need to be.

Reply to Objection 1. Prudence is the principal of all the virtues simply. The others are principal, each in its own genus.	Reply to Objection 1. Prudence is the foremost virtue of moral virtue as such, irrespective of kind. But other virtues are foremost over particular kinds of moral virtue.

Each virtue is foremost among its subjective parts, or species – as we might say today, its departments, or kinds. Thus, temperance in general is foremost among such virtues as abstinence, sobriety, chastity, and purity, which are species of temperance. Similarly, justice in general is foremost among such virtues as distributive and commutative justice, which are species of justice.[12] Surprisingly, St. Thomas holds that fortitude does not have species. The explanation of this puzzle is that the species of a virtue is determined by the end to which it is directed, and fortitude is directed to only one special matter – regulating the fear of difficult things which can pull the will away from following reason, especially death. The fear of other difficult things certainly differs from the fear of death in degree, but according to St. Thomas, it does not differ from it in kind. By contrast with fortitude, prudence does have species – prudence concerning one's own good and prudence concerning the common good, along with their subspecies. Unlike the other three cardinal virtues, however, prudence is foremost not only among its own species, but also among the other moral virtues.

We are now in position to explain why the four cardinal virtues are ranked as they are. The chief consideration is that man's good lies in reason. Since it is better to *be* something than merely to bring it about, and prudence simply *is* the right ordering of practical reason, prudence ranks first. Since it is better to bring something about (as justice does) than merely to remove obstacles to it (as fortitude and temperance do), justice ranks second. Since the fear of difficulty, especially the danger of death, has greater power to draw us away from the good of reason than any other obstacle, fortitude ranks third. Since the attraction to pleasure, especially the pleasure of touch, has the next greatest power to draw us away from the power of reason, temperance ranks fourth. And since a general virtue is more important than one of its species, all of the other moral virtues rank afterward.[13]

---

[12] Commutative justice concerns the preservation of equity in relations among individuals, for example giving equal value in exchange. Distributive justice concerns the preservation of equity in the allocation of goods in the community as a whole, for example giving honor to those who deserve honor.

[13] Concerning the species of temperance, see II-II, Q. 143, Art. 1; concerning the species of justice, II-II, Q. 61, Art. 1; concerning the species of fortitude, II-II, Q. 123, Arts. 1–4, and Q. 128, Art. 1; concerning the species of prudence, II-II, Q. 47, 10–12, and Q. 50, Arts. 1–4; and concerning the order of the cardinal virtues, II-II, Q. 123, Art. 12.

Reply to Objection 2. That part of the soul which is rational by participation is threefold, as stated above.	**Reply to Objection 2.** The Objector takes reason to be one thing and right desire to be another. Yes, reason is only one thing in itself, but as we have already explained, there are three other things in the soul which must be brought to *share* in reason – three ways in which desire must be made right.

What the Objector overlooks is that right desire is brought about by the *participation* of other powers in reason. So rather than thinking of two things (reason and right desire), he should be thinking of four things (first reason in itself; then the way in which the will is brought to participate in reason, the way in which the irascible power is brought to participate in reason, and the way in which the concupiscible power is brought to participate in reason).

Reply to Objection 3. All the other virtues among which one ranks before another, are reducible to the above four, both as to the subject and as to the formal principle.	**Reply to Objection 3.** All virtues on which other virtues depend are themselves rooted in the four cardinal virtues. Not only do they have the same subjects as these four, but they also share the same four modes of formal dependence on reason.

In terms of our previous image of the moral virtues as a branching tree, St. Thomas is pointing out that the Objector is seeing the tree incorrectly, for the smaller branches are not independent of the four great boughs – rather they fork out from them. Because every branch and twig ultimately grows from the same four great boughs, only these four should be called cardinal.

Whether Any Other Virtues Should Be Called Principal Rather Than These?

TEXT	PARAPHRASE
Whether any other virtues should be called principal rather than these?	Should any other moral virtues be considered pivotal or paramount in place of the traditional four?

St. Thomas is about to consider three other virtues besides prudence, justice, fortitude and moderation which might be proposed as pivotal or paramount: Magnanimity, humility, and patience. The context for the discussion is the *Summa*'s ongoing effort to untangle the various and sundry lists of virtues which the tradition had absorbed from both philosophical and theological sources, and to bring them into systematic order. So if it seems surprising that he doesn't also consider three other possible candidates – faith, hope, and charity or love, the "spiritual" or "theological" virtues suggested by St. Paul in his first letter to the young church at Corinth[1] – the answer is that he does consider them, but not here. In one Article, for example, he has the Objector protest,

Further, the end is principal as compared to the means. But the theological virtues are about the end; while the moral virtues are about the means. Therefore the theological virtues, rather than the moral virtues, should be called principal or cardinal."[2]

What this complaint overlooks is that whereas prudence, justice, fortitude and temperance are pivotal among the *acquired* moral virtues – the ones attainable by our natural powers, though not without God's help – faith, hope and love are pivotal among the *infused* moral virtues – the ones attainable only by supernatural grace. For this reason St. Thomas calls them "superhuman"

---

[1] I Corinthians 13:13.   [2] I-II, Q. 61, Art. 1, Obj. 2.

virtues, "virtues of man as sharing in the grace of God,"[3] and at present he is considering only the human virtues. We return to the spiritual virtues when we arrive at Question 62.

St. Thomas might have considered a different query: Should any of the four, prudence, justice, fortitude, or temperance, be *removed* from the list of cardinal virtues? In each generation, it seems that certain virtues fall into disrepute. The cardinal virtue which is considered silliest in our own time is probably temperance, because of our tendency to consider pleasure the Supreme Good and the consequent difficulty we have in believing that any pleasure could be bad for us. St. Thomas makes short work of this opinion in the section of the *Treatise on Man's Last End* devoted to the question, "Whether man's happiness consists in pleasure?" where he says pleasure is "quite a trifle as compared with the good of the soul."[4]

Objection 1. [1] *It would seem that other virtues should be called principal rather than these. For, seemingly, the greatest is the principal in any genus.* [2] *Now "magnanimity has a great influence on all the virtues" (Ethic. iv, 3). Therefore magnanimity should more than any be called a principal virtue.*	Objection 1. Apparently at least one other moral virtue should be called more important than the traditional four. Why? Because whatever virtue is greatest in *every* genus of virtue must be ranked before any others – and as Aristotle explains, in every genus the greatest deeds are spurred by magnanimity. Therefore magnanimity has a greater claim than any other virtue to be called principal.

[1] The "principal" or chief element of a genus is its greatest element. The Objector is about to suggest that magnanimity is the greatest element in the genus of virtue because it has the greatest influence on all the other elements.

[2] Magnanimity has been described as an ornament or crown of the other moral virtues, because it stretches the mind to do great things – not deeds of the sort which commonly attract fame, like unjustly establishing an empire, amassing a superfluous fortune, or making numerous sexual conquests, but deeds which are *morally* great. We may say that it converts ordinary virtue into heroic virtue, since a person of magnanimity has all the rest of the moral virtues, but takes them further. Whereas ordinary courage enables someone to stand firm in the peril of death, magnanimity makes him willing to die for others. Whereas ordinary temperance enables him to resist forbidden things, magnanimity leads him to forsake even permitted things for the sake of something great. Whereas ordinary prudence and justice enable him to act reasonably and equitably, magnanimity causes him to become the sort of person described in the vision of Daniel: "And those who are wise shall shine like the brightness

---

[3] I-II, Q. 58, Art. 3, ad 3, which becomes in turn the basis for I-II, Q. 61, Art. 1, ad 2.
[4] I-II, Q. 2, Art. 6. The *Treatise on Man's Last End* is also called the *Treatise on Happiness*.

of the firmament; and those who turn many to righteousness, like the stars for ever and ever."[5]

St. Thomas agrees with the Objector that true magnanimity – by contrast with its counterfeits – is not a mask for pagan pride and vanity, but a real and majestic virtue which Christians should endorse. In one place, commenting on a suggestion of Marcus Tullius Cicero, he suggests that it is a kind of confidence, but one in which "man hopes in himself, yet under God."[6] We might also think of it as something like nobility, provided that we are thinking of the nobility of virtue, not the nobility of class. When Aristotle wrote of magnanimity, perhaps he was thinking mostly of impressively grand and good men of the aristocratic class; when St. Thomas writes of magnanimity, he is doubtless thinking of the saints.

Both St. Thomas and Aristotle say that magnanimity is about *honors*: It brings the desire to be truly honorable and truly honored under the guidance of reason. Why so much bother about honor? We must understand that the magnanimous person *desires* to be heroically virtuous; he *wants* to shine like the brightness of the firmament. As Léon Bloy wrote, "There is but one sadness, and that is for us not to be saints."[7] In the same vein, C. S. Lewis remarks, "It would seem that Our Lord finds our desires not too strong, but too weak .... We are far too easily pleased."[8] But as the ancients said, the perversion of the best is the worst. Precisely because the desire to do great things and shine like the brightness of the firmament can so easily overthrow us, it needs to be brought under the governance of reason.

Magnanimity, then, is not the sheer and unregulated desire to do great things, or even to do morally great things, but one of a set of virtues which enable the mind to resist both pride and despair in the face of both the intense desire to do heroically virtuous deeds and the anxiety of failure.[9] We see then that although it may never have occurred to Aristotle to couple magnanimity with humility, in a Christian view these two virtues are partners; in fact, the truest greatness depends on a certain kind of littleness. This is why St. Thérèse of Lisieux, speaking of God, was able to write the startling words,

He made me understand my own *glory* would not be evident to the eyes of mortals, that it would consist in becoming a great *saint*! This desire could certainly appear daring if one were to consider how weak and imperfect I was, and how, after seven years in the religious life, I still am weak and imperfect. I always feel, however, the same bold confidence of becoming a great saint because I don't count on my merits since I have *none*, but I trust in Him who is Virtue and Holiness.[10]

---

[5] Daniel 12:3 (RSV-CE).   [6] II-II, Q. 128, Art. 1, ad 2.

[7] Leon Bloy, *The Poor Woman*, quoted by Jacques Maritain, *The Responsibility of the Artist*, Chapter 4. Available online at www3.nd.edu/~maritain/jmc/etext/resart4.htm. Bloy's character Clotilde writes these words in her last message to the artist Lazare Druide.

[8] C. S. Lewis, *The Weight of Glory, and Other Addresses* (New York: HarperCollins, 1949, 2001), p. 26.

[9] II-II, Q. 129, esp. Arts. 1 and 4.

[10] Thérèse de Lisieux, *Story of a Soul: The Autobiography of St. Thérèse of Lisieux*, 3rd ed., trans. John Clarke (Washington, DC: ICS Publications, 1996), p. 60. Compare p. 207: "God cannot inspire unrealizable desires. I can, then, in spite of my littleness, aspire to holiness."

Objection 2. [1] *Further, that which strengthens the other virtues should above all be called a principal virtue.* [2] *But such is humility: for Gregory says (Hom. iv in Ev.) that "he who gathers the other virtues without humility is as one who carries straw against the wind." Therefore humility seems above all to be a principal virtue.*	Objection 2. It might also be argued that a virtue which gives greater firmness to other virtues is more important than any of them. But as St. Gregory the Great observes, that is what humility does. So strongly do the other virtues depend on humility that trying to attain them without it is like gathering chaff in the wind. Apparently, then, the virtue of humility excels all the rest.

[1] At first it may seem that Objections 1 and 2 apply exactly the same argument to different virtues: We might put it, "Any virtue which improves all the other virtues should be called a principal virtue." Actually, the arguments are different. In Objection 1, magnanimity was called a principal virtue because it incites those who have attained the other virtues to great deeds, but in Objection 2, humility is called a principal virtue because without it, the other virtues cannot even be attained. St. Thomas fully agrees that humility is gravely important; therein lies the force of the Objection.

[2] Following is the context of St. Gregory's remark. Notice that he does not regard the desire for heroic virtue as a vice, but, like St. Thomas, he thinks such desire must be properly governed:

Let each of you, then, strive to be great in virtue, but nonetheless let him know that he is not so in some degree. Otherwise he may proudly attribute his greatness to himself and lose whatever good he has; he might even be rejected because of his sin of pride....

If holy men think themselves worthless even when they do courageous deeds, what will those who swell up with pride even without doing any virtuous work say to excuse themselves? Whatever good works are at hand are worth nothing unless they are seasoned with humility. No marvelous deed done with pride raises you up – it weighs you down! A person who gathers virtues without humility is like one carrying dust in a wind; he is worse blinded by what we see him carrying.

My friends, in everything you do hold on to humility as the root of good works. Do not look at the things which make you better now, but at those which make you still bad. When you set before yourselves the example of those who are better, you may always be able to rise above your humble place.[11]

The Angelic Doctor's own comment on the relation between humility and magnanimity is that "a twofold virtue is necessary with regard to the difficult good: one, to temper and restrain the mind, lest it tend to high things immoderately; and this belongs to the virtue of humility: and another to strengthen the mind

---

[11] Gregory the Great, *Homilies on the Gospels*, Homily 4, in *Forty Gospel Homilies by Gregory the Great*, trans. Dom Hurst (Piscataway, NJ: Gorgias Press, 2009), pp. 26–27. To prevent confusion, I have substituted "courageous" for "brave," because in this book I have given the terms different meanings (see the example of the "brave" bank robber in I-Ii, Q. 55, Art. 4).

against despair, and urge it on to the pursuit of great things according to right reason; and this is magnanimity."[12]

Objection 3. [1] *Further, that which is most perfect seems to be principal.* [2] *But this applies to patience, according to James 1:4:* "*Patience hath a perfect work.*" *Therefore patience should be reckoned a principal virtue.*	Objection 3. Still further, whatever is most complete would also seem to be most important. But patience is the most complete virtue, for as the Apostle James argues in his letter, it is through patience that any deed is fully carried out. It follows that patience deserves to be designated a principal virtue.

[1] The word *perfectum* causes a bit of trouble here, because although its English cognate usually refers to something flawless, the Latin term more often means something complete or fully developed. Such is the case here.

[2] The context of the quotation is St. James' exhortation,

My brethren, count it all joy when you shall fall into diverse temptations; knowing that the trying of your faith works patience. And patience has a perfect work; that you may be perfect and entire, failing in nothing."[13]

Although "patience has a perfect work" is the most straightforward translation of the Latin clause *patientia opus perfectum habet*, it does not convey much to English speakers. Bearing in mind that the term *habet* has a variety of meanings besides "has," including "holds" (which suggests preservation), "considers" (which suggests holding in mind), "manages" (which suggests taking in hand), and "keeps" (which suggests guarding), we might render the passage as follows:

Count it as nothing but joy, my brothers, when various temptations assault you, bearing in mind that the testing of your faith accomplishes patience. Patience completes and preserves the work, so that you too are complete and whole, deficient in nothing.

The Objector, then, is suggesting that patience should be considered a cardinal virtue because without it, none of the work of any other virtue can reach completion.

On the contrary, Cicero reduces all other virtues to these four (De Invent. Rhet. ii).	On the other hand, Marcus Tullius Cicero claims in *On Rhetorical Invention* that all of the other virtues depend on the four we have named.

In the context of the work, Marcus Tullius Cicero has just equated virtue with *honestum*, that which is to be sought for its own sake rather than for the sake of something else. The term *honestum* might be rendered "the honest and honorable," taking the honest in the double sense of truthfulness and good

[12] II-II, Q. 161, Art. 1.
[13] James 1:2–4 (DRA), changing the archaic "divers" to "diverse," "worketh" to "works," and "hath" to "has."

faith, and taking the honorable in the double sense of receiving honor and being worthy to receive it. He goes on to say:

It has four parts: prudence, justice, fortitude, and temperance.... Prudence is the knowledge of the good, the evil, and the indifferent.... Justice is a habit of the soul which renders to each his proper dignity while preserving the well-being of all.... Fortitude is the deliberate undertaking of dangers and enduring of toils.... Temperance is the firm and moderate control exercised by reason over lust and other improper impulses of the soul.[14]

I answer that, [1] As stated above (Article 2), these four are reckoned as cardinal virtues, in respect of the four formal principles of virtue as we understand it now. These principles are found chiefly in certain acts and passions. [2] Thus the good which exists in the act of reason, is found chiefly in reason's command, but not in its counsel or its judgment, as stated above (Question 57, Article 6). [3] Again, good as defined by reason and put into our operations as something right and due, is found chiefly in commutations and distributions in respect of another person, and on a basis of equality. [4] The good of curbing the passions is found chiefly in those passions which are most difficult to curb, viz. in the pleasures of touch. [5] The good of being firm in holding to the good defined by reason, against the impulse of passion, is found chiefly in perils of death, which are most difficult to withstand.

[6] Accordingly the above four virtues may be considered in two ways. First, in respect of their common formal principles. In this way they are called principal, being general, as it were, in comparison

Here is my response. As already explained, we recognize these four virtues as cardinal in the light of the four formal principles we have discovered at the bottom of certain acts and passions. But to explain it again: The good which consists in the exercise of practical reason itself is found mainly, though not exclusively, in its command rather than its counsel or judgment. This rational good is put into operations by conforming them to what is right and due – mainly, though not exclusively, in exchanges or distributions which preserve equality among various people. It is applied to the passions by bridling especially, though not exclusively, those passions which resist reason most obstinately, in particular the excitements of touch. But the good of holding firmly to the good of reason when passion urges pulling back is found especially, though not exclusively, in face of the danger of death, which is so difficult to withstand.

And so the four virtues we have been discussing may be examined from two points of view. First, let us consider them from the viewpoint of the formal principles in which all of them *share*. From this point of view, the virtues in question are called foremost because in a certain sense all other virtues partake of them. For (1) *any* virtue may be said to partake of prudence insofar as it brings the activity of reason

---

[14] Marcus Tullius Cicero, *On [Rhetorical] Invention*, Book 2, Chapter 53, Sections 159–160, 163–164 (translation mine). The Latin text is available online at http://scrineum.unipv.it/wight/invs1.htm.

with all the virtues: [7] so that, for instance, any virtue that causes good in reason's act of consideration, may be called prudence; [8] every virtue that causes the good of right and due in operation, be called justice; [9] every virtue that curbs and represses the passions, be called temperance; [10] and every virtue that strengthens the mind against any passions whatever, be called fortitude. [11] Many, both holy doctors, as also philosophers, speak about these virtues in this sense: [12] and in this way the other virtues are contained under them. Wherefore all the objections fail.

[13] Secondly, they may be considered in point of their being denominated, each one from that which is foremost in its respective matter, [14] and thus they are specific virtues, condivided with the others. Yet they are called principal in comparison with the other virtues, on account of the importance of their matter: —— [15] so that prudence is the virtue which commands; [16] justice, the virtue which is about due actions between equals; [17] temperance, the virtue which suppresses desires for the pleasures of touch; —— [18] and fortitude, the virtue which strengthens against dangers of death. [19] Thus again do the objections fail: because the other virtues may be principal in some other way, but these are called principal by reason of their matter, as stated above. ——

itself into good order; (2) *any* virtue may be said to partake of justice insofar as it brings deeds into conformity with the good of what is right and due; (3) *any* virtue may be said to partake of temperance insofar as it holds the passions back and keeps them down when they urge what is contrary to reason; and (4) *any* virtue may be said to partake of fortitude insofar as it makes the soul stand firm when the passions fight against what reason commands. ——

This is how many people speak of the cardinal virtues – not only doctors of sacred doctrine, but also philosophers. And since, from this point of view, every moral virtue whatsoever turns out to partake of all four of these cardinal virtues, the objections fail.

Now let us consider them from the other point of view – according to the *chief element* in the particular matter with which each virtue is concerned. Taken in this sense, the cardinal virtues are not general virtues (as in the previous way of thinking), but special virtues, each one distinct from the others. And yet in this sense too they are called foremost among other virtues, just because these matters of concern are so important. For (1) prudence is the virtue concerned chiefly with the commands of reason; (2) justice, the virtue concerned chiefly with the actions which are due between equals; (3) temperance, the virtue which chiefly reins in the desire for the excitements of touch; and (4) fortitude, the virtue which gives us firmness chiefly when we are in peril of death. ——

And so the objections fail in this respect too. For although other virtues might be foremost in other senses, the four virtues traditionally called cardinal are foremost because of the importance of the matters with which they are concerned. ——

[1] As we have seen before, the four formal principles of the virtues are the four patterns from which their activity arises. Notice that in the rest of the paragraph, St. Thomas mentions not only what each virtue generically concerns, but also what it chiefly concerns. He returns to the generic considerations (the

formal principles viewed as things that are *shared*) in paragraph two, and he returns to the principal considerations (the formal principles viewed as things that are *not* shared) in paragraph three.

[2] Although St. Thomas says simply "reason," he is actually thinking of practical, not speculative or theoretical, reason. Two of the three activities of practical reason, counsel and judgment, have parallels in "speculative" or theoretical reason. On the other hand, the third activity, command, does not correspond to anything in theoretical reason. St. Thomas therefore concludes that the chief good of practical reason *as such* is command.[15]

[3] Commutations are reciprocal acts between individuals, especially exchanges. Distributions are assignments of offices and honors, especially by public authority for the common good. The former preserves "arithmetic" equality, for each party gives equal value to the other. The latter preserves "proportional" equality, for each party receives what he deserves; to put it another way, the ration of reward to desert is the same for everyone.

[4] It is certainly possible for a strong pleasure of taste, hearing, sight, and smell to exceed a weak pleasure of touch. Generally speaking, however, the pleasures of touch are the strongest, and their urgings most difficult to resist, especially in the context of sex.

[5] Likewise, it is certainly possible for a particular fear to exceed the fear of bodily death. Generally speaking, however, the fear of bodily death is the hardest to overcome. Rationally speaking, isn't spiritual death, eternal ruin, much worse? Yes, but there is never an occasion to "overcome" the fear of spiritual death; to suppose that there is would be to regard a lesser good as more important than our ultimate final good in God.

[6] One way to view prudence, justice, temperance, and fortitude is to see them as names for four general qualities of the human mind. Even though one of these general qualities is most prominent in, say, facing the fear of death, and another is most conspicuously on display in, say, resisting the pleasures of touch, what we have in view here is how each quality "overflows" into all the others. Thus in a certain sense even fortitude can be called temperate, even temperance can be called courageous, and so on.[16] We are about to see what these four qualities are.

[7] Viewed as a general quality of mind which all virtues require, *prudence* is a perfectly developed discretion about everything.

[8] Viewed in the same way, *justice* is the rectitude of mind by which we do what we should and avoid what we should not.

[9] Viewed in the same way, *temperance* is the moderation of all our passions and activities so that they remain within their proper bounds.[17]

[10] Viewed in the same way, *fortitude* is the strength or firmness of mind which enables us to do what is reasonable despite temptations to deviate.[18]

---

[15] I-II, Q. 57, Art. 6.   [16] I-II, Q. 61, Art. 4 and ad 1.
[17] II-II, 41, 2.   [18] II-II, 123, 2.

[11] Among the doctors of sacred doctrine who speak of the cardinal virtues in the former way are St. Augustine of Hippo, St. Gregory the Great, and St. Ambrose of Milan; among philosophers, especially Marcus Tullius Cicero. We will see more of this when we come to I-II, Question 65, Article 1.

[12] The Objections are defeated because *all* virtues require the same four general mental qualities of discretion, rectitude, moderation, and strength (which are here named prudence, justice, temperance, and fortitude). Magnanimity, humility, and patience – the three virtues the Objectors would like us to call cardinal – do not reveal any *additional* mental qualities which work in all the virtues; they do not bring to light mental qualities *over and above* discretion, rectitude, moderation, and firmness of mind. Quite the contrary! Just as all the other virtues do, magnanimity, humility, and patience depend on discretion, rectitude, moderation, and firmness of mind.

[13] Prudence, justice, temperance, and fortitude may also be viewed, not as names for four general qualities of mind, as above, but instead as names for four highly particular dispositions – each of them concerned primarily with some special matter. Among other thinkers, this is how Aristotle speaks of them – and how St. Thomas himself *most often* speaks of them.

[14] If we think of the four cardinal virtues in the previous sense, as four general qualities of mind, what makes them cardinal is that each one overflows into the others. Viewed as four special dispositions, however, each one does *not* overflow into the others. Rather what makes each one cardinal is that the matter with which it deals is so important.

[15] Viewed as a specific disposition rather than as a general quality of mind, prudence is the virtue which brings the operation of practical reason called "command" into its full and appropriate development.

[16] Viewed as a specific disposition rather than as a general quality of mind, justice is the virtue which causes each person to give others what is due to them. We may add that the phrasing "between equals" is a little misleading, for St. Thomas does not mean, say, that a parent need not treat a child as he deserves. However, what St. Thomas elsewhere calls "the equality of justice" operates differently between equals than between unequals. For example, the principles of what each owes to the other are the same between all parents, and the same between all children, but they are not the same between parents and children, for what the mother and father owe to their child is their *care*, whereas what a child owes to his mother and father is to *honor* them, although, strictly speaking, he can never repay all that they have done for him.

[17] Viewed as a specific disposition rather than as a general quality of mind, temperance is the virtue which enables us to resist the temptations of pleasure. Since St. Thomas is discussing that with which each virtue is *chiefly* concerned, his reference to the pleasures of touch does not mean that fortitude is not concerned with other pleasures, but that with this most clamorous pleasure it finds that it must take special care.

[18] Viewed as a specific disposition rather than as a general quality of mind, fortitude is the virtue which enables us to resist the assaults of fear. Again, since St. Thomas is discussing what each virtue is *chiefly* concerned with, his reference to the fear of death does not mean that temperance is not concerned with other fears, but that this fear characterizes it most distinctively.

[19] We saw above how to defeat the objections if prudence, justice, temperance, and fortitude are viewed as four general qualities of mind. We now see that if we take them instead as four special dispositions, each concerned chiefly with a particular matter, the Objections still fail. For magnanimity, humility, and patience do not bring to light matters *different from yet just as important as* the matters with which prudence, justice, temperance, and fortitude are concerned. Rather they turn out to be *lesser virtues linked* with prudence, justice, temperance, and fortitude, for the matters with which they are concerned are of the same general types with which prudence, justice, temperance, and fortitude are concerned, but less complete or less important.[19] St. Thomas provides the details not here, but later in the *Summa*, where we find that:

- Magnanimity turns out to be an aspect of the cardinal virtue of fortitude, for by urging the soul on to great things, magnanimity strengthens it against the fear of failure.[20]
- Humility turns out to be an aspect of the cardinal virtue of temperance, for by withdrawing the soul from things too high for it, humility holds it back from presumption.[21]
- Patience turns out to be primarily an aspect of fortitude, for by enabling the soul to bear evils without being disordered by sorrow, patience enables it to advance to better things.[22]

---

[19] Such lesser virtues linked with a cardinal virtue are called its "potential parts."

[20] II-II, Q. 129, Art. 5, and Q. 140, Art. 2, ad 1.

[21] II-II, Q. 162, Art. 1, ad 3, and Q. 162, Art. 2.

[22] Though in a certain way, St. Thomas suggests, patience may also be viewed as an aspect of the cardinal virtue of justice, because it is not fitting to bear all evils in the same way; for example, sometimes it behooves us to fight for the common good. II-II, Q. 136, Art. 4 and ad 3.

Whether There Are Any Theological Virtues?

TEXT	PARAPHRASE
Whether there are any theological virtues?	The tradition maintains that besides attaining the cardinal virtues, human beings may also attain certain "spiritual" or "theological" virtues. Are there such things?

Besides the four cardinal virtues, the tradition also identifies three "theological" or spiritual virtues: Faith, hope, and charity or love. The suggestion that we may need spiritual virtues over and above the ordinary qualities of good character is ridiculous to the secular sort of mind. Do such virtues exist?

In one sense, it may seem obvious that they exist, but we must be careful, because the popular culture gives each of these four terms different meanings than what the tradition intends when it calls them spiritual virtues. Confidence that my friend will not betray me is not the spiritual virtue of faith; optimism that I will get a raise in salary is not the spiritual virtue of hope; giving money to worthy causes is not the definition of charity; and even though the merely natural loves are good, the love called charity is different from the love of a man and a woman, the love of a mother for her child, or the love of two friends. On the other hand, mundane acts, affections, and dispositions can certainly partake of these virtues. According to the tradition, for example, erotic love is *lifted up* into charity through the sacrament of marriage, in which two polar and complementary opposites, the husband and wife, are really, permanently, and exclusively made one, receiving the grace to be bound with the same love that binds Christ with the Church. Rather than pushing aside natural love, charity transfuses and transforms it.

What then are these three alleged virtues? *Faith* concerns beliefs about God. However, not all belief about God is faith. To believe something which is false is not faith; for example it is not faith to believe that God is evil. To believe something which is true, yet desire it not to be true, is not faith; for example it is not faith to believe that God exists but wish that He did not. To believe something true just because it is proven is a very good thing, and it may, as St. Thomas says, be a preamble to faith, but is not the same thing as faith; for example it is not faith to believe God exists solely because of the philosophical arguments for His existence which St. Thomas offers earlier in the *Summa*. And yet to believe blindly, with no good reason whatsoever, is not faith either. Characteristically, faith involves believing in truths for which there are good reasons which God enables us to accept with complete subjective confidence – for example, believing in the Resurrection because of the well-tested testimonies of numerous reliable witnesses – but which fall short of the sort of certainty which the blessed enjoy in the next life by the vision of God Himself, seeing Him as He sees us.[1]

Hope resembles faith in that both virtues cause us to cling to God, provided that we cooperate with the gift of grace. However, hope and faith bring about this result in different ways. Faith causes us to cling to him because we believe that what He tells us is true. By contrast, Hope makes us cling to Him because we trust His help in attaining the complete and utter fulfillment in Him for which He made us.[2]

Charity or spiritual love is friendship for God Himself, who is our ultimate good, and who desires us to be united with Him in a fellowship of everlasting happiness. Love of God turns out to be closely related to loving our neighbor, because our neighbor is made in God's image. In fact, St. Thomas argues that the act of loving God, and the act of loving our neighbor so that he may be in God, belong to the same species or kind of act, since in both cases the object of the act is God Himself.

Interestingly, St. Paul identifies charity not just as a theological virtue but as the *greatest* theological virtue, exceeding faith and hope:

Love never ends; as for prophecies, they will pass away; as for tongues, they will cease; as for knowledge, it will pass away. For our knowledge is imperfect and our prophecy is imperfect; but when the perfect comes, the imperfect will pass away. When I was a child, I spoke like a child, I thought like a child, I reasoned like a child; when I became a man, I gave up childish ways. For now we see in a mirror dimly, but then face to face.

[1] See II-II, Q. 2, Art. 1, and Q. 4, esp. Arts. 1, 8. Concerning the provables as "preambles" to faith, see I, Q. 1, Art. 2, ad 1: "The existence of God and other like truths about God, which can be known by natural reason, are not articles of faith, but are preambles to the articles; for faith presupposes natural knowledge, even as grace presupposes nature, and perfection supposes something that can be perfected. Nevertheless, there is nothing to prevent a man, who cannot grasp a proof, accepting, as a matter of faith, something which in itself is capable of being scientifically known and demonstrated."

[2] See II-II, Q. 17, Art. 6.

Now I know in part; then I shall understand fully, even as I have been fully understood. So faith, hope, love abide, these three; but the greatest of these is love.[3]

St. Thomas agrees: For what the redeemed now believe in faith and desire in hope they will one day experience not only in foretaste, but fully. Charity is the very life of the communion with God which we will then enjoy more perfectly.[4]

Objection 1. [1] *It would seem that there are not any theological virtues. For according to Phys. vii, text. 17, "virtue is the disposition of a perfect thing to that which is best: and by perfect, I mean that which is disposed according to nature."* [2] *But that which is Divine is above man's nature. Therefore the theological virtues are not virtues of a man.*	**Objection 1.** Apparently there is no such thing as a spiritual virtue. For as Aristotle explains in the seventh book of his *Physics*, a virtue is a dispositional tendency which a "perfect" thing – a thing which is in the condition natural to it – has toward what is best for it. But a *spiritual* virtue seems to pertain to the Divine nature, not to human nature; so even if there are spiritual virtues, they are not *human* virtues.

[1] The Objector is paraphrasing certain remarks in Aristotle, *Physics*, Book 7, Chapter 3. We must bear in mind that the original meaning of the term "physics" is the study of the principles of nature [Greek, *phusis*], of things which are subject to development and decay according to the potentialities implanted in them. Consider for example the natural development of an oak tree from an acorn. The acorn is "imperfect," meaning incomplete or immature; the oak tree is "perfect," meaning complete or mature. The qualities which the oak possesses in its mature condition – qualities which not only display its maturity but also tend to preserve it – may be called its excellences, or virtues, and so with the qualities which anything possesses in its mature condition. Thus Aristotle says that each excellence or virtue "puts that which possesses it in a good or bad condition with regard to its proper affections, where by 'proper' affections I mean those influences that from the natural constitution of a thing tend to promote or destroy its existence." St. Thomas remarks in his *Commentary* on the work that "when a thing possesses its nature completely, then it is called perfect."[5]

[2] The purpose of the Objector's allusion to Aristotle is merely to make the point that the virtues or excellences of a human being are those which bring his human nature to its complete development. But to call a virtue "theological" suggests that it pertains to the *Theos* – to God – in other words, that it is not about human nature at all.

---

[3] 1 Corinthians 13:8–13 (RSV-CE).

[4] See esp. II-II, Q. 23, Arts. 1, 3, 5, and 6, and II-II, Q. 25, Art. 1.

[5] Aristotle, *Physics*, trans. R. P. Hardie and R. K. Gaye (public domain), Book 7, Chapter 3; Thomas Aquinas, *Commentary on Aristotle's Physics*, Book 7, Lecture 6, trans. Richard J. Blackwell, Richard J. Spath, and Edmund Thirlkel (Notre Dame, IN: Dumb Ox Books, 1999), p. 473.

Objection 2. [1] *Further, theological virtues are quasi-Divine virtues. But the Divine virtues are exemplars, as stated above (Question 61, Article 5),* [2] *which are not in us but in God. Therefore the theological virtues are not virtues of man.*	**Objection 2.** Moreover, the so-called spiritual virtues are something like Divine virtues. Now there are such things as Divine virtues, but as we found earlier in the *Summa*, they are exemplar virtues, which are found not in humans, but in God. The problem is not that they are *not virtues*, but that they are not virtues *for us*; they are superhuman.

[1] The Objector is hoping to turn St. Thomas's own previous words against the tradition. In I-II, Question 61, Article 5, St. Thomas paraphrased St. Augustine's explanation that the soul needs to follow something in order to attain virtue. St. Augustine had pointed out that it would make no sense for the soul to follow *itself* to attain virtue, because in that case it would be trying to attain virtue by following something that does not yet have virtue. Nor would it be sufficient for the soul to follow a completely wise man to attain virtue, because even supposing that the man is completely wise, he can be taken away from us. The conclusion is that "God then remains, in following after whom we live well, and in reaching whom we live both well and happily."[6]

But what would it *mean* for a person seeking virtue to follow after God? Here St. Thomas alludes to yet another thinker, Macrobius Ambrosius Theodosius, who, after discussing three other levels of virtue,[7] argues as follows:

The fourth type comprises the virtues that are present in the divine Mind itself, the *nous*, from the pattern of which all the other virtues are derived. For if we believe that there are ideas of other things in the Mind, then with much greater assurance must we believe that there are ideas of the virtues. There the divine Mind itself is prudence; it is temperance because it always looks back on itself with unremitting attention; it is courage because it is always the same and is never changed; it is justice because, by eternal law, it never turns from constant application to its work.[8]

St. Thomas endorses Macrobius's suggestion:

Consequently the exemplar of human virtue must needs pre-exist in God, just as in Him pre-exist the types of all things. Accordingly virtue may be considered as existing originally in God, and thus we speak of "exemplar" virtues: so that in God the Divine

---

[6] St. Augustine, *On the Morals of the Catholic Church* (public domain), Chapter 6, available online at www.newadvent.org/fathers/1401.htm.

[7] St. Thomas himself discusses these three levels in I-II, Q. 61, Art. 5; they are the same four cardinal virtues, but as practiced by persons at different stages of moral development. Social virtues are those which enable us to behave well in the conduct of human affairs. Perfecting virtues (literally, "cleansing") are those of persons who are "on their way," who are coming to resemble God more and more. Perfect virtues (literally, virtues of the "cleansed") are those of persons who have already reached this resemblance.

[8] Macrobius Ambrosius Theodosius, *Commentary on the Dream of Scipio*, trans. William Harris Stahl, Book 1, Chapter 8, Section 10 (New York: Columbia University Press, 1952, 1990), p. 123. We will deal more extensively with Macrobius in connection with II-II, Q. 80, Art. 1.

Mind itself may be called prudence; while temperance is the turning of God's gaze on Himself, even as in us it is that which conforms the appetite to reason. God's fortitude is His unchangeableness; His justice is the observance of the Eternal Law in His works.

[2] This is where the Objector comes in. Though he reaches his conclusion by a different path than the previous Objector, his point is very similar: Virtues can properly be called "theological" only if they are exemplar virtues, virtues in the mind of God alone. But in this case they are not in the mind of man.

Objection 3. [1] *Further, the theological virtues are so called because they direct us to God, Who is the first beginning and last end of all things.* [2] *But by the very nature of his reason and will, man is directed to his first beginning and last end. Therefore there is no need for any habits of theological virtue, to direct the reason and will to God.* ⎯	Objection 3. Still further, the reason these alleged virtues are called "theological" or spiritual is that they are supposed to direct us to God, the first beginning and ultimate goal of all things. What this supposition overlooks is that man is directed toward his first beginning and ultimate goal just by the nature of his reason and will. All that is necessary for reason and will to guide him along the path is that they be themselves; no dispositions to so-called spiritual virtues need to be added.

[1] Although, a little later, St. Thomas gives three different reasons for calling these virtues theological, he agrees with the Objector that the first reason is that they direct us to God. God is called the "first beginning" because He is the Creator; it is He who endowed us with our distinctive potentialities, such as rationality. In turn, He is called the "last end" because he is our ultimate and final good. All action presupposes some good to be attained; God is Good Himself, in Person, to enjoy whom leaves nothing to be desired.

[2] Man, who is by nature rational, aims at God by means of his mind and by a will guided by his mind, because he desires to know God as He is. He is *made* this way. Now the eyes do not have to acquire any additional virtues over and above their natural excellences in order to see; their nature simply is to see. And the heart does not have to acquire any additional virtues over and above its natural excellences in order to pump blood; its nature simply is the pumping of blood. So the Objector reasons that man's reason and will do not have to acquire any "theological" or spiritual virtues over and above their natural excellences in order to reach God; their nature simply is to reach God.

On the contrary, [1] *The precepts of the law are about acts of virtue.* [2] *Now the Divine law contains precepts about the acts of faith, hope, and charity: for it is written (Sirach 2:8, seqq.): "Ye that fear the Lord believe Him," and again, "hope in Him," and again, "love Him."* [3] *Therefore*	On the other hand, Divine law commands us to perform acts of virtue, and among these are the acts of faith, hope, and love, for Scripture tells those who fear God to believe Him, to hope in Him, and to hold dearly to Him. It follows from this that faith, hope, and love are virtues which direct us to

faith, hope, and charity are virtues directing us to God. Therefore they are theological virtues.	God – and these are precisely the virtues traditionally called "theological" or spiritual.

[1] Divine law is given by God to put us into right relation with God. Since man, a rational creature who is made in God's image, is united to God by his mind, Divine law includes precepts about everything which puts the mind into proper order. But, argues St. Thomas, "this is effected by the acts of all the virtues: since the intellectual virtues set in good order the acts of the reason in themselves: while the moral virtues set in good order the acts of the reason in reference to the interior passions and exterior actions." His conclusion is that the Divine law does propose – and is right to propose – precepts about the acts of all the virtues.[9]

[2] In his usual abbreviated way, St. Thomas is referring to a trio of exhortations in the Old Testament book of Sirach:

> You that fear the Lord, believe him: and your reward shall not be made void.
> You that fear the Lord, hope in him: and mercy shall come to you for your delight.
> You that fear the Lord, love him, and your hearts shall be enlightened.[10]

By choosing this Old Testament passage instead of the Pauline remark quoted above, St. Thomas seems to say, "See, the teaching about the three theological virtues is not just part of the New Testament; it was in the Old Testament too!" A word about the "fear of the Lord" may be in order because it is so often misunderstood. Scripture mentions two different fears in relation to God. One of them is the faintheartedness which imagines that the loving God wills evil to us; the other is the adoring awe and reverence which dreads anything which might separate us from Him, and which bears in mind that His inexorable love will not tolerate anything which mars His image in us. The former fear is forbidden: "Fear not!" But the latter is commanded: "Fear Him!" An interesting passage in the Gospel of Luke plays on these two senses of fear:

I tell you, my friends, do not fear those who kill the body, and after that have no more that they can do. But I will warn you whom to fear: fear him who, after he has killed, has power to cast into hell; yes, I tell you, *fear him!* Are not five sparrows sold for two

---

[9] I-II, Q. 100, Art. 2.

[10] Sirach 2:8–10 (DRA), changing "ye" to "you." Sirach, also known as Ecclesiasticus (not to be confused with Ecclesiastes, a different book), belongs to the category of Old Testament writings called Wisdom. Although it is not included in the version of the Bible used by most Protestants, some varieties of Protestantism hold it in high esteem "for example of life and instruction of manners." Verse 10 is not found in the text used by more recent translators. However, for the virtue of love, St. Thomas could just as easily have used a later verse in the chapter, "They that fear the Lord, will not be incredulous to his word: and they that love him, will keep his way." The verse, numbered 18 in the DRA, corresponds in the newer translations to verse 15.

pennies? And not one of them is forgotten before God. Why, even the hairs of your head are all numbered. *Fear not; you are of more value than many sparrows.*[11]

[3] Since each of the three verses in the trio is addressed to those who fear God, and the kind of fear intended is the reverent awe with which they seek Him rather than ignoring, avoiding, or fleeing from Him, it follows that each of the three virtues mentioned directs us to God. Since directing us to God is the first mark of what is called a theological virtue – a mark to which St. Thomas returns in the *respondeo* – they are theological virtues.

Thus far, St. Thomas is not presenting his own argument, but explaining the tradition against which the Objectors are protesting. He now proceeds to give his own view.

I answer that, [1] Man is perfected by virtue, for those actions whereby he is directed to happiness, as was explained above (Question 5, Article 7). [2] Now man's happiness is twofold, as was also stated above (Question 5, Article 5). One is proportionate to human nature, a happiness, to wit, which man can obtain by means of his natural principles. [3] The other is a happiness surpassing man's nature, and which man can obtain by the power of God alone, by a kind of participation of the Godhead, about which it is written (2 Peter 1:4) that by Christ we are made "partakers of the Divine nature." [4] And because such happiness surpasses the capacity of human nature, man's natural principles which enable him to act well according to his capacity, do not suffice to direct man to this same happiness. Hence it is necessary for man to receive from God some additional principles, whereby he may be directed to supernatural happiness, [5] even as he is directed to his connatural end, by means of his natural principles, [6] albeit not	Here is my response. We saw earlier in the *Summa* that virtue renders the acts which direct man to happiness complete. But as we have also seen, man's happiness – his felicity[12] – is not one thing, but two.
	One happiness is commensurate to his nature – that is, he can reach it from starting points he finds within himself. But the other happiness exceeds anything that his nature can accomplish. He can reach it only by virtue of God Himself – in fact, by a kind of sharing in God. St. Peter goes so far as to say that in Christ we become "partakers of the Divine nature."
	Just because partaking of the Divine nature does exceed man's powers, man finds that although the seeds of action implanted in him are adequate for attaining natural happiness, they cannot lift him up to supernatural happiness. For him to reach the latter, God must plant additional seeds in him – principles must be implanted in him which direct him to this supernatural happiness in the same way that his natural principles direct him to his natural happiness.

[11] Luke 12:4–7 (RSV-CE), emphasis added.

[12] My paraphrase uses two words for happiness at this point just because St. Thomas does: He says *beatitudo sive felicity* ("beatitude or felicity"), using *sive*, the form of the Latin word for "or" that means they are different expressions for the same thing. Thus, we are not to suppose that beatitude is one kind of happiness and felicity is the other – indeed, throughout the rest of the passage, he uses only one word, *beatitudo*, for both kinds of happiness.

without Divine assistance. [7] *Such like principles are called "theological virtues":* [8] *first, because their object is God, inasmuch as they direct us aright to God:* [9] *secondly, because they are infused in us by God alone:* [10] *thirdly, because these virtues are not made known to us, save by Divine revelation, contained in Holy Writ.*	(Although even in seeking his natural happiness, he needs Divine help!). ⏤ These additional seeds of action, which have God for their object, are called theological virtues – for they direct us to God, they are poured into us by God alone, and we learn of them only from God's revelation, as recorded in Sacred Scripture.

[1] St. Thomas has explained in several previous places in the *Summa* that happiness cannot exist without a rightly directed will. Aristotle had considered happiness a reward for acts of virtue, and the Angelic Doctor agrees.[13] It is not enough to do the same outward deed that a virtuous person does *but do it without virtue*, the way even a habitual liar might tell the truth in a situation in which he thinks that a lie might be discovered. One must have the virtues themselves – and live by them.

[2] Here St. Thomas is speaking of that "imperfect" or incomplete happiness which man can obtain in this life merely by his natural powers, a happiness which is realized in the practice of virtue. It is imperfect for two different reasons. First, we are not completely happy so long as there remains something more to desire and seek. Second, there always does remain something more, for just because we are rational beings, our minds are restless with wonder and longing unless they know the cause of all things, *know* the Divine Essence as they are known to Him. Our natural powers fall desperately short of that, for the created mind simply cannot grasp the Uncreated Mind which brought it into being: "[E]very knowledge that is according to the mode of created substance, falls short of the vision of the Divine Essence, which infinitely surpasses all created substance. Consequently neither man, nor any creature, can attain final Happiness by his natural powers."[14] —

[3] Although man can attain only incomplete happiness left to his own powers, God does not leave him to his own powers; rather He pours His own power into His followers so that they can share in His own inner life. St. Peter opens his second letter with the daring words to which St. Thomas alludes:

May grace and peace be multiplied to you in the knowledge of God and of Jesus our Lord. His divine power has granted to us all things that pertain to life and godliness, through the knowledge of him who called us to his own glory and excellence, by which he has granted to us his precious and very great promises, that through these you may escape from the corruption that is in the world because of passion, *and become partakers of the divine nature.* For this very reason make every effort to supplement your faith with virtue, and virtue with knowledge, and knowledge with self-control, and

[13] I-II, Q. 4, Art. 4, and Q. 5, Art. 7.   [14] I-II, Q. 3, Art. 8, and Q. 5, Art. 5.

self-control with steadfastness, and steadfastness with godliness, and godliness with brotherly affection, and brotherly affection with love.[15]

[4] St. Thomas may seem to be repeating himself, but he is adding depth and detail. Natural happiness is radically incomplete, a mere "likeness" of our complete good.[16] Its imperfection arises not just from the fact that the human race has fallen into sin (although that is true too). Rather it arises from the fact that our natural powers would not have been enough to see God even if there had never been a Fall. God must *raise man beyond* himself. The point is not to climb up to Him, but to hold on as He pulls us up – not to generate His life in ourselves, but to allow Him to pour it into us. Redeemed men and women do not become God, for they retain their human natures. However, their natures are transfigured by the Divine nature of which they are invited to partake. This is the doctrine of which the secular movement called transhumanism might be viewed as the mockery and counterfeit.[17]

The possibility of partaking of the Divine nature raises an interesting point about human nature. No creature can have a natural potentiality to rise beyond its own nature – the very thought is absurd, like pulling oneself up by one's shoelaces. We must be *lifted*. But unless God had *made* man liftable, this could not happen, for not even God can do what is contradictory. Our liftability, then, is a genuine aspect of our created nature. St. Thomas's term for it is the "obediential potentiality," the passive potentiality to receive God's direct influence.[18]

obediential potentiality

---

[15] 2 Peter 1:2–7, emphasis added.

[16] I-II, Q. 3, Art. 6.

[17] Transhumanism is the ideology that proposes to use nanotechnology, biotechnology, information technology, and cognitive science to "transcend" human nature – which in this case means destroying human nature, since the result of this kind of "transcendence" would no longer be a "nature," as St. Thomas understands it, but an artifact. Some of the applications that have been discussed are military or industrial, for example, workers who never go on strike or soldiers who can fight for days on end and never have to sleep. Still others are aimed at giving human beings godlike qualities. Once limited to the readers and writers of science fiction, such disturbing aspirations have now become widespread in the military, industry, and government. See, for example, Mihail C. Roco and William Sims Bainbridge, eds., *Converging Technologies for Improving Human Performance: Nanotechnology, Biotechnology, Information Technology and Cognitive Science* (Dordrecht, Netherlands: Kluwer Academic, 2003), www.wtec.org/ ConvergingTechnologies/Report/NBIC_report.pdf. For a breathless popular treatment of the theme, see Gary Marcus and Christof Koch, "The Future of Brain Implants," *Wall Street Journal*, March 14, 2014, www.wsj.com/articles/SB10001424052702304914904579435592981780528?ref=/news-books-best-sellers (the title of the print version, published the following day, is "The Plug-and-Play Brain"). I have criticized transhumanism in "What If We Changed Our Nature?," available online at www.undergroundthomist.org/what-if-we-changed-our-nature, and in Sections 6–7 of "Diplomacy and Theology in the Dialogue on Universal Ethics," *Nova et Vetera*, English ed., 9, no. 3 (2011): 707–735, http://undergroundthomist.org/sites/default/files/ Diplomacy-and-Theology-in-the-Dialogue-on-Universal-Ethics_0.pdf.

[18] III, Q. 11, Art. 1.

St. Thomas's use of the term "principles" may be puzzling, and my paraphrase renders the idea in several different ways. The thing to bear in mind is that in Latin, *principia* are beginnings or starting points. So man's "natural principles" are the seeds of human action, the potentialities which become actualized in human life just according to our nature. On the other hand, the "additional principles" which direct us to supernatural happiness are additional seeds of action poured into us by God. These additional seeds turn out to be the spiritual virtues. We could never "whip them up" by our own effort; rather they are infused into us by God. The power is entirely His; yet He does not force Himself upon us, because by making us rational beings He has also made us free. We have already encountered this paradox in I-II, Question 55, Article 4, Reply to Objection 6, for as we saw there, the fact that infused virtue is poured into us by God, rather than generated by our own efforts, does not mean that God pours it into us without our consent. To be sure, there are things which we do in connection with His grace, but even these things are brought about by Him with our cooperation, for He works *in* the nature of our will, not by doing violence to our will.

In the present Article, St. Thomas does not actually call the principles of the virtues "seeds," but he does in many other places, for example I, Question 63, Article 2, to which we will return. The expression is especially helpful because it conveys the idea of an effect which is present *virtually* in its cause, like an oak tree and an acorn.

[5] Our "connatural" end is what we seek and are able to achieve *according to* our nature. In some contexts the term "connatural" refers to "second nature," and that sense is apropos here too, because although the cardinal virtues are difficult, it becomes second nature to exercise them in the way that our natural happiness requires.

[6] The words "albeit not without Divine assistance" guard us from a possible misunderstanding. From what St. Thomas has said before this, it may at first seem that he thinks we can achieve our connatural happiness without God's help – that we need Divine assistance only for our supernatural happiness. Not so: Happiness *of either kind* requires Divine assistance, but connatural and supernatural happiness require Divine assistance *in different ways*. The difference is that to achieve our connatural end, we require divine assistance to *support* our natural principles, but to achieve our supernatural end, we require divine assistance to *supplement* them so that they transcend their intrinsic limits.

[7] St. Thomas's phrasing here slightly obscures an important distinction which he makes a little later, in I-II, Question 63, Article 3, to which we will return – for two things are poured into us, not one. There, he explains that just as the natural virtues are perfections of certain natural inclinations to virtue, so also the theological virtues are perfections of certain additional supernatural inclinations to virtue. The natural inclinations are built into us (in our God-given nature), and the natural virtues which crown them are acquired by

discipline (though not without God's help). By contrast, the supernatural inclinations are poured into us by God (though not without our consent), and the theological virtues which crown them are also poured into us by Him (though not without our continuing cooperation).

[8] This is the criterion of the theological virtues which is mentioned in both Objection 3 and the *sed contra*: They are aimed at God, and direct us on the right path to Him. There is no thought here of "many roads to God." Although God's Providence leads people onto the one road in many different ways, there is only one road, and every path is to be judged according to whether it ultimately joins *with* that road or turns away from it. St. Thomas now proceeds to add two more reasons for calling such virtues theological.

[9] The point here is that although in our God-given freedom we must consent to God's help, nothing we can do by our natural power will lift us up to Him. Unless He pours His divine life into us, we will eternally miss our destiny in Him. However, it is important to understand that just as there are acquired virtues other than the four cardinal virtues, so there are infused virtues other than the three spiritual virtues. Just as the four cardinal virtues are the *roots* of the other acquired virtues, so the three theological virtues are the *roots* of the other infused virtues.

Now things become really interesting, because under the influence of the theological virtues, the cardinal virtues are themselves transformed. The difference lies in orientation. For example:

- Acquired prudence helps us to make good decisions for the sake of earthly life, such as marriage and education, but infused prudence helps us make good decisions for the sake of eternal life with God.
- Acquired justice helps us respect the rights of others as seen in the light of reason, but infused justice helps us to respect their rights as seen in the additional light of love.
- Acquired fortitude helps us to face frightening things for the sake of the goods of this life or to resist what endangers them, but infused fortitude helps us to face frightening things, even martyrdom, for the sake of the kingdom of heaven.[19]
- Acquired temperance helps us to moderate our desires for the sake of earthly goods like health, but infused temperance helps us to moderate our desires for the sake of spiritual purity.

We see then that the infused virtues bring about a transformation of human psychology, not in the sense that they are contrary to human nature – for in fact human nature was prepared ahead of time to receive them – but in the sense

---

[19] I hope it is clear that by martyrs, I am not referring to such persons as suicide bombers, who are not martyrs but murderers and self-murderers.

that the transformation exceeds the capacities which human nature possesses by itself. This vast change affects all aspects of the human person, including intellect, appetite, and will. From this point of view, says St. Thomas, the infused virtues "deserve to be called virtues simply," since they direct us to our ultimate end in God. By contrast, the acquired virtues are virtues only *secundum quid*, "in a restricted sense," because although they direct us with respect to a particular kind of action, in a way which is *compatible with* our ultimate end in God, they do not actually direct us *to* this ultimate end.[20] In one of St. Thomas's major early works, he also remarks that although the acquired virtues make us fit for the life of the civil community, the infused virtues make us fit for the spiritual life of that community which is the Church.[21] Similarly, in I-II, Question 61, Article 5, following Macrobius, he distinguishes among the forms which the cardinal virtues take at different levels of development: As "social" virtues, they enable us to conduct ourselves well in the community; as "cleansing" virtues, they incline us to God; and as cleansed virtues, they repose in God. The social virtues are acquired, but the cleansing virtues and cleansed virtues are infused.[22]

St. Thomas distinguishes not only among different spiritual virtues, but also between spiritual virtues and spiritual *gifts*, which may be further divided into spiritual *fruits* and spiritual *beatitudes*. In the *Summa*, this is the subject of a long investigation, but for present purposes, a few paragraphs will suffice. In one sense, all the spiritual virtues are gifts because they are influences poured into the faithful by God. However, the term "gifts" is applied in a special sense to additional graces which make them especially ready to receive this inflow. In this way, the spiritual gifts prompt acts *even higher* than the ordinary acts of virtue – acts of what is sometimes called "heroic" or "divine" virtue, as seen in the lives of especially holy persons. Interestingly, St. Thomas remarks that "even the Philosopher," that is, Aristotle, a pagan, had some faint glimmering of this matter.[23]

A popular misconception attributes to St. Thomas an analogy actually expressed by a later writer, João or Johannes Poinsot, known as John of St. Thomas, according to which the exercise of the spiritual virtues is like rowing a boat using oars, but that the enjoyment of the spiritual gifts is like being blown across the water by the wind. The image is attractive; a person who is granted

---

[20] I-II, Q. 65, Art. 2. This makes it likely that in most places where St. Thomas refers to the virtues, he is speaking of infused virtues.

[21] *Unde et in alia vita hominem perficiunt, acquisitae quidem in vita civili, infusae in vita spirituali, quae est ex gratia, secundum quam homo virtuosus est membrum Ecclesiae.* I am paraphrasing freely. Thomas Aquinas, *Commentary on the Sentences of Peter Lombard*, Dist. 33, Q. 1, Art. 2, Qc. 4. The Latin text of the work is available online at www.corpusthomisticum.org/iopera.html.

[22] In this context he also mentions the "exemplar" virtues, but these are the virtues as they preexist in God Himself.

[23] I-II, Q. 68, Art. 1; for the remark on Aristotle, see ad 1.

the gifts may *feel* as though he is being blown along. For three reasons, however, I believe St. Thomas himself would regard Poinsot's analogy as misleading. In the first place, he would view the image of laborious rowing as going too far because it treats the spiritual virtues as though they were acquired purely by our own efforts rather than infused. In the second, he would view the image of being blown effortlessly across the water as going too far in the opposite direction, for it treats the gifts of the spirit as though God, in infusing His grace, bypassed human will altogether. Finally, although Poinsot offers the analogy to explain what he considers the spiritual point of an incident in the Gospels in which Jesus calms a storm on the Lake of Galilee, surely this is a misunderstanding, because Jesus does not help the disciples by stirring up the wind, but by calming it.[24] Yet even though Poinsot mischaracterizes and exaggerates the distinction between the virtues and the gifts, the gifts really are different than the infused virtues, and they are a great boon.

What about fruits and beatitudes? These are not so much dispositions of character as things that *result* from dispositions of character. The distinction can be confusing, because several terms, for example "patience," are applied to things in more than one of these categories. However, when a term is used for a disposition which is poured into us by grace, it refers to an infused virtue; if it is used for the additional grace which disposes us to receive this inflow even more readily, it refers to a spiritual gift; if it is used for the delight we experience in acting according to such dispositions, it refers to a spiritual fruit; and if it is used for the perfect excellence of this delight, it refers to a spiritual beatitude.[25]

Consider for example the beatitude described in Jesus' announcement, "Blessed are those who hunger and thirst for righteousness, for they shall be satisfied."[26] The statement embodies three claims. What kind of people possess the supreme happiness called blessedness? Those who hunger and thirst for righteousness. What is it that so delights them? To be made righteous. Why do they find righteousness so delightful? Because, by God's grace, they are the kind of people who hunger and thirst for it. This beatitude has nothing to say about people who don't hunger and thirst for righteousness; it is about the kind of people who do. To those who have that longing, God promises satisfaction – and because they trust in this promise, they have a foretaste of that blessedness now.

[10] We can know *that* God is by natural reason. We can also know certain things *about* God by natural reason – for example, that He is eternal and

---

[24] For the incident, see Mark 6:45–52. For the analogy, see John of St. Thomas, *The Gifts of the Holy Ghost*, trans. Dominic Hughes (New York: Sheed and Ward, 1951), Chapter 2, Section 29 (pp. 56–57). My remarks on the analogy have gained from the discussion of Andrew Pinsent, "Wisdom and Evil," in Paul Moser and Michael McFall, eds., *The Wisdom of the Christian Faith* (New York: Cambridge University Press, 2012), pp. 105–106.

[25] I-II, Q. 69, Art. 1; and Q. 70, Art. 2.   [26] Matthew 5:6 (RSV-CE).

all-powerful. But to know *what* God is – to see the Divine Essence as it is, to know God as we are known – transcends our natural powers. This is not a problem that would have vanished if only we had been created with stronger minds, because no matter how strong a created mind may be, it must inevitably fall infinitely short of the Creator. God, therefore, (1) offers to *lift us up* to Himself, (2) makes known, by revelation, what we must do to avail ourselves of His offer, and (3) bestows on those who truly seek Him the help we need to do so. Just because these means of grace exceed anything human reason could have found out for itself, it is sometimes called unreasonable to believe in them. But given the limitations of human reason, it is reasonable to believe that a God who does wish to be known would not have left us to our inadequate devices.[27]

Reply to Objection 1. [1] *A certain nature may be ascribed to a certain thing in two ways. First, essentially: and thus these theological virtues surpass the nature of man.* [2] *Secondly, by participation, as kindled wood partakes of the nature of fire: and thus, after a fashion, man becomes a partaker of the Divine Nature, as stated above: so that these virtues are proportionate to man in respect of the Nature of which he is made a partaker.*	Reply to Objection 1. A thing may be said to have a particular nature in two different senses. In one sense, its nature is its essence, and in this sense, the spiritual virtues do exceed human nature. But in another sense, a thing can be said to share in the nature of something else, as we say that a burning thing shares in the nature of fire. This is the sense in which man may partake in a way in the Divine nature. So although the spiritual virtues are not commensurate with man's essence, they are certainly commensurate with his participation in the Divine nature.

[1] The essence of a thing is the formal principle which makes it is the kind of thing that it is. In the case of man, the essence is *rational animal*, for unlike the other animals, we are rational, but unlike the angels, who are also rational, we are animal.[28] But finite rationality is not enough; to think that our finite created minds could reach the infinite Mind of the Creator is something like thinking that our eyes could gaze at the sun. The problem is not that the sun which makes all things visible is not visible enough, but that it is too visible for our weak eyes to take in.[29] This is what the Objector has in mind – and so far he is right.

---

[27] Problems such as how to discern among conflicting claims to Divine revelation, or conflicting interpretations of the Scriptures, are practical difficulties rather than objections to believing in Divine revelation in principle. Moreover, they are difficulties to which St. Thomas believes that God has provided the solution, through Divine grace and through His guidance of the Church.

[28] This does not mean that men and women always act rationally but that they are members of the species of animal characterized by the potentiality of doing so.

[29] A point fatally overlooked in Plato's Allegory of the Cave, according to which the escapee from the Cave is eventually able to gaze straight upon the Sun of Being merely by his own powers.

[2] What the Objector forgets is that in its own way, one thing can be made to share in the nature of another thing. Wood cannot set itself on fire, but wood is of such a nature that fire can set it on fire; sponges cannot make themselves wet, but sponges are of such a nature that water can make them wet; cruets cannot fill themselves with oil, but cruets are of such a nature that oil can fill them with oil. It is in this way that we become partakers of the Divine nature, for although we are not holy, and cannot make ourselves holy, we are of such a nature that God can make us holy. The blessed have not *become, in their own being*, what God is, but they have truly become partakers of the Divine nature.

exemplar vs. exemplate

Reply to Objection 2. These virtues are called Divine, not as though God were virtuous by reason of them, but because of them God makes us virtuous, and directs us to Himself. Hence they are not exemplar but exemplate virtues.	Reply to Objection 2. In calling these virtues Divine, we do not mean that they make God virtuous, but that by means of them, God makes *us* virtuous and leads us to Him. They are not *exemplar* virtues, models of virtue as it pre-exists in God Himself. Rather they are *exemplate* virtues, qualities in us which partake of these models.

Although the qualities of God are Divine, not everything which is called Divine is a quality of God. In particular, the theological virtues are called Divine because (1) they are poured into us by God, and (2) they make us reflect Him in our own finite way. Just because they are poured into us by God, they are called "infused," and just because they do reflect their Divine example, they are called "exemplate."

Reply to Objection 3. [1] The reason and will are naturally directed to God, inasmuch as He is the beginning and end of nature, but in proportion to nature. [2] But the reason and will, according to their nature, are not sufficiently directed to Him in so far as He is the object of supernatural happiness.	Reply to Objection 3. Certainly natural reason and will are directed to God, just in the sense that all nature proceeds from Him and finds its goal in Him. But it is quite another thing to suppose that natural reason and will are directed to God in the sense that they can attain their object *by themselves*. To reach their object of supernatural beatitude, they are insufficient.

[1] God is the Creator of *all* things, not just us, and *all* things aim at Him according to their nature. For example, He created even the mollusks, and for a mollusk to seek what is good for mollusk nature is in a way for the mollusk to seek God. Not, or course, that the mollusk thinks of God; the mollusk does not think of anything! Yet everything which the mollusk seeks is good to it only by virtue of the fact that it reflects the uncreated Goodness of the Creator; the very striving and burgeoning of these creatures reflects God's limitless life.[30]

---

[30] Concerning this point, see I, Q. 103, Art. 4.

It is in this sense that Scripture speaks of things which know nothing of God praising God – fire and hail, snow and frost, cattle, serpents, and flying birds.[31] Now mollusks seek what is good for them according to mollusk nature, by the guidance the Creator implanted in their instincts; they do not know that all this is about God. But human beings seek what is good for them according to the guidance the Creator implanted in their created will and intellect; this is a more excellent way, because *we can* know that all this is about God.

[2] Yet the mere fact that human reason and will are naturally aimed at God does not mean that they have within themselves the force to attain Him. Our nature is like a bow, bent by a great longing which for all its strength is insufficient to drive our souls across the infinite gulf which separates us from our target. The theological virtues "direct" us to God, not in the sense that they enable us to cross that gulf, but in the sense that they dispose us to receive Him. We cannot, of ourselves, reach God; He must come to us.

---

[31] See esp. Psalm 148.

Whether Virtue Is in Us by Nature?

TEXT	PARAPHRASE
Whether virtue is in us by nature?	Are we naturally virtuous?

Is virtue implanted in the constitution of human beings – does it in some sense belong to us just because we possess a human nature? The query sounds very modern: Many secular people believe that we are naturally good, and corrupted only by some disorder of social life which might perhaps be corrected by social engineering. During my freshman year of college I attended a lecture by the well-known democratic socialist Michael Harrington, one of the great influences on President Lyndon Johnson's "War on Poverty." A questioner put to Harrington the objection that socialism could never work because of human selfishness. Harrington replied that people are selfish only because of the scarcity of goods; that goods are scarce only because of capitalism; that socialism would put an end to scarcity; and therefore, that under socialism, people would no longer be selfish. —

In the Christian view, our situation is much more complex. Human beings were created in the image of God, in a condition of original justice – all of their powers in harmony with one another. Because rational beings have free will, this did not make it impossible for them to sin, and through the abuse of their freedom, they overreached. The result was unhappy, for although they had the same nature as before – the same minds, the same passions – this good thing was now in bad condition: Their minds, having refused submission to God, were no longer able to command the willing submission of their appetites. We suffer the same disorder. Complicating the question of whether we are "naturally" virtuous is the fact that although the term "natural" is sometimes used for things we do without having to learn them, it is also used for things we *must* learn in order to reach our full and appropriate development. In the former sense, it is "natural" to breath; in the latter sense, it is "natural" to make friends.

What then shall we say – are we are naturally virtuous or not? Or is this one of those cases in which a simple "Yes" or "No" does not suffice? St. Thomas responds to the query not just theologically but also philosophically, considering what it means for something to be true of us "by nature," reviewing the history of the problem from the pre-Socratic philosopher Anaxagoras to his own time.

Objection 1. [1] *It would seem that virtue is in us by nature. For Damascene says (De Fide Orth. iii, 14): "Virtues are natural to us and are equally in all of us."* [2] *And Antony says in his sermon to the monks: "If the will contradicts nature it is perverse, if it follow nature it is virtuous."* [3] *Moreover, a gloss on Matthew 4:23, "Jesus went about," etc., says: "He taught them natural virtues, i.e. chastity, justice, humility, which man possesses naturally."*	Objection 1. Apparently the answer to the question is "Yes," for this view is supported by eminent authorities. John of Damascus says in the fourth book of his great work that virtues are natural and belong to everyone in equal measure. St. Anthony says in his famous address to monks that the will is perverse if it challenges nature, but virtuous if it preserves the natural condition. Finally, the commentary called the Ordinary Gloss says that when Jesus went about Galilee preaching the Gospel of the Kingdom, he was teaching natural righteousness – chastity, justice, humility, and other such things which man possesses naturally.

[1] According to some of the Fathers of the Church, especially in the East, the development of virtue is not an acquisition of something we lack, but an uncovering of something which is already present in us but obscured by the muck of sin. On this view, even though we do not all *exercise* the virtues to the same degree, we all *possess* them to the same degree because we are all made in the *imago Dei*. Such is the view of St. John of Damascus:

For the virtues are natural qualities, and are implanted in all by nature and in equal measure, even if we do not all in equal measure employ our natural energies. By the transgression [the Fall] we were driven from the natural to the unnatural. But the Lord led us back from the unnatural into the natural. For this is what is the meaning of *in our image, after our likeness.* [Genesis 1:26] And the discipline and trouble of this life were not designed as a means for our attaining virtue which was foreign to our nature, but to enable us to cast aside the evil that was foreign and contrary to our nature: just as on laboriously removing from steel the rust which is not natural to it but acquired through neglect, we reveal the natural brightness of the steel.[1]

St. Thomas sharpens the edge of the Objection by having the imaginary Objector mention the first part of the first sentence, "for the virtues are natural qualities, and are implanted in all by nature and in equal measure," but omit the second part, "even if we do not all in equal measure employ our natural energies."

[1] St. John of Damascus, *An Exposition of the Orthodox Faith*, Book 3, Chapter 14 (public domain), available on the internet at www.newadvent.org/fathers/3304.htm.

[2] The Anthony whom the Objector is paraphrasing is St. Anthony the Great, whose address to a group of monks who had asked to hear him is contained in St. Athanasius's *Life of Anthony*. The Latin translation of this book was widely read in the middle ages. For our purposes, the critical passage is the following:

For the Lord aforetime has said, *The kingdom of heaven is within you* [Luke 17:21]. Wherefore virtue has need at our hands of willingness alone, since it is in us and is formed from us. For when the soul has its spiritual faculty in a natural state virtue is formed. And it is in a natural state when it remains as it came into existence. And when it came into existence it was fair and exceeding honest. For this cause Joshua, the son of Nun, in his exhortation said to the people, *Make straight your heart unto the Lord God of Israel* [Joshua 24:23], and John, *Make your paths straight* [Matthew 3:3]. For rectitude of soul consists in its having its spiritual part in its natural state as created. But on the other hand, when it swerves and turns away from its natural state, that is called vice of the soul. Thus the matter is not difficult. If we abide as we have been made, we are in a state of virtue, but if we think of ignoble things we shall be accounted evil. If, therefore, this thing had to be acquired from without, it would be difficult in reality; but if it is in us, let us keep ourselves from foul thoughts. And as we have received the soul as a deposit, let us preserve it for the Lord, that He may recognize His work as being the same as He made it.[2]

[3] Matthew 4:23 (DRA) says "And Jesus went about all Galilee, teaching in their synagogues, and preaching the gospel of the kingdom: and healing all manner of sickness and every infirmity, among the people." According to one of the remarks quoted in the Ordinary Gloss[3] – a widely used medieval commentary stitched together from comments by previous writers – this means Jesus is teaching "natural justice, such as chastity and humility and other such things that man possesses naturally."[4]

The main point is clear: The Objector is continuing to buttress his case for the view that the virtues are in us by nature. In view of the phrasing of the Gloss, however, a secondary point may be mysterious: Why does it say that chastity, humility, and so on are parts of *justice?* Aren't these virtues all distinct? The answer is that in Latin, just as in English, the term "justice" (*iustitia*) is sometimes used not as a name for a specific virtue, but as a synonym for virtue in general. As though to cover his bases, in the Objector's paraphrase the term is actually used twice, once in each sense: "He taught them natural *justice*, such as chastity, *justice*, humility, which man possesses naturally" (emphasis mine).[5] The Blackfriars translation renders the two instances of the term as "virtues" and "justice"; my paraphrase, as "righteousness" and "justice."

---

[2] St. Athanasius of Antioch, *Life of Anthony*, Section 20 (public domain), available on the internet at www.newadvent.org/fathers/2811.htm.
[3] A facsimile of the Latin text of the *Glossa Ordinaria* is available on the internet at http://lollardsociety.org/?page_id=409.
[4] *Doces naturales iustitias, castitatem scilicet & humilitate & similia que homo naturaliter habet.*
[5] *Docet naturales iustitias, scilicet castitatem, iustitiam, humilitatem, quas naturaliter habet homo.*

Objection 2. [1] *Further, the virtuous good consists in accord with reason, as was clearly shown above (55, 4, ad 2).* [2] *But that which accords with reason is natural to man; since reason is part of man's nature. Therefore virtue is in man by nature.*	**Objection 2.** Moreover, we have seen earlier in the *Summa* that the good of virtue lies in the fact that it follows reason. But seeing that man's nature is rational, whatever follows reason is natural. It follows that virtue is natural.

[1] As we saw in I-II, Q. 55, Art. 4, the good to which virtue directs us is "the good as fixed by reason."

[2] Our good is that to which we are naturally inclined – not what we happen to desire as individuals, but what we are made to desire as human beings. We share certain natural inclinations with the beasts, but our highest natural inclinations are those we possess as rational beings, beings made to seek and to know truth and to live in a partnership in goodness which is shaped by that truth. In us, even the inclinations which we do share with other animals are taken up into rationality and transformed by it. Mating is transformed into marriage, generation is transformed into family and care for posterity, the attraction of the pack is transformed into civil life, and the mere desire for the presence of another beast is transformed into friendship.

Objection 3. [1] *Further, that which is in us from birth is said to be natural to us.* [2] *Now virtues are in some from birth: for it is written (Job 31:18): "From my infancy mercy grew up with me; and it came out with me from my mother's womb."* [3] *Therefore virtue is in man by nature.*	**Objection 3.** Still further, we commonly call the qualities which are in us from birth "natural." But in some persons, virtue is manifest from birth. Job makes this claim about himself when he cries that compassion has been seen in him since infancy, and has been with him since his emergence from the womb. So virtue is in us by nature.

[1] The term "natural" is often used in this sense today as well, especially in controversies about natural and unnatural sexuality.

[2] Job is protesting to God that he does not deserve the suffering which has befallen him. If he has failed to show mercy to the poor, then let him be punished! But on the contrary, he has shown compassion from his birth:

If I have denied to the poor what they desired, and have made the eyes of the widow wait: If I have eaten my morsel alone, and the fatherless hath not eaten thereof: (For from my infancy mercy grew up with me: and it came out with me from my mother's womb:) If I have despised him that was perishing for want of clothing, and the poor man that had no covering: If his sides have not blessed me, and if he were not warmed with the fleece of my sheep: If I have lifted up my hand against the fatherless, even when I saw myself superior in the gate: Let my shoulder fall from its joint, and let my arm with its bones be broken.[6]

---

[6] Job 31:16–20 (DRA).

I have dropped the conventions of quotation because the Objector is not quite quoting the Latin of the crucial verse, but paraphrasing it closely.

[3] At first the Objector seems to be arguing that because virtue is in *some* of us from birth, it must be in *all* of us by nature. This would be extremely silly reasoning, but the Objections are never merely silly. It might next seem that the Objector is *weakening* the view that virtue is in us by nature, as though to say "Even if virtue is not in all of us by nature, at least it is in some of us by nature." But in the light of such authorities as John of Damascus, quoted by Objection 1, I think Objector 3 is making a different claim: That because virtue is *manifest* in some of us from birth, and we all have the same nature, it must be *present* in all of us from birth, even if not always manifest.

This is the interpretation I have adopted in the paraphrase, and the Latin supports it fully. Both the Vulgate and the Objector's paraphrase use the term *crevit*,[7] which carries not only the meaning of growing up, as in "from my infancy mercy grew up with me," but also the meaning of becoming visible or manifest.

| On the contrary, [1] *Whatever is in man by nature is common to all men, and is not taken away by sin,* [2] *since even in the demons natural gifts remain, as Dionysius states (Div. Nom. iv). [3] But virtue is not in all men; and is cast out by sin. Therefore it is not in man by nature.* | On the other hand, if something is in us by nature, then we all have it, and not even sin can remove it from us. Pseudo-Dionysius emphasizes the point by explaining that natural good persists even in demons. But this is not the case with the virtues, for in the first place we do not all have them, and in the second place sin pushes them out of us. It follows that the proposition that virtue is in man naturally is false. |

[1] Sin can impair our nature, as cloudy moisture impairs the transparency of glass.[8] Each of the natural powers in which virtue can reside is wounded:

[A]ll the powers of the soul are left, as it were, destitute of their proper order, whereby they are naturally directed to virtue; which destitution is called a wounding of nature.... Therefore in so far as the reason is deprived of its order to the true, there is the wound of ignorance; in so far as the will is deprived of its order of good, there is the wound of malice; in so far as the irascible is deprived of its order to the arduous, there is the wound of weakness; and in so far as the concupiscible is deprived of its order to the delectable, moderated by reason, there is the wound of concupiscence.[9]

But sin does not *take away* our nature, as if moisture not only fogged the glass but shattered it. For If men and women no longer possessed their human nature, they would no longer be human beings, but something else.

[2] This point is taken from the following words of Pseudo-Dionysius in his work, *On the Divine Names*:

---

[7] Objector: *ab infantia crevit mecum miseratio.*   [8] I-II, Q. 85, Art. 2.   [9] I-II, Q. 85, Art. 3.

For in what, pray, do we consider the wickedness of the devils to consist except their ceasing from the quality and activity of divine virtues? ... [T]hey are not utterly without the Good, seeing that they exist and live and form intuitions and have within them any movement of desire at all; but they are called evil because they fail in the exercise of their natural activity. The evil in them is therefore a warping, a declension from their right condition; a failure, an imperfection, an impotence, and a weakness, loss and lapse of that power which would preserve their perfection in them.... Hence the devils are not evil in so far as they fulfil their nature, but in so far as they do not.... And we maintain that the angelic gifts bestowed upon them have never themselves suffered change, but are unblemished in their perfect brightness, even if the devils themselves do not perceive it through blinding their faculties of spiritual perception. Thus, so far as their existence is concerned, they possess it from the Good, and are naturally good, and desire the Beautiful and Good in desiring existence, life, and intuition, which are existent things. And they are called evil through the deprivation and the loss whereby they have lapsed from their proper virtues.[10]

[3] The *sed contra* is making two arguments at once, which can be put in a pair of syllogisms:
The first:

1. Whatever is natural is in all men.
2. But virtue is not in all men.
3. Therefore virtue is not natural.

The second:

1. Whatever is natural is incapable of being utterly destroyed by sin.
2. But virtue can be utterly destroyed by sin.
3. Therefore virtue is not natural.

I answer that, [1] *With regard to corporeal forms,* [2] *it has been maintained by some that they are wholly from within, by those, for instance, who upheld the theory of "latent forms" [Anaxagoras; Cf. I, 45, 8; 65, 4].* [3] *Others held that forms are entirely from without, those, for instance, who thought that corporeal forms originated from some separate cause.* [4] *Others, however, esteemed that they are partly from within, in so far as they pre-exist*	Here is my response. The query before us is how the *form* of virtue comes to be in us – whether the pattern of its activity does, or does not, inhere in our nature. To answer, we must consider both bodily and nonbodily forms, but let us begin with bodily forms. Three views on the subject of bodily forms have been maintained. (1) Some have said that they arise from causes intrinsic to bodies; this is the theory of so-called latent forms. (2) Others have said that they arise from causes distinct from bodies. (3) A third group has held that certain bodily forms come from within in

[10] *Dionysius the Areopagite: On the Divine Names and the Mystical Theology*, trans. C. E. Rolt (public domain), Chapter 4, Section 23, available on the internet at www.ccel.org/ccel/rolt/dionysius.i.html. See also Sections 18, 24, and 27.

potentially in matter; and partly from without, in so far as they are brought into act by the agent.

[5] *In like manner with regard to sciences and virtues,*
[6] *some held that they are wholly from within, so that all virtues and sciences would pre-exist in the soul naturally, but that the hindrances to science and virtue, which are due to the soul being weighed down by the body, are removed by study and practice, even as iron is made bright by being polished. This was the opinion of the Platonists.*
[7] *Others said that they are wholly from without, being due to the inflow of the active intellect, as Avicenna maintained.*
[8] *Others said that sciences and virtues are within us by nature, so far as we are adapted to them, but not in their perfection: this is the teaching of the Philosopher (Ethic. ii, 1), and is nearer the truth.*

[9] *To make this clear, it must be observed that there are two ways in which something is said to be natural to a man; one is according to his specific nature, the other according to his individual nature.*
[10] *And, since each thing derives its species from its form, and its individuation from matter, and, again, since man's form is his rational soul, while his matter is his body, whatever belongs to him in respect of his rational soul, is natural to him in respect of his specific nature;* [11] *while whatever belongs to him in respect of the particular temperament of his body, is natural to him in respect of his individual nature.*

the sense that they exist in matter as potentialities, but from without in the sense that potentialities are actualized through the intervention of an agent.

Turning now to nonbodily forms, such as the forms of the sciences and virtues in our souls, we again find three views. (1) Some have said that they arise entirely from causes intrinsic to the soul. On this view, the soul is oppressed by the body, which hinders the sciences and virtues. However, just as iron is made lustrous by polishing off the rust, so the soul is made bright by study and training, which polish off these hindrances. This was the Platonist opinion. (2) Others have said that nonbodily forms arise entirely from a cause distinct from the soul. They believed that sciences and virtues are poured into the soul by an external agent called the "active intellect." This was the opinion of Avicenna. (3) A third group has held that although the sciences and virtues can be said to be in us naturally, they are not present in their completeness, but as aptitudes. [And so long as we do not attempt to apply it to the theological virtues,] this theory – maintained by Aristotle in the second book of the *Nicomachean Ethics* – is really true.

To see why this is true, we must remember that something may be called natural to man in two different senses. In one sense, what is natural pertains to the nature of the *species* of man; in the other, it pertains to the nature of *this particular man*. Now each thing derives its nature from its form, and its individuality from its matter. In the case of man, the form is his rational soul, and the matter is his body. For this reason, whatever is true of him because of his rational soul pertains to his *species* nature, while whatever is true of him because of the particular character of his body pertains to his *individual* nature. And these two senses of nature are related, for whatever is natural to us because we have human *bodies* is natural to us because our bodies are informed by human *souls*. The soul makes the

For whatever is natural to man in respect of his body, considered as part of his species, is to be referred, in a way, to the soul, in so far as this particular body is adapted to this particular soul. ⌣

[12] *In both these ways virtue is natural to man inchoatively.* ⌣ [13] *This is so in respect of the specific nature, in so far as in man's reason are to be found instilled by nature certain naturally known principles of both knowledge and action, which are the nurseries of intellectual and moral virtues, and in so far as there is in the will a natural appetite for good in accordance with reason.* [14] *Again, this is so in respect of the individual nature, in so far as by reason of a disposition in the body, some are disposed either well or ill to certain virtues: because, to wit, certain sensitive powers are acts of certain parts of the body, according to the disposition of which these powers are helped or hindered in the exercise of their acts,* [15] *and, in consequence, the rational powers also, which the aforesaid sensitive powers assist. In this way one man has a natural aptitude for science, another for fortitude, another for temperance:* [16] *and in these ways, both intellectual and moral virtues are in us by way of a natural aptitude, inchoatively, but not perfectly,* [17] *since nature is determined to one,* [18] *while the perfection of these virtues does not depend on one particular mode of action, but on various modes, in respect of the various matters, which constitute the*

body the species of body that it is; *this* body corresponds to *this* soul. ⌣

Virtue is natural to man in both of these senses, but only as a sketch or beginning, not as something finished. It is natural to the *species* of man in two ways: First, in that his reason contains certain naturally known starting points of both knowledge and of action (the former being seeds of intellectual virtue, the latter of moral virtue); second, in that his will contains a natural appetite for good *in conformity with* reason. ⌣

In turn, virtue is natural to *this particular* man, in the sense that the particular dispositions of his body may give him either a strong or weak inclination to a given virtue. Why should this be the case? Because each of the various sensitive powers is the activity of some bodily process. So in the first place, depending on the dispositions of these processes, any given sensitive power may be either spurred into action or held back, and in the second place, since the sensitive powers are the servants of the rational powers, the rational powers are affected by these processes too. So it is that one man has a natural aptitude for, say, science (an intellectual virtue), while others have natural aptitudes for, say, fortitude or temperance (both moral virtues).

We see then that in both of these senses of the natural – what is natural to the species of man, and what is natural to this particular man – both intellectual and moral virtues are in us by nature. But as the argument also shows us, they belong to us only as aptitudes or beginnings; they are not finished work. Why? Because nature's mode of action is fixed – when nature alone determines what we do, we always act in the same way. But virtue's mode of action is to choose the right course of action when more than one course is possible and nature alone does *not* fix what we do. Just what the right choice is depends on all sorts of things, including the circumstances of each case and the particular kind of thing with which each virtue is concerned. What then is the answer to the query "Is virtue *sphere of virtue's action, and according to various circumstances.*

[19] *It is therefore evident that all virtues are in us by nature, according to aptitude and inchoation, but not according to perfection, except the theological virtues, which are entirely from without.*

[20] *This suffices for the Replies to the Objections. For the first two argue about the nurseries of virtue which are in us by nature, inasmuch as we are rational beings. The third objection must be taken in the sense that, owing to the natural disposition which the body has from birth, one has an aptitude for pity, another for living temperately, another for some other virtue.*

in us by nature?" If it is taken to mean that an aptitude for acquired virtue and a prod toward it belong to our nature, we must reply "Yes." But if it is taken to mean that the perfection of acquired virtue belongs to our nature, we must reply "No." In the case of the theological virtues, not even the aptitude and the prod exist in us by nature, because they are poured into us entirely from outside.

How the Objections may be answered should now be clear. Objections 1 and 2 concern those seeds of virtue which are in us by nature because we are naturally rational. Provided that these two Objections are taken only in this sense, they are quite true. Objection 3 concerns the natural bodily dispositions which various persons have from birth, so that this fellow has an aptitude for mercy, that one for the living temperately, still another for some other virtue. Provided that it is taken only in this sense, this Objection too is quite true. None of the Objections stands against our conclusions.

[1] Since the question is how the form of virtue comes to be in us, it might seem strange that St. Thomas begins with the forms of material bodies. After all, virtue is a property of the soul, which is immaterial. The chief reason for beginning with the forms of material bodies is that the theories which have been held about corporeal forms are paralleled by those which have been held about immaterial forms, and in a few paragraphs St. Thomas intends to develop the comparison.

But there may be another reason too, for the immaterial soul *simply is* the form of the material body. We are not speaking here just of the shape of our flesh; we are speaking of the theme being played upon our flesh, the pattern of an embodied human life. I am *human* because I possess the human essence, because my body is informed by a human soul; and I am *this* human because the matter of my body is *this* matter rather than some other matter. Now since the complete human being is neither the body alone, nor the soul alone, but the composite of body and soul, each one affects the other. Not only is does it seem more natural to kneel if I am reverent, but it is easier to be reverent if I kneel; not only is it easier to be cheerful if I am healthy, but it is easier to be healthy if I am cheerful. The unity of body and soul affects the question of how the form of virtue makes its home in us, for the very possibility of human virtue depends on a human soul. But it is also true that the general disposition of the body may make it easier or more difficult for this possibility to be realized – a fact which St. Thomas is soon to explain.

[2] The Pre-Socratic philosopher Anaxagoras thought that the forms of all things are latently present within every particular thing. On this view, what makes a thing the particular thing that it happens to be is merely the disclosure or unveiling of one of these forms. Earlier in the *Summa* St. Thomas has rejected this hypothesis, commenting that it "arose from ignorance concerning matter, and from not knowing how to distinguish between potentiality and actuality. For because forms pre-exist in matter in potentiality, [the proponents of this view] asserted that they pre-exist simply."[11]

[3] The medieval Islamic philosopher Avicenna maintained that corporeal forms subsist separately from the body. St. Thomas has previously explained that a body's form is not something separate from the body, but something which *informs* the body; it is the very thing that makes it the kind of body that it is.[12]

[4] Aristotle held that a corporeal form may be said to exist in matter *in the sense of a potentiality* if the matter is capable of receiving that form. However, some agent distinct from the matter must act upon it for that form to be realized. Think of someone pressing a signet ring into wax.

[5] We now turn to immaterial forms, such as the forms of various sciences and virtues, viewing their patterns as dispositions in our minds. As before, St. Thomas is using the term "sciences" not for social practices but for intellectual virtues – for dispositions by which the mind connects first principles of theoretical reason with particular conclusions. In this case, though, by "virtues" he means not intellectual but moral virtues – dispositions by which the mind connects the first principles of practical reason with particular acts.

[6] Here St. Thomas suggests that just as some, like Anaxagoras, have mistakenly held that corporeal forms pre-exist in bodies not just as potentialities but simply, so some, like Plato, have mistakenly held that the incorporeal forms of the moral and intellectual virtues pre-exist in minds, not just as potentialities but simply. Those who held the former view thought that a given body becomes what it is not because it *acquires* a particular corporeal form, but because one of the corporeal forms it already possesses is unveiled. In much the same way, those who held the latter view thought that a virtuous mind becomes what it is not because it *acquires* virtues, but because the virtues it already possesses are stripped of influences which weigh them down. On this view, the human being is not a soul united with a body, but a soul encumbered by a body. Plato has Socrates express this view on the day of his execution, explaining to his friends that until the soul is rescued by the love of wisdom, she "could only view real existence through the bars of a prison,

---

[11] I, Q. 45, Art. 8, substituting the term "actuality" for the archaic equivalent "act" used in the Blackfriars translation.
[12] Ibid.

not in and through herself; she was wallowing in the mire of every sort of ignorance; and by reason of lust had become the principal accomplice in her own captivity."[13]

[7] Here St. Thomas suggests that just as Avicenna thought that corporeal forms originate entirely outside of bodies, so he thought, mistakenly, that the incorporeal forms of the moral and intellectual virtues originate entirely outside of minds. The reason St. Thomas considers the hypothesis mistaken is that knowing is the intellect's "act" – that which actualizes the intellect, that which it is *for* – and nothing can perform its proper act except by means of some power inherent in it. So the human intellect must have some power of its own, which St. Thomas, following Aristotle, calls the "active intellect." To be sure, this power does not make human intellect independent of the Divine intellect. Rather it is a power the Creator gives human intellect so that it can *reflect* His intellect. The active intellect performs the work of abstracting from the inflow of the senses the universal forms that make the things we perceive what they are, be these things men, hands, or trees. Afterward, we exercise another power, the "passive intellect," to retain and consider them.

[8] Aristotle writes that "Neither by nature, then, nor contrary to nature do the [moral and intellectual] virtues arise in us"; rather nature makes us ready to receive them, and their development is completed by habituation or discipline.[14] St. Thomas paraphrases that they are naturally within us not in their fully developed state, but "by way of aptitude" (*secundum aptitudinem*).

The Blackfriars translation, which has St. Thomas say that this view is "nearer to the truth," is incorrect. What St. Thomas actually says is "and this is true" (*et hoc verius est*). Perhaps the translators thought it necessary to soften his words because of the way he qualifies his conclusion, a few lines below, with respect to the theological virtues. I have preferred to deal with this small difficulty in a different way, by adding a line to the paraphrase.

[9] If I say that by nature my friend Dorothy is a rational animal, I am speaking of her "specific" or species nature – something she shares with all other humans, the essence which *makes* her human. But if I say that she is naturally good at making puns, I am speaking of her individual nature – her distinction from other humans, something which sets her apart. True, only a rational being could understand puns in the first place, but a being could be rational and yet not understand them. St. Thomas is not the originator of the distinction between individual and species nature; Marcus Tullius Cicero, for example, had written that:

We must realize also that we are invested by Nature with two characters, as it were: One of these is universal, arising from the fact of our being all alike endowed with reason and with that superiority which lifts us above the brute. From this all morality and propriety are derived, and upon it depends the rational method of ascertaining our

---

[13] Plato, *Phaedo*, trans. Benjamin Jowett (public domain).
[14] Aristotle, *Nicomachean Ethics*, trans. W. D. Ross, Book 2, Chapter 1 (public domain).

duty. The other character is the one that is assigned to individuals in particular. In the matter of physical endowment there are great differences; some, we see, excel in speed for the race, others in strength for wrestling; so in point of personal appearance, some have stateliness, others comeliness. Diversities of character are greater still."[15]

The *normative* sense of the term "natural" is not individual nature, but species nature. Otherwise, there would be a different natural law for every person, something St. Thomas denies. All of us should live up to our rationality, which is a privilege of our species nature and the very hallmark of our flourishing. But if Dorothy suffers the misfortunate of being naturally attracted to drunkenness, it doesn't follow that she should indulge the attraction. In fact she should resist it.

[10] Dan is a man, not a dog or a fish, because he possesses the form or essence which makes men men. But he is *this particular* man, not Dorothy or Edward, because his human soul is united with *this particular* body. To put this point still another way, we are individuated by our matter. My soul, my embodied human life, is different from your soul, your embodied human life, not because the very essence of humanity is different for you and me, but because in me the one essence *man* is united with a different body than in you, and so has led a different history. It isn't that we have the same soul but different bodies. Rather our souls are different *because* they inform different bodies. If we differed from each other *essentially*, then each of us would belong to a different species, like the talking beasts and birds in folk stories.[16]

Now the species nature of man is "rational animal" – what distinguishes our species from other animals is our rational souls. It follows that whatever is true of Dan just because of his species nature is true of him because he has a rational soul. To be sure, if we were to find some day that there are other species of rational animals besides us – say, on Mars – then we may have to add to the definition of our species nature to show how we are different from not only from subrational animals but also from Martians; but so far this suffices.

[11] What individuates Dan – what makes him not just human but *this* human – is the particular matter which is informed by this rational soul. In all sorts of ways, his body differs not just from nonhuman bodies, but even from other human bodies. Now the sheer essence of man does not make him, say, cheerful, melancholy, humorous, or good at poker. But the dispositions of his body – of his nervous system, his endocrine system, and so on – surely can incline him in such ways.

[15] Marcus Tullius Cicero, *De Officiis* [On duties], trans. Walter Miller (Cambridge, MA: Harvard University Press, 1913), Book 1, Section 107 (public domain).

[16] Interestingly, St. Thomas suggests that this *is* how it is among the angels, which are individuated not by matter (being immaterial) but by essence. If this conjecture is correct, then it follows that even though they may be classified into ranks – seraphim, cherubim, and so on, as the tradition has held – each individual angel belongs to a different species; each is the only one of its kind. See I, Q. 50, Art. 4.

Thus, St. Thomas reasons, whatever is true of Dan just because he has *this particular* body pertains to his individual rather than species nature. But whatever is true of Dan just because he has a *human* body pertains to his species rather than individual nature – and is true of him because it is informed by a *human* soul. What St. Thomas says, by the way, is that this particular body and this particular soul are "proportionate" (*proportionatum*), but he is not speaking in the arithmetic sense; the Latin term has a much broader meaning than its English cognate. The Blackfriars translation tries to convey the idea by saying that this particular body is "adapted" to this particular soul; my own paraphrase is a little more elaborate.

[12] To say that virtue is "natural to man inchoatively" is to say that man's nature contains only a beginning of virtue, only something which can grow up to be virtue. We may think of each of the virtues as the mature development of a natural inclination to some good which is either intrinsic to reason or obedient to it.

[13] Often St. Thomas calls these "seeds" of virtue, bearing in mind that a seed is a beginning which is aimed at an end; the Blackfriars translators like to call them "nurseries" of virtue, as we see a few sentences below. The seeds of the intellectual virtues are the first principles of theoretical reason; the seeds of the moral virtues are the first principles of practical reason.[17]

[14] St. Thomas is maintaining the *general* hypothesis that differences in personality have a physiological basis. For present purposes, exactly how this works is not important. He accepts the best theory of the medical science of his day, according to which individual temperament is determined by the relative proportion of certain crucial bodily fluids, the "four humors," and their associated bodily organs.[18] Although this theory now appears quite false, the fact that physiology and temperament are connected is well established. Our scientists may not have much to say about the relative proportion of blood, black bile, yellow bile, and phlegm, but they have plenty to say about the levels of serotonin, GABA, dopamine, epinephrine, and norepinephrine, and although they may laugh at the suggestion that "love springs from the liver,"[19] they are quite open to the suggestion that it springs from the limbic system.

[15] The argument here is not simply that the condition of the body affects both the sensitive and the intellectual powers; rather St. Thomas is suggesting that *because* it affects the sensitive powers, it affects the intellectual powers. The more readily I lose my temper, the more readily I am tempted to believe that the other fellow is in the wrong; the more delicious I find chocolate, the more likely I am to think that I should eat it; the more jittery I am, the more difficult I will find it to concentrate. Even apart from discipline and habituation, all such things influence our development. So it is, St. Thomas thinks, that one person is naturally attracted to contemplation, but another would rather play;

---

[17] See the discussion earlier in this book, in the commentary on I-II, Q. 58, Art. 4.
[18] See for example I-II, Q. 48, Art. 2.   [19] I-II, Q. 48, Art. 2, ad 1.

that one has that loftiness of spirit which makes him scoff at petty dangers, but another is afraid of everything; that one finds it easy to resist the beckoning of lust, but to another it is like a sucking whirlpool.

[16] So the answer to the question "Do some people naturally have certain moral or intellectual virtues without having to acquire them?" is "No," but the answer to the question "Do some people find it easier to develop certain moral or intellectual virtues?" is "Yes."

[17] Whenever one of my natural powers is sufficient to determine my course of action by itself, I always do the same thing. By the nature of the respiratory power, I draw breath; by the nature of the tactile power, I feel; by the nature of the visual power, I see what is there. St. Thomas expresses the point by saying that each of these powers is in potentiality, or is determined, to only one act.

This does *not* mean that my natural powers *always are* sufficient to determine my course of action by themselves. For example, I might drink either temperately or intemperately. Whenever a natural power is in potentiality to more than one act – whenever, by itself, it is open to more than one course of action – then what I do is settled by something more than nature. For example, I don't eat beyond the point of satiety merely because of natural hunger, but because of choice and habit.[20]

[18] Since virtue determines my course of action when my natural powers are insufficient to determine my course of action, it would be absurd to think that my natural powers are sufficient to *give me virtue*. For one of these modes of action is determinate, while the other requires an exercise of judgment. To be sure, using the term "natural" in a somewhat different sense, I have a natural power to make judgments – but the bare possession of the power does not determine what use I will make of it. Judgment among alternatives really is judgment among alternatives. If it were a determinate outworking of subrational forces, it would be illusion.

[19] Here four conclusions are affirmed:

1. The virtues in general are in all of us by nature, in the sense that the seeds or inclinations from which they develop are in us by nature: This is what it means to say that they are in us "according to inchoation."
2. A particular virtue may be in a particular person by nature, in the sense that his natural endowments make it easier for him to acquire it than for others to: This is what it means to say that it is in someone "according to aptitude."
3. No virtue is in anyone by nature, in the sense that he receives it from nature full and intact.

---

[20] See I-II, Q. 49, Art. 4, esp. ad 2: "Power sometimes has a relation to many things: and then it needs to be determined by something else. But if a power has not a relation to many things, it does not need a habit to determine it.... For this reason the natural forces do not perform their operations by means of habits: because they are of themselves determined to one mode of operation."

4. We receive the theological virtues through the inflow of grace – they are neither in our nature of itself, nor in someplace other than our nature, but poured into our nature from outside (though we must cooperate).

[20] Objection 1 held that the development of virtue is not an acquisition of something we lack, but an uncovering of something which is already present in us but obscured by the muck of sin. St. Thomas would say that the task is not to remove the sinful rust which keeps our natural virtue from shining out of us, but to encourage good growth from the seed of virtue and remove the bad growth of vice. This raises a question, for how could vice grow from the same seed as virtue? Because vice responds to the same natural inclinations, but in a disordered way. For example, the husband and the philanderer are both responding to the procreative inclination, but the philanderer tries to divorce it from the good of procreation.

Objection 2 held that since our virtue lies in following reason, and our nature is rational, therefore virtue is natural to us. But our nature is not rational in the sense that from birth we reason well; it is rational in the sense that we always act for reasons, even if for bad ones, and can learn to tell bad ones from good ones. So since virtue lies in following reason, and since the fulfillment of our rational nature requires learning and discipline, the acquisition of virtue requires learning and discipline too.

Objection 3 held that virtue is manifest in some of us from birth (presumably, therefore, present in the rest of us too, even if not manifest). St. Thomas replies that if the notion of being virtuous from birth is taken to mean that some of us naturally possess the *aptitudes* for certain virtues, it is true, but if it is taken to mean that these persons naturally possess the *complete form* of these virtues, it is false. I may be "born with a generous heart" in the sense that I have always enjoyed giving things to others, but the wrong gift may hurt instead of help; I must still learn what I should give, to whom, on what occasions, for what reasons, and to what degree. I may have always preferred study to play, but not everything is a suitable method or object of study; it is one thing to wonder what it is for a being to live, but quite another to ask what will happen if I pull the wings from a fly.

Whether Any Virtue Is Caused in Us by Habituation?

TEXT	PARAPHRASE
Whether any virtue is caused in us by habituation?	According to the tradition, some kinds of virtue are brought about in us by practicing the acts which correspond to them until they become habitual. Is this true?

St. Thomas asks whether *any* virtue can be caused by habituation – not whether *all* virtues are caused by habituation – because he has already presented reasons for thinking that some virtues are brought about in us by other means. In particular, the infused virtues, such as faith, hope, and charity, are poured into us by Divine grace, and one might suppose that all virtues are like this. So it is necessary to ask whether *any* moral or intellectual virtues are brought about by habituation – by the repetition of acts. According to the tradition, the answer to the question is "Yes," and the preceding discussion has assumed this to be correct. But now the assumption must be justified.

Those virtues traditionally thought achievable by habituation are called the "acquired" virtues. The terminology may cause confusion: Don't we "acquire" the infused virtues too? But the term "acquired virtues" is used only for virtues acquired by human effort; in this sense the infused virtues, which are gifts, are not "acquired," but received or accepted. It is deadly to overlook this difference. On the other hand, it should not be exaggerated either, for the question before us is not whether repeated acts are helpful at all with respect to infused virtue, but whether they *cause* it. As St. Thomas says later, "Virtue is twofold, ... acquired and infused. Now the fact of being accustomed to an action contributes to both, but in different ways; for it causes the acquired virtue; while it disposes to infused virtue, and preserves and fosters it when it already exists."[1]

---

[1] I-II, Q. 92, Art. 1, ad 1.

Another reason why the terminology may cause confusion is that a virtue itself is a kind of "habit," or disposition, so that to ask whether virtues can be acquired by habituation is to ask whether habits are acquired by habituation. In English, the question sounds tautological, as though we were asking, "Are things acquired by habituation acquired by habituation?" No such confusion arises in Latin, where the word for "habituation," *assuetudine*, is etymologically unrelated to the word for "habit," *habitus*. In our own language we can prevent confusion by translating the word *habitus* by non-question-begging words and phrases such as "disposition" or "dispositional tendency."

Dispositions in general come to be in us in all sorts of ways. Some are even natural. For instance, the heart has a natural "habit" or disposition to pump blood, and the mind has a natural dispositional tendency to recognize that there is a difference between good and evil, such that the former is to be done and pursued and the latter avoided. Neither of these dispositions is a moral or intellectual *virtue*, however. The former is merely bodily. Although the latter is a quality of the mind, it is only a seed or beginning from which virtue – somehow – develops. We are asking about that "somehow." The question is whether any moral or intellectual virtues develop in us by repeated acts.

But is this query necessary? Doesn't everyday experience show us the power of habituation? Yes and no. Certainly everyday experience shows us that *certain moral and intellectual dispositions* develop in us by repeated acts. But some of these are bad ones, and fairly persuasive reasons can be set forward for thinking that even the good ones fall short of true virtues. St. Thomas considers three such reasons, the first two theological, the third based on the nature of causation.

Objection 1. [1] *It would seem that virtues cannot be caused in us by habituation. Because a gloss of Augustine [Cf. Lib. Sentent. Prosperi cvi.], commenting on Romans 14:23, "All that is not of faith is sin,"* [2] *says: "The whole life of an unbeliever is a sin: and there is no good without the Sovereign Good. Where knowledge of the truth is lacking, virtue is a mockery even in the best behaved people."* [3] *Now faith cannot be acquired by means of works, but is caused in us by God, according to Ephesians 2:8: "By grace you are saved through faith." Therefore no acquired virtue can be in us by habituation.*	Objection 1. It seems that virtues are not the result of habituation. For in connection with St. Paul's remark that everything that does not come from faith is sin, a collection based on the works of St. Augustine declares that everything in the life of those who lack faith is sin; that apart from the Supreme and Unchangeable Good there is no good at all; *and that wherever truth is unknown, virtue is false – even in those who have "the best morals."* Very well, then, virtue depends on faith. But as we see in St. Paul's teaching, "*by grace you are saved through faith*," faith is brought about in us by God, not by the repetition of deeds. Since virtue depends on faith, and faith cannot be acquired by habituation, neither can virtue be acquired that way.

[1] The Objector is referring to Sentence 106 in *Sentences Taken from Augustine,* by Prosper of Aquitaine, a commentary widely used in the middle ages. Prosper is speaking about St. Augustine's views of St. Paul's much-discussed remark, in his letter to the young Church at Rome, that everything which does not arise from faith is sin. Much depends on what St. Paul meant by this comment. Taken in the bluntest, most literal way, with no attention to context or figurative expressions, his remark may seem to mean that nothing which any nonbeliever ever does can ever be in any sense good – and as we are about to see, that is just how the Objector takes it. St. Augustine himself mentions St. Paul's remark in a number of places, which it will be more convenient to discuss a little later in the context of the *respondeo* or "I answer that."

[2] In the paraphrase, I have suppressed the quotation marks – which do not exist in the original – because the Objector is paraphrasing. Prosper says, "The whole life of a nonbeliever is sin, and nothing is good without the Supreme Good. For where there is no acknowledgement of the Supreme and Unchangeable Truth, virtue is false, even in those who are most moral [*optimis moribus*]." The Objector makes the minor change of altering *agnitio*, recognition or acknowledgement, to *cognitio*, recognition or knowledge, and he greatly strengthens *veritatis*, truth, to *summae et incommutabilis veritatis*, supreme and unchangeable truth, thereby clarifying the fact that the truth in question is the Truth of God Himself.

[3] The complete statement in St. Paul's letter to the Christians in Ephesus, quoted by the Objector only in part, reads "For by grace you are saved through faith, and that not of yourselves, for it is the gift of God; not of works, that no man may glory."[2] The Objector argues that if there is no virtue without faith, and there is no faith without grace, then there can be no virtue without grace.

Objection 2. [1] *Further, sin and virtue are contraries, so that they are incompatible.* [2] *Now man cannot avoid sin except by the grace of God, according to Wisdom 8:21: "I knew that I could not otherwise be continent, except God gave it."* [3] *Therefore neither can any virtues be caused in us by habituation, but only by the gift of God.*	**Objection 2.** Moreover, virtue gives rise to acts of virtue, not acts of sin. But apart from divine grace, we do sin – for example, Solomon says he would never have been able to avoid sin unless God had given him the virtue to do so. It follows that virtue comes from God's gift, not from habituation.

[1] Virtue is a disposition; here, "sin" means an act. In calling virtue and sin contrary, the Objector means that virtue disposes us to perform good acts instead of sins. In calling them incompatible, he means that if we truly possess virtue, then we literally cannot commit sins. He thinks the latter point follows from the former: *Because* virtue and sin are contraries, *therefore* they are incompatible.

[2] Ephesians 2:8–9 (DRA).

[2] What Solomon is actually saying in this verse is that he knew he could not possess "her" except by God's gift. Who is "she"? Perhaps because of the preceding verse, in which he has just commented that he kept his body undefiled, the Vulgate takes him to mean that he could not possess *continence* unless God gave it: "And as I knew that I could not otherwise be continent, except God gave it, and this also was a point of wisdom, to know whose gift it was: I went to the Lord, and besought him." Ever since the previous chapter, however, Solomon has been speaking of Wisdom, poetically personified as feminine: "I called upon God, and the spirit of wisdom came upon me: and I preferred her before kingdoms and thrones, and esteemed riches nothing in comparison of her.... I loved her above health and beauty, and chose to have her instead of light: for her light cannot be put out."[3] For this reason, modern translators take him to be saying that he could not possess *wisdom, or prudence,* unless God gave it.

RSV-CE: "But I perceived that I would not possess wisdom unless God gave her to me – and it was a mark of insight to know whose gift she was – so I appealed to the Lord and besought him."

NABRE: "And knowing that I could not otherwise possess her unless God gave it – and this, too, was prudence, to know whose gift she is – I went to the Lord and besought him."

Surprisingly, however, the Objector's argument is actually strengthened by this change of view among translators, because he is speaking about virtue in general. If it refers to continence, as he thinks, then it provides an example of how moral virtue depends on God's grace; but if it refers to prudence, as we think today, then it shows how the intellectual virtue which guides *all* moral virtue depends on God's grace.

[3] The argument works like this: If we have virtue, we cannot sin. But we cannot avoid sin – that is, we cannot have virtue – except by God's grace. Therefore the cause of virtue is God's grace; and therefore its cause is not habituation.

| *Objection 3.* [1] *Further, actions which lead toward virtue, lack the perfection of virtue.* [2] *But an effect cannot be more perfect than its cause.* [3] *Therefore a virtue cannot be caused by actions that precede it.* | Objection 3. Yet further, good deeds we perform before we actually have virtue are less complete than the acts of virtue. Such deeds cannot *cause* virtue, because an effect cannot be more complete than its cause. Therefore, virtue cannot be brought about by preceding deeds. |

[1] To suggest that moral and intellectual virtue can be caused by habituation is to suggest that we acquire courage by doing courageous things over

---

[3] Wisdom 7:7b, 8, 10 (DRA).

and over, temperance by doing temperate things over and over, "science" by deriving conclusions from first principles over and over, and so on, until at last they become second nature. But the Objector suggests that individual deeds, even good ones, fall far short of the virtues which dispose us to perform them.

[2] The Objector is borrowing the idea that an effect cannot be more perfect than its cause from St. Thomas's own analysis of causality. The underlying intuition is that since every effect *depends* upon its efficient cause, the effect must *pre-exist virtually* in its efficient cause, as the oak pre-exists in the acorn. In different places the idea is put in different ways: An efficient cause is more *perfect or complete* than its effect, more *noble or excellent* than its effect, or more *powerful* than its effect.[4]

Here, of course, we are inquiring into the causes of the virtues, but the idea that an effect cannot be more perfect than its cause also plays a great role in some of the classical arguments for the existence of God: for the universe must have had a cause, and its First Cause must have been more perfect than the things that the universe contains. How, for example, could such a thing as a person, "the most perfect thing in all nature," arise from impersonal matter? For that matter, how could even matter arise from nothing? If we protest that the universe has always existed, this is no answer, because, granted that the universe does not exist *necessarily*, even a universe which had always existed would need a cause of having always existed.

[3] In a nutshell: If causes are always *more* perfect than their effects, but prior deeds are *less* perfect than virtues, then prior deeds cannot cause virtues.

On the contrary, [1] *Dionysius says (Div. Nom. iv) that good is more efficacious than evil.* [2] *But vicious habits are caused by evil acts. Much more, therefore, can virtuous habits be caused by good acts.*	**On the other hand,** as Pseudo-Dionysius explains, good is stronger than evil in bringing about its effects. So since even evil acts are strong enough to habituate us to vice, good acts must even more effective in habituating us to virtue.

[1] Good is more efficacious than evil because good can bring about effects by itself, but evil is able to bring about effects only by way of the good which it parasitizes. In an age which confuses realism with cynicism, it is easy to dismiss the proposition that good is stronger than evil as Polyannish and naive, as though it meant something like "Good guys always win." Considered closely, however, it seems almost obviously true. A healthy body is more efficacious than a body afflicted with the evil of disease; a sound mind is more efficacious than a mind afflicted with the evil of foolishness; a person of fortitude is more efficacious than a coward. The crux of the argument is that evil is a privation – not a being, but a deficiency in a being, not a "something," but a "something

---

[4] See I, Q. 2, Art. 2; I, Q. 4, Art. 2; I-II, Q. 66, Art. 1; and I-II, Q. 112, Art. 1.

missing." For example, although health is the proper order of a living body, sickness is nothing but the lack of such order. Now a "something," such as the body, can bring about an effect of its own nature. But a "something missing," such as sickness, can bring about an effect only through indirectly – in this case, through the body itself.

Here is how Pseudo-Dionysius develops the point in his work *On the Divine Names:*

Evil in itself has neither being, goodness, productiveness, nor power of creating things which have being and goodness; the Good, on the other hand, wherever It becomes perfectly present, creates perfect, universal and untainted manifestations of goodness; while the things which have a lesser share therein are imperfect manifestations of goodness and mixed with other elements through lack of the Good. In fine, evil is not in any wise good, nor the maker of good; but everything must be good only in proportion as it approaches more or less unto the Good, since the perfect Goodness penetrating all things reaches not only to the wholly good beings around It, but extends even unto the lowest things, being entirely present unto some, and in a lower measure to others, and unto others in lowest measure, according as each one is capable of participating therein.[5]

Here is St. Thomas's own explanation:

It must be said that every evil in some way has a cause. For evil is the absence of the good, which is natural and due to a thing. But that anything fail from its natural and due disposition can come only from some cause drawing it out of its proper disposition. For a heavy thing is not moved upwards except by some impelling force; nor does an agent fail in its action except from some impediment. But only good can be a cause; because nothing can be a cause except inasmuch as it is a being, and every being, as such, is good.

And if we consider the special kinds of causes, we see that the agent, the form, and the end, import some kind of perfection which belongs to the notion of good. Even matter, as a potentiality to good, has the nature of good. Now that good is the cause of evil by way of the material cause was shown above (Question 48, Article 3). For it was shown that good is the subject of evil. But evil has no formal cause, rather is it a privation of form; likewise, neither has it a final cause, but rather is it a privation of order to the proper end; since not only the end has the nature of good, but also the useful, which is ordered to the end. Evil, however, has a cause by way of an agent, not directly, but accidentally.[6]

[2] The more lies we tell, the stronger becomes our tendency to lie; the more often we fall short of temperance, the stronger becomes our disposition to miss the mark again. In short, we acquire the vices by doing vicious things. But if

---

[5] *Dionysius the Areopagite: On the Divine Names and the Mystical Theology*, trans. C. E. Rolt (public domain), Chapter 4, Section 20, available on the internet at www.ccel.org/ccel/rolt/dionysius.i.html. I have changed "hath" into "has," "approacheth" to "approaches," "reacheth" to "reaches," and "extendeth" to "extends."

[6] I, Q. 49, Art. 1.

even the repetition of vicious acts builds up vice, still more should we expect the repetition of virtuous acts build up virtue. Why "still more" rather than "just as much"? Because good is more efficacious than evil, as Pseudo-Dionysius says.

I answer that, [1] *We have spoken above (51, A2, 3) in a general way about the production of habits from acts; [2] and speaking now in a special way of this matter in relation to virtue, we must take note that, as stated above (55, A3, 4), man's virtue perfects him in relation to good.* [3] *Now since the notion of good consists in "mode, species, and order," as Augustine states (De Nat. Boni. iii) or in "number, weight, and measure," as expressed in Wisdom 11:21, man's good must needs be appraised with respect to some rule.* [4] *Now this rule is twofold, as stated above (19, A3, 4), viz. human reason and Divine law. And since Divine law is the higher rule, it extends to more things, so that whatever is ruled by human reason, is ruled by the Divine law too; but the converse does not hold.* [5] *It follows that human virtue directed to the good which is defined according to the rule of human reason can be caused by human acts: inasmuch as such acts proceed from reason, by whose power and rule the aforesaid good is established. On the other hand, virtue which directs man to good as defined by the Divine law, and not by human reason, cannot be caused by human acts, the principle of which is reason, but is produced in us by the Divine operation alone.* [6] *Hence Augustine in giving the definition of the latter virtue inserts the words, "which God works in us without us" (Super Ps. 118, Serm. xxvi).* [7] *It is also of these virtues that the First Objection holds good.*	Here is my response. Earlier in the *Summa*, we have discussed how certain dispositions can arise from repeated acts, but we have done so only in a general way. Concerning the particular sort of disposition called virtue, let us begin with a point made much earlier: Human virtue makes man completely fit to achieve what is good for him. But the mind grasps good in terms of "mode, species, and order" (as St. Augustine puts it), or "number, weight, and measure" (as the book of Wisdom puts it). Thus, human good must be considered by the mind according to some yardstick, some regulative principle. We have found this rule to be double – on one hand, human reason, on the other, Divine law. Of these two, Divine law is superior, and as such, it takes in more territory. Consequently, although whatever falls under human reason also falls under Divine law too, not everything that falls under Divine law falls under human reason too. Two conclusions follow: (1) Those human virtues which are ordered to the good as measured by the rule of human reason *can* be brought about by human acts – providing that these acts really do arise from reason. For it is precisely in the power and rule of human reason that such good lies. But (2) those virtues which are ordered to the good as measured by the Divine law, rather than by human reason, *cannot* be brought about by human acts the starting points of which lie solely in human reason. They can be brought about in us only by the work of God Himself. This is why, in defining such virtues, St. Augustine includes the words, "which God brings about in us, without us." So Objection 1 is true – provided that it is said with respect to the latter virtues. But if said of the latter, it is false.

[1] St. Thomas is referring to his explanation earlier in the *Summa* that agents differ in such a way that although some can acquire habits by repeated acts, others cannot. Consider an agent such as fire. Fire can heat something else, but it cannot heat itself; it transmits the effect of its acts, but it cannot receive them. Just for this reason, this sort of agent cannot bring about a "habit" or dispositional tendency in itself. But a man is a different kind of agent, because he acts not only acts on others but also on himself. Consequently, unlike fire he *can* bring about a habit in himself. "Wherefore if the acts be multiplied a certain quality is formed in the power which is passive and moved, which quality is called a habit: just as the habits of moral virtue are caused in the appetitive powers, according as they are moved by the reason, and as the habits of science are caused in the intellect, according as it is moved by first propositions."[7]

But habituation takes time. Just as fire must gradually overcome the wood, counteracting its tendencies *not* to burn, so human reason must gradually master the appetites, counteracting their tendencies to go whichever way seems attractive to the senses. "Therefore a habit of virtue cannot be caused by one act, but only by many." Furthermore St. Thomas points out that there is more than one "passive principle" in us, more than one power in us to be acted upon, and these are not affected by the same things in the same ways. For example:

- Even a single consideration of a self-evident proposition convinces us so that we acquire the disposition of firm assent.
- However, we may have to consider a merely probable proposition many times before we acquire the disposition of opinion.
- The same thing may have to happen over and over, or be thought about many times, before we acquire the disposition to remember it.
- Yet even a single dose of a sufficiently powerful medicine may sometimes be sufficient to bring about the bodily disposition of health.[8]

[2] The very term "virtue" implies an excellence with respect to some good. For example, the virtue of the eyes lies in discerning visible objects in order to see as well as possible, and the virtue of the thumb lies in opposing the fingers in order to grasp as well as possible. In the same way, the virtue of a man *as such* lies in following reason in order to do good works as well as possible.[9]

[3] St. Augustine writes "these three things, therefore, mode, species, and order, are so to speak general goods in things made by God, whether in spirit or in body."[10] Why these three? According to St. Thomas, because "in order for a thing to be perfect and good it must have a form," but three different considerations precede and follow upon its form:

---

[7] I-II, Q. 51, Art. 2.   [8] I-II, Q. 51, Art. 3.   [9] I-II, Q. 55, Arts. 3.

[10] [H]aec ergo tria, modus, species, ordo, tamquam generalia bona sunt in rebus a Deo factis, sive in spiritu, sive in corpore. St. Augustine, *On the Nature of the Good*, Chapter 3; the Latin text is available at www.augustinus.it/latino/natura_bene/index.htm.

- The *principles* of the form tell us the rule by which the thing operates and the yardstick by which it is measured.[11] mode, measure
- *What form the thing has* is determined by its species, meaning the genus to species, number which it belongs along with its difference from other things in that species.
- The form in turn determines *the end toward which the thing tends*, and therefore indicates the order which it needs to acquire so that it can reach that end. order, weight.

These three things are called by various equivalent expressions, including "mode" and "measure" for the first, "species" and "number" for the second, and "order" and "weight" for the third.[12]

[4] The rule by which man's good is appraised depends on human reason, because the goodness of the will depends on its object, and its object is presented to it by reason.[13] But in an even higher way, the rule depends on the law of God:

> Wherever a number of causes are subordinate to one another, the effect depends more on the first than on the second cause: since the second cause acts only in virtue of the first. Now it is from the eternal law, which is the Divine Reason, that human reason is the rule of the human will, from which the human derives its goodness.... It is therefore evident that the goodness of the human will depends on the eternal law much more than on human reason: and when human reason fails we must have recourse to the Eternal Reason.[14]

Eternal law is the pattern of the wisdom by which God created and governs the universe. In itself, the eternal law is beyond our finite minds, but we can understand it in its reflections. One reflection is natural law, the reflection of eternal law in the created rational mind as it apprehends the pattern of creation itself; it is the *sharing* of the human mind in God's wisdom. The other reflection is Divine law, the reflection of eternal law in the words of Holy Scripture.[15] Why do we need two reflections? Why wouldn't natural law be enough? We are about to see.

[5] Later on in the *Summa*,[16] St. Thomas explains that "it is by law that man is directed how to perform his proper acts in view of his last end. And indeed if man were ordained to no other end than that which is proportionate to his natural faculty, there would be no need for man to have any further direction of the part of his reason, besides the natural law and human law which

---

[11] St. Thomas derives from Aristotle's *Metaphysics*, Book 10 (Iota), the argument that the principle in any genus is the rule and measure of that genus. He develops the argument most fully in connection with law, as a rule and measure of human acts based on reason, in I-II, Q. 90, Art. 1. For discussion, see my *Commentary on Thomas Aquinas's Treatise on Law*.

[12] See I, Q. 5, Art. 5, which draws from the passage in St. Augustine's *On the Nature of the Good* quoted above, and Q. 45, Art. 7, which draws from his *On the Trinity*, Book 6, Chapter 10.

[13] I-II, Q. 19, Art. 3.   [14] I-II, Q. 19, Art. 4.   [15] See I-II, Q. 91, Arts. 1, 2, and 4.

[16] I-II, Q. 91, Art. 4. For further discussion, see J. Budziszewski, *Commentary on Thomas Aquinas's Treatise on Law*, pp. 95–111.

is derived from it. But since man is ordained to an end of eternal happiness which is inproportionate to man's natural faculty ... therefore it was necessary that, besides the natural and the human law, man should be directed to his end by a law given by God."

In brief, we were made not just for earthly flourishing, but for a yet higher end that *transcends* our natural experience, one that exceeds what our natural powers of reason can achieve or imagine. The happiness of the life to come is not simply a longer-lasting version of the happiness of this life, but an infinitely higher quality of happiness, the complete joy of *union* with God, of knowing Him as we are known. At first it seems puzzling that two different things, one lower and one higher, could both be called "ends" or goals. This difficulty is only apparent. In St. Thomas's view, temporal happiness is a real end in the sense that it is desirable in itself, not just as a means to something else. But it cannot be our final end, because for that it would have to be completely satisfying, leaving nothing further to be desired. Eternal happiness, or beatitude, has both of these properties. It is the "sweetness" of "the ultimate and most complete participation in his goodness," which lies in "the vision of His essence, so that we live together in His company, as His friends."[17]

How do we know that man *is* ordained to a supernatural end? From Revelation, of course, but not only from Revelation. This is the conclusion of a long and complex, but brilliantly illuminating philosophical argument, most of which is contained in the *Treatise on Man's Last End*.[18] In short, everything we do is for the sake of an end. The end we seek is final and perfect happiness that leaves nothing else to be desired. Since we desire such happiness – and since God and nature, which is His creation, do nothing in vain[19] – it is impossible that such happiness be impossible. After knocking down a series of other hypotheses – that final and perfect happiness lies in wealth, fame, power, pleasure, and so on – St. Thomas concludes that it this happiness does not lie in any created good whatsoever; therefore it must lie in union with God. Now since man cannot be united with God through his body or his senses, he must be united to God through his mind (though the Angelic Doctor remarks that the body and senses do receive a certain completing "overflow").[20] But since the mind could not be satisfied by anything less than seeing God as He is, that is how it beholds Him. Final and perfect happiness, then, consists in nothing else that the vision of God in His essence – as He is.

---

[17] *Ultima autem et completissima participatio suae bonitatis consistit in visione essentiae ipsius, secundum quam ei convivimus socialiter, quasi amici, cum in ea suavitate beatitudo consistat.* Thomas Aquinas, *Commentary on the Sentences of Peter Lombard*, III, Dist. 19, Q. 1, Art. 5, Qc. 1.

[18] I-II, QQ. 1–5.

[19] Even Darwinism assumes that in the long run, nature brings about nothing unless it has adaptive value for the organism.

[20] III, Q. 3, Art. 3.

But how do we know that the attainment of this end lies beyond our natural powers? Consider first that our natural knowledge begins from sense experience. This being the case, it cannot go further than what we can learn from sensible things. Now although God is the cause of such things, He is infinitely greater than all of them taken together. Therefore, even if we knew everything that could be known from them, we would still fall short of knowing *Him*. It follows that the vision of God cannot be attained by our natural powers, but requires supernatural grace.[21] ——

[6] We have discussed the significance of these words of St. Augustine previously, in connection with I-II, Q. 55, Art. 4. ⌐

[7] The first Objection maintained that *no* virtues can be caused in us by habituation, because *all* virtues come about only through the infusion of divine grace. St. Thomas agrees that infused virtues cannot be caused in us by habituation, and of these virtues, the Objection holds good. What we see from the *respondeo*, however, is that the infused virtues are not the only virtues.

But isn't St. Thomas ducking the issue? After all, the Objector had argued that according to St. Paul, *all* that is not of faith – an infused virtue – is sin. So the infused virtues *are* the only virtues, aren't they?

At first it may seem that this view must be correct, but we should not be too quick to assume that St. Paul is speaking literally. Hyperbole is used more extensively in the Bible than in contemporary English, not to exaggerate but to emphasize. For example, where Christ says "If any one comes to me and does not hate his own father and mother and wife and children and brothers and sisters, yes, and even his own life, he cannot be my disciple," He is not urging literal hatred, but dramatizing a difference in degree of love. Likewise, when St. Paul writes that for the sake of Christ he has suffered the loss of all things and counts them as *skubala* – as garbage or excrement, in the Latin translation *stercora* or dung – he does not literally mean that such things as love for his friends are no better than what is thrown to the dogs, but that all else is worth losing for Christ.[22]

Here, from various works of St. Augustine, are some of his remarks on the Pauline statement:[23]

A man's free-will, indeed, avails for nothing except to sin, if he knows not the way of truth; and even after his duty and his proper aim shall begin to become known to him, unless he also take delight in and feel a love for it, he neither does his duty, nor sets about it, nor lives rightly." (*On the Spirit and the Letter*, Chapter 5.)

But this will, which is free in evil things because it takes pleasure in evil, is not free in good things, for the reason that it has not been made free. Nor can a man will any good thing unless he is aided by Him who cannot will evil – that is, by the grace of God

---

[21] I, Q. 12, Art. 4.   [22] Luke 14:26 (RSV-CE); Philippians 3:8.
[23] I draw the following quotations from the public-domain translations at www.newadvent.org/fathers.

through Jesus Christ our Lord. For "everything which is not of faith is sin." (*Against Two Letters of the Pelagians*, Book 1, Chapter 7.)

[W]ithout [faith], even those things which seem good works are turned into sins: "For everything which is not of faith is sin." (*Ibid.*, Book 3, Chapter 14.)

For although God's commandment appears sometimes to be kept by those who do not love Him, but only fear Him; yet where there is no love, no good work is imputed, nor is there any good work, rightly so called; because "whatsoever is not of faith is sin" [Romans 14:23] and "faith works by love" [Galatians 5:6]. (*On the Grace of Christ, and on Original Sin*, Book I, Chapter 27.)

But a more complete picture of St. Paul's mind emerges from the following, longer passage.

What, then, have we to say when conjugal chastity is discovered even in some unbelievers? Must it be said that they sin, in that they make a bad use of a gift of God, in not restoring it to the worship of Him from whom they received it? Or must these endowments, perchance, be not regarded as gifts of God at all, when they are not believers who exercise them; according to the apostle's sentiment, when he says, "Whatsoever is not of faith is sin?" (Romans 14:23) But who would dare to say that a gift of God is sin? For the soul and the body, and all the natural endowments which are implanted in the soul and the body, even in the persons of sinful men, are still gifts of God; for it is God who made them, and not they themselves. When it is said, "Whatsoever is not of faith is sin," only those things are meant which men themselves do. When men, therefore, do without faith those things which seem to appertain to conjugal chastity, they do them either to please men, whether themselves or others, or to avoid incurring such troubles as are incidental to human nature in those things which they corruptly desire, or to pay service to devils. Sins are not really resigned, but some sins are overpowered by other sins. God forbid, then, that a man be truly called chaste who observes connubial fidelity to his wife from any other motive than devotion to the true God. (*On Marriage and Concupiscence*, Chapter 4.)

Taken in the sense of the latter passage, the Pauline remark would not mean that without grace it is impossible *to do anything good in any sense*, but that without grace it is impossible to do anything from the pure love of God. We see an example of the sort of thing St. Augustine is criticizing in the famous "Plan" of thirteen virtues which Benjamin Franklin drew up for himself at the age of twenty. Item 11 was "Chastity: Rarely use venery but for health or offspring; Never to dullness, weakness, or the injury of your own or another's peace or reputation."[24] Suppose, in this spirit, a man abstained from adultery merely to avoid scandals, lawsuits, and getting caught. Viewed in Franklin's sense, he would completely chaste. Viewed in the light of divine charity, as St. Augustine would have us do, he would be very far from chaste.

---

[24] Benjamin Franklin, *Autobiography*, Chapter 8 (public domain), available at www.earlyamerica. com/lives-early-america/autobiography-benjamin-franklin/autobiography-benjamin-franklin-chapter-eight.

St. Augustine makes much the same argument in the fascinating discussion in *City of God*, Book 5, Chapters 12–21, in which he argues that the supposedly virtuous Romans of the republican age were not motivated by true virtue but merely by the love of glory, a vice which imitated virtue by prompting men of the political class to perform deeds of conspicuous benefit to the community just to be praised. Not only was the motive wrong, but in the long run, it was overwhelmed by the baser motives which, for a time, it had suppressed, such as the love of wealth and power. For if one loves glory most of all, and if it turns out that glory can be gained just as easily by spectacular bad deeds as by "good" ones – why not?[25]

Substantially, St. Thomas agrees, but his language is less hyperbolic. The crux of his view is that man has a twofold end. Temporal happiness is a true end for human beings in the sense that it is good in itself, but it is insufficient; we keep asking "Is this all there is?" Only eternal happiness is an end in the unqualified sense that it utterly fulfills us, leaving nothing further to be desired. This distinction concerning happiness necessarily leads to another distinction concerning virtue. For the acquired virtues, which lead to temporal happiness, are virtues in the qualified sense that they direct us to our imperfect natural good, but only the infused virtues are virtues in the unqualified sense that they direct us to our perfect supernatural good. To put it another way, all deeds prompted by the virtues are good deeds (*bona opera*), but only those prompted by the infused virtues are both good and meritorious (*opera bona et meritoria*).[26] As St. Catherine of Siena represents God as explaining, "No virtue, my daughter, can have life in itself except through charity."[27]

Although the acquired virtues are incomplete, they are far from nothing. Although they cannot make us fit for the spiritual life of the City of God, they do assist us in the natural life of the City of Man. And though the infused virtues cannot be brought about in us by habituation, the acquired virtues can.

We now pass directly to the second Objection.

Reply to Objection 2. [1] *Mortal sin is incompatible with divinely infused virtue, especially if this be considered in its perfect state.* [2] *But actual sin, even mortal, is*	**Reply to Objection 2.** Divinely infused virtue, especially considered in its full development, cannot exist in us alongside any mortal sin. But humanly acquired virtue *can* exist in us alongside actual

[25] For discussion, see J. Budziszewski, "The Lower Is Not the More Solid," *Communio: International Catholic Review* 38, no. 2 (2011), available at http://undergroundthomist.org/sites/default/files/The-Lower-Is-Not-the-More-Solid_o.pdf.

[26] As St. Thomas explains in II-II, Q. 10, Art. 4, "unbelievers are without grace indeed, yet some good of nature remains in them. Consequently it is evident that unbelievers cannot do those good works which proceed from grace, viz. meritorious works; yet they can, to a certain extent, do those good works for which the good of nature suffices."

[27] St. Catherine of Siena, *Dialogue* (1378), trans. Algar Thorold (public domain).

compatible with humanly acquired virtue; because the use of a habit in us is subject to our will, as stated above (Question 49, Article 3): [3] and one sinful act does not destroy a habit of acquired virtue, since it is not an act but a habit, that is directly contrary to a habit. [4] Wherefore, though man cannot avoid mortal sin without grace, so as never to sin mortally, yet he is not hindered from acquiring a habit of virtue, whereby he may abstain from evil in the majority of cases, and chiefly in matters most opposed to reason. [5] There are also certain mortal sins which man can nowise avoid without grace, those, namely, which are directly opposed to the theological virtues, which are in us through the gift of grace. This, however, will be more fully explained later (109, 4).

sin – yes, even mortal sin – because, as explained previously, the exercise of such dispositions is subject to our will. For an acquired disposition of virtue is not utterly corrupted by a single act of sin: Although it is not possible to have contrary dispositions of character at the same time, it is quite possible to have a disposition and yet commit an act which is out of character with it. For this reason, although without the help of grace it is impossible for anyone to keep from committing *any moral sin at any time*, still, nothing prevents him from acquiring a virtuous disposition by which he can abstain from evil deeds most of the time, especially the deeds most outrageously contrary to reason.

However, this conclusion must be qualified. *Certain* mortal sins – the ones which are *directly* opposed to the theological virtues – cannot be avoided *ever, in any way*, without grace, because it is only by the gift of grace that we receive them. This will be made clear later on.

[1] Mortal sin is sin which destroys right relationship with our final end, who is God; venial sin is sin which impairs this relationship but does not destroy it. Since what ultimately directs us to God is that love of God called charity, mortal sin can also be described as sin which corrupts charity. But charity, along with the virtues dependent on charity, are infused virtues. Consequently, mortal sin cannot coexist with the infused virtues.[28]

[2] Suppose I am devoid of true charity for God and neighbor, and therefore in a condition of mortal sin. I may yet have a dispositional tendency to, say, acts of fortitude. However, these will be acts of *acquired* fortitude. I will be incapable of *infused* fortitude, because my will is focused on a lower object.

[3] Even one mortal sin destroys charity. To speak only of the acquired virtues, however, we see that although it is impossible to be habitually disposed to one kind of act and at the same time *habitually disposed* to the opposite kind, it is quite possible to be habitually disposed to a certain kind of act and yet *commit one act* of the opposite kind. For example, even though I am temperate, I might some time yield to the temptation of a third piece of cake. If I should happen to yield to such temptations over and over, eventually my temperance will be destroyed, but it will not be destroyed by a single act.

---

[28] Concerning moral and venial sin, see I-II, Q. 88, Arts. 1–2. Concerning the sense in which all infused virtue depends on charity, see I-II, Q. 62, Art. 4, and Q. 66, Art. 6.

[4] Only God Himself can repair the corruption of charity. Therefore, apart from His grace, one cannot avoid mortal sin. This is not just a matter of avoiding certain acts, such as murder; the problem is much deeper, because it lies in the condition of the will. On the other hand, even a person devoid of charity might avoid the acts themselves – at least most of the time – especially when even natural reason, without help from Divine law, can see that they are wrong.

[5] What St. Thomas explains "later," in I-II, Q. 109, Arts. 2–4, is that man might fulfill the commandments of Divine law in two different senses. In the first sense, he merely does as he is commanded. In the second, he does it out of charity. If we had never fallen – if human nature had remained in its original integrity – then we would love God not for anything else, but for Himself, and we would love ourselves, our friends, and all other things for His sake.[29] This, by the way, would not mean loving them less well, but loving them better, for what makes humans lovable is His image in them, and perfect love for Him *extends* to love of them.[30] Having rebelled against God, we fall far short of this, pursuing our private good above everything. Without the gratuitous help of God which cures this corruption of nature, human beings can fulfill the law in the first sense – that is, we can perform the right outward deeds – but we do not and cannot perform them very well: Absurdly, we imagine that so long as we have not murdered or cheated anyone lately, we are all right. Moreover, we cannot full the law in the second sense at all, because we have no charity. Thus we need grace to fulfill the law in both senses, but especially in the second.

Reply to Objection 3. [1] As stated above *(1; 51, 1), certain seeds or principles of acquired virtue pre-exist in us by nature.* [2] *These principles are more excellent than the virtues acquired through them:* [3] *thus the understanding of speculative principles is more excellent than the science of conclusions,* [4] *and the natural rectitude of the reason is more excellent than the rectification of the appetite which results through the appetite partaking of reason, which*	Reply to Objection 3. As explained previously, acquired virtues naturally pre-exist in us, though only as seeds or "principles," that is, beginnings. These seeds are of greater nobility than the acquired virtues themselves. Thus, the natural understanding of the principles of theoretical reason is nobler than the working out of their conclusions, which is at the heart of the acquired intellectual virtue called "science." And the natural rectitude of practical reason is nobler than the rectification of desire brought about by its participation in reason, which is at the heart of the acquired moral virtues.

[29] Concerning why God is to be loved for Himself, see II-II, Q. 27, Art. 3. Concerning how man before the Fall loved God more than he loved himself, see I-II, Q. 109, Art. 3.

[30] II-II, Q. 27, Art. 8. See also II-II, Q. 23, Art. 1, ad 2: "so much do we love our friends, that for their sake we love all who belong to them, even if they hurt or hate us; so that, in this way, the friendship of charity extends even to our enemies, whom we love out of charity in relation to God, to Whom the friendship of charity is chiefly directed."

rectification belongs to moral virtue. [5] *Accordingly human acts, in so far as they proceed from higher principles, can cause acquired human virtues.*	So the axiom that no effect can be more perfect than its cause has not been violated after all. Just to the degree that they do proceed from these nobler beginnings, human acts *can* bring about acquired human virtues.

[1] We have already discussed these "seeds" in our exploration of I-II, Question 62, Article 1, and I-II, Question 63, Article 1. None of the dispositional tendencies of the powers of the human soul (such as the intellect and the appetite) are due entirely to nature. However, some are due partially to nature, for their seeds or beginnings are natural, but what grows from these seeds depends on other causes. For example, by the very nature of the intellect, once someone grasps what parts and wholes are, he immediately perceives that every whole is larger than each of its parts – but which things are wholes and which things are parts must be learned from experience. In a similar way, the appetite is by its very nature inclined to certain objects, but when, how, in what ways, and on what occasions we should pursue these objects must also be learned from experience.

[2] The seeds of the virtues are more excellent than the virtues because the virtues pre-exist in them virtually, much as flowers are contained virtually in flower seeds. Without the seeds of flowers, flowers could not come to be; without the seeds of virtues, virtues could not come to be. "Now it is plain that the effect pre-exists virtually in the efficient cause: and although to pre-exist in the potentiality of a material cause is to pre-exist in a more imperfect way, since matter as such is imperfect, and an agent as such is perfect; still to pre-exist virtually in the efficient cause is to pre-exist not in a more imperfect, but in a more perfect way."[31]

[3] An illustration: It is more fundamental to grasp that nothing can both be and not be in the same sense at the same time than to be able to see, as a result, that the door cannot be both closed and open.

[4] An illustration: It is more fundamental to grasp that the sexual inclination is naturally directed to procreation and family, than to turn away, for this reason, from anonymous sex. "[I]t is not the function of virtue to deprive the powers subordinate to reason of their proper activities," St. Thomas writes, "but to make them execute the commands of reason, by exercising their proper acts."[32]

[5] The Objector had argued as follows:

1. According to the hypothesis of habituation, the repetition of actions by a person without virtue can bring about virtue.
2. But such actions are less excellent than virtue, and no cause can be less excellent than its effect.
3. Therefore such actions cannot be the cause of virtue.

---

[31] I, Q. 4, Art. 2.   [32] I-II, Q. 59, Art. 5.

St. Thomas corrects the Objector by calling attention to the fact that the repetition of actions is merely an extrinsic cause of the virtues. Their intrinsic cause is the seeds or principles of virtues which exist in us by nature; were it not for these, the repetition of actions could have no effect. So the Objector is right that such actions are less excellent than virtue – but what he misses is that the seeds themselves are *more* excellent than virtue.

Whether the Moral Virtues Are Connected with One Another?

TEXT	PARAPHRASE
Whether the moral virtues are connected with one another?	The various moral virtues have traditionally been held to depend on each other in such a way that if one is deficient, the others will be deficient too. Is this true?

Can we pick and choose among the virtues – is it possible to possess some of them without the others? The classical tradition supposes that this is impossible; if you are defective in any virtue, then to some degree you will be defective in each of them, so that if you are serious about cultivating any of them you must cultivate all of them. In fact, not only does each virtue depend on the others, but also the judgment involved in the practice of each virtue depends on the judgment involved in the practice of the others. This interconnection among the virtues has also been discovered by other world wisdom traditions. For example, Confucius writes in *The Doctrine of the Mean*, "If one is not obedient to his parents, he will not be true to friends."[1]

Yet often, we view the virtues as disconnected. "He may be a crooked businessman, but he's good to his mom." "Even a bad man can be a good statesman." "There is honor among thieves." "I may not know what's good, but I know what's bad." The first saying, about the businessman, supposes that a man who lacks justice can be just to his mother and father – which unreasonably supposes that trying to be the best people we can is *not* a part of the payment of our debt to our parents. The one about the statesman supposes that a man who cannot be trusted to keep faith with his wife and friends *can* be trusted to keep faith with the citizens – or perhaps that being "good" means

[1] Confucius, *The Doctrine of the Mean*, trans. James Legge, Chapter 20, Section 17 (public domain).

merely being crafty about getting one's way. The one about thieves absurdly posits that people who are habitually dishonest to honest people will be scrupulously honest to dishonest ones. And the final saying supposes that one can understand vice without knowing the first thing about virtue. ⌐

According to one common view of human social life, disconnection is but the half of the problem. In this view not only can the virtues be disconnected from one another, they may even oppose each other. Consider how many people think that to practice loyalty to my friend, I must be willing to lie and cheat for him – something which on the classical view is absurd, because the truest friendship is a partnership in a virtuous life. ⌐

In politics the opposition among the virtues is commonly thought to be sharper still. Although Machiavelli argues in *The Prince* that ruling requires the virtues of the "lion" and the "fox" (by which he means debased versions of fortitude and prudence), the thrust of his argument is that the other two cardinal virtues, temperance and justice, merely get in the way. In our own time, in much the same vein, Thomas Nagel has urged political "ruthlessness" on grounds that private morality and public morality are not the same.[2] Although William Galson prefers the more soothing term "toughness," he too means ruthlessness: He views doing evil so that good may come as merely a "moral cost," the avoidance of which must be weighed against other objectives, and regards it as virtuous to achieve a mean *between virtue and vice*.[3] Although this dirty hands scenario is presented as Aristotelian in spirit, it is far from what Aristotle had in mind. Because it amounts to suggesting that sometimes it is right to do wrong, St. Thomas would regard it as incoherent. ⌐

Judith Shklar argues *against* the Machiavellian view, holding that we should put the avoidance of cruelty above other things – as she puts it, we should "put cruelty first."[4] Here too there is a difficulty, but this time it is more subtle. Shklar, obviously, rank-orders vices. Now the classical tradition also rank-orders virtues and vices, but its reason for doing so is different. According to that tradition, since all virtues are interconnected and all acts of duty are compatible, a person who has done nothing wrong will never find himself in

---

[2] Thomas Nagel, "Ruthlessness in Public Life," in Stuart Hampshire, ed., *Public and Private Morality* (Cambridge, MA: Cambridge University Press, 1978), pp. 75–92.

[3] "[H]ow is the actual or would-be leader to keep his or her moral balance? My answer takes the form of an Aristotelian schema: by embracing toughness as the mean between extremes. Three continua seem especially relevant.... The third ranges from what Hampshire calls "innocence" (the focus on maintaining the unsullied purity of one's soul) to calculation (the focus on attaining external objectives, whatever the consequences for one's soul).... [Toughness is] the disposition that enables leaders to recognize harsh necessities without blinding themselves to moral costs." William A. Galston, "Toughness as a Political Virtue," *Social Theory and Practice* 17, no. 2 (1991): 175–197, quoting from pp. 175–176.

[4] Judith N. Shklar, "Putting Cruelty First," in *Ordinary Vices* (Cambridge, MA: Harvard University Press, 1984), and "The Liberalism of Fear," in *Political Thought and Political Thinkers* (Chicago: University of Chicago, 1998).

a situation in which he must choose between forbidden alternatives.[5] Now if this is true – if we are never forced by circumstances to choose between, say, avoiding acts of cruelty and avoiding other acts of vice – then what exactly is the reason for rank-ordering vices?

In the classical tradition, the chief reason is to determine the wrongdoer's degree of guilt. In Shklar's thinking, the reason is different. She reasons that since no constitutional system or system of human laws can entirely prevent evils, we should focus on preventing the worst ones, especially those which hurt others. Up to this point, St. Thomas agrees.[6] The problem is that Shklar also agrees with another Thomas, the seventeenth-century thinker Thomas Hobbes, that we can avoid the greatest evil *without agreeing upon the greatest good.* Here St. Thomas would *not* agree – for the understanding of goods and evils is all connected. People who cannot see eye to eye about the virtues will not be able to agree about the vices either – *not even what it means to be cruel.*[7]

| Objection 1. [1] *It would seem that the moral virtues are not connected with one another. Because moral virtues are sometimes caused by the exercise of acts, as is proved in Ethic. ii, 1,2. [2] But man can exercise himself in the acts of one virtue, without exercising himself in the acts of some other virtue. Therefore it is possible to have one moral virtue without another.* | Objection 1. Apparently, moral virtues need not be connected. For as Aristotle shows in *Nicomachean Ethics,* moral virtues can be developed in us by repeatedly performing the acts which correspond to them – and yet a man can perform the acts of one virtue without performing the acts of another. Since, by performance, he can habituate himself to the acts of one virtue without habituating himself to the acts of another, he can also end up *having* the former virtue without *having* the latter. |

[1] We become virtuous by behaving as though we already had virtue – by doing the things virtuous people do. As Aristotle says, "the virtues we get by first exercising them, as also happens in the case of the arts as well. For the things we have to learn before we can do them, we learn by doing them,

[5] He *may* find himself in such a situation if he *has* done something wrong; for example, if he has promised to do something immoral, he must choose between committing the immoral act and violating his promise. See Thomas Aquinas, *Commentary on St. Paul's Letter to the Romans,* Chapter 14, Lecture 2, Sec. 1120, ad 2: "[N]othing forbids a person to be perplexed in certain circumstances, although no one is perplexed absolutely" (trans. Fabian Larcher; see www.pteditor.com). The distinction between absolute or simple perplexity (*perplexus simpliciter*) and qualified perplexity (*perplexus secundum quid*), also called perplexity arising from a supposition (*perplexum aliquo supposito*), is especially important to the question of whether an erring conscience binds. See also *Disputed Questions on Truth,* Q. 17, Art. 4, as well as S.T., I-II, Q. 19, Art. 5, and III, Q. 64, Art. 6, ad 3.

[6] See I-II, Q. 96, Art. 2.

[7] A point also made by Alasdair MacIntyre, esp. in "The Privatization of Good," *Review of Politics* 52, no. 3 (1990): 344–377. The article includes replies by Donald P. Kommers and W. David Solomon, with MacIntyre's responses.

e.g. men become builders by building and lyre-players by playing the lyre; so too we become just by doing just acts, temperate by doing temperate acts, brave by doing brave acts." A little later he elaborates, "by abstaining from pleasures we become temperate, and it is when we have become so that we are most able to abstain from them; and similarly too in the case of courage; for by being habituated to despise things that are terrible and to stand our ground against them we become courageous, and it is when we have become so that we shall be most able to stand our ground against them."[8]

[2] Suppose I habituate myself to despise dangers and stand my ground against things that kindle terror, but I make no effort to abstain from any pleasures. In that case, the Objector thinks, I will acquire fortitude but not temperance – for otherwise, anything that habituated me to acts of fortitude would also habituate me to acts of temperance, which is clearly not the case. So he concludes that the virtues are *not* interconnected.

Objection 2. [1] *Further, magnificence and magnanimity are moral virtues. Now a man may have other moral virtues without having magnificence or magnanimity: for the Philosopher says (Ethic. iv, 2, 3) that "a poor man cannot be magnificent," and yet he may have other virtues; [2] and (Ethic. iv) that "he who is worthy of small things, and so accounts his worth, is modest, but not magnanimous." [3] Therefore the moral virtues are not connected with one another.*	Objection 2. Moreover, magnificence and magnanimity are moral virtues. But one can have other moral virtues without having these two, for as Aristotle explains, a poor man may have other virtues but not the virtue of magnificent use of wealth, and a person of modest merits and deserts may be regarded as moderately virtuous but not as having the heroic virtue of magnanimity. It follows that the moral virtues are not interconnected after all.

[1] We tend to use a single term, "generosity," for all virtuous giving. In keeping with the tradition, however, St. Thomas makes a distinction, because the sorts of considerations which enter into the making of great gifts are different than those which enter into the making of small ones. For the virtue which guides generosity even in small matters, such as alms, he uses the term "liberality"; for the virtue which guides generosity in large matters, such as endowing public libraries, he uses the term "magnanimity" (we might say "well-judged philanthropy"). Thus Aristotle had written, "a poor man cannot be magnificent, since he has not the means with which to spend large sums fittingly; and he who tries is a fool, since he spends beyond what can be expected of him and what is proper."[9]

---

[8] Aristotle, *Nicomachean Ethics*, trans. W. D. Ross (public domain), Book 2, Chapters 1 and 2, respectively. To prevent confusion, I have substituted "courageous" for "brave," because in this book I have given the terms different meanings (see the example of the "brave" bank robber in I-Ii, Q. 55, Art. 4).

[9] Aristotle, *Nicomachean Ethics*, trans. W. D. Ross (public domain), Book 4, Chapter 2.

liberality vs. magnanimity

[2] As we saw earlier in this commentary, magnanimity is the virtue which moves us to exercise the rest of the virtues to a heroic degree – to achieve deeds which are morally great. After the words from the *Nicomachean Ethics* which the Objector is paraphrasing, Aristotle goes on to say that magnanimity "implies greatness, as beauty implies a goodsized body."[10] ___

[3] Later on in the *Summa*, the procedure seen in the present Article is reversed. Here, the Objector denies that the virtues are interconnected, because magnificence and magnanimity are virtues, yet one can have the other virtues without having these two. But in the *Treatises on Justice and Fortitude*, the Objector denies that magnificence and magnanimity are virtues, because the virtues *are* interconnected, yet one can have the other virtues without having these two.[11] By contrast with both Objectors, St. Thomas wishes to maintain *both* that magnificence and magnanimity are real virtues *and yet* that the virtues are interconnected.

Objection 3. [1] *Further, as the moral virtues perfect the appetitive part of the soul, so do the intellectual virtues perfect the intellective part.* [2] *But the intellectual virtues are not mutually connected: since we may have one science, without having another.* [3] *Neither, therefore, are the moral virtues connected with one another.*	Objection 3. Still further, the moral virtues bring the desiring powers of the soul to their full and appropriate development, in the same way that the intellectual virtues bring the intellectual powers of the soul to theirs. Yet we see that the intellectual virtues are not mutually dependent – it is quite possible to have one intellectual virtue without another. So there is no reason to think that the moral virtues are dependent upon each other either.

[1] Moral virtues calibrate and correct our desires; the intellectual virtues calibrate and correct our reasoning. Although this includes both theoretical and practical reasoning – reasoning about both *what is* and *what is to be done* – the Objector wishes to draw our attention toward theoretical reasoning.

[2] For example, I might possess geometrical without physical science – I might grasp the manner in which geometrical conclusions depend on geometrical first principles without grasping the manner in which the conclusions of physics depend on physical first principles.

---

[10] Ibid., Book 4, Chapter 3.

[11] I-II, Q. 129, Art. 3, Obj. 2: "Further, he that has one virtue has them all, as stated above. But one may have a virtue without having magnanimity: since the Philosopher says that 'whosoever is worthy of little things and deems himself worthy of them, is temperate, but he is not magnanimous.' Therefore magnanimity is not a virtue." II-II, Q. 117, Art. 1, Obj. 3: "Further, the virtues are connected with one another. But liberality does not seem to be connected with the other virtues: since many are virtuous who cannot be liberal, for they have nothing to give; and many give or spend liberally who are not virtuous otherwise. Therefore liberality is not a virtue."

[3] The argument works like this:

1. Moral and intellectual virtues are analogous, because each kind brings one of the powers of the soul to its full and appropriate development.
2. Because they are analogous, the moral virtues will be interconnected if and only if the intellectual virtues are interconnected.
3. But the intellectual virtues are *not* interconnected.
4. Therefore, the moral virtues are not interconnected either.

Objection 4. [1] *Further, if the moral virtues are mutually connected, this can only be because* [2] *they are united together in prudence.* [3] *But this does not suffice to connect the moral virtues together. For, seemingly, one may be prudent about things to be done in relation to one virtue, without being prudent in those that concern another virtue:* [4] *even as one may have the art of making certain things, without the art of making certain others.* [5] *Now prudence is right reason about things to be done. Therefore the moral virtues are not necessarily connected with one another.*	Objection 4. Still further, the only possible reason why the moral virtues might be thought to depend on each other would be that they are connected through their mutual dependence on prudence. However, an analogy shows that this reason is insufficient. For just as prudence is properly ordered reason about things to be done, so craftsmanship is properly ordered reason about things to be made. But a person can possess the craftsmanship to *make* one kind of thing and yet lack the craftsmanship to *make* another – so in the same way it seems that one should be able to possess the prudence to recognize what one virtue requires us to *do* and yet lack the prudence to recognize what another virtue requires us to *do.*

[1] "This can only be": Although the Objector claims that there can be only one reason for thinking that the moral virtues depend on each other, actually, as we see below in the *respondeo*, there are two. However, each takes a different view of what the cardinal virtues are. In one, they are viewed as certain general qualities that good acts of every kind require, while in the other they are viewed as particular virtues, each with its own subject matter. The Objector is viewing them in the latter way.

[2] The Objector is alluding to a well-known argument to which we return several times in the course of this Article. Reduced to simplest terms, the argument unfolds in three steps.

1. Each of the moral virtues depends on prudence.
2. Prudence in turn depends on each of the moral virtues, so that the relation runs in both directions.
3. Therefore, by transitivity, each moral virtue depends on each of the others.

For example, if fortitude depends on prudence but prudence in turn depends on temperance, then fortitude indirectly depends on temperance – and if temperance depends on prudence but prudence in turn depends on fortitude, then temperance indirectly depends on fortitude. This argument is illustrated by the diagram below, simplified to represent only the four cardinal virtues; single-headed arrows indicate dependence, double-headed arrows indicate mutual dependence, and dashed arrows indicate indirect dependence.

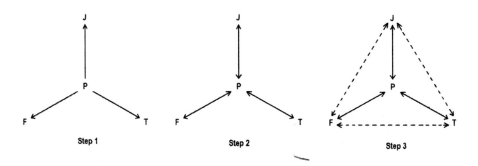

[3] The argument for the interconnection of the virtues *through prudence* supposes that prudence is one thing. But according to the Objector, it is actually several things – for example, prudence about justice, prudence about temperance, and prudence about fortitude – and these things are essentially unrelated. The argument for this conclusion depends on an analogy between prudence (right reason about what is to be done) and art (right reason about what is to be made).

[4] Just because a craftsman can make objects of one kind, such as wood, it does not follow that he can make objects of another kind, such as stone.

[5] So if the analogy holds, then just because a person is prudent about the affairs of one moral virtue, such as fortitude, it does not follow that he is prudent about the affairs of another moral virtue, such as temperance.

On the contrary, [1] *Ambrose says on Luke 6:20: "The virtues are connected and linked together, so that whoever has one, is seen to have several":* [2] *and Augustine says (De Trin. vi, 4) that "the virtues that reside in the human mind are quite inseparable from one another":* [3] *and Gregory says (Moral. xxii, 1) that "one virtue without the other is either of no account whatever, or very imperfect":* [4] *and Cicero says (Quaest. Tusc. ii): "If you confess to not having one particular virtue, it must needs be that you have none at all."*	**On the other hand,** there stands the authority of St. Ambrose of Milan, St. Augustine of Hippo, St. Gregory the Great, and Marcus Tullius Cicero. For Ambrose maintains that the virtues are connected and concatenated in such a way that to have one virtue is to have still others; Augustine explains that the virtues in the soul are mutually inseparable; Gregory holds that one virtue without the others is either not a virtue at all, or extremely incomplete; and Cicero says that to lack a single virtue is to be stripped of them all.

[1] The passage St. Thomas has in mind is the discussion of Luke 6:20–23 in St. Ambrose of Milan's *Exposition of the Gospel of Luke*, where Ambrose, in relating the beatitudes to the cardinal virtues, comments on their interdependence. St. Thomas supplies the passage in his *Catena Aurea* or "Golden Chain," a commentary on the Gospels threaded together from passages by the Patristic writers. Here is how it runs there:[12]

In that [Christ] says, *Blessed are the poor*, you have temperance; which abstains from sin, tramples upon the world, seeks not vain delights. In *Blessed are they that hunger*, you have righteousness [justice]; for he who hungers suffers together with the hungry, and by suffering together with him gives to him, by giving becomes righteous, and his righteousness abides forever. In *Blessed are they that weep now*, you have prudence; which is to weep for the things of time, and to seek those which are eternal. In *Blessed are ye when men hate you*, you have fortitude; not that which deserves hatred for crime, but which suffers persecution for faith. For so you will attain to the crown of suffering, if you slight the favour of men, and seek that which is from God. Temperance therefore brings with it a pure heart; righteousness, mercy; prudence, peace; fortitude, meekness. The virtues are so joined and linked to one another, that he who has one seems to have many; and the saints have each one especial virtue, but the more abundant virtue has the richer reward.[13]

[2] Seeking for comparisons to explain the inseparability of the Father, Son, and Holy Spirit, St. Augustine writes,

For in like manner the virtues which are in the human mind, although each has its own several and different meaning, yet are in no way mutually separable; so that, for instance, whosoever were equal in courage, are equal also in prudence, and temperance, and justice. For if you say that such and such men are equal in courage, but that one of them is greater in prudence, it follows that the courage of the other is less prudent, and so neither are they equal in courage, since the courage of the former is more prudent. And so you will find it to be the case with the other virtues, if you consider them one by one. For the question is not of the strength of the body, but of the courage of the mind.[14]

[3] St. Thomas makes use of this passage from St. Gregory the Great's *Morals on the Book of Job* in another place as well, the *sed contra* for I-II, Question 58, Article 4, "Whether there can be moral without intellectual virtue?" which we considered earlier.

And so one virtue without another is either none at all or but imperfect. For that (as it has seemed best to some persons) I may speak of the four first virtues, viz. prudence,

---

[12] As St. Thomas mentions, sometimes in the *Catena* he paraphrases the views of other writers rather than quoting them exactly.

[13] Thomas Aquinas, *Catena Aurea: Commentary on the Four Gospels, Collected out of the Works of the Fathers*, Volume 3, Part 1 (Oxford: Oxford University Press, 1843), pp. 211–212, online at www.saintsbooks.net/BooksList.html#Scripture. I have modernized the archaisms (for example, changing "thou hast" to "you have").

[14] Augustine, *On the Trinity*, Book 6, Chapter 4, Section 6, online at http://newadvent.org/fathers/1301.htm.

temperance, fortitude, and justice, they are severally so far perfect, in proportion as they are mutually joined to one another. But separated they can never be perfect. For neither is it real prudence which has not justice, temperance, fortitude, nor perfect temperance which has not fortitude, justice, and prudence, nor complete fortitude which is not prudent, temperate, and just, nor genuine justice which has not prudence, fortitude, and temperance.[15]

[4] Marcus Tullius Cicero relies on a different theory than we saw criticized in Objection 4. In the theory on display there, moral virtues are specialized according to their subject matter but interconnected through their mutual and reciprocal dependence on prudence. But in Cicero's view, the cardinal virtues are general qualities which are mutually co-implicated in all acts of moral virtue. Thus he writes:

Will temperance permit you to do anything to excess? Will it be possible for justice to be maintained by one who through the force of pain discovers secrets, or betrays his confederates, or deserts many duties of life? Will you act in a manner consistently with courage, and its attendants, greatness of soul, resolution, patience, and contempt for all worldly things? Can you hear yourself called a great man when you lie groveling, dejected, and deploring your condition with a lamentable voice; no one would call you even a man while in such a condition. You must therefore either abandon all pretensions to courage, or else pain must be put out of the question.

You know very well that, even though part of your Corinthian furniture were gone, the remainder might be safe without that; but if you lose one virtue (though virtue in reality cannot be lost), still if, I say, you should acknowledge that you were deficient in one, you would be stripped of all.[16]

I answer that, [1] *Moral virtue may be considered either as perfect or as imperfect.* [2] *An imperfect moral virtue, temperance for instance, or fortitude, is nothing but an inclination in us to do some kind of good deed, whether such inclination be in us by nature or by habituation.* [3] *If we take the moral virtues in this way, they are not connected: since we find men who, by natural temperament or by being accustomed, are prompt in doing deeds of liberality, but are not prompt in doing deeds of chastity.*	Here is my response. When we speak of the moral virtues, we must make clear whether we are speaking of fully developed virtues, or incipient and incomplete virtues. An incipient moral virtue – say, incomplete temperance or fortitude – is nothing but an inclination within us, either from natural temperament or through custom, to perform some kind of good deed. As we find by observation, *imperfect* moral virtues are *not* mutually dependent and interconnected. For example, consider how often we see men who are quick to act generously, but who do not readily practice sexual purity.

[15] *Morals on the Book of Job by St. Gregory the Great,* trans. John Henry Parker, J. G. F. Rivingon, and J. Rivington (public domain), Book 22, Chapter 2, online at www.lectionarycentral.com/GregoryMoraliaIndex.html.

[16] Cicero, *Tusculan Disputations,* trans. C. D. Yonge (public domain), Book 2 ("On Bearing Pain"), Chapters 13–14.

[4] *But the perfect moral virtue is a habit that inclines us to do a good deed well; and if we take moral virtues in this way, we must say that they are connected, as nearly as all are agreed in saying.* [5] *For this two reasons are given, corresponding to the different ways of assigning the distinction of the cardinal virtues.* [6] *For, as we stated above (61, A3,4), some distinguish them according to certain general properties of the virtues: for instance, by saying that discretion belongs to prudence, rectitude to justice, moderation to temperance, and strength of mind to fortitude, in whatever matter we consider these properties to be.* [7] *In this way the reason for the connection is evident: for strength of mind is not commended as virtuous, if it be without moderation or rectitude or discretion: and so forth.* [8] *This, too, is the reason assigned for the connection by Gregory, who says (Moral. xxii, 1) that "a virtue cannot be perfect" as a virtue, "if isolated from the others: for there can be no true prudence without temperance, justice and fortitude": and he continues to speak in like manner of the other virtues (cf. 61, 4, Objection 1). Augustine also gives the same reason (De Trin. vi, 4).* [9] *Others, however, differentiate these virtues in respect of their matters, and it is in this way that Aristotle assigns the reason for their connection (Ethic. vi, 13).* [10] *Because, as stated above (Question 58, Article 4), no moral virtue can be without prudence; since it is proper to moral virtue to make a right choice, for it is an elective habit. Now right choice requires not only the inclination to a due end, which inclination is the direct outcome of moral virtue, but also correct choice*

By contrast, a fully developed moral virtue is a habitual inclination not just to do a good deed, but to do it in the right way. *Fully developed* moral virtues *are* mutually dependent and interconnected. Although almost everyone who has written about this matter declares that this is so, they give two different reasons, depending how they distinguish the cardinal virtues.

As we saw earlier in the *Summa*, some writers distinguish the cardinal virtues according to certain general qualities that good acts of every kind require. Thus they view prudence as discretion about *all* matters, justice as rectitude about *all* matters, temperance as moderation about *all* matters, and fortitude as firmness of mind about *all* matters. Viewing the cardinal virtues in this way, their interconnection is obvious. For we do not praise firmness of mind *without moderation, rectitude, or discretion* as virtuous; each quality must be seasoned by the other three. This is the reason Augustine and Gregory give for the connection, since, as Gregory explains, virtues which are disconnected are incomplete (for example, there is no prudence without justice, temperance, and fortitude, and he continues in this vein), and Augustine offers much the same explanation.

But other writers, such as Aristotle, distinguish the virtues not according to general qualities which all action requires, but according to their respective subject matters. In this way too the connection of the virtues becomes clear. How so?

We begin with a point we have established long before: Every moral virtue depends on prudence. To spell this out a little further, every moral virtue requires correct choice, but to make the right choice, one must not only desire the right end, but also choose the right means to achieve it. Each in its own department, the moral virtues make us desire the right ends. But prudence is what counsels, judges, and commands concerning the right means.

of things conducive to the end, which choice is made by prudence, that counsels, judges, and commands in those things that are directed to the end. [11] In like manner one cannot have prudence unless one has the moral virtues: since prudence is "right reason about things to be done," and the starting point of reason is the end of the thing to be done, to which end man is rightly disposed by moral virtue. [12] Hence, just as we cannot have speculative science unless we have the understanding of the principles, so neither can we have prudence without the moral virtues: [13] and from this it follows clearly that the moral virtues are connected with one another.

Now let us turn this around. Not only does every moral virtue depend on prudence, but prudence depends in turn on every moral virtue. For prudence is rightly ordered reason about what is to be done – but how can we begin to reason about what is to be done unless we know to what end we are doing it? We are inclined to the right "whys," the right ends, by the moral virtues. So in just the same way that deriving true conclusions depends on grasping the true starting points, the proper choice of means to ends depends on desiring the right ends.

From the preceding reasoning it should be clear that the moral virtues are mutually interconnected.

[1] The English words "perfect" and "imperfect" are misleading here, because the respective senses of the Latin words *perfecta* and *imperfecta* are not so much "flawless" and "flawed" as "complete" and "incomplete." Some other suggestive terms for complete virtue might be "fully formed virtue" or "virtue properly so-called."

[2] A person of merely "imperfect" temperance is temperamentally inclined to restrain himself, as temperance requires, but he lacks judgment about when to exercise this inclination. Thus, he may fast even when he ought to be feasting. Similarly, because a person of "imperfect" fortitude is temperamentally resistant to fear, he may be inclined to brave acts, but he may have difficulty distinguishing true courage from rashness.

[3] Here St. Thomas is explaining why the moral virtues may *seem* to be unconnected; taken in their imperfect forms, they have only such relations as may arise from the accidents of personal psychology (and from the ways in which cardinal vices give rise to other vices[17]). St. Thomas's example – someone who is temperamentally inclined to generosity but not to sexual purity – is featured in the stock fictional character, the "hooker with a heart of gold." Although such a woman may exist, because she lacks chastity even her "heart of gold" will be gravely flawed.

[4] If the so-called hooker with a heart of gold ever truly came to possess liberality or generosity – if she came to understand what it is appropriate to give, to whom, on what occasions, and for what reasons – she would desist from her profession, for its whole point is to give what should not be given. The same applies to the unchaste man: If he truly possessed the virtue of the appropriate giving of gifts, then rather than bestowing presents and pleasures on his latest sexual

---

[17] For which, see I-II, Q. 84, Art. 4.

partners, he would either abstain from sexual intercourse, or else give himself permanently, completely, and exclusively to his wife. So although "imperfect" generosity can coexist with unchastity, a man or woman of true generosity is also chaste.

[5] To "assign the distinction" of the cardinal virtues is to indicate how and why they are distinguished. We considered the two ways of assigning the distinction earlier, in I-II, Question 61, Article 3, but while there, St. Thomas's reason for discussing them was to explain why only these four should be called "cardinal" virtues, here his reason is to explain why each of them – and therefore every other moral virtue too – depends on each of the others.

[6] The first way of assigning the distinction is to identify formal qualities which are shared by *all* of the many moral virtues. It turns out that there are four such qualities, prudence, justice, temperance, and fortitude, for as we have seen, (1) *any* virtue may be said to partake of prudence insofar as it brings the activity of reason itself into good order; (2) *any* virtue may be said to partake of justice insofar as it brings deeds into conformity with the good of what is right and due; (3) *any* virtue may be said to partake of temperance insofar as it holds the passions back and keeps them down when they urge what is contrary to reason; and (4) *any* virtue may be said to partake of fortitude insofar as it makes the soul stand firm when the passions fight against what reason commands.

[7] Since every moral virtue whatsoever – generosity, humility, patience, and so on – partakes of the *same* four formal qualities, each in its own way, two conclusions follow. The first is that if all four qualities are present in the right way, then every moral virtue is well developed. The second is that if any of these four are missing or disordered, then every moral virtue is deficient. It follows that no moral virtue can be fully developed unless all of them are.

[8] The *sed contra* had mentioned four sources for the view that moral virtues are interconnected: Ambrose, Augustine, Gregory, and Cicero. Although here, where he is discussing the first explanation for their interconnection, he mentions only Gregory and Augustine, he might have mentioned any of the four. Cicero's reliance on the first explanation is clear from the quotation in the *sed* contra; St. Thomas had also emphasized it in I-II, Question 61, Article 4, ad 1. He makes Ambrose's reliance on the first explanation plain in a number of passages in the *Summa*, for example I-II, Question 61, Article 4, Obj. 2 and ad 2, and II-II, Question 169, Article 2, ad 2.

[9] St. Thomas is thinking of the following passage of Aristotle's *Nicomachean Ethics*, which merely *presupposes* that the moral virtues differ according to their subject matter (as Aristotle had said a little earlier, "The virtue of a thing is relative to its proper work"[18]), but *explains* that they are connected through their mutual reliance on prudence:

It is clear, then, from what has been said, that it is not possible to be good in the strict sense without practical wisdom, nor practically wise without moral virtue. But in this way we may also refute the dialectical argument whereby it might be contended that the

[18] Aristotle, *Nicomachean Ethics*, trans. W. D. Ross (public domain), Book 6, Chapter 2.

virtues exist in separation from each other; the same man, it might be said, is not best equipped by nature for all the virtues, so that he will have already acquired one when he has not yet acquired another.... [T]he choice will not be right without practical wisdom any more than without virtue; for the one determines the end and the other makes us do the things that lead to the end.[19]

[10] Each moral virtue depends on prudence, because although the moral virtues direct us to right ends, by themselves they don't show us the right way to pursue these ends. Prudence, for example, requires enough fear to avoid being rash, and enough daring to avoid being cowardly, but how much to give fear and daring their way varies from case to case. Correct decision in these varying circumstances requires deliberating well, attaining the right judgment, and applying this judgment to action.

[11] Prudence in turn depends on each of the moral virtues, because they supply the goals to which prudence finds the right means. Were it not for the virtue of temperance, for example, prudence would be jerked around by a riot of conflicting impulses and desires, trying to find means to satisfy or at least conciliate them all. This is what Aristotle has in mind when he says that temperance "preserves" prudence.[20] In its own way, however, each of the other moral virtues may also be said to preserve prudence. Consider fortitude, which deals with fear and daring. The prudent man must fear error, yet he must also be capable of risking error in pursuit of right judgment; he must value the counsel of others, yet he must also be capable of bearing their contempt if he is right and they think him a fool. Without such acquired dispositions, the quest for prudence would be impossible, so fortitude too preserves prudence.

[12] Just as true principles are the starting points of all "speculative" or theoretical reasoning – reasoning about what is the case – so right desires are the starting points of all practical reasoning – reasoning about what is to be done.

[13] All moral virtues are connected with all other moral virtues *through* their mutual dependence on prudence. Given any two moral virtues P and Q, P depends on prudence, which depends on Q; therefore P depends on Q. Moreover Q depends on prudence, which depends on P; therefore Q depends on P. So P and Q are mutually dependent, and this is the meaning of their "connection."

Reply to Objection 1 (and 2). [1] *Some moral virtues perfect man as regards his general state, in other words, with regard to those things which have to be done in every kind of human life. Hence man needs to exercise himself at the same time in the matters of all moral virtues.* [2] *And if he exercise himself, by good deeds, in all such matters, he*	Reply to Objection 1 (and 2). Certain moral virtues make us fit to conduct ourselves with respect to matters with which everyone has to deal; they enable persons in every walk of life to do well. We must practice the good deeds which correspond to every such virtue, and if we do, we will acquire all of them. But if someone practices the deeds of one of them but not another – for example, if he

[19] Ibid., Book 6, Chapter 13.   [20] Ibid., Book 6, Chapter 5.

will acquire the habits of all the moral virtues. But if he exercise himself by good deeds in regard to one matter, but not in regard to another, for instance, by behaving well in matters of anger, but not in matters of concupiscence; he will indeed acquire a certain habit of restraining his anger; but this habit will lack the nature of virtue, through the absence of prudence, which is wanting in matters of concupiscence. [3] In the same way, natural inclinations fail to have the complete character of virtue, if prudence be lacking.

[4] *But there are some moral virtues which perfect man with regard to some eminent state, such as magnificence and magnanimity; and since it does not happen to all in common to be exercised in the matter of such virtues, it is possible for a man to have the other moral virtues, without actually having the habits of these virtues.* [5] *provided we speak of acquired virtue.* [6] *Nevertheless, when once a man has acquired those other virtues he possesses these in proximate potentiality. Because when, by practice, a man has acquired liberality in small gifts and expenditure, if he were to come in for a large sum of money, he would acquire the habit of magnificence with but little practice: even as a geometrician, by dint of little study, acquires scientific knowledge about some conclusion which had never been presented to his mind before.* [7] *Now we speak of having a thing when we are on the point of having it, according to the saying of the Philosopher (Phys. ii, text. 56): "That which is scarcely lacking is not lacking at all."*

[8] *This suffices for the Reply to the Second Objection.*

works hard to restrain his anger, but not to restrain his lust – then although he will certainly learn a certain restraint concerning anger, it will fall short of complete virtue. Why is this so? Because it will lack those elements of prudence which were perverted though his failure to learn to hold his lust in check as well. The same limitation affects natural inclinations: Without prudence, they too fall short of true virtue.

On the other hand, certain other moral virtues make us fit to conduct ourselves not with respect to universal concerns, but with respect to especially lofty ones. The virtues of magnificence and magnanimity are good examples, for since the opportunity to practice the acts of magnificence and magnanimity does not come to everyone in common, a man might fail to acquire these two virtues even though he has acquired all of the others (though let us remember that what holds for acquired virtues does not necessarily hold for infused virtues).

However, even though such a man does not possess these two virtues in actuality, still, if he really has acquired all the others, then he does possess these two virtues in potentiality. Moreover, their actuality is not distant. For consider someone who has truly acquired the virtue of generosity in small gifts and expenditures. If abundant wealth should now fall to his lot, then with just a little more practice and discipline he will be able to acquire the virtue of magnificence, because it is like generosity, but on a much larger scale. What we have just seen has a close parallel in the case of intellectual virtue, for someone who has deep knowledge of geometrical theorems will be able to master a new theorem with only a little additional study. This is why, when we are at the verge of acquiring something, we speak as though we already have it; Aristotle remarks that what falls just barely short seems to us not to be short.

From this Reply, the answer to Objection 2 should also be clear.

[1] Everyone requires fortitude, because everyone must confront his fear; everyone requires temperance, because everyone must moderate his desires; and everyone requires justice, because everyone must give others what is due to them. These are not virtues for a few, but virtues for all. So it is with all the everyday moral virtues, such as patience, perseverance, modesty, humility, chastity, sobriety, studiousness, friendliness, gratitude, filial piety (in the sense of giving what is due to our parents), and religion (in the sense of giving what is due to God).

[2] Suppose I work at restraining my anger, but do nothing to restrain my sensual desires. No doubt I will become better at restraining my anger, but it does not follow that I will have acquired the corresponding virtue, which is called meekness. Why not? Because meekness is not simply avoiding anger; it is avoiding *unreasonable* anger. To distinguish between reasonable and unreasonable anger, I require prudence. But my judgment of the reasonable and unreasonable in general will be malformed, just because I have not exercised practical reason properly in restraining my sensual desires.

[3] The way in which a natural inclination may fall short of true virtue is parallel to the way in which an acquired inclination may fall short of true virtue: Both require the guidance of prudence, without which both are deficient. For example, someone may be "born with a generous heart," yet fall short of the virtue called liberality or generosity, because he cannot distinguish appropriate from inappropriate gifts, and the same is true of someone who has acquired the inclination to give gifts, but has not developed good judgment about what gifts are suitable, to whom, for what reasons, or on what occasions.

[4] Anyone, even a poor man, can practice the discipline necessary to acquire the virtue of liberality or generosity, because it lies not in the amount given, but in the interior disposition of the giver. St. Thomas emphasizes the point in II-II, Question 117, Article 1, Reply to Objection 3, alluding to St. Ambrose, who had remarked about an incident in Luke 21:3–4, "The Lord preferred the two mites of the widow to all the gifts of the rich, for she gave all that she had, but they only gave a small part out of all their abundance. It is the intention, therefore, that makes the gift valuable or poor, and gives to things their value."[21] We may make the same observation in daily life; the author of this book once had the privilege of being invited by a poor woman to share a piece of cake in a tiny shack with cardboard walls, cellophane windows, a tarpaper roof, and a wood-burning stove. Yet although anyone can acquire the virtue of liberality or generosity, not everyone can acquire the virtue of magnificence or philanthropy, for the latter virtue requires good judgment in the giving of very large sums, and only those who have great wealth can acquire the requisite

---

[21] St. Ambrose of Milan, *On Duties*, Book 1, Section 149. Available online at www.newadvent.org/fathers/34011.htm.

experience.[22] In much the same way, although anyone can practice the other everyday virtues as well, not everyone has the opportunity to practice them in lofty affairs – yet it is only by the experience of doing so that one can acquire the virtue of magnanimity or heroic virtue.

[5] St. Thomas inserts this remark to remind us that at present he is speaking only of acquired virtues, not of infused virtues – only of those developed by human effort, not of those which are poured into us by the grace of God. For an instance of infused rather than acquired magnanimity, we might consider St. Thérèse of Lisieux, whose gift was to perform even the smallest of everyday acts with heroic humility and hiddenness. The case is paradoxical, because in her afflictions and low station she did not have the conventional opportunities for great deeds; the opportunity she seized was the very fact of her afflictions and low station. This sort of "opportunity" cannot even be recognized as such, except by grace, and would have been invisible to Aristotle.

[6] Rather than saying that the poor but virtuous man with no opportunity to practice acts of magnificence *lacks* magnificence, or that he possesses it in *remote* potentiality, St. Thomas says that he possesses it in *proximate* potentiality, meaning that only the action of the agent is required to make it actual. This is a very strong statement. I am in proximate potentiality of remembering my acquaintance's name if it is on the very tip of my tongue; I am in proximate potentiality of seeing my child's face when all I have to do to see her in front of me is open my eyes.

[7] As usual, St. Thomas is paraphrasing. In the passage that he has in mind, Aristotle says "Chance or fortune is called 'good' when the result is good, 'evil' when it is evil. The terms 'good fortune' and 'ill fortune' are used when either result is of considerable magnitude. Thus one who comes within an ace of some great evil or great good is said to be fortunate or unfortunate. The mind affirms the essence of the attribute, ignoring the hair's breadth of difference."[23]

[8] The foregoing explanation has provided a Reply to both Objection 1 and Objection 2. The first Objector had held that moral virtues are unconnected because a man can exercise himself in the acts of one moral virtue, thereby attaining it, without exercising himself in the acts of another moral virtue, thereby attaining that one too. But as we have just seen, although certain dispositions can be acquired in this way, they will fall short of complete virtues because the prudence on which they depend will also be deficient.

---

[22] In another passage, offered by St. Thomas in the *Catena Aurea*, where Ambrose is discussing Luke 6:24–26, Ambrose remarks, "For as that poor man is more praiseworthy who gives without grudging, so is the rich man more guilty, who ought to return thanks for what he has received, and not to hide without using it the sum which was given him for the common good. It is not therefore the money, but the heart of the possessor which is in fault." Thomas Aquinas, *Catena Aurea: Commentary on the Four Gospels, Collected out of the Works of the Fathers*, Volume 3, Part 1 (Oxford: Oxford University Press, 1843), p. 213.

[23] Aristotle, *Physics*, trans. R. P. Hardie and R. K. Gaye (public domain), Book 2, Chapter 5.

The second Objector had held that moral virtues are unconnected because a man may acquire all the other moral virtues and yet lack the moral virtues of magnificence or magnanimity. St. Thomas has replied that although someone who possesses all the other moral virtues may not possess magnificence or magnanimity in actuality, he does possess them in proximate potentiality; he has the interior dispositions by which, with a little practice, he would attain the virtue of magnificence if he came into great wealth, and attain the virtue of magnanimity if he came into the opportunity for great deeds. We must be careful not to misunderstand, because St. Thomas is speaking only of persons who really do possess these interior dispositions. Some persons who do not have them may seem to have them merely because they have not yet been presented with the opportunity to do either great wrong or great good. Such are those who ruin themselves only after winning the lottery, or break out into enormities only after attaining high office.

Reply to Objection 3. [1] *The intellectual virtues are about diverse matters having no relation to one another, as is clearly the case with the various sciences and arts.* [2] *Hence we do not observe in them the connection that is to be found among the moral virtues, which are about passions and operations, that are clearly related to one another.* [3] *For all the passions have their rise in certain initial passions, viz. love and hatred, and terminate in certain others, viz. pleasure and sorrow.* [4] *In like manner all the operations that are the matter of moral virtue are related to one another, and to the passions. Hence the whole matter of moral virtues falls under the one rule of prudence.*

[5] *Nevertheless, all intelligible things are related to first principles. And in this way, all the intellectual virtues depend on the understanding of principles; even as prudence depends on the moral virtues, as stated.* [6] *On the other hand, the universal principles which are the object of the virtue of understanding of principles, do not depend on the conclusions, which are the objects*

Reply to Objection 3. As the diversity of the sciences and arts makes obvious, intellectual virtues concern all sorts of things which are mutually unrelated. Just for this reason, we do not find among them the connections we find among moral virtues, which concern passions and deeds – which do bear mutual relations. For example, all passions begin in the same primal passions, such as love and hate, and conclude in the same subsequent passions, such as delight or sadness. In the same way, the affairs that the moral virtues address are related not only to each other, but also to the passions themselves. This is why a single rule of prudence regulates the diverse matters of all of the moral virtues.

True, all things which can be grasped by the mind depend on the same first principles – for example, prudence itself depends on the moral virtues, as we have seen. Yet the parallel between the moral and intellectual virtues goes no further. For prudence and the moral virtues influence each other *reciprocally*, because in a certain way desire moves reason, and in another way reason moves desire – but understanding and the other

of the other intellectual virtues, as do the moral virtues depend on prudence, because the appetite, in a fashion, moves the reason, and the reason the appetite, as stated above (9, 1; 58, 5, ad 1).	intellectual virtues do *not* influence each other reciprocally, because the universal principles which are the starting points of the intellectual virtue of understanding do not depend on the conclusions of the other intellectual virtues.

[1] The various arts and sciences have no principles in common *properly and essentially*. For example, carpentry *as such* depends only on the principles of making things of wood; ignorance of the properties of bricks will not prevent the carpenter making, say, a wooden chair. However, St. Thomas is not denying that these pursuits may have principles in common *accidentally*, as we will see at the very end of our commentary on the Reply to Objection 4.

[2] By contrast, the moral virtues do have principles in common properly and essentially. Why? One reason is that they all concern the passions of the soul, which are intrinsically connected with each other; the other is that they all concern "operations" or deeds, which are intrinsically connected *both* with the passions *and* with each other.

[3] Broadly speaking, every passion of the soul regards the same goods and evils. However, some passions, such as joy, sorrow, love, and hatred, regard them simply as things *to be* acquired or avoided, while others, such as daring, fear, and hope, regard them as things *which are difficult* to acquire or avoid. Now since these two sets of passions regard goods and evils from different points of view, they belong to different powers of the soul (called the concupiscible and irascible powers).[24] But because both sets regard the *same* goods and evils – even though from these different points of view – they also *influence* each other. For example, it would be impossible to regard some good as an object of love without also regarding it as an object of hope of attainment and fear of loss. For this reason, not only are the moral virtues which regulate the concupiscible power mutually connected, and not only are the moral virtues which regulate the irascible power mutually connected, but also, the moral virtues which regulate the concupiscible power are mutually connected with the ones with regulate the irascible power. For example, one might think that one could have fortitude, which regulates fear, without temperance, which regulates desire, but in fact this is impossible, because fear and desire influence each other; a glutton, for example, has excessive fear of missing his next meal because he has excessive desire for the pleasures of taste.

[4] Just as the passions are connected with each other, so deeds or operations are connected, both with each other and with passions. Suppose I rob

[24] 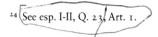 See esp. I-II, Q. 23, Art. 1.

you of your money for fear of being unable to supply my drug habit, and when you resist, I become angry and strike you. In the first place, my passions of fear, desire, and anger are all connected. In the second, my deeds of robbing you, feeding my drug habit, and striking you are all connected. And in the third, my deficiencies of justice and temperance are connected – justice, because I have taken for myself what is due to you, and temperance, not only because I inappropriately desire the pleasures or consolations which drugs give me, but also because, through intemperate anger, I inappropriately seek to revenge myself upon you.

[5] Here St. Thomas offers a clarification: When he insisted above that the various arts and sciences have no principles in common properly and essentially, he was not denying that they share a foundation in the universal principles of being. In particular, nothing that the mind apprehends can be grasped apart from such principles of theoretical reason as the principle of noncontradiction: Neither the carpenter, the bricklayer, or the practitioner of geometry will get far if he supposes that something can both *be* and *not be* in the same sense at the same time.

[6] But someone might suggest that *just for this reason*, the intellectual virtues are in exactly the same position as the moral virtues – which would overturn the whole Reply to the Objection. The argument would run like this:

1. Intellectual virtues depend on the understanding of first theoretical principles in exactly the same way that moral virtues depend on first practical principles.
2. Therefore, either intellectual virtues are connected just as moral virtues are connected – or else the moral virtues *lack* connection just as the intellectual virtues lack connection.

For this reason, St. Thomas takes a moment to explain what would be wrong with such reasoning. The problem with it is that although the intellectual virtues do depend on understanding of first principles or starting points, the converse is not true: Understanding of principles does not depend on the intellectual virtues. Because I understand the principle of noncontradiction, I can acquire the intellectual virtue involved in geometry, but it is not because I have acquired the intellectual virtue involved in geometry that I understand the principle of noncontradiction. First theoretical principles are *per se nota*, known in themselves.

By contrast, the dependence between prudence and the moral virtues is mutual or reciprocal, as we have seen above. St. Thomas has also made the point earlier: "Reason, as apprehending the end, precedes the appetite for the end: but appetite for the end precedes the reason, as arguing about the choice of the means, which is the concern of prudence."[25]

---

[25] I-II, Q. 58, Art. 5, ad 1.

Reply to Objection 4. [1] *Those things to which the moral virtues incline, are as the principles of prudence:* [2] *whereas the products of art are not the principles, but the matter of art.* [3] *Now it is evident that, though reason may be right in one part of the matter, and not in another, yet in no way can it be called right reason, if it be deficient in any principle whatever. Thus, if a man be wrong about the principle, "A whole is greater than its part," he cannot acquire the science of geometry, because he must necessarily wander from the truth in his conclusion. Moreover, things "done" are related to one another, but not things "made," as stated above (ad 3). Consequently the lack of prudence in one department of things to be done, would result in a deficiency affecting other things to be done:* [4] *whereas this does not occur in things to be made.*	Reply to Objection 4. Moral virtue stands in a different relationship to the things to which it inclines than craftsmanship stands to the products that it makes. For the thing at which each moral virtue aims is intrinsic to the virtue, and prudence concerns nothing but how to fulfill such inclinations. By contrast, the products which each craft produces are extrinsic to the craft – they are merely the matter to which the craftsman happens to direct it.
	Plainly, even if reason is on the right path concerning one aspect of a matter, it cannot be called "right reason" if it is defective in another aspect. For example, if someone fails to grasp that every whole is greater than one of its parts, he will not possess the intellectual virtue of geometry, because his conclusions will inevitably miss the truth by a mile. Moreover, as we saw in the reply to the previous Objection, our deeds depend on each other in a way that our products do not. That is, any shortcoming of prudence concerning certain deeds produces corresponding mistakes about other deeds, but the parallel with products does not hold because craftsmanship is not ruled by prudence.

[1] The Objector had argued that right reason concerning things to be *done* is analogous to right reason about things to be *made*; therefore, just as someone can be good at one craft without being good at another, so someone can possess one moral virtue without possessing another. To show that the analogy is defective, St. Thomas argues that the principles or starting points of right reason work differently in the cases of things to be done and things to be made. He begins by showing that on the case of prudence, or right reason about things to be done, the starting points are supplied by the moral virtues themselves: For instance, the aim of fortitude is to make fear obey reason, and the aim of temperance is to make desire obey reason. Prudence *begins* with these inclinations, then identifies the course of action which fulfills them.

[2] One might think that it is the just same with the practice of a craft – for doesn't the craftsman begin planning the work by deciding what to make? He does, but this misses the point. A moral virtue such as temperance *supplies* the inclination to the end; to know that a person is temperate is to know that he aims at bringing desire under the regulation of reason. By contrast, a craft such as carpentry does *not* supply the inclination to the end; one may know that a

person has mastered carpentry without knowing anything about what wooden things he wants to make, or even whether he wants to make any at all. We may express this fact by saying that the products of carpentry are not carpentry's principles, but only the matter with which carpentry is concerned.

[3] The argument presented here is highly elliptical, and the order in which its premises are presented renders it still more obscure. Reordered, it runs something like this:

1. Anyone who fails to grasp even one of the starting points of geometry will err badly in geometrical conclusions.

2. This illustrates the more general point that anyone who fails to grasp even one of the starting points in *any* domain of reasoning will err badly in its conclusions.

3. But the starting points of morality are supplied by the moral virtues. Moreover, even though the various crafts constitute *distinct* domains of reasoning, morality constitutes a *single* domain of reasoning, for reasons already explored in the Reply to Objection 3. (These, we recall, were the connection among passions, the connection among actions, and the connection of actions with passions.)

4. Therefore, even though one may possess one craft even while being deficient in others, one cannot fully possess any virtue without fully possessing all of them.

[4] "Whereas this does not occur in things to be made": Is this contrast a little strong? Can't a mistake concerning one craft bring about mistakes in the practice of others? This can certainly happen; for example, if a carpenter is making a wooden hod to carry mortar, he must know that mortar is soft and wet, even though, in themselves, the properties of mortar concern bricklaying, not carpentry. But such connections among the crafts are accidental, rather than proper and essential. It isn't because of the nature of carpentry that the carpenter must know something about bricklaying, but because in this case he happens to have been asked to make something that a bricklayer uses. By contrast, the connection among the moral virtues is not accidental, but essential; it goes right down to the things that the moral virtues are aiming at.

Whether the Seven Capital Vices Are Suitably Reckoned?

TEXT	PARAPHRASE
Whether the seven capital vices are suitably reckoned?	Is the traditional view correct in enumerating vainglory, envy, anger, sloth, covetousness, gluttony, and lust as the chief or originating vices from which the particular kinds of vice tend to arise?

Since the virtues are interconnected, and since all virtues hinge on certain chief or cardinal virtues, it makes sense to ask whether there are chief vices too. The answer is yes: Capital vices are those from which other vices arise, mainly through determining the end which is sought. Because the end conditions the choice of means, they are like leaders and directors of all the other vices.[1] This is dreadful news for those who cherish the hope of indulging one special vice without being infected by others. Just as we must practice all of the virtues to be fully developed in any of them, so we cannot let one vice into the house without opening the door wide to its brothers.

The interconnection among vices may seem strange, because it implies a kind of *order* among sins. How can sin have order? Isn't it essentially disorder? Yes and no. Insofar as turns us away from God, it deprives us of *proper* order, but insofar as it pursues some good (even though in the wrong way), it certainly possesses a perverse kind of order.[2] We see the same thing in physical disease, which proceeds in a recognizable way even though the body is deprived of the

---

[1] I-II, Q. 84, Art. 3.

[2] I-II, Q. 84, Art. 3, ad 2: "Sin lacks order in so far as it turns away from God, for in this respect it is an evil, and evil, according to Augustine ... is 'the privation of mode, species and order.' But in so far as sin implies a turning to something, it regards some good: wherefore, in this respect, there can be order in sin."

order of health. However, because virtue and vice originate in different ways, the parallel between cardinal virtues and capital vices is not exact; capital vices are neither the same in number, nor interconnected in precisely the same fashion. This subtlety turns out to be crucial later on.

In this Article, St. Thomas focuses on the order among sins in the individual, but there is also an order of sins in society. Every age imagines that its own favorite capital vice "doesn't hurt anyone." Consider just one of our own favorite capital vices. We begin by separating sex from procreation. Along one line of development, this innovation leads to the taking of innocent life, for since conception occurs anyway, we invent justifications for doing away with children; even infanticide is now widely accepted among medical ethicists.[3] Along another line of development, it leads to insensitivity to women, whom we expect to have male patterns of sexual response, and almost to prostitute themselves for male enjoyment. Along still another, it disorders marriage, for the husband and wife no longer see themselves as long-range partners in turning the wheel of the generations. Along yet another, it leads to the abuse of children who are allowed to live, because live-in boyfriends tend to resent their girlfriends' babies, and girlfriends are ambivalent about babies that their boyfriends did not father. Especially among the comfortable, those children who are desired are more and more viewed as lifestyle enhancements rather than as expressions of hope for the future. At the other end of the social order are poverty, because single women must provide for their children by themselves; adolescent violence, because male children grow up without a father's influence; and venereal disease, because formerly rare infections spread rapidly through sexual contact. In all classes, there develops a Peter Pan attitude in which young men and women are afraid to grow up, partly because there seems less and less in prospect but toiling for money so that one can have fun when one is not toiling. The blessing of Psalm 128:3, "your wife will be like a fruitful vine within your house; your children will be like olive shoots around your table,"[4] comes to seem not an expression of a universal aspiration, but almost incomprehensible. Eventually we come to hold our very nature in contempt, as illustrated by the author who declared in a family planning journal that pregnancy "may be defined as an illness" which "may be treated by evacuation of the uterine

---

[3] See, for example, Alberto Giubilini and Francesca Minerva, "After-Birth Abortion: Why Should the Baby Live?," *Journal of Medical Ethics*, www.jme.bmj.com, published online February 27, 2012. The authors write, "What we call 'after-birth abortion' (killing a newborn) should be permissible in all the cases where abortion is, including cases where the newborn is not disabled." The editor, Julian Savulescu, nonplused by public criticism of the article, pointed out in the journal's blog that its arguments for infanticide are "are largely not new and have been presented repeatedly in the academic literature and public fora by the most eminent philosophers and bioethicists in the world." The novelty of the article, he says, lies not in its arguments for infanticide, "but rather their application in consideration of maternal and family interests."

[4] RSV-CE.

contents."[5] One suspects that even this is not the end. The progression from one thing to another is straightforward; if we do not see it, the reason can only be that we do not want to.

A certain roadblock must be removed from the highway before we can go on. Since the term "sin" can refer either to the act of sin or the habit of sin, St. Thomas uses the terms "sin" and "vice" all but interchangeably in this Article. I find that although my students do not mind the term "vice" too much, the term "sin" disturbs them; it "seems religious." This aversion is something like our strange preference for the psychoanalytic term "psyche" over the traditional term "soul," even though "psyche" is merely a word for "soul." Perhaps such prejudices are inevitable in an intellectual culture which tries so hard to scrub its young people of faith, but the irrational prejudice that faith is the enemy of reason raises a high barrier to following St. Thomas's reasoning.

Far be it from me to suggest that St. Thomas isn't doing theology. Even so, nine tenths of what he does in this Article (I don't say ten tenths) is straight psychological analysis with no need to dip into Revelation. Even his audacious view that God is our ultimate and final good rests firmly on natural reason. Consider that although, in a sense, we "repose" in every good which we possess – a point to which we will return – any such repose in merely temporal goods is short-lived, for every temporal good leaves something to be desired. Yet how strange and inexplicable it would be if perfect and complete happiness were impossible! For in that case, we would have to say that our nature is founded on futility, driven by desires that have no purpose. Such a view would be absurd even if we tried to get by on Darwin alone, without reference to St. Thomas's God – for it cannot be "adaptive" for an organism to howl for something that it cannot help desiring and yet cannot ever have.

Objection 1. [1] *It would seem that we ought not to reckon seven capital vices, viz. vainglory, envy, anger, sloth, covetousness, gluttony, lust.* [2] *For sins are opposed to virtues. But there are four principal virtues, as stated above (Question 61, Article 2). Therefore there are only four principal or capital vices.*	Objection 1. Since we have found there to be four chief virtues, and since sins and virtues are contraries, there must be only four chief vices, yet the traditional list includes seven.

[1] We must consider what each of these vices is, and why it is capital. First, however, let us consider the "queen of all vices," which is pride.

Pride, or *superbia* – not to be confused with vainglory, although it is closely associated with it – is a disordered pursuit of excellence, an excessive desire to be uplifted. The problem is not that one tries to be the best that one can be – that is good. Rather the problem is that one overreaches in some way. Not

---

[5] Warren M. Hern, "Is Pregnancy Really Normal?," *Family Planning Perspectives* 3, no. 1 (1971), online at www.drhern.com/pregnorml.htm; the quotations are from the conclusion.

only is this contrary to reason, but it is especially dangerous because although pride is not the only possible cause of sin, it can give rise to any kind of sin. Other sins may arise from it *directly*, because for the sake of our own excellence we may desire any wrong thing whatsoever; for example I may resent the excellence of someone else, which is envy. Other sins may also arise from it *indirectly*, because it arouses contempt for the restraint of Divine law. Some writers list pride as one of the capital vices, putting it in the place of vainglory. As we will see, however St. Thomas agrees with St. Gregory the Great in giving it a still higher place as the queen of all vices, with the seven capital vices her generals. To see why, we must bear in mind that in every vice, there are two elements: The formal element is to turn away from the unchangeable good which is God, and the material element is to turn instead to some changeable good. Now the dreadfulness of pride is not due to what it seeks, for the inordinate pursuit of uplifting is no more alien to virtue than the inordinate pursuit of other changeable goods. Its extreme gravity arises from the reason for which it turns from God Himself: For although in all other vices, we turn from God through ignorance, weakness of will, or the desire for something other than God, in pride we turn away from Him *just because we are unwilling to submit to Him*. St. Augustine had identified pride as the sin of our first parents, who sought to decide solely by themselves what was good and evil for them to do, to know solely by their own power what good or evil would happen to them, and to attain supreme happiness solely by their own natural power instead of in reliance on God. St. Thomas agrees. One might wonder why humility, the virtue opposite to pride, is not listed as a cardinal virtue. However, because it moderates a desire – the impetuous desire to be lifted up – St. Thomas classifies it as one of the virtues linked with the cardinal virtue of temperance.[6]

We turn now to the capital vices proper. The first of them, vainglory, *inanis gloria*, is the immediate offspring of pride. Vainglory does not lie in desiring glory *per se*, for whatever is good in any person should be appreciated, and it is not sinful to know, to approve, or to desire the appreciation of something good about one's self. The problem lies in seeking hollow or false glory. Glory is hollow or false (*inanis vel vanae*) if it is sought for something unworthy, from those who are not good judges of worth, or for a bad reason – for example, for the pleasure of feeling puffed up rather than for the honor of God or the good of one's neighbor.[7] Thus, I ought to desire that this book be worthy to lead many to love God and to understand and practice virtue; this is fitting.

---

[6] For pride as a vice, see II-II, Q. 162, Arts. 1–2; for pride in relation to the capital vices, see II-II, Q. 162, Art. 8; for what makes gives pride its extreme gravity, see II-II, Q. 162, Art. 6; for pride as the sin of our first parents, see II-II, Q. 163, Arts. 1–2; for humility as a potential part of temperance, opposed to pride, see II-II, Q. 161, Art. 4, and II-II, Q. 162, Art. 1, ad 3.

[7] For vainglory as the immediate offspring of pride, see II-II, Q. 132, Art. 4. For its definition, see II-II, Q. 132, Art. 1.

Just for this reason, I should desire that any excellence in the book be loved and honored. But I should desire exactly the same thing for worthy books by other persons, and I should *not* desire that my book be admired for anything in it which may happen to be unworthy.

Envy, *invidia*, is sorrow about our neighbor's good or excellence because it seems to reduce our own good or excellence. He thinks that in order to be high, *others must be low*. This is a capital vice because it incites us to many sorts of sins in order to climb above others, to make them less, or to make them seem less.[8]

Anger, *ira*, viewed as a capital vice, is not the same as being angry. At times, in fact, one *should* be angry; for example, I should be angry with criminals and desire that they be brought to justice. The problem lies in *immoderate anger* – in being angrier than rightly ordered reason demands. In particular, excessive anger can cause many kinds of sin, either by leading us to view personal revenge as just and good, or by provoking us to act without thinking.[9] To be sure, there is such a thing as having too little anger – for example, not being indignant about great crimes – but in this Article we are considering the capital vices themselves, not the vices opposite to them. Excessive anger is a much more common and dangerous failing than insufficient anger, with a much greater tendency to father other vices.

Sloth, *tristitia* or *acedia*, is not laziness (though it is connected with laziness), but a kind of sadness or weariness – an "oppressive sorrow which so weighs upon man's mind that he wants to do nothing," a "sluggishness of the mind which neglects to begin good." The problem does not lie not in sorrow which is fitting due to loss, for it is right to grieve sometimes; nor does it lie in that good sorrow which prompts us to change our ways when we have been in error; nor does it lie in despondency which is beyond our control because there is something wrong with our brain chemistry. Rather it lies in a voluntary and habitual tendency to indulge excessive sadness in a way which withdraws us from good, especially spiritual good. One form of sloth lies in excessive grief about real evil – for example if I am so swallowed up in sorrow for my repented and forgiven sins that I am drawn away from doing good. Another form is to be grieved about good itself because it involves work – for example if I turn away from the good of charity or spiritual love because it requires me to take care of my ailing wife or father. Sloth is a capital vice, one from which other vices grow, because "just as we do many things on account of pleasure, both in order to obtain it, and through being moved to do something under the impulse of pleasure, so again we do many things on account of sorrow, either that we may avoid it, or through being exasperated into doing something under pressure thereof."[10]

---

[8] II-II, Q. 36, Arts. 1 and 4.   [9] II-II, Q. 158, Arts. 1 and 6.
[10] For the definition of sloth, see II-II, Q. 35, Art. 1; for sloth as a capital vice, see I-II, Q. 35, Art. 4.

Covetousness or avarice, *avaritia,* also called greed, *aviditas,* is "immoderate love of possessing." It lies not in merely seeking enough wealth to live in a manner fitting to one's position in life, but in seeking even more. Covetousness is a capital vice because for the sake of wealth one may commit all sorts of sins, erroneously thinking that in this way one can attain the sufficiency of happiness.[11]

Gluttony, *gula,* concerns the unregulated desire for food and drink. Probably it is best to think of it not simply as too much *desire* for food or drink, but as too much *interest* in food or drink – for it can be as wrong to make unreasonable demands that one's food always be exactly right. One might think that gluttony would be unconnected with other sins, but the underlying problem is disordered desire concerning bodily pleasures, and from this cause spring all sorts of sins.[12]

Finally lust, *luxuria,* is not sexual desire in itself, but wrongly directed sexual desire. Conjugal desire exists for the procreation of the children and the loving union of the procreative partners, who are husband and wife. Within this context and for these purposes it is good; outside this context and against these purposes it is wrong.[13] It might seem redundant to regard both lust and gluttony as capital sins, because both involve unregulated desire for bodily pleasures. However, lust deserves a special place because "venereal pleasures above all debauch a man's mind." The Latin word translated "debauch" is *solvunt,* which means to loosen, set sail, or scatter; we might say that lust has greater power than any other pleasure to *unstring* the mind, to release it from all order and scatter it to the winds, so that it the person commits many other sins besides.[14] In his great work *Inferno,* Dante Alighieri poetically depicts what it really means to give one's reason over to sexual desire by representing the souls in the Circle of Lust as blown endlessly up and down, hither and yon, now in one direction, now in another, in the grip of a driving gale which "snatches [them] up … whisks them about and beats and buffets them."[15] The tempest of wind that they are suffering is the same one they surrendered to in life, merely stripped of its facile illusions; it is nothing but what they have desired.

[2] The Objector holds that since there are four principal or cardinal virtues (prudence, justice, fortitude, and temperance), there must be only four principal or capital vices (presumably lack of prudence, lack of justice, lack of courage, and lack of temperance.

Notice the tacit assumption, to which St. Thomas later calls attention: That since virtue and sin are contraries, they must arise in parallel ways – that vice is caused by the mere absence of something which is present in virtue.

By the way, although in some cases the expressions "sin" and "vice" can be used interchangeably, their meanings are not identical. Sins [*peccata*] are evil

---

[11] II-II, Q. 118, Arts. 1 and 7.   [12] II-II, Q. 148, Arts. 1 and 5.
[13] II-II, Q. 152, Arts. 2–3.   [14] II-II, Q. 153, Art. 1; see also Art. 4.
[15] Dante Alighieri, *Inferno*, trans. Anthony Esolen, Canto 5, lines 32–33.

acts, vices [*vitia*] are *dispositions* to commit evil acts, and virtues [*virtutes*] are dispositions to commit good acts.

Objection 2. [1] *Further, the passions of the soul are causes of sin, as stated above (Question 77). [2] But there are four principal passions of the soul; [3] two of which, viz. hope and fear, are not mentioned among the above sins, whereas certain vices are mentioned to which pleasure and sadness belong, since pleasure belongs to gluttony and lust, and sadness to sloth and envy. Therefore the principal sins are unfittingly enumerated.*	Objection 2. Moreover, we have found that the passions of the soul can prompt sins, and there are four leading passions of the soul – pleasure and sadness, hope and fear. Surely, then, a complete list of the leading vices would have to address all four of these passions. The traditional list does address two of them: Gluttony and lust pertain to pleasure, and sloth and envy pertain to sadness. However, none of the vices on the list pertain to hope or to fear. Therefore the list is incomplete.

[1] St. Thomas does not mean that the movements of the sensitive appetite are evil in themselves, but they need to be under the direction of reason. They become causes of sin when they subvert reason instead of accepting its guidance.

Passions can either *distract* reason or *cloud* it. In the former case, our energies are so divided that we do not reason with sufficient attention. In the latter case our, the imagination is so powerfully caught up by the object of our emotion that reason merely endorses the goal that appetite presents to the imagination.[16]

[2] According to St. Thomas, the passions are generated in the following order: "Love and hatred are first; desire and aversion, second; hope and despair, third; fear and daring, fourth; anger, fifth; sixth and last, joy and sadness, which follow from all the passions: yet so that love precedes hatred; desire precedes aversion; hope precedes despair; fear precedes daring; and joy precedes sadness."[17] Now the expression "principal passions" refers to *culminative* passions, but this term may be taken in two senses. Joy and sadness are culminative in the sense that all the other passions find their rest in them: "In them all the other passions have their completion and end." But fear and hope are called "principal passions" in the sense that they are the last link in the movement of desire: "For in respect of good, movement begins in love, goes forward to desire, and ends in hope; while in respect of evil, it begins in hatred, goes on to aversion, and ends in fear." Because one rests in something present but moves toward something future, another way to put the matter is that "joy relates to present good, sadness relates to present evil; hope regards future good, and fear, future evil."[18]

---

[16] I-II, Q. 77, Art. 1.   [17] I-II, Q. 25, Art. 3.   [18] I-II, Q. 25, Art. 4.

Notice that in the passage I have just been summarizing (I-II, Question 25, Article 4), St. Thomas says that the principal passions of the soul are *joy* and sadness, hope and fear. Here, though, he allows the Objector to call the four principle passions *pleasure* and sadness, hope and fear, substituting *delectatio* for *gaudium*, and he lets him get away with it even in his Reply. Since in the strict sense, joy refers to rational delight, while pleasure refers both to rational and to bodily delight,[19] this may seem to be a mistake, but surprisingly, it isn't. St. Thomas frequently employs the classical figure of speech called metonymy, in which a part stands for a whole. In one form of metonymy, the best kind of P is used as a placeholder for all kinds of P.[20] This is what St. Thomas is doing in Question 25, where he uses rational delight as a symbol for all kinds of delight. So when the Objector says "pleasure" instead of "joy," he really means the same thing, but he is using words in their literal senses instead of their metonymical senses – probably because his focus is not on rational but on bodily delight. Although later on St. Thomas criticizes him, he doesn't criticize him *for this.*

But what *is* pleasure? According to St. Thomas, to experience a pleasure is merely to experience *repose* of either the sensitive or the rational appetite in some loved good. Thus, although pleasure is a good in a certain secondary sense (just because it *completes* the possession of the good), it is not *the* good because it always implies some good other than itself, such as love, knowledge, friendship, the sexual union of husband and wife, or friendship with God.[21]

This view of pleasure – one of St. Thomas's most distinctive doctrines – may be contrasted with the view of philosophical hedonists, who think that the good is nothing but what we desire, and the only thing we actually desire is pleasure. Did you think you desired love, knowledge, friendship, or any of those other things? According to them, you were mistaken; you only desired the pleasure of those things. If this view were correct, then if you were offered a life devoid of all *real* love, knowledge, friendship, and so forth, receiving in its place the perpetual delivery, via electrode, of just the right voltage to the pleasure center of your brain, you should accept the offer. This would be merely to hallucinate the good, and hallucinating the good is not the same as experiencing it, any more than hallucinating a cat is the same as seeing it. In one case, the cat isn't really there; in the other case, the good isn't.

---

[19] See I-II, Q. 31, Art. 3, "Whether delight [*delectationis*] differs from joy [*gaudium*]?"

[20] For example, the best kind of government is sometimes used to refer to all kinds of legitimate government, and the best kind of law is sometimes used to refer to all kinds of law. The older writers also frequently used the opposite kind of metonymy, in which the *worst* kind of P is used to refer to all kinds of P. This is why the Church has traditionally understood the Decalogue's prohibition of adultery to forbid all kinds of sexual impurity, and the prohibition of false witness to forbid all kinds of lying. For further discussion, see J. Budziszewski, *Commentary on Thomas Aquinas's Treatise on Law* and *Companion to the Commentary* (both Cambridge: Cambridge University Press, 2014).

[21] I-II, Q. 33, Art. 4.

[3] Gluttony pertains to pleasures of taste; lust pertain to pleasures of sexual touch; sloth is disinclination to pursue the good either because of excessive sorrow about evil, or excessive sorrow because the good is laborious; and envy is sorrow for the good of our neighbor. Of these four, the one most frequently misunderstood is sloth; we confuse it with laziness, which is not its essence, but merely its effect. As pleasure is repose in some loved good, sadness is repose in evil.[22]

Objection 3. *Further, anger is not a principal passion. Therefore it should not be placed among the principal vices.*	**Objection 3.** Still further, anger is not one of the leading passions, so it does not deserve to be listed among the leading vices.

In much the same vein as the second Objection, which protested that the list of capital vices fails to pay enough attention to several of the principal passions, the third Objection complains that it pays *too much* attention to a passion which is *not* principal. His reasoning seems to be that each of the capital vices must pertain directly to some principal passion – either to joy, to sadness, to hope, or to fear. Why then is anger on the list of capital vices, since it does not pertain directly to any of these?

Objection 4. [1] *Further, just as covetousness or avarice is the root of sin,* [2] *so is pride the beginning of sin, as stated above (Question 84, Article 2).* [3] *But avarice is reckoned to be one of the capital vices. Therefore pride also should be placed among the capital vices.*	**Objection 4.** Still further, a cardinal vice is one that gives rise to other vices. Since we have seen previously that covetousness is sin's root, and pride is its beginning, it would seem that both covetousness and pride are cardinal vices. But although covetousness is on the traditional list, pride is not. It should be.

[1] The traditional view that covetousness is the "root" of all sins comes from a passage in St. Paul's first letter to his young friend Timothy, whom he was grooming to be an apostle: "For they that will become rich, fall into temptation, and into the snare of the devil, and into many unprofitable and hurtful desires, which drown men into destruction and perdition. For the desire of money is the root of all evils; which some coveting have erred from the faith, and have entangled themselves in many sorrows."[23]

[2] The equally traditional view that pride is the "beginning" of sin comes from the following passage in Sirach: "The beginning of the pride of man is to fall off from God: Because his heart is departed from him that made him: for pride is the beginning of all sin: he that holds it, shall be filled with maledictions, and it shall ruin him in the end."[24]

---

[22] I-II, Q. 25, Art. 1. [23] 1 Timothy 6:9–10 (DRA).
[24] Sirach 10:14–15 (DRA). I have modernized the archaism "holdeth."

[3] The Objector reasons that "root" and "beginning" mean much the same thing, so if we are to list the root vice as a capital vice, then surely we should also list the beginning vice as a capital vice.

Objection 5. Further, some sins are committed which cannot be caused through any of these: as, for instance, when one sins through ignorance, or when one commits a sin with a good intention, e.g. steals in order to give an alms. Therefore the capital vices are insufficiently enumerated.	Objection 5. Still further, some of the sins men commit arise from causes independent of any of the traditional seven capital vices. For example, someone may stray because of ignorance, or commit a sin because of a good intention (such as stealing in order to give alms). We see then that the traditional list must be expanded.

The Objector seems to reason that since we use the term "capital vices" to refer to the causes of sin, the list of capital vices ought to include *every* cause of sin, and plainly it doesn't. Presumably he would have us list ignorance, misguided good intentions, and other causes as capital vices, just as we list vainglory, envy, and all the rest.

On the contrary, stands the authority of Gregory who enumerates them in this way (Moral. xxxi, 87[25]).	On the other hand, we have this list of seven capital vices by the authority of St. Gregory the Great, in his *Morals on the Book of Job.*

St. Gregory writes, "For pride is the root of all evil, of which it is said, as Scripture bears witness: Pride is the beginning of all sin. But seven principal vices, as its first progeny, spring doubtless from this poisonous root, namely, vainglory, envy, anger, sloth, covetousness, gluttony, lust." A little later he explains how these vices govern in the occupied territory of the soul:

For vainglory is wont to exhort the conquered heart, as if with reason, when it says, You ought to aim at greater things ...

Envy is also wont to exhort the conquered heart, as if with reason, when it says, In what are you inferior to this or that person? ...

Anger is also wont to exhort the conquered heart, as if with reason, when it says, The things that are done to you cannot be borne patiently ... .

Sloth is also wont to exhort the conquered heart as if with reason, when it says, What ground have you to rejoice, when you endure so many wrongs from your neighbors? ...

[25] Correcting the Blackfriars citation, which gives the chapter as 17 instead of 87. St. Thomas himself refers only to Book 31.

Covetousness also is wont to exhort the conquered mind, as if with reason, when it says, It is a very blameless thing, that you desire some things to possess ...

Gluttony is also wont to exhort the conquered heart, as if with reason, when it says, God has created all things clean, in order to be eaten ...

Lust also is wont to exhort the conquered heart, as if with reason, when it says, Why not enlarge yourself now in your pleasure, when you know not what may follow you?[26]

I answer that, I answer that, [1] As stated above (Question 84, Article 3), the capital vices are those which give rise to others, especially by way of final cause. [2] Now this kind of origin may take place in two ways. First, on account of the condition of the sinner, who is disposed so as to have a strong inclination for one particular end, the result being that he frequently goes forward to other sins. But this kind of origin does not come under the consideration of art, because man's particular dispositions are infinite in number. [3] Secondly, on account of a natural relationship of the ends to one another: and it is in this way that most frequently one vice arises from another, so that this kind of origin can come under the consideration of art.	Here is my response. Capital vices are those from which other vices spring up, especially in the sense that the capital vices are their ends or purposes. But we may view the origination of other vices from two points of view. First we may consider the condition of the sinner himself – that is, we may inquire into the *idiosyncratic* relations among ends. For if someone has an extreme and habitual inclination to seek some special purpose, then in order to attain it he may commit all kinds of sins. This is not a proper mode of investigation, because such inclinations are innumerable. Second we may consider the *natural* relations among ends. This *is* a proper mode of investigation, because such relations are the most common ways in which one vice gives rise to another.
[4] Accordingly therefore, those vices are called capital, whose ends have certain fundamental reasons for moving the appetite; and it is in respect of these fundamental reasons that the capital vices are differentiated. [5] Now a thing moves the appetite in two ways. First, directly and of its very nature: thus good moves	Just for this reason, we give the designation "capital" to vices aimed at purposes by which appetite is *especially* provoked – and we distinguish the capital vices from each other according to the rational distinctions among them. But now we encounter a further complication, for there are two ways in which appetite may be provoked. One way is that desire is incited *directly, by the very nature of the good,* so that good which a person has in view moves appetite to pursue it, and for the same reason the evil that he has in view provokes appetite to flee. The other way is that desire

---

[26] *Morals on the Book of Job by St. Gregory the Great,* trans. John Henry Parker, J. G. F. Rivingon, and J. Rivington (public domain), Book 31, Chapters 87 and 90, available on the internet at www.lectionarycentral.com/GregoryMoraliaIndex.html. I have modified the translations by substituting the synonymous expressions "vainglory" for "vain glory," "sloth" for "melancholy," and "covetousness" for "avarice," as well as modernizing archaisms such as "Why enlargest thou not thyself?"

the appetite to seek it, while evil, for the same reason, moves the appetite to avoid it. [6] Secondly, indirectly and on account of something else, as it were: thus one seeks an evil on account of some attendant good, or avoids a good on account of some attendant evil.

[7] Again, man's good is threefold. For, in the first place, there is a certain good of the soul, which derives its aspect of appetibility, merely through being apprehended, viz. the excellence of honor and praise, and this good is sought inordinately by "vainglory." [8] Secondly, there is the good of the body, and this regards either the preservation of the individual, e.g. meat and drink, which good is pursued inordinately by "gluttony," or the preservation of the species, e.g. sexual intercourse, which good is sought inordinately by "lust." [9] Thirdly, there is external good, viz. riches, to which "covetousness" is referred. These same four vices avoid inordinately the contrary evils.

[10] Or again, good moves the appetite chiefly through possessing some property of happiness, which all men seek naturally. [11] Now in the first place happiness implies perfection, since happiness is a perfect good, to which belongs excellence or renown, which is desired by "pride" or "vainglory." [12] Secondly, it implies satiety, which "covetousness" seeks in riches that give promise thereof. [13] Thirdly, it implies pleasure, without which happiness is impossible, as stated in Ethic. i, 7; x, 6,7,[8] and this "gluttony" and "lust" pursue.

[14] On the other hand, avoidance of good on account

is incited *indirectly and because of something else*, so that a person pursues an evil for the sake of an associated good, or flees a good because of an associated evil.

(I) As the first way in which appetite is provoked – the one in which it is incited directly and by the nature of the good – we must bear in mind that man is directed to a triple good rather than a single one. In the first place are goods of the soul, nonmaterial goods which are such that as soon as the mind grasps them it considers them desirable. For example, the good of distinguished praise and honor come under this heading, the unregulated pursuit of which is vainglory. In the second place are the goods of the body, which pertain to the preservation of either the individual or the species. Under the former heading come food and drink, the unregulated pursuit of which is gluttony; under the latter, coitus, the unregulated pursuit of which is lust. In the third place are external goods, such as wealth, to which avarice is directed. We may add that these four vices are disordered not only in how they pursue the goods we have been discussing, but also in how they avoid the opposite evils.

A good thing may also incite appetite primarily through its participation in some property of happiness, which all men desire naturally. Such properties turn out to be threefold. First come properties happiness has because of its completeness, such as distinction and eminence. These are the goals of pride [superbia] or vainglory [gloria]. Second come properties happiness has because of its sufficiency. This is why avarice seeks wealth; it seems to promise having enough. Third is the flavor of pleasure, without which, as Aristotle reminds us, happiness cannot exist. And this is what gluttony and lust strive for.

(II) As to the second way in which appetite is provoked – the one in which we flee some good because of an associated evil – again we encounter a complication, because this can happen in two ways. One way is to

of an attendant evil occurs in two ways. [15] *For this happens either in respect of one's own good, and thus we have "sloth," which is sadness about one's spiritual good, on account of the attendant bodily labor:* [16] *or else it happens in respect of another's good, and this, if it be without recrimination belongs to "envy," which is sadness about another's good as being a hindrance to one's own excellence,* [17] *while if it be with recrimination with a view to vengeance, it is "anger."* [18] *Again, these same vices seek the contrary evils.*	turn against one's own good because of an associated evil. In this case we have the capital vice of sloth, in which spiritual good saddens us not in itself but because of the associated bodily labor. The other way is to turn against someone else's good because of an associated evil. Here again we must distinguish, because when this happens without combativeness, it is envy – sorrow about another person's good because it seems to hinder one's own excellence. But when one rises up against the other person with the intention of vengeance, then it is anger. And just as these three cardinal vices of sloth, envy, and anger may flee goods because of associated evils, they may seek the opposite evils because of associated goods.

[1] Figuratively, a capital vice (*vitia capitalia*) is a *head* vice – a vice from which other vices arise. The main way in which a capital vice gives rise to other kinds of sin is by being their final cause – that is, by providing a reason or purpose for sinning.[27]

[2] Suppose, for instance, that I ardently desire to become known as the Popcorn King, and will do anything to achieve my goal. To raise capital for my popcorn enterprises, I defraud my investors; to foil competition, I steal all the sources of supply; to remove impediments, I have other popcorn magnates assassinated. From one sin I go forward to many others. Yet we can hardly generalize from a motive which perhaps no one possesses but me.

[3] Suppose that instead of listing all possible particular motives – a task that would be endless – we list the underlying commonalities among them. For example, even though I may be the only person who wants to become known as the Popcorn King, surely I am not the only one who desires glory of some kind, and we can certainly generalize about the ways in which the unregulated appetite for glory can give rise to other vices.

[4] The capital vices, then, are vices which proceed from certain very general motives or ends when they are insubordinate to reason and Divine law – one from the unregulated desire for glory, another from the unregulated desire for wealth, and so on. From each such vice springs a host of other vices.

[5] Whatever we desire, we desire to attain some good or to avoid some evil. As St. Thomas remarks, "Everything naturally desires good, nor can anyone

---

[27] I-II, Q. 84, Art. 3.

desire anything for himself, save under the aspect of good: for 'evil is outside the scope of the will.'"²⁸

[6] Certainly it is possible to seek evil for the sake of something else, but not even those who are said to "love iniquity" desire evil for its own sake. For example, the murderer may murder to have a sufficiency of wealth, to gain glory among his friends, to exercise his skill, to make himself safe from his rivals, or even, perversely, to enjoy pleasure. The fact that his evil deed is motivated by desire for some good does not make the deed itself good, for one must not only pursue good and avoid evil (which we cannot help but do), but pursue them in the right way. In particular, though murder may be directed to some good, it cannot be directed to our ultimate good, and so cannot be made right by any circumstance whatsoever.²⁹

[7] The distinction among goods of the soul, goods of the body, and external goods is very old; it was already customary even in Aristotle's day.³⁰ Honor and praise are goods of the soul (although they are empty when undeserved); so is the rule of reason; so are the virtues; so are prayer and contemplation; so is happiness itself.

[8] Goods of the body are "quite a trifle as compared with the good of the soul," because the body is at the service of the soul. Indeed the soul is what makes it a *human* body in the first place, for the soul is the pattern of an embodied human life.³¹

[9] External goods are least important, because just as the body is at the service of the soul, external goods are at the service of the body. As St. Thomas remarks later, "The good of external things is the lowest of human goods: since it is less than the good of the body, and this is less than the good of the soul, which is less than the Divine good."³² The expression "the Divine good" refers to the uncreated good of God Himself, which human beings cannot share by their own power, but in which the redeemed souls participate in heaven by a special act of His love.

[10] Happiness is what everyone seeks for itself; no one seeks happiness for the sake of something else. True happiness is perfect, meaning that it is fully developed and complete; it is sufficient, meaning that it leaves nothing to be desired; and it is pleasurable, meaning that we experience the delight of repose in it. St. Thomas's insight is that just because these three qualities of perfection, sufficiency, and pleasure do belong to true happiness, we tend to be attracted to whatever possesses perfection, sufficiency, or pleasure, even if it is not the same thing as true happiness.

This insight is intensely suggestive of St. Augustine's views about *mimesis* or imitation. Addressing God, he says:

---

²⁸ I-II, Q. 29, Art. 4, alluding to a remark of Pseudo-Dionysius in *The Divine Names*, Book 4. Compare I, Q. 82, Art. 2, ad 1; I-II, Q. 1, Art. 6; and I-II, Q. 94, Art. 2.
²⁹ I-II, Q. 27, Art. 1, ad 1.   ³⁰ Aristotle, *Nicomachean Ethics*, Book 1, Chapter 8.
³¹ I-II, Q. 2, Art. 5 and ad 1, Art. 6.   ³² II-II, Q. 118, Art. 5.

Ambition seeks honour and glory, although You alone are to be honoured before all and glorious forever. By cruelty the great seek to be feared, yet who is to be feared but God alone: from His power what can be wrested away, or when or where or how or by whom? The caresses by which the lustful seduce are a seeking for love: but nothing is more caressing than Your charity, nor is anything more healthfully loved than Your supremely lovely, supremely luminous Truth. Curiosity may be regarded as a desire for knowledge, whereas You supremely know all things. Ignorance and sheer stupidity hide under the names of simplicity and innocence: yet no being has simplicity like to Yours: and none is more innocent than You, for it is their own deeds that harm the wicked. Sloth pretends that it wants quietude: but what sure rest is there save the Lord? Luxuriousness would be called abundance and completeness; but You are the fullness and inexhaustible abundance of incorruptible delight. Wastefulness is a parody of generosity: but You are the infinitely generous giver of all good. Avarice wants to possess overmuch: but You possess all. Enviousness claims that it strives to excel: but what can excel before You? Anger clamours for just vengeance: but whose vengeance is so just as Yours? Fear is the recoil from a new and sudden threat to something one holds dear, and a cautious regard for one's own safety: but nothing new or sudden can happen to You, nothing can threaten Your hold upon things loved, and where is safety secure save in You? Grief pines at the loss of things in which desire delighted: for it wills to be like to You from whom nothing can be taken away.

.... Thus even those who go from You and stand up against You are still perversely imitating You. But by the mere fact of their imitation, they declare that You are the creator of all that is, and that there is nowhere for them to go where You are not.[33]

Compare St. Thomas:

Creatures of themselves do not withdraw us from God, but lead us to Him; for "the invisible things of God are clearly seen, being understood by the things that are made" (Romans 1:20). If, then, they withdraw men from God, it is the fault of those who use them foolishly. Thus it is said (Wisdom 14:11): "Creatures are turned into a snare to the feet of the unwise." And the very fact that they can thus withdraw us from God proves that they came from Him, for they cannot lead the foolish away from God except by the allurements of some good that they have from Him.[34]

[11] For example, because the perfection of happiness sets it above other things and gives it vividness and distinction (*claritas*), we are attracted to the excellent and distinguished. Excellence and distinction really are goods; they are not bad in themselves. This is why we seek deserved honor and praise. But to pursue excellence and distinction in a habitually disordered way is vice. Disordered pursuit of excellence is pride; disordered pursuit of distinction, vainglory.

[33] St. Augustine of Hippo, *Confessions*, 2d ed., trans. Frank J. Sheed (Indianapolis: Hackett, 2006), Book 2, Chapter 6, Sections 13–14, pp. 31–32.
[34] I, Q. 65, Art. 1, ad 3.

[12] Again, because it seems to promise having enough, we are attracted to wealth. To seek enough material goods to maintain ourselves according to our stations is good, but to pursue wealth excessively is covetousness or avarice.

[13] As we have seen above, pleasure is *repose* in some good; therefore it *completes* the possession of that good; therefore, one cannot have happiness without pleasure. On the other hand, it is quite dreadfully possible to have pleasure without happiness! Now just because it is possible to repose in the objects of any of the appetites, including the bodily appetites (even if not for long), we are attracted to the pleasures of taste and touch – but these goods too must be pursued only according to reason. To enjoy dinner is good, but it would be gluttony, say, to eat, purge, then return to the table. For the husband and wife to enjoy sexual union with an attitude of welcome to the possibility of children is good, but it would be lust, say, to deliberately make the act sterile, or to sleep with someone other than each other.

[14] Again a distinction; taking each in turn, St. Thomas is showing us the perspectives from which we must view the capital vices in order to see why the list includes just the ones that it does.

[15] Sometimes people think it must be wrong to pursue one's ultimate good too ardently. For isn't that "selfishness"? On the contrary, in St. Thomas's view it is impossible to pursue one's ultimate good too ardently. If I am indifferent to the good of my neighbors, for example, the problem is not that I am pursuing my good too ardently, but that I am not pursuing it ardently enough, for my ultimate good lies in that God whose nature is to love and in whose image both I and my neighbors are made; hence, even though I may think that my selfishness is a way to hold onto myself, I am actually losing myself. The general name for disinclination to seek our ultimate, spiritual good ardently is *acedia* or sloth. Just because this good really is ultimate, it may seem impossible that anyone would *not* seek it enough, but in fact pursuing it with insufficient ardor is all too common because of our sorrow about the difficulties that are associated with the pursuit. We grieve and even fall into despair because of what we would have to give up, do, or suffer in order to accept the gift which is infinitely better. This is why the older writers described sloth not as laziness, but as sadness or melancholy.

One might also expect that St. Thomas would have dwelt on the spiritual difficulties that discourage us from following God, such as dryness in prayer. Surprisingly, he centers our attention on the *bodily* difficulties that discourage us from following God – the sheer bodily laboriousness of what have traditionally been called the "corporal works of mercy." This is precisely where Christ laid his emphasis in the parable of the separation of the sheep from the goats:

Then the King will say to those at his right hand, "Come, O blessed of my Father, inherit the kingdom prepared for you from the foundation of the world; for I was hungry and you gave me food, I was thirsty and you gave me drink, I was a stranger and you welcomed me, I was naked and you clothed me, I was sick and you visited me, I was in prison and you came to me." Then the righteous will answer him, "Lord, when did we see thee hungry and feed thee, or thirsty and give thee drink? And when did we see thee a stranger and welcome thee, or naked and clothe thee? And when did we see thee sick or in prison and visit thee?" And the King will answer them, "Truly, I say to you, as you did it to one of the least of these my brethren, you did it to me." Then he will say to those at his left hand, "Depart from me, you cursed, into the eternal fire prepared for the devil and his angels; for I was hungry and you gave me no food, I was thirsty and you gave me no drink, I was a stranger and you did not welcome me, naked and you did not clothe me, sick and in prison and you did not visit me." Then they also will answer, "Lord, when did we see thee hungry or thirsty or a stranger or naked or sick or in prison, and did not minister to thee?" Then he will answer them, "Truly, I say to you, as you did it not to one of the least of these, you did it not to me." And they will go away into eternal punishment, but the righteous into eternal life."[35]

[16] The Latin word rendered in the Blackfriars translation as "recrimination" is *insurrectionem*, which means literally to rise up against someone. Just because it seems to my crooked way of thinking that some good which you enjoy makes my own good less, I may grieve – but it does not necessarily follow that I blame you for having it and want you to be punished. Envy is the name of the vice which causes me to sorrow for your good, but without recrimination.

[17] On the other hand, if I not only sorrow for some good which you enjoy but also blame you for having it, so that I do want you to be punished for it, then I am guilty not of envy, but of anger. Notice, though, that the *vice* of anger is not the same as the *passion* of anger. For suppose you have murdered; then I *ought* to be aroused to desire your punishment. Provided that my anger is reasonable and proportionate, it would pertain not to the capital vice of anger, but to the virtue of justice. To say this is not to preclude the possibility of mercy, to which we return later on in this commentary.

[18] Though we naturally pursue good and avoid evil – though, in fact, we *cannot help* but pursue good and avoid evil, and we are always doing it – nevertheless, just as in the earlier part of the *respondeo* we saw that we may seek goods and avoid evils in the wrong way, so in this part of the *respondeo* we see that we may wrongly flee goods *in order* to avoid evils and seek evils *in order* to attain goods.

Reply to Objection 1. [1] Virtue and vice do not originate in the same way: since virtue is caused by the subordination of the appetite to reason, [2] or to the immutable good, which is God, [3] whereas vice arises from the appetite for mutable good. [4] Wherefore there is no need for the principal vices to be contrary to the principal virtues.	Reply to Objection 1. The Objector assumes that virtue and vice are caused in the same way, but this is incorrect. Virtue arises when desire is ruled by reason, or by the one unchangeable good which is God; vice arises when desire unreasonably latches onto some changeable good. Thus it is unnecessary for the leading vices to be inverted images of the leading vices, as the Objector thinks.

[35] Matthew 25:34–45 (RSV-CE).

[1] We have seen already that if our appetites are to be subordinate to reason, four things are needed: The power of practical reason itself must be brought into right order, and this is prudence; our desires for the "delectable" goods must be brought into right order, and this is temperance; our desires for the "arduous" goods must be brought into right order, and this is fortitude; and finally, no matter what desires may come into play, all of the operations by which we give and receive from others must be brought into right order, and this is justice. So, insofar as we consider only our natural powers, there are four cardinal virtues. (The spiritual or theological virtues require the transformation of motive by divine grace.)

[2] The word St. Thomas uses here is the inclusive "or" (*vel*); he is not thinking of subordination to reason and subordination to God as mutually exclusive. Indeed, as he says later, "the light of natural reason, whereby we discern what is good and what is evil, which is the function of the natural law, is nothing else than an imprint on us of the Divine light. It is therefore evident that the natural law is nothing else than the rational creature's participation of the eternal law."[36] Why then doesn't St. Thomas use the synonymous "or" (*sive*), which means "this, or in other words, that"? Because God made us not only for temporal happiness, which lies within our natural powers, but also for eternal happiness, which transcends our natural powers; "therefore it was necessary that, besides the natural and the human law, man should be directed to his end by a law given by God."[37]

[3] The *formal* aspect of vice in general is to turn away from the unchanging good. In this respect the contrast between virtue and vice is exact. But to understand how each vice arises, we must also understand what it is *for the sake of which* one turns away from the unchanging good.[38]

[4] Thus it is not enough to say (for example) that temperance is opposed by intemperance, for temperance is opposed in a variety of ways by a variety of vices. Thus, running down the list of capital vices, we find that vainglory is but one of several vices opposed to magnanimity, which is linked with fortitude. Sloth and envy are among the vices opposed to charity – the former because it resists one's own good, the latter because it resists one's neighbor's good. The capital vice of anger refers to *excessive* anger; anger in accord with rightly ordered reason is a virtue, not a vice; this virtue has no name, but is yet another aspect of temperance. Excessive anger is directly opposed to meekness, which moderates the passion of anger itself, and indirectly opposed to clemency, which moderates the impulse to punish. Covetousness is one of several

---

[36] I-II, Q. 91, Art. 2. These matters are discussed thoroughly in J. Budziszewski, *Commentary on Thomas Aquinas's Treatise on Law* (Cambridge: Cambridge University Press, 2014).

[37] I-II, Q. 91, Art. 4.

[38] II-II, Q. 162, Art. 6: "Two things are to be observed in sin, conversion to a mutable good, and this is the material part of sin; and aversion from the immutable good, and this gives sin its formal aspect and complement." See also I-II, Q. 72, Art. 1.

vices opposed to liberality or generosity, which is connected with justice; the opposite vice is prodigality. Gluttony and lust are opposed to temperance, but in the opposite way, so is insensibility: For "nature has introduced pleasure into the operations that are necessary for man's life," so if anyone were so insusceptible to pleasure that he resisted even things necessary to well-being, such as nourishment, he would be doing wrong.[39]

So even though virtue really is opposed to vice – and even though for every virtue we can clearly identify the various vices which are contrary to it – we should not expect the list of capital vices to be a mirror image of the list of cardinal virtues, as the Objector thinks.

Reply to Objection 2. [1] Fear and hope are irascible passions. [2] Now all the passions of the irascible part arise from passions of the concupiscible part; [3] and these are all, in a way, directed to pleasure or sorrow. [4] Hence pleasure and sorrow have a prominent place among the capital sins, as being the most important of the passions, as stated above (Question 25, Article 4).	**Reply to Objection 2.** The Objector complains that none of the capital vices arise from hope or fear. However, hope and fear are irascible passions; the irascible passions arise from the concupiscible passions; and each of the concupiscible passions aims at pleasure or sorrow. Therefore, pleasure and sorrow are more fundamental than hope and fear, and the list of capital vices reflects this fact.

[1] We saw earlier that the irascible passions pertain to goods viewed as arduous and difficult to obtain. Hope is certainly one of the irascible passions, "for we do not speak of any one hoping for trifles, which are in one's power to have at any time." So is fear, for its object is a future evil "which surpasses the power of him that fears, so that it is irresistible."[40]

[2] The concupiscible passions pertain to delectable goods, to goods viewed simply as good; they are called "delectable" because they promise pleasure (*delectatio*). Irascible passions arise from concupiscent passions, in the sense that we view something as an arduous and difficult good only if we already view it as good.[41]

[3] Pleasure pertains to present good, but sorrow belongs to present evil – to the weariness arising from the mind's apprehension of something that opposes the good.[42]

[4] This answers the Objector, who had assumed that because there are four principal passions, all four must be equally important to the enumeration of

---

[39] For vainglory, see II-II, Q. 132; for sloth, Q. 35; for envy, Q. 36; for anger, Q. 158; for covetousness, Q. 118; for gluttony, Q. 148; and for lust, QQ. 153–154. The quotation about insensibility is from II-II, Q. 142, Art. 1.
[40] I-II, Q. 40, Art. 1; I-II, Q. 41, Art. 4.   [41] I-II, Q. 23, Art. 1; see also II-II, Q. 25, Art. 1.
[42] I-II, Q. 25, Art. 4; see also I-II, Q. 35, Art. 2, and I-II, Q. 38, Art. 1.

the capital vices. We now see that just as we should not expect the list of capital vices to mirror the list of cardinal virtues, so we should not expect it to mirror the list of principal passions.

A point of translation: St. Thomas writes that pleasure and sorrow are *principaliter connumerantur in* the capital sins. The Blackfriars translation tales the phrase to mean that they *have a prominent place among* the capital sins, making it seem as though pleasure and sorrow of every kind are sinful in themselves, which of course is not the case. I take St. Thomas to mean that pleasure and sorrow are *of primary importance to classifying or reckoning* the capital sins. Hence my paraphrase above, "pleasure and sadness are more fundamental than hope and fear, and the classification of capital vices reflects this fact."

Reply to Objection 3. [1] *Although anger is not a principal passion, yet it has a distinct place among the capital vices, because it implies a special kind of movement in the appetite,* [2] *in so far as recrimination against another's good has the aspect of a virtuous good, i.e. of the right to vengeance.*	Reply to Objection 3. Anger is distinguished from other leading vices because even though it is not a principal passion, it has a singular way of kindling desires. It stirs them up by presenting an assault on another person's good as something honest and honorable – as something that shares in the goodness of a just punishment.

[1] Every vice involves some passion which has become disobedient to reason. But *principal* passions are passions in which other passions *culminate*, whereas *capital* vices are vices from which other vices *arise*. Therefore, there is no reason why the list of principal passions and the list of capital vices should be in one-to-one correspondence. In particular, if there is some passion which gives rise to vice in a distinct way which none of the four principal passions express, then it deserves a place on the list of capital vices. Anger is just such a passion, for it can certainly give rise to vice, and it is not a movement of pleasure, sadness, hope, or fear *per se*.

[2] The distinctive way in which anger gives rise to vice is that it views another's good as *something for which he deserves punishment*. "So what if that bastard has more talent than I do? He doesn't deserve it!" "What a thief – he took the job that should have gone to me!" "So she likes him better than me, eh? I'll get back at him for that."

Reply to Objection 4. [1] *Pride is said to be the beginning of every sin, in the order of the end, as stated above (Article 2): and it is in the same order that we are to consider the capital sin as being principal.* [2] *Wherefore pride, like a universal vice, is not counted along with the others, but is reckoned as the "queen*	Reply to Objection 4. Capital vices are considered capital because they supply motives for sinning. Pride, however, is called the beginning of all sins because it supplies the overarching motive of the capital vices themselves. For this reason, it should be considered not one among other capital vices, but the universal

of them all," as Gregory states (Moral. xxxi, 87).[43] [3] *But covetousness is said to be the root from another point of view, as stated above (Articles 1, 2).*	vice – as St. Gregory puts it, the "queen of them all." As we have seen previously, covetousness is called is called the root of all sins in a different sense.

[1] The awkward phrase "in the order of the end" means "with respect to what I am aiming at." Each capital sin begins by aiming at some temporal good. But I aim at that good, whatever it is, in order to be lifted up in some way, and pride is doing so in a disordered way. So with respect to what I am aiming at, every capital vice is a beginning of sin, but pride is so to speak a beginning of the beginning. St. Thomas puts it like this in I-II, Question 84, Article 2:

In voluntary actions, such as sins, there is a twofold order, of intention, and of execution. In the former order, the principle is the end, as we have stated many times before. Now man's end in acquiring all temporal goods is that, through their means, he may have some perfection and excellence. Therefore, from this point of view, pride, which is the desire to excel, is said to be the "beginning" of every sin.

[2] St. Gregory thinks of pride as the queen, the capital vices as her generals, and the army of subordinate vices as their soldiers:

For when pride, the queen of sins, has fully possessed a conquered heart, she surrenders it immediately to seven principal sins, as if to some of her generals, to lay it waste....

But the leaders are well said to exhort, the armies to howl, because the first vices force themselves into the deluded mind as if under a kind of reason, but the countless vices which follow, while they hurry it on to every kind of madness, confound it, as it were, by bestial clamor.

Alluding to the war horse of Job 39:25, who hears the trumpet and says "Ha!," who smells the battle from afar, who hears the urging of the commanders and the ululating cries of the swarming soldiers, St. Gregory goes on to say:

But the soldier of God, since he endeavors skillfully to pursue the contests with vices, smells the battle afar off; because while he considers, with anxious thought, what power the leading evils possess to persuade the mind, he detects, by the sagacity of his scent, the exhortation of the leaders. And because he beholds the confusion of subsequent iniquities by foreseeing them afar off, he finds out, as it were, by his scent the howling of the army.[44]

---

[43] Again I have corrected the incorrect citation given in the Blackfriars translation (this time Chapter 27).

[44] *Morals on the Book of Job by St. Gregory the Great*, trans. John Henry Parker, J. G. F. Rivingon, and J. Rivington (public domain), Book 31, Chapters 87, 90, and 91, available on the internet at www.lectionarycentral.com/GregoryMoraliaIndex.html.

[3] Though pride is a beginning of all sins with respect to their *end or pur-pose,* covetousness is a beginning with respect to their *means,* because "by riches man acquires the means of committing any sin whatever."[45]

Reply to Objection 5. [1] *These vices are called capital because others, most frequently, arise from them: so that nothing prevents some sins from arising out of other causes.* [2] *Nevertheless we might say* [3] *that all the sins which are due to ignorance, can be reduced to sloth, to which pertains the negligence of a man who declines to acquire spiritual goods on account of the attendant labor; for the ignorance that can cause sin, is due to negligence, as stated above (Question 76, Article 2).* [4] *That a man commit a sin with a good intention, seems to point to ignorance, in so far as he knows not that evil should not be done that good may come of it.*	Reply to Objection 5. The Objector assumes that the capital vices are called capital because they are the *only* causes of sins. Actually they are called capital because they are the *most frequent* causes of sins. Certainly some sins might arise from other causes. We might rest here, but let us continue a little further. For (1) although the Objector is correct to say that some sins arise from ignorance, such ignorance is due to sloth – to the cardinal vice which causes a person to neglect spiritual goods just because their acquisition is toilsome. And (2) although the Objector is right to say that someone might sin with a good intention, this sort of sin also arises from negligence – he has not bothered to learn that we must not do evil for the sake of good.

[1] St. Thomas drives this point home in many places, for example in his discussion of covetousness a few Articles earlier, where he says "Just as in natural things we do not ask what always happens, but what happens most frequently, for the reason that the nature of corruptible things can be hindered, so as not always to act in the same way; so also in moral matters, we consider what happens in the majority of cases, not what happens invariably, for the reason that the will does not act of necessity." So, for example, "when we say that covetousness is the root of all evils, we do not assert that no other evil can be its root, but that other evils more frequently arise therefrom."[46]

[2] The previous point alone is enough to defeat the Objection, for the Objector had thought the list of capital vices must include *all* causes of sin, and this is not the case. "Nevertheless," says St. Thomas, still more can be said against the Objection, and we are about to see what.

[3] The Objector thinks the list of capital vices fails to recognize that ignorance can cause sin. Yet indirectly, it does recognize the fact, for truly culpable ignorance results from the capital vice of sloth. St. Thomas explains

---

[45] I-II, Q. 84, Art. 1. See also Art. 2: "In the order of execution, the first place belongs to that which by furnishing the opportunity of fulfilling all desires of sin, has the character of a root, and such are riches."

[46] I-II, Q. 84, Art. 1, ad 3.

elsewhere that although no one can be blamed for ignorance of what he could not have known, anyone who neglects finding out what he has a duty to know has committed a sin of omission. He includes in this the fundamentals of faith, the universal principles of right and wrong, and the particular duties of his position in life (for example, that rulers should rule justly, that parents should care for their children, and that the guardians of the city gates should not abandon their stations).[47] It might be questioned whether literally everyone can find out the fundamentals of faith, but certainly everyone in his audience was able to.

[4] The Objector also thinks the list of capital vices fails to recognize that sin can be caused by a misguided good intention. Yet indirectly, the list of capital vices recognizes this fact too. Suppose, for example, I destroy human embryos to extract stem cells for medical research. Then I have committed the sin of deliberately taking some innocent human lives with the intention of helping others; my sin results from either ignorance or disregard of the fact that I must not do evil so that good will result, and we have just seen that culpable ignorance results from sloth.

Is ignorance of the principle that we must not do evil so that good will result really culpable? Yes, because the wrong of doing evil so that good will result is fundamental – this is one of the principles that we are "adapted by birth" to know, or as St. Thomas also says, that we have a "natural habit" of knowing. So, even though I am not necessarily thinking of this moral principle at all times, I have a dispositional tendency to be aware of it – a tendency which is due not merely to instruction, but to the way the human mind is made.[48] If I am *not* aware of the principle, something must be wrong – perhaps I am trying not to think of it. And if I *am* aware of it, but disregard it, I am equally to blame.

---

[47] I-II, Q. 76, Art. 2.
[48] For the language of natural aptitude to know – more literally, of being adapted by birth to know – see again I-II, Q. 72, Art. 2. For the language of the natural habit of knowing, see I-II, Q. 94, Art. 1.

PART II

THE VIRTUE OF JUSTICE, ESPECIALLY IN RELATION TO LAW

Taken in the sense of that general justice which is called "legal" because it puts man in harmony with the law which directs the acts of all of the virtues to the common good, justice stands foremost among all the moral virtues, because the common good transcends the individual good of one person. But even taken as one moral virtue among others, justice excels all the others for two reasons. The first reason concerns the subject in which it lies: For although justice is found in the more excellent part of the soul, the rational appetite or will, other moral virtues are found merely in the sensitive appetite, the seat of the passions that they regulate. The second reason concerns the object at which it aims: For although the other virtues are commendable merely for promoting the sole good of the virtuous person himself, justice is praiseworthy for making the virtuous person well disposed towards others.

– Thomas Aquinas[1]

---

[1] II-II, Q. 58, Art. 12, slightly paraphrased, and interpolating some clarifying language from Art. 5.

Whether Mercy Is a Virtue?

TEXT	PARAPHRASE
Whether mercy is a virtue?	Our tradition of moral thought has considered mercy a virtue. But is it?

St. Thomas says "Mercy is compassion in our own heart for someone else's misery, impelling us to succor him if we can, for we call it mercy [*misericordiam*] from the fact that someone has a heart [*cor*] which is in suffering [*miserum*] for the suffering of another."[2]

The tradition is very precise about the sorts of things which succor may include. Bodily works of mercy may be classified under the headings of feeding the hungry, giving drink to the thirsty, clothing the naked, harboring the harborless, visiting the sick, ransoming the captive, and burying the dead. Spiritual works of mercy include instructing the ignorant, counseling the doubtful, comforting the sorrowful, reproving the sinner for the sake of the amendment of his life, forgiving injuries, bearing with those who trouble and annoy us, and praying for everyone. St. Thomas discusses these works at some length in II-II, Question 32.[3]

That succor includes comforting the sorrowful and healing the sick may seem obvious. That it includes instructing the doubtful and even reproving the wrongdoer may seem surprising in an age of skepticism and reluctance to "judge," but after reflection, these points are not difficult either. The real sticking point comes with forgiving injuries.

---

[2] So I render his words in II-II, Q. 30, Art. 1: *Misericordia est alienae miseriae in nostro corde compassio, qua utique, si possumus, subvenire compellimur, dicitur enim misericordia ex eo quod aliquis habet miserum cor super miseria alterius.*

[3] See especially Art. 2. The term St. Thomas uses for the works of mercy is *eleemosynarum,* which the Blackfriars translation archaically renders as "almsdeeds." As we see, however, it includes much more than giving material assistance to poor people.

How so? The second part of this book is concerned primarily with the virtue of justice. St. Thomas's tradition firmly holds that in God's salvation "mercy and truth have met each other: justice and peace have kissed."[4] But to most people today it is not easy to see how justice, which involves punishment, and mercy, which involves remission or forgiveness of punishment, can both be virtues. Contemporary culture swings between an excessively softhearted interpretation of mercy which leaves no room for justice, and an excessively hardhearted interpretation of justice which leaves no room for mercy. It is futile to seek to understand either justice or mercy part from the other; we must seek to understand both of them.

Objection 1. [1] *It would seem that mercy is not a virtue. For the chief part of virtue is choice as the Philosopher states (Ethic. ii, 5).* [2] *Now choice is "the desire of what has been already counselled" (Ethic. iii, 2). Therefore whatever hinders counsel cannot be called a virtue.* [3] *But mercy hinders counsel, according to the saying of Sallust (Catilin.): "All those that take counsel about matters of doubt, should be free from ... anger ... and mercy, because the mind does not easily see aright, when these things stand in the way."* [4] *Therefore mercy is not a virtue.*	Objection 1. Apparently mercy is not a virtue, for as Aristotle reminds us, the crux of virtue is choice, and to choose is to desire what one has settled upon through previous deliberation. This being so, nothing which impedes deliberation can be virtuous. A statesman quoted by Sallust put the point memorably when he said in the Roman Senate that men who deliberate about uncertain matters must be devoid of anger and mercy, because these things obstruct the mind's view of the truth. It follows that mercy is not a virtue.

[1] Aristotle explains in *Nicomachean Ethics*, Book 2, Chapter 4, that an act is not virtuous unless the agent has knowledge, *chooses* the act for its own sake, and proceeds from a firm character. In the following chapter, he further emphasizes the importance of choice with the somewhat obscure comment that virtue either is choice, or involves choice. In his *Commentary on Aristotle's Nicomachean Ethics*, St. Thomas explains the remark by pointing out that the interior act of virtue *is* a choice, the exterior act of virtue *proceeds* from the choice, and the disposition of virtue *causes* the choice.

[2] Because of slippage among the Greek, the Latin, and the English, our translations of Aristotle do not make his point very clear. However, in his *Commentary on Aristotle's Nicomachean Ethics*, St. Thomas explains it by saying that although choice is voluntary, not everything voluntary is a choice, but only what is both voluntary and *praeconsiliatum* – both voluntary and done as a result of previous counsel. Counsel means good deliberation. We saw in I-II,

---

4 Psalm 84:11 (DRA), numbered in most modern translations 85:10.

Question 58, Article 4, that it is one of the three subordinate virtues associated with the cardinal virtue of prudence.

[3] The "matters of doubt" which the Objector has in mind are matters of moral and legal judgment. Sallust, the Roman historian whom he closely paraphrases, was not giving his own opinion, but quoting from a speech given in the Roman Senate by Gaius Caesar. Gaius was responding to the question of the consul in office at that time, who had asked the Senate what should be done with certain men who had been judged guilty of treason. Although the consul-elect had just recommended that they be put to death, Gaius warned:

Fathers of the Senate, all men who deliberate upon difficult questions ought to be free from hatred and friendship, anger and pity. When these feelings stand in the way the mind cannot easily discern the truth, and no mortal man has ever served at the same time his passions and his best interests. When you apply your intellect, it prevails; if passion possesses you, it holds sway, and the mind is impotent.

Gaius went on to argue that that although the traitors certainly deserved death – although, indeed, perhaps not even death would be commensurate to their guilt – such a penalty would violate prevailing law and custom. In accordance with the Law of Portius, the Senate should merely confiscate the traitors' goods and allow them to go into exile under permanent guard.[5]

[4] Interestingly, although Gaius mentions the distraction of pity, in the case at hand he is concerned primarily about the distraction of hatred and anger. Reversing Gaius's emphasis, the Objector reasons something like this:

1. Passion interferes with counsel.
2. But counsel is necessary to virtuous choice.
3. Nothing which causes interference with virtuous choice is a virtue.
4. Therefore no passion is a virtue.
5. But mercy is a passion.
6. Therefore mercy is not a virtue.

Objection 2. [1] *Further, nothing contrary to virtue is praiseworthy.* [2] *But nemesis is contrary to mercy, as the Philosopher states (Rhet. ii, 9),* [3] *and yet it is a praiseworthy passion (Rhet. ii, 9).* [4] *Therefore mercy is not a virtue.*	Objection 2. Moreover, nothing opposed to virtue deserves praise. But as Aristotle points out, even though nemesis, or indignation, is opposed to mercy, it does deserve praise. So mercy must not be a virtue.

[1] The Objector's premise that nothing contrary to virtue is praiseworthy is St. Thomas's too. However, it contrasts sharply with a view commonly taken in our own time, that things which are despicable from the viewpoint of

5 Sallust, *The War with Cataline*, Sections 49–51, available online at http://penelope.uchicago.edu/ Thayer/E/Roman/Texts/Sallust/Bellum_Catilinae*.html.

virtue may actually be praiseworthy from some other point of view. Consider for example the majority opinion in the 1982 US Supreme Court case *New York v. Ferber*, which concerned a New York state statute which banned the knowing promotion of sexual performances by children by means of the distribution of material which depicted them. Although the Court allowed the statute to stand, its unanimous decision emphasized that the statute would nevertheless have to be set aside in any case in which the works which depicted such performances had "serious literary, artistic, political, or scientific value." Speaking for the majority, Justice White wrote that "how often ... it may be necessary to employ children to engage in conduct clearly within the reach of [the statute] in order to produce educational, medical, or artistic works cannot be known with certainty," so that it could be identified only "through case-by-case analysis."[6] So, for example, a movie of children who have been induced to do unspeakable things[7] on camera would have to be permitted if it were artistic enough. This is like permitting an act of murder and rape if only it is carried out with flair. In a Thomistic point of view, we should not say that something contrary to virtue might be praiseworthy from another perspective, but that evil perverts the good qualities which might otherwise be praiseworthy.

[2] "Most directly opposed to pity is the feeling called nemesis," says Aristotle. His countrymen gave the name *Nemesis* to the goddess who brought retribution to those who arrogantly had set themselves up against the divine order, grasping for things beyond their merit. Though Aristotle considers it fitting to attribute *nemesis* to the gods, he views it first and foremost as a human passion, "pain caused by the sight of undeserved good fortune,"[8] which in English we call "indignation." This is also the sense in which the term is used by both the Objector and St. Thomas himself.

[3] Aristotle writes, "Pain at unmerited good fortune is, in one sense, opposite to pain at unmerited bad fortune, and is due to the same moral qualities. Both feelings are associated with good moral character; it is our duty both to feel sympathy and pity for unmerited distress, and to feel *nemesis* at unmerited prosperity; for whatever is undeserved is unjust, and that is why we ascribe *nemesis* even to the gods."[9] He says a little later, "If you are pained by the unmerited distress of others, you will be pleased, or at least not pained, by

---

[6] *New York v. Ferber*, 458 U.S. 747 (1982).

[7] The statute defined "sexual performances" as performances including actual or simulated sexual intercourse, deviate sexual intercourse, sexual bestiality, masturbation, sadomasochistic abuse, or lewd exhibition of the genitals.

[8] Aristotle, *Rhetoric*, trans. W. Rhys Roberts (public domain), Book 2, Chapter 9, available at https://ebooks.adelaide.edu.au/a/aristotle/a8rh/complete.html, substituting the original Greek term *Nemesis* for the English word "indignation."

[9] Ibid.

their merited distress. Thus no good man can be pained by the punishment of parricides or murderers."[10]

We may pause to suggest that the pagan philosopher was never so close to Christianity in one way, and never so far from it in another. In St. Thomas's view, it is not that we fittingly project our indignation into the divine order, but that the certain judgment of conscience is the voice of God in us.[11]

[4] If *nemesis* is praiseworthy, but contrary to mercy or pity, then mercy or pity cannot be praiseworthy – and so it must not be a virtue.

Objection 3. [1] *Further, joy and peace are not special virtues* [2] *because they result from charity, as stated above (28, 4; 29, 4).* [3] *Now mercy, also, results from charity; for it is out of charity that we weep with them that weep, as we rejoice with them that rejoice. Therefore mercy is not a special virtue.*	Objection 3. Still further, we do not classify joy and peace as distinct virtues, because they are merely consequences of the virtue of charity. But mercy is another such consequence, for it is charity which impels us to weep with those who weep and rejoice with those who rejoice. So by the same token, mercy is not a distinct virtue either.

[1] To say that joy and peace are not "special" virtues is to say that they are not distinct *species* of virtue. The Objector hopes to show that mercy is not a distinct species of virtue either. Unlike the previous two Objectors, his object is not to deny that acts of mercy are *virtuous*, but to deny that rather to deny that mercy is a *distinct virtue*.

[2] In its proper sense, charity is the friendship of man with God, founded on the love which desires to repose in His goodness, a love inseparable from love of one's neighbors, who are made in God's image. Because joy is the mind's delight in any present good, but especially in God Himself, whoever has charity has joy. Because peace includes concord with one's neighbors,[12] whoever is in charity with them also has peace. So rather than being distinct species of virtue, joy and peace are merely effects, or overflows, of the virtue of charity.

[3] The Objector is reasoning by analogy: If the fact that joy and peace result from charity is a sufficient reason to deny that joy and peace are distinct virtues, then the fact that mercy results from charity is a sufficient reason to deny that mercy is a distinct virtue. Thus, if St. Thomas chooses to defend the tradition, he will have to break the analogy. The most straightforward way to do this would be to deny the *sufficiency* of this reason, and argue that some

---

[10] Ibid.
[11] See Thomas Aquinas, *Disputed Questions on Truth*, Q. 17, Art. 5, trans. James V. McGlynn (available at www.dhspriory.org/thomas/QDdeVer17.htm).
[12] See II-II, Q. 29, Art. 1.

other factor must also be considered. As we see in the Reply, that is exactly what he does.

Objection 4. [1] *Further, since mercy belongs to the appetitive power, it is not an intellectual virtue,* [2] *and, since it has not God for its object, neither is it a theological virtue.* [3] *Moreover it is not a moral virtue, because neither is it about operations, for this belongs to justice;* [4] *nor is it about passions, since it is not reduced to one of the twelve means mentioned by the Philosopher (Ethic. ii, 7).* [5] *Therefore mercy is not a virtue.*	**Objection 4.** Besides: Mercy is not an intellectual virtue because it pertains our desires and aversions; it is not a theological virtue because it does not direct us to God; it is not the sort of moral virtue that justice is, because it does not regulate the form of moral deeds; and it is not the sort of moral virtue that moderates the passions, because it does not fall into any of the twelve categories discussed by Aristotle. Therefore it is not a virtue at all.

[1] Could mercy be an *intellectual* virtue? According to the Objector, no, because mercy pertains to the appetites, not to the power of reasoning. For in II-II, Question 30, Article 1, St. Thomas had argued that since mercy concerns the misery of one's neighbor, its motive is "anything contrary to the will's natural appetite, namely corruptive or distressing evils, the contrary of which man desires naturally."

[2] Could mercy be a theological virtue? No again, says the Objector, for in this case it would have God as its object – it would concern God's misery. But the divine nature, which is eternally perfect, cannot suffer misery.[13]

[3] Could mercy be the sort of virtue which brings "operations," or deeds, under the direction of reason? No again, says the Objector. His wording is admittedly confusing, but the point is straightforward. Although in the other moral virtues the mean lies between opposite extremes of *passion*, in justice the mean lies between opposite extremes of *actions* – for justice lies in giving to others what they deserve, and one may miss the mark by giving either too little or too much. Of course, I may experience delight in acting justly, and in order give you what is due to you I must quell any passion which makes me desire not to do so. However, *what in fact is due to you* does not depend on my interior condition, and there are no special passions which correspond to the extremes which the mean of justice achieves. Given this understanding of justice, it seems to the Objector that mercy cannot pertain to justice, because in cases where someone deserves punishment, it gives too little; it involves *remitting* some of the punishment that is due.[14]

---

[13] Although Christians believe that Christ, the God-Man, suffered, He suffered in his human nature, not in His divine nature. He is not Man alone, God alone, or partly Man and partly God, but *fully* Man and *fully* God, two natures in one Person.

[14] See I-II, Q. 59, Art. 5.

[4] Could mercy be the sort of virtue that *does* seek the mean between extremes of passion? Once more the Objector says no. For in the *Nicomachean Ethics*, Books 2, Chapter 7, Aristotle identifies twelve such means, but as we see from the following list, mercy does not correspond to any of them:

1. With regard to feelings of fear and confidence, the mean is fortitude.
2. With regard to pleasures and pains, temperance.
3. With regard to giving and taking of money, liberality or generosity.
4. With regard to giving and taking of money on a grand scale, magnificence.
5. With regard to honor and dishonor for great deeds, magnanimity.
6. With regard to ordinary honor and dishonor, temperate desire for recognition.
7. With regard to anger, good temper.
8. With regard to the truth about one's self, the frankness which lies between mock-modesty and boastfulness.
9. With regard to one aspect of pleasantness in social life, tactful wittiness.
10. With regard to another aspect, amiability.
11. With regard to shame, modesty.
12. With regard to indignation, pain at the *undeserved* reward (or suffering) of another.

We must remember that neither Aristotle nor St. Thomas thinks every passion fits under the formula that virtue lies in a mean. For instance, there is no right amount or right occasion for envy, which is sorrow *just because* someone enjoys reward, or for spitefulness, which is delight *just because* someone suffers.[15]

[5] If mercy is neither an intellectual virtue, like prudence, nor a theological virtue, like charity, nor the sort of moral virtue that justice is, nor the sort of moral virtue that temperance and fortitude are, then what is left? Nothing, says the Objector; those are the only kinds of virtue that there are. So mercy is not a virtue.

| On the contrary, [1] *Augustine says (De Civ. Dei ix, 5):* [2] *"Cicero in praising Caesar expresses himself much better and in a fashion at once more humane and more in accordance with religious feeling, when he says: 'Of all thy virtues none is more marvelous or more graceful than thy mercy.'" Therefore mercy is a virtue.* | On the other hand, the traditional view is well represented by St. Augustine, when he writes, "Cicero, in lauding Caesar, speaks [of mercy] much more suitably, humanely, and reverently [than the Stoics do], saying, 'Of all your virtues, none is more admirable or graceful than your mercy." |

[15] See Aristotle, *Nicomachean Ethics*, Book 2, Chapter 6.

[1] St. Thomas is exactly quoting St. Augustine, who is *almost* exactly quoting Cicero's speech "For Ligarius."[16] Augustine is not expressing any view at all concerning Cicero's flattery of Caesar; he is interested solely in Cicero's praise of mercy.

[2] Not just for its praise of mercy, but for its view of the passions in general, the context of St. Augustine's remark is worth reproducing at some length. Having just criticized the Stoic view of the passions, he goes on to explain that:[17]

[The Christian doctrine of the passions] subjects the mind itself to God, that He may rule and aid it, and the passions, again, to the mind, to moderate and bridle them, and turn them to righteous uses. In our ethics, we do not so much inquire whether a pious soul is angry, as why he is angry; not whether he is sad, but what is the cause of his sadness; not whether he fears, but what he fears. For I am not aware that any right thinking person would find fault with anger at a wrongdoer which seeks his amendment, or with sadness which intends relief to the suffering, or with fear lest one in danger be destroyed. The Stoics, indeed, are accustomed to condemn compassion. But how much more honorable had it been in that Stoic we have been telling of, had he been disturbed by compassion prompting him to relieve a fellow-creature, than to be disturbed by the fear of shipwreck!

Now comes the portion from which St. Thomas quotes. He uses the first of the following three sentences here, in the *sed contra*, and he uses the third, as we will see, in the *respondeo*:

Far better and more humane, and more consonant with pious sentiments, are the words of Cicero in praise of Caesar, when he says, "Among your virtues none is more admirable and agreeable than your compassion." And what is compassion but a fellow-feeling for another's misery, which prompts us to help him if we can? And this emotion is obedient to reason, when compassion is shown without violating right, as when the poor are relieved, or the penitent forgiven.

St. Augustine goes on to criticize the Stoics, who argue, like Objector 1, that mercy is a passion inimical to virtue, even though they admit that it is present in the soul of the virtuous man:

Cicero, who knew how to use language, did not hesitate to call this a virtue, which the Stoics are not ashamed to reckon among the vices, although, as the book of the eminent Stoic, Epictetus, quoting the opinions of Zeno and Chrysippus, the founders of the school, has taught us, they admit that passions of this kind invade the soul of the wise man, whom they would have to be free from all vice. Whence it follows that these very passions are not judged by them to be vices, since they assail the wise man

---

[16] The only difference is that Cicero speaks of Caesar's "many" virtues. Whether because he overlooks it, or because he finds it a little too fulsome, St. Augustine drops the adjective. For the Latin text of Cicero's speech, see www.thelatinlibrary.com/cicero/lig.shtml; the quotation is from Section 37.

[17] Augustine of Hippo, *City of God Against the Pagans*, trans. Marcus Dods (public domain), Book 9, Chapter 5, available online at. http://newadvent.org/fathers/1201.htm

without forcing him to act against reason and virtue; and that, therefore, the opinion of the Peripatetics or Platonists and of the Stoics is one and the same.

I answer that, [1] *Mercy signifies grief for another's distress. Now this grief may denote, in one way, a movement of the sensitive appetite, in which case mercy is not a virtue but a passion; whereas, in another way, it may denote a movement of the intellective appetite, in as much as one person's evil is displeasing to another.* [2] *This movement may be ruled in accordance with reason, and in accordance with this movement regulated by reason, the movement of the lower appetite may be regulated.* [3] *Hence Augustine says (De Civ. Dei ix, 5) that "this movement of the mind" (viz. mercy) "obeys the reason, when mercy is vouchsafed in such a way that justice is safeguarded, whether we give to the needy or forgive the repentant."* [4] *And since it is essential to human virtue that the movements of the soul should be regulated by reason, as was shown above (I-II, 59, A4,5), it follows that mercy is a virtue.*	**Here is my response.** The word "mercy" conveys sorrow for someone else's misery, but this sorrow may be taken in two different senses. If we mean merely that our feelings are stirred up, then we are not speaking of a virtue, but of a passion. But we may also mean that in beholding another person suffering evil our *mind* is displeased, and that as a result, our passions, or lower appetites, are brought in line with reason's requirements. Explaining what these requirements of the mind are, St. Augustine says that no matter whether we are relieving those who are poor or pardoning those who are penitent, the mental processes of mercy serve reason precisely when they conserve justice. And since, as we have been arguing, the very idea of human virtue is that the soul be under reason's direction, it follows that mercy is a virtue.

[1] The distinction St. Thomas is making here is often difficult for readers in our own day to grasp, because of the influence upon us of thinkers like David Hume, who famously wrote as follows:

Reason is, and ought only to be the slave of the passions, and can never pretend to any other office than to serve and obey them.... A passion is an original existence, or, if you will, modification of existence, and contains not any representative quality, which renders it a copy of any other existence or modification. When I am angry, I am actually possessed with the passion, and in that emotion have no more a reference to any other object, than when I am thirsty, or sick, or more than five foot high. It is impossible, therefore, that this passion can be opposed by, or be contradictory to truth and reason; since this contradiction consists in the disagreement of ideas, considered as copies, with those objects, which they represent.... It is not contrary to reason to prefer the destruction of the whole world to the scratching of my finger. It is not contrary to reason for me to choose my total ruin, to prevent the least uneasiness of an Indian or person wholly unknown to me. It is as little contrary to reason to prefer even my own acknowledged lesser good to my greater, and have a more ardent affection for the former than the latter.[18]

[18] David Hume, *Treatise on Human Nature*, Book 2, Chapter 3, Section 3.

St. Thomas views passion not as an "original" existence, but as a response of the sensitive appetite to something which seems good or bad to it. But that is not the end of the matter, for now the mind must consider the matter and decide what response is rationally appropriate. What it wills *as a result* of its consideration is not sensitive appetite, but *rational* appetite: "Now reason directs, not only the passions of the sensitive appetite, but also the operations of the intellective appetite, i.e. the will, which is not the subject of a passion."[19]

Unfortunately, Hume ignores this distinction, tendentiously using the word "passion" for all desire whatsoever, whether sensitive or rational. In this sense, certainly reason is the slave of the passions, but the claim has become empty. It is like saying "rational impulses are always in accord with either rational or sub-rational impulses."

[2] Sensitive appetite can and should coincide with rational appetite, although it may not. Suppose, for example, that my sorrow for a convicted criminal is so great that I feel like letting him go. My mind, recognizing that he needs and deserves to be punished, sets aside the feeling and judges that he should be sentenced to imprisonment. On the other hand, suppose my compassion is so weak that I feel indifferent to the prisoner's suffering, saying to myself "Let him rot." My mind reflects that the ruin of a soul is a terrible thing, so I set aside the feeling and visit him in prison.

In the former case, my mind may even counsel me to moderate my excessive sympathy. In the latter case, it may encourage me to try to feel more compassionate than I do. So sensitive and rational appetite do interact – St. Thomas not only admits but insists on the point. But except in the case of weak-willed persons, this does not make the mind "a slave of the passions."

[3] We have already encountered this quotation (with slightly different wording) in our discussion of the *sed contra*. What remains is to explain how it may be accordance with reason to give to the needy and forgive the penitent. The former case is easy; not only in love but in justice, we owe succor to those who suffer undeservedly. The latter case is difficult, because not only does forgiveness indicate the restoration of fellowship with the wrongdoer, but it *may* even involve remission of deserved punishment. Isn't this falling away from justice, which requires giving each person what is due to him, honor for good, penalty for evil?

If we consider *how punishment serves* justice, the answer is no, forgiveness is not necessarily contrary to it. Both human and divine justice require punishment for the same three reasons:[20]

1. To correct the wrongdoer himself, "since the very fact that man endures toil and loss in sinning, is of a nature to withdraw man from sin."
2. To correct others, "who seeing some men fall from sin to sin, are the more fearful of sinning."

[19] I-II, Q. 59, Art. 4.
[20] For the following quotations, see I-II, Q. 87, Art. 2, ad 1, and II-II, Q. 67, Art. 4, ad 3.

3. To relieve the person whom the wrongdoer has injured, "who is compensated by having his honor restored in the punishment of the man who has injured him."

It follows that with although deserved punishment may not be lessened indiscriminately, it may be lessened, with no falling away from justice, just to the degree that it does not impair these three purposes. To be sure, one must never punish the wrongdoer *more* than he deserves, not even to correct him, to correct others, or to relieve the person whom he has injured; but if the three conditions have been satisfied, then one may punish him less.

On the part of the human judge, then, the three conditions for mercy – for giving the wrong does *less* than he deserves – would seem to be as follows:

1. The judge must have well-grounded confidence that the wrongdoer has in fact been corrected.
2. He must have good reason to believe that lessening the wrongdoer's punishment will not shock the community into carelessness about wrongdoing.
3. He must make sure that lessening the punishment will not make a mockery of the person who has been injured by treating the injury as though it did not matter.

Since mercy concerns not only the wrongdoer, but also the person whom he has injured and the community whose moral order has been disturbed, all three conditions must be satisfied. Depending on the degree to which they are satisfied or not satisfied, one may remit deserved punishment, decline to remit it, or remit part but not all of it.

Of God's own mercy, St. Thomas writes,

God acts mercifully, not indeed by going against His justice, but by doing something more than justice; thus a man who pays another two hundred pieces of money, though owing him only one hundred, does nothing against justice, but acts liberally or mercifully. The case is the same with one who pardons an offence committed against him, for in remitting it he may be said to bestow a gift. Hence the Apostle [St. Paul] calls remission a forgiving: "Forgive one another, as Christ has forgiven you" (Ephesians 4:32). Hence it is clear that mercy does not destroy justice, but in a sense is the fulness thereof. And thus it is said: "Mercy exalteth itself above judgment" (James 2:13).[21]

Indeed, so far is God's mercy from contradicting His justice that even when God punishes, His justice *presupposes* His mercy. We could not even speak of what we deserve unless we had already, beyond all desert, been created as moral beings capable of desert. What is "due" to us in one sense depends *just on the kind of beings God has made us*, and exceeds what we deserve by our deeds. The passage in which St. Thomas explains this point begs to be quoted in full:

[21] I, Q. 21, Art. 3, ad 2.

Mercy and truth are necessarily found in all God's works, if mercy be taken to mean the removal of any kind of defect. Not every defect, however, can properly be called a misery; but only defect in a rational nature whose lot is to be happy; for misery is opposed to happiness. For this necessity there is a reason, because since a debt paid according to the divine justice is one due either to God, or to some creature, neither the one nor the other can be lacking in any work of God: because God can do nothing that is not in accord with His wisdom and goodness; and it is in this sense, as we have said, that anything is due to God. Likewise, whatever is done by Him in created things, is done according to proper order and proportion wherein consists the idea of justice. Thus justice must exist in all God's works. Now the work of divine justice always presupposes the work of mercy; and is founded thereupon. For nothing is due to creatures, except for something pre-existing in them, or foreknown. Again, if this is due to a creature, it must be due on account of something that precedes. And since we cannot go on to infinity, we must come to something that depends only on the goodness of the divine will—which is the ultimate end. We may say, for instance, that to possess hands is due to man on account of his rational soul; and his rational soul is due to him that he may be man; and his being man is on account of the divine goodness. So in every work of God, viewed at its primary source, there appears mercy. In all that follows, the power of mercy remains, and works indeed with even greater force; as the influence of the first cause is more intense than that of second causes. For this reason does God out of abundance of His goodness bestow upon creatures what is due to them more bountifully than is proportionate to their deserts: since less would suffice for preserving the order of justice than what the divine goodness confers; because between creatures and God's goodness there can be no proportion.[22]

As he later summarizes, "the effect of the divine mercy is the foundation of all the divine works. For nothing is due to anyone, except on account of something already given him gratuitously by God. In this way the divine omnipotence is particularly made manifest, because to it pertains the first foundation of all good things."[23]

[4] Mercy in the sense of *mere passion* is *not* a virtue, but mercy in the sense of the habitual disposition to succor others in accordance with reason *is* a virtue. This important distinction figures into the reply to several of the Objections.

| Reply to Objection 1. *The words of Sallust are to be understood as applying to the mercy which is a passion unregulated by reason: for thus it impedes the counselling of reason, by making it wander from justice.* | Reply to Objection 1. The words which Sallust quotes are not about mercy in the second sense, but in the first – they refer to a sheer passion, unregulated by reason. *In that sense* mercy does interfere with reason's deliberation, pushing it from the path of justice, but in the proper sense it does not. |

Although, as we have seen in the *respondeo*, the virtue of mercy is not the same as the sheer passion of mercy, virtue does require that the passions be trained to cooperate. Thus St. Thomas writes:

---

[22] I, Q. 21, Art. 4.   [23] I-II, Q. 25, Art. 3, ad 3.

Moral virtues, which are about the passions as about their proper matter, cannot be without passions. The reason for this is that otherwise it would follow that moral virtue makes the sensitive appetite altogether idle: whereas it is not the function of virtue to deprive the powers subordinate to reason of their proper activities, but to make them execute the commands of reason, by exercising their proper acts.[24]

So although undisciplined passions do hinder counsel, just as the Objector fears, trained and moderated passions do reason's bidding. We might compare them with a spirited horse which is eager to run at the direction of its rider.

Reply to Objection 2. [1] *The Philosopher is speaking there of pity and nemesis, considered, both of them, as passions.* [2] *They are contrary to one another on the part of their respective estimation of another's evils, for which pity grieves, in so far as it esteems someone to suffer undeservedly, whereas nemesis rejoices, in so far as it esteems someone to suffer deservedly, and grieves, if things go well with the undeserving:* [3] *"both of these are praiseworthy and come from the same disposition of character" (Rhet. ii, 9).* [4] *Properly speaking, however, it is envy which is opposed to pity, as we shall state further on (36, 3).*	Reply to Objection 2. In the passage to which the Objector refers, Aristotle is viewing both mercy and nemesis, or indignation, merely as passions. These passions are certainly opposed to each other in one sense, for they arise in response to different views of the evil another person is suffering. Mercy sorrows, so far as it views suffering as undeserved; nemesis rejoices, so far as it views suffering as deserved; and nemesis sorrows, so far as it views good fortune as undeserved. But in another sense, he says the two passions are not opposed, for they are both praiseworthy and they both arise from the same moral character. So the Objector has got all this wrong. However, we view the relation of mercy to its opposite somewhat differently than Aristotle does. Strictly speaking, the opposite of mercy is not indignation, but envy – a point we will explain later on.

[1] St. Thomas seems to consider the inference to be drawn from this comment too obvious to state. His point is that although the passions of mercy and indignation oppose each other, it does not follow that the virtues which moderate and discipline these passions oppose each other.

[2] Sorrowing *as such* is opposed to rejoicing *as such*, but grieving over *undeserved* suffering is in no way opposed to rejoicing over *deserved* suffering, nor is rejoicing over the *relief* of undeserved suffering opposed to sorrowing over the *relief* of deserved suffering. We may add that rejoicing over deserved suffering when the conditions for mercy are *not* satisfied is fully compatible with grieving that mercy has been denied when the conditions for mercy *are* satisfied. All these things are compatible with virtue; virtue may even command them.

---

[24] I-II, Q. 59, Art. 5.

The tenderhearted may protest that we should not rejoice *even over deserved suffering*. But surely a distinction is needed here. Certainly we should rejoice over the fact *that justice has been done*.

> Those moral virtues ... which are not about the passions, but about operations, can be without passions. Such a virtue is justice: because it applies the will to its proper act, which is not a passion. Nevertheless, joy results from the act of justice; at least in the will, in which case it is not a passion. And if this joy be increased through the perfection of justice, it will overflow into the sensitive appetite; in so far as the lower powers follow the movement of the higher. Wherefore by reason of this kind of overflow, the more perfect a virtue is, the more does it cause passion.[25]

But we should not rejoice that the wrongdoer has done something deserving of punishment, nor should we rejoice that the conditions for mercy have so far not been met. Rather we should hope for the wrongdoer's amendment, so long as it remains possible. Among other things, justice is a means to bring his amendment about.

We may also reflect that what we know or do not know about what happens after this life makes a difference to the prospects of moderating *nemesis*. In St. Thomas's view, although the duties of earthly judges are very grave, final judgment belongs to God, for even someone who slips the net of temporal justice will have to answer to eternal justice. Although this does not make a difference to the punishment which is due to the wrongdoer, it certainly makes it easier for us humans to keep reason from being overwhelmed by rage and despair if we have been unable to pin the crime on him.

[3] Aristotle writes, "Both feelings [pity and *nemesis*] are associated with good moral character; it is our duty both to feel sympathy and pity for unmerited distress, and to feel indignation at unmerited prosperity; for whatever is undeserved is unjust, and that is why we ascribe indignation even to the gods."[26]

[4] St. Thomas has already answered the Objector; now he promises an extra. For if mercy is a virtue, and each virtue is opposed by various vices, but in each such case one vice is chief, then of course we will want to know by what vice mercy is chiefly opposed. The answer isn't *nemesis*, so what is it? The answer is envy, which rejoices not in my neighbor's good but in his evil, not because he deserves punishment but merely because he is not me.

Aristotle had written that although it might be thought that envy is opposed to pity *in the same way* as indignation is opposed to it, actually they are opposed to it in different ways.[27] In II-II, Q. 36, Art. 3, ad 3, St. Thomas elaborates:

---

[25] I-II, Q. 59, Art. 5.

[26] Aristotle, *Rhetoric*, trans. W. Rhys Roberts (public domain), Book 2, Chapter 9.

[27] "It might indeed be thought that envy is similarly opposed to pity, on the ground that envy is closely akin to indignation, or even the same thing. But it is not the same. It is true that it also is a disturbing pain excited by the prosperity of others. But it is excited not by the prosperity of the undeserving but by that of people who are like us or equal with us." Ibid., Book 2, Chapter 9.

According to the Philosopher, envy is contrary both to nemesis and to pity, but for different reasons. For it is directly contrary to pity, their principal objects being contrary to one another, since the envious man grieves over his neighbor's good, whereas the pitiful man grieves over his neighbor's evil, so that the envious have no pity, as he states in the same passage, nor is the pitiful man envious. On the other hand, envy is contrary to nemesis on the part of the man whose good grieves the envious man, for nemesis is sorrow for the good of the undeserving according to Psalm 72:3: "I was envious of the wicked, when I saw the prosperity of sinners,"[28] whereas the envious grieves over the good of those who are deserving of it. Hence it is clear that the former contrariety is more direct than the latter. Now pity is a virtue, and an effect proper to charity: so that envy is contrary to pity and charity.

Reply to Objection 3. [1] *Joy and peace add nothing to the aspect of good which is the object of charity, wherefore they do not require any other virtue besides charity.* [2] *But mercy regards a certain special aspect, namely the misery of the person pitied.*	Reply to Objection 3. Since joy and peace do not further specify the good of fellowship with God at which charity aims, they depend on the virtue of charity alone. But mercy does further specify this good – and therefore, it is appropriately considered a virtue – for it is concerned specifically with the suffering of the person for whom our hearts are grieved.

[1] Prudence, fortitude, temperance, justice, faith, hope, and charity can be thought of as compendium virtues, for each of them has many "parts" or subordinate virtues. The question here is whether joy, peace, and mercy are parts of charity. As to joy and peace, the answer is no. Certainly they *result* from charity, but neither of them designates a particular mode in which acts of charity may be carried out. We remember that the Objector thinks the same is true of mercy.

[2] But the Objector is mistaken. By contrast with joy and peace, mercy does designate a particular mode in which acts of charity may be carried out. It is the mode in which charity works when it acts to relieve the suffering of others. Therefore, mercy is one of the subordinate virtues corresponding to the chief virtue of charity.

Reply to Objection 4. [1] *Mercy, considered as a virtue, is a moral virtue having relation to the passions, and it is reduced to the mean called nemesis, because "they both proceed from the same character" (Rhet. ii, 9).* [2] *Now the Philosopher proposes these means*	Reply to Objection 4. Viewed as a virtue rather than as a passion, mercy is a moral virtue because it regulates passions; nemesis is but a name for the mean which it achieves. That is why Aristotle says that mercy and nemesis arise from the same moral character. True, even though Aristotle considers nemesis praiseworthy,

[28] Vulgate, *quia zelavi super iniquis pacem peccatorum videns*; DRA, "Because I had a zeal on occasion of the wicked, seeing the prosperity of sinners."

| *not as virtues, but as passions, because, even as passions, they are praiseworthy. Yet nothing prevents them from proceeding from some elective habit, in which case they assume the character of a virtue.* | he describes it as a passion, not a virtue. Even so, if through repeated choices we have disciplined ourselves so that we habitually achieve the mean of this passion, then this acquired disposition is a virtue. |

[1] Like other moral virtues, mercy is a mean between two opposite vices. In one direction we find the vice of angry grief over my neighbor's deserved good, which is envy. In the other we find the vice of failing to grieve over my neighbor's undeserved good. It may seem strange to think of mercy and indignation as connected, but a merciful person does feel proper indignation. On one hand, he is indignant over undeserved suffering – "He shouldn't have to suffer!" – so he comes to the aid of the sick and defends those who are persecuted for doing good. On the other, he is indignant over undeserved prosperity – "He shouldn't be rewarded for that!" – so he tries to make sure that merit is honored, the dishonorable is not honored, and wrongdoers do not profit from their crimes.

[2] To understand St. Thomas's point, we must bear in mind that there are two related means, not just one. In the first place there is a mean of *passion:* I must neither feel what I should not feel, nor fail to feel what I should feel. In the second place there is a mean of *deliberate choice:* I must neither do what I should not do, nor fail to do what I should do. St. Thomas, then, is pointing out that when Aristotle speaks of *nemesis* or indignation as a mean, he is viewing it as a mean of passion. Taken this way, even though it is good, it is not strictly speaking a virtue. Yet the fact that Aristotle himself views *nemesis* as a mean of passion does not prevent *us* from viewing mercy as the associated mean of deliberate choice. Mercy, in this sense, *is* a virtue. Hence, the Objection is defeated.

Whether Justice Is Fittingly Defined as Being the Perpetual and Constant Will to Render to Each One His Right?

TEXT	PARAPHRASE
Whether justice is fittingly defined as being the perpetual and constant will to render to each one his right?	According to a classical definition, justice is "a constant and perpetual will to give to each person his right." Does this time-honored formula suitably express the essence of justice?

In Latin, the words *justice* and *right* are very similar – respectively, *iustitia* and *ius* – allowing plays on words which are difficult in in English unless we translate *iustitia* as "righteousness," as the older writers did. We might paraphrase the definition by saying that justice, or righteousness, is a constant and perpetual will to give each person *what it is right to give him*, for his right is what is his, what he deserves, what is properly due to him. This fact is important to bear in mind, because in our day, the expression "right" is most often used in a different sense, one which indicates a liberty to do something – for example the right to bear arms, to speak freely, or to worship according to conscience. Giving a person his right may *include* respecting his proper liberties, but the idea is much broader.

Although the definition echoes much earlier authorities, its particular words come down to us from Ulpian, one of the most famous of the Roman jurisconsults, whose words are quoted in the *Digest*, or *Pandects* – one of the four parts of the *Corpus Iuris Civilis*, prepared under the supervision of Tribonius at the instruction of the emperor Justinian with the aim of harmonizing the sprawling mass of Roman law. In context, the passage runs as follows:

Justice is a steady and enduring will to render unto everyone his right. 1. The basic principles of right are: to live honorably, not to harm any other person, to render to each his own. 2. Practical wisdom in matters of right is an awareness of God's and men's affairs, knowledge of justice and injustice.[1]

Down the long centuries, this definition has had a profound and stabilizing influence on Western jurisprudence. It enters English-speaking jurisprudence largely through the great work of St. Thomas's contemporary, Henry de Bracton, *On the Laws and Customs of England.*

Each of the six Objections targets some element in the definition. Objections 1 and 2 deny that justice "a will"; Objection 3 denies that it is "perpetual"; Objection 4, that it is both "perpetual" *and* "constant" as though these were different qualities; and Objections 5 and 6, that it "renders to each one his right."

Objection 1. [1] *It would seem that lawyers* [2] *have unfittingly defined justice as being "the perpetual and constant will to render to each one his right"* [Digest. i, 1; De Just. et Jure 10. *For, according to the Philosopher* (Ethic. v, 1), *justice is a habit which makes a man "capable of doing what is just, and of being just in action and in intention."* [3] *Now "will" denotes a power, or also an act. Therefore justice is unfittingly defined as being a will.*	Objection 1. This definition of justice, drawn from ancient legal authorities, seems unsuitable. As Aristotle explains, justice is a *disposition or habit* by which the just man both does what is just, and is himself just, both in his deeds and his intentions. But the term "will," in the definition, denotes either a *power* or an *act.* So at least in this respect, the definition is defective.

[1] "Lawyers" is incorrect; the Latin expression *iusisperiti* refers to legal authorities, especially the jurisconsults consulted in the composition of the *Digest.* Elsewhere in the *Summa* the term is usually translated "jurists."

[2] Aristotle says "We see that all men mean by [the virtue of] justice that kind of state of character which makes people disposed to do what is just and makes them act justly and wish for what is just; and similarly by [the vice of] injustice that state which makes them act unjustly and wish for what is unjust."

[3] The Objector suggests that if the virtue of justice lies in the *will* to do something, then it is either the act of willing something, or the power or capacity to will it. But this cannot be the case, he holds, because a virtue is neither an act nor a power, but a "habit" or disposition.

[1] Alan Watson, ed., *The Digest of Justinian*, rev. ed., vol. 1 (Philadelphia: University of Pennsylvania Press, 1998), p. 2. The translator of the passage I am quoting (in the system of the *Digest* itself, Book 1, Title 1, Section 10) is Geoffrey MacCormack. In Latin, the passage reads *Iustitia est constans et perpetua voluntas ius suum cuique tribuendi. Iuris praecepta sunt haec: honeste vivere, alterum non laedere, suum cuique tribuere. Iuris prudentia est divinarum atque humanarum rerum notitia, iusti atque iniusti scientia.*

| *Objection 2.* [1] *Further, rectitude of the will is not the will; else if the will were its own rectitude, it would follow that no will is unrighteous.* [2] *Yet, according to Anselm (De Veritate xii), justice is rectitude. Therefore justice is not the will.* | Objection 2. Moreover, as Anselm points out, justice is rectitude – that is, rectitude of the will. But the rectitude of the will is not the same as the will itself; if it were, then every will would be just, which is absurd. So justice is not the will, and in this respect too, the formula is inadequate. |

[1] The traditional formula defines justice as a will. But according to another definition, justice is not the will *per se*, but a certain quality which some wills have and others do not – rectitude for its own sake.

One might suggest that the Objector is merely being quarrelsome, for the traditional definition of justice does not identify justice with the will *per se*, but with a certain *kind* of will. Viewing it this way, the two definitions might seem to be the same; that is, it may seem that a perpetual and constant will to give each person his right *simply is* a will characterized by rectitude. Surprisingly – as we will see in his Reply – St. Thomas does not even concede this much.

[2] The definition the Objector prefers is found in the dialogue *On Truth*, by Anselm of Canterbury:

TEACHER: As I see it, you are asking for a definition of that justice which is praiseworthy, even as its opposite, viz., injustice, is blameworthy.

STUDENT: That's the justice I am seeking.

TEACHER: It is evident that this justice is not in any nature which does not know rightness. For whatever does not will rightness does not merit to be praised for having it, even if it does have it. But that which does not know rightness is not able to will it.

STUDENT: That's true.

TEACHER: Therefore, the rightness which brings praise to a thing which has rightness is present only in a rational nature, which alone perceives the rightness we are talking about.

STUDENT: It follows.

TEACHER: Therefore, since all justice is rightness, the justice which makes the one who keeps it worthy of praise is present only in rational natures.

STUDENT: It cannot be otherwise.

TEACHER: Then where do you think this justice is to be found in man, who is rational?

STUDENT: It is nowhere except either in his will or in his knowledge or in his action.

TEACHER: What if someone understands rightly or acts rightly but does not will rightly: will anyone praise him on account of justice?

STUDENT: No.

TEACHER: Therefore, this justice is not rightness of knowledge or rightness of action but is rightness [rectitudo] of will.

* * *

STUDENT: When a just man wills what he ought, then – insofar as he is to be called just – he keeps uprightness-of-will only for its own sake. By contrast, someone who wills what he ought to will but does so only if compelled to or only if induced by external rewards, does not keep uprightness-of-will for its own sake but keeps it for the sake of something else – if he should at all be said to keep it.

TEACHER: Then, that will is just which keeps its uprightness on account of that uprightness itself.

STUDENT: Either that will is just or no will is.

TEACHER: Therefore, justice is uprightness-of-will kept for its own sake.

STUDENT: Yes, this is the definition of "justice" I was seeking.[2]

Objection 3. Further, no will is perpetual save God's. If therefore justice is a perpetual will, in God alone will there be justice.	Objection 3. Still further, although the formula defines justice as a *perpetual* will, only God's will is perpetual. So if justice is a *perpetual* will, only God can be just, which seems incorrect.

With the tacit premise reinserted, the argument works like this:

1. Only God is eternal.
2. Therefore only God's will is perpetual.
3. But justice is a perpetual will.
4. Therefore only God can be just.

Because the conclusion is implausible, the Objector rejects the premise expressed in line 3.

Objection 4. Further, whatever is perpetual is constant, since it is unchangeable. Therefore it is needless in defining justice, to say that it is both "perpetual" and "constant."	Objection 4. We may also point out that since whatever is perpetual is unchangeable, it must also be constant; the two words mean the same thing. Therefore, to define justice as something *both* perpetual *and* constant, as though the two words had different meanings, is inappropriate.

The Objector's tacit criterion for a fitting definition is that every word in it should have a distinct meaning; there should be nothing superfluous. Thus, if justice is said to be both perpetual and constant, perpetuity and constancy should be different things. Unfortunately, he protests, they aren't.

Lawyers and judges employ a similar criterion for construing the meaning of statutes, but with a difference. Whenever they examine a statute, they assume that it *is* suitably drafted, so every word in it *must* have a distinct meaning. If

---

[2] Anselm of Canterbury, *On Truth*, Section 12, in *Complete Philosophical and Theological Treatises*, trans. Jasper Hopkins and Herbert Richardson (Minneapolis, MN: Arthur J. Banning Press, 2000), pp. 182–184.

the Objector were to proceed in this way, then instead of protesting that perpetuity and constancy mean the same thing, he would try to work out how their meanings are different. As we will see in the Reply, this is very much what St. Thomas does.

Objection 5. [1] *Further, it belongs to the sovereign to give each one his right.* [2] *Therefore, if justice gives each one his right, it follows that it is in none but the sovereign: which is absurd.*	Objection 5. Yet again, the one who "gives to each person his right" is the magistrate. So if the definition of justice really were to give each person his right, then only a magistrate could be just, and this is absurd.

[1] To render the Latin word *principem* as "sovereign" in this context is entirely too strong; "magistrate" or "public official" is quite sufficient. Literally, the term means someone who is foremost in position or honor. In Roman republican times, it was applied to a senior senator – to one of the *maiores* or "great men." Much later it was applied to the emperors, who came to call themselves "living law." However, both in the Reply and in other places in the *Summa*, St. Thomas applies the expression "living law" not to kings, but to judges.[3]

[2] Of course the magistrate should be just – what is absurd is that *only* the magistrate can be just. The Objector suggests that if this is the logical consequence of the traditional definition, then the tradition definition must be wrong.

Objection 6. Further, Augustine says (De Moribus Eccl. xv) that "justice is love serving God alone." Therefore it does not render to each one his right.	Objection 6. Besides, as St. Augustine says, justice is love for the service of God alone. But whatever is rendered to God *alone* is thereby withheld from others, so it cannot be correct to define justice as giving each person his right.

Actually, St. Augustine characterizes not only justice but all four of the cardinal virtues in terms of the love of God. In context, the passage which the Objector quotes runs as follows.

As to virtue leading us to a happy life, I hold virtue to be nothing else than perfect love of God. For the fourfold division of virtue I regard as taken from four forms of love. For these four virtues (would that all felt their influence in their minds as they have their names in their mouths!), I should have no hesitation in defining them: that temperance is love giving itself entirely to that which is loved; fortitude is love readily bearing all things for the sake of the loved object; justice is love serving only the loved object, and therefore ruling rightly; prudence is love distinguishing with sagacity between what

---

[3] Compare I-II, Q. 95, Art. 1, Obj. 2 and ad 2; II-II, Q. 60, Art. 1; and II-II, Q. 67, Art. 3.

hinders it and what helps it. The object of this love is not anything, but only God, the chief good, the highest wisdom, the perfect harmony. So we may express the definition thus: that temperance is love keeping itself entire and incorrupt for God; fortitude is love bearing everything readily for the sake of God; justice is love serving God only, and therefore ruling well all else, as subject to man; prudence is love making a right distinction between what helps it towards God and what might hinder it.[4]

Plainly, the justice of which St. Augustine speaks in this lovely passage is infused justice, not acquired justice. One might suppose that to show how the Objector is mistaken, it would suffice to point this fact out. As we see in the Reply, however, St. Thomas thinks the Objector has even got infused justice wrong.

On the contrary... [This section remains tacit.]	On the other hand, the definition of justice as "a constant and perpetual will to give to each person his right" is itself a testimonial of the tradition.

Since the function of the *sed contra* is to restate the traditional view, and the formula of justice into which we are looking already does that, St. Thomas does not need to compose an explicit *sed contra*. I have filled in what he might have said had he done so.

I answer that, [1] The aforesaid definition of justice is fitting if understood aright. [2] For since every virtue is a habit that is the principle of a good act, a virtue must needs be defined by means of the good act bearing on the matter proper to that virtue. [3] Now the proper matter of justice consists of those things that belong to our intercourse with other men, as shall be shown further on (2). [4] Hence the act of justice in relation to its proper matter and object is indicated in the words, "Rendering to each one his right [ius]," [5] since, as Isidore says (Etym. x), "a man is said to be just [iustus] because he respects the rights [ius] of others." [6] Now in order that an act bearing upon any matter whatever be virtuous,	Here is my response. Properly understood, the traditional definition of justice is quite adequate. Concerning justice as "giving to each person his right": Each virtue is a habit that gives rise to a particular kind of good act. Consequently, each virtue must be defined *by that kind* of good act – that is, by one having to do with the virtue's particular field of operation. As we will explain more fully later, the field of operation of justice is deeds concerning others. For this reason, in relation to its proper matter and object the act of justice is described as "giving to each person his right." Isidore has this point in mind when he remarks that a man is said to have rightness or justice (*iustus*) simply because he preserves the right or the just (*ius*).

[4] St. Augustine of Hippo, *Of the Morals of the Catholic Church*, Chapter 15, available online at www.newadvent.org/fathers/1401.htm.

it requires to be voluntary, stable, and firm, because the Philosopher says (Ethic. ii, 4) that in order for an act to be virtuous it needs first of all to be done "knowingly," secondly to be done "by choice," and "for a due end," thirdly to be done "immovably."

[7] Now the first of these is included in the second, since "what is done through ignorance is involuntary" (Ethic. iii, 1). Hence the definition of justice mentions first the "will," in order to show that the act of justice must be voluntary; [8] and mention is made afterwards of its "constancy" and "perpetuity" in order to indicate the firmness of the act.

[9] Accordingly, this is a complete definition of justice; save that the act is mentioned instead of the habit, which takes its species from that act, because habit implies relation to act. And if anyone would reduce it to the proper form of a definition, he might say that "justice is a habit whereby a man renders to each one his due by a constant and perpetual will": [10] and this is about the same definition as that given by the Philosopher (Ethic. v, 5) who says that "justice is a habit whereby a man is said to be capable of doing just actions in accordance with his choice."

Concerning justice as a "constant and perpetual will": For any act, concerning any matter, to be virtuous, it must be (1) voluntary, (2) stable, and (3) firm. Aristotle makes essentially the same point when he says that it must be done (1) with knowledge, (2) voluntarily, (3) for its own sake, and (4) unchangeably, because his second condition implies his first one – as he himself points out, nothing done without knowledge is voluntary. So the traditional definition refers to the will to indicate the act's voluntariness, and to constancy and perpetuity to indicate its firmness.

We see then that the traditional definition of justice is complete except for one thing. Since habits are identified by the acts which are associated with them, the traditional definition refers to the act of doing justice, rather than to the disposition or habit which is specified by this act. This slight deviation from the proper form of a definition is easy to fix; it would be enough to say that justice is the habit by which a man constantly and perpetually wills to give each person his right. This is very nearly how Aristotle defines justice when he calls it the habit by which a man chooses to act justly.

[1] If the traditional definition is fitting *if understood aright*, then the Objections understand it incorrectly. However, they are not straw men; each of them corresponds to what St. Thomas considers a real confusion about justice.

[2] The virtue of P is the habitual disposition to perform the act of P; thus, the virtue of justice is the habitual disposition to perform the act of justice. This is a particularly important reminder because the hypothetical Objector seems to forget that habits are defined in terms of acts.

[3] Each virtue has its own subject matter, its own sphere of action; for example, the subject matter of fortitude is fearful things, especially those posing risk of death. In the same way, the subject matter of justice is our relations with others, usually other persons. For example, it is just that customers pay bakers

what they owe them and that soldiers give obedience to the lawful commands of their officers.

St. Thomas adds in II-II, Question 58, Article 2 that at times we also speak figuratively about justice, as though the "others" were not other persons but the various other sources of action within a single person. In this sense, it is just that the heart delivers blood to the organs, and just that the appetites obey reason. In the *Nicomachean Ethics*, Book 5, Chapter 11, Aristotle called this idea "metaphorical justice." Metaphorical justice is even more prominent in Plato's *Republic*, which relies on an analogy between the soul and a city.

[4] St. Thomas has just presented a highly compressed demonstration: Justice is that which puts our relations with other persons into right order; in order to do so, it must cause us to give each person what is right to give him; *hence* this is what it does.

What then *is* the other person's right? St. Thomas has explained in II-II, Question 57, Article 1, that deeds are just when they preserve "a kind of equality" among different persons. The kind of equality he has in mind is proportional equality, for example the payment of a wage to someone in proportion to the service he has provided. What is right or due to him is what brings this kind of equality about, as determined by an act of judgment.

Of course our relations with others involve a great many things besides what is due to them, just like sailing a boat in a flotilla involves a great many things besides not colliding with the other boats. Of itself, justice regards only the right. It does not consider that if the swindler goes to prison, the world will lose a great violin player. Nor is justice the greatest virtue – charity goes far beyond it. But not even charity will permit that justice be undermined; there can be no love in violation of justice, and in this sense, justice comes first. As we see later, even mercy is reconcilable with justice. One may go above justice, but one may never go below it.

[5] In the tenth book of his *Etymologies*, or *Origins*, the great scholar Isidore of Seville had written that "justice (*iustus*) derives its name from the fact that it preserves right (*ius*) and lives according to the law." Here St. Thomas uses only the first part of the statement – that justice preserves right.[5] Later on he will discuss the relation between justice and law.

[6] St. Thomas's paraphrase of Aristotle's conditions for an act to be virtuous is terse, and the meaning of the phrase "for a due end" (*propter debitum finem*) is somewhat obscure. I take it to mean "for its own sake." Not only does this make much more sense in context, but also it squares with what St. Thomas writes in his *Commentary on Aristotle's Nicomachean Ethics*, which the translator renders as follows:

---

[5] St. Thomas: *Iustus dicitur quia ius custodit.* Isidore: *Iustus dictus quia iura custodit et secundum legem vivit.*

[Aristotle] says, therefore, in order that actions be justly and temperately performed, it is not enough that the things done be good but the agent must work in a proper manner. Regarding this manner, he says we must pay attention to three things. (1) The first, pertaining to the intellect or reason, is that one who performs a virtuous action should not act in ignorance or by chance but should know what he is doing. (2) The second is taken on the part of the appetitive power. Here two things are noted. One is that the action be not done out of passion, as happens when a person performs a virtuous deed because of fear. *But the action should be done by a choice that is not made for the sake of something else, as happens when a person performs a good action for money or vainglory. The actions should be done for the sake of the virtuous work itself which, as something agreeable, is inherently pleasing to him who has the habit of virtue.* (3) The third, taken from the nature of a habit, is that a person should possess a virtuous choice and operate according to it resolutely – that is, consistently on his part – and with stability so as not to be moved by any external thing.[6]

[7] Aristotle writes that "to distinguish the voluntary and the involuntary is presumably necessary for those who are studying the nature of virtue, and useful also for legislators with a view to the assigning both of honors and of punishments. Those things, then, are thought involuntary, which take place under compulsion or owing to ignorance; and that is compulsory of which the moving principle is outside."[7]

[8] It might be protested that St. Thomas has not yet distinguished between constancy and perpetuity, but he does this in the Reply to Objection 4.

[9] St. Thomas concedes that if the definition is taken literally, then it ought to refer not to just acts, but to the habit of performing them. But the correction of this trivial flaw requires only a minor and technical adjustment, and the triviality of the flaw is becomes even clearer in the Reply to Objection 1, where he comments on how common definitional practices are to be taken.

[10] Although Aristotle's and Ulpian's definitions are approximately equivalent, Ulpian's is a more complete and precise. First, whereas Aristotle says justice is a habit, Ulpian says it is a habit of doing something constantly and perpetually. (Though it might be protested that every habit seeks the mean constantly and perpetually, this spells it out.) Second, whereas Aristotle says it is a habit which makes a man able to choose, Ulpian says it is a habit by which a man wills, which comes to the same thing. Third, whereas Aristotle says it is a habit of performing just acts, Ulpian says it is a habit of giving each person his right, which specifies just acts more precisely.

---

[6] Thomas Aquinas, *Commentary on Aristotle's Nicomachean Ethics*, Book 2, Lecture 4, trans. C. J. Litzinger, rev. ed. (Notre Dame, IN: Dumb Ox Books, 1993), p. 97, emphasis added. Available online at www.dhspriory.org/thomas/english/Ethics.htm.

[7] Aristotle, *Nicomachean Ethics*, trans. W. D. Ross (public domain), Book 3, Chapter 1.

***Reply to Objection 1.** [1] Will here denotes the act, not the power: and it is customary among writers to define habits by their acts: [2] thus Augustine says (Tract. in Joan. xl) that "faith is to believe what one sees not."*	Reply to Objection 1. In the definition of justice, the term "will" should be taken to mean the act of willing, not the power of willing. Writers often define dispositions or habits according to the acts that are associated with them. St. Augustine provides an example of this practice when he defines the *disposition* of faith according to the *act* of believing what we do not see.
—	

[1] The argument here is highly elliptical. Elaborated more fully, it works like this:

1. Tacit premise: The Objector is right that in general, the term "will" refers to either the act of willing something or the power to will something.
2. Explicit premise: In the definition of justice, the term "will" refers to the act.
3. Another tacit premise: Moreover, the Objector is right that strictly speaking, justice is neither an act nor a power, but a habit.
4. Another explicit premise: But the Objector overlooks the common practice of defining habits *by means* of acts.
5. Conclusion: Although a literalist might fault the words of the definition of justice, taken as intended it *does* refer to the habit.

The definitional practice mentioned in point 4 employs the figure of speech in which a part represents a whole. Along with the classical writers whom he cites, St. Thomas makes frequent use of both metonymy and synecdoche – part for whole, and whole for part. I have given other examples in the *Commentary on Thomas Aquinas's Treatise on Law*:

1. Isidore sometimes uses the term "law" not for all kinds of law but for the best kind of law, the kind supremely deserving of the name.
2. St. Thomas sometimes uses the term "kingship" not for the good government of a king but for any good form of government, even a democracy.
3. According to St. Thomas, the Decalogue uses the single greatest debt to others, our debt to our parents, to represent all debts to others – indeed, justice in general – and the single greatest duty among spouses, faithfulness, to represent all aspects of marital integrity – indeed, sexual purity in general.

I emphasize this point because failure to recognize the classical figures of speech is one of the most common reasons for misinterpreting St. Thomas's writings (not to mention those of other writers).

[2] To illustrate the general principle that habits or dispositions may be defined by their characteristic acts, St. Thomas mentions the habit of faith, which is defined by the characteristic act of faith: Believing those matters which God has revealed, even though they cannot be seen with the eyes. This does not mean believing in them with no good reason; it means having confidence in

the good reasons we have to believe in them, even though these good reasons cannot be backed up by the bodily senses. (We believe in invisible things such as protons and neutrons in the same way.)

They believed, not because they knew, but that they might come to know. For we believe in order that we may know, we do not know in order that we may believe. For what we shall yet know, neither eye has seen, nor ear heard, nor has it entered the heart of man. For what is faith, but believing what you see not? Faith then is to believe what you see not; truth, to see what you have believed, as He Himself says in a certain place.[8]

By what "He Himself says in a certain place," St. Augustine probably means what the resurrected Christ says to Thomas, who had formerly been doubtful: "Have you believed because you have seen me? Blessed are those who have not seen and yet believe."[9] Compare the astonishing remark of the unknown author of the letter to the Hebrews: "Now faith is the substance [*substantia*] of things to be hoped for, the evidence [*argumentum*] of things that appear not."[10] St. Thomas comments about this passage, "faith is said to be the 'substance of things to be hoped for,' for the reason that in us the first beginning of things to be hoped for is brought about by the assent of faith, which contains virtually [*virtute*, in potentiality] all things to be hoped for."[11] In other words, faith is not merely subjective confidence in the invisible reality believed, but a foretaste of it – and this foretaste is real evidence.[12]

Before closing this digression on faith, we might also comment on St. Augustine's insight that sometimes, rather than knowing something so that one can believe it, one must believe something so that one can know it. Everyone who has ever come to love another person should understand what he is talking about. Up to a certain point, trust is not necessary to find things out about another person – but to enter into the much more intimate knowledge which the lover shares with the beloved, trust is utterly prerequisite.[13] So it is with the knowledge of God.

Reply to Objection 2. Justice is the same as rectitude, not essentially but causally; for it is a habit which rectifies the deed and the will.	Reply to Objection 2. Yes, justice is rectitude – not in the sense that rectitude is the essence of justice, but in the sense that justice brings rectitude about. It *straightens* both our deeds and our wills.

---

[8] St. Augustine of Hippo, *Tractates on the Gospel of John*, Tractate 40, available online at http://newadvent.org/fathers.

[9] John 20:29 (RSV-CE).   [10] Hebrews 11:1 (DRA).   [11] II-II, Q. 4, Art. 1.

[12] Concerning this important point, see Benedict XVI, encyclical letter *Spe Salvi* ("On Christian Hope"), Section 7.

[13] See especially I-II, Q. 32, Art. 2, ad 3, Art. 3, ad 3, and Art. 8, ad 3. For further discussion, see J. Budziszewski, *The Line through the Heart: Natural Law as Fact, Theory, and Sign of Contradiction* (Wilmington, DE: ISI Books, 2009), Chapter 4, "The Natural, the Connatural, and the Unnatural."

The Objector had taken Anselm of Canterbury to mean that justice *simply is* rightness or rectitude – that these things are essentially the same. St. Thomas disagrees. As in I-II, Question 61, Article 3, which we have discussed previously, whenever he speaks of the virtues he presents them as *causes*: The good man is good, and his actions are good, *because* he possesses the virtues which predispose him to act well. In a passage to which St. Thomas often refers,[14] Aristotle takes the same view:

> Every virtue or excellence both brings into good condition the thing of which it is the excellence and makes the work of that thing be done well; e.g. the excellence of the eye makes both the eye and its work good; for it is by the excellence of the eye that we see well. Similarly the excellence of the horse makes a horse both good in itself and good at running and at carrying its rider and at awaiting the attack of the enemy. Therefore, if this is true in every case, the virtue of man also will be the state of character which makes a man good and which makes him do his own work well.[15]

Why does this matter? Because if rightness were the *essence* of justice, as the Objector thinks, then the Objector would be correct, for no human will is *simply identical* with rightness. But if justice is what *makes* the will right, as St. Thomas maintains, then the Objector is mistaken, and the traditional definition stands.

Reply to Objection 3. [1] *The will may be called perpetual in two ways. First on the part of the will's act which endures for ever, and thus God's will alone is perpetual. Secondly on the part of the subject, because, to wit, a man wills to do a certain thing always, and this is a necessary condition of justice* [2] *For it does not satisfy the conditions of justice that one wish to observe justice in some particular matter for the time being, because one could scarcely find a man willing to act unjustly in every case; and it is requisite that one should have the will to observe justice at all times and in all cases.*	Reply to Objection 3. The will may be called "perpetual" in two senses. If we use the term to mean that the act of will has everlasting duration, then yes, only God's will may be called perpetual. But if we use the term to mean merely that a man wills to do something without ceasing, then his will may also be called perpetual. In the latter sense, perpetuity is a requirement of justice. For justice is not fulfilled merely because someone wishes to serve justice only for the hour and only in one sort of business. Indeed, it would hardly even be possible to find someone who willed to violate justice in every single case. What the virtue of justice requires is that a man wills to act justly at *all* times and *all* things.

[14] In the *Summa* alone, he mentions it at least three times in the Objections (I-II, Q. 56, Art. 1, Obj. 2; I-II, Q. 66, Art. 3, Obj. 2; and II-II, Q. 136, Art. 1, Obj. 2), three times in the *sed contra* (I-II, Q. 55, Art. 2; I-II, Q. 55, Art. 3; and II-II, Q. 157, Art. 2), and five times in the *respondeo* (I-II, Q. 99, Art. 2; II-II, Q. 47, Art. 4; II-II, Q. 81, Art. 2; II-II, Q. 109, Art. 1; and II-II, Q. 123, Art. 1).

[15] Aristotle, *Nicomachean Ethics*, Book 2, Chapter 6.

[1] Perpetuity in the first sense means that *the agent goes on willing forever.* Perpetuity in the second sense means that *the agent wills to keep doing the same thing.* Only God's will can be perpetual in the first sense, but even man's will can be perpetual in the second.

[2] Here St. Thomas is answering the question "Why is perpetuity in the second sense important?"

Reply to Objection 4. Since "perpetual" does not imply perpetuity of the act of the will, it is not superfluous to add "constant": for while the "perpetual will" denotes the purpose of observing justice always, "constant" signifies a firm perseverance in this purpose.	Reply to Objection 4. Since the expression "perpetual" does not mean that the act of will has everlasting duration, the addition of the term "constant" is not at all redundant. For the former term indicates that the will proposes to conserve justice at all times, but the latter indicates that rather than abandoning this purpose, it firmly perseveres in it.

If perpetuity did mean that the agent goes on willing forever, then it really would be superfluous to add constancy as a second condition. But if perpetuity means that the agent keeps willing to do the same thing, then it is important to add that so long as he lives, he continues to do so, and this is constancy.

Reply to Objection 5. [1] *A judge renders to each one what belongs to him, by way of command and direction,* [2] *because a judge is the "personification of justice,"* [3] *and "the sovereign is its guardian" (Ethic. v, 4).* [4] *On the other hand, the subjects render to each one what belongs to him, by way of execution.*	Reply to Objection 5. In one way, the judge gives each person his own: By commanding and arranging how this is to be done. For as Aristotle explains, he is living justice and the guardian of justice. But in another way, the subjects give each person his own: By actually doing it.

[1] The judge gives each person what is due to him only in the sense that he *tells what is to be done* so that each person receives what is due to him.

[2] Rules are not self-interpreting. The judge is living justice, "justice animate," for he is not a dead rule, but a rational mind capable of understanding the rule and applying it to cases in such a way as to fulfill its intention of justice. The expression comes from Aristotle: "When people dispute, they take refuge in the judge; and to go to the judge is to go to justice; for the nature of the judge is to be a sort of animate justice."[16]

[3] The *function* of the judge is to guard justice; it does not follow that all judges do so. As Aristotle explains,

For justice exists only between men whose mutual relations are governed by law; and law exists for men between whom there is injustice; for legal justice

[16] Ibid., Book 5, Chapter 4.

Justice is ~~takes~~ "a constant and perpetual will to give to each person his right."

is the discrimination of the just and the unjust. And between men between whom there is injustice there is also unjust action (though there is not injustice between all between whom there is unjust action), and this is assigning too much to oneself of things good in themselves and too little of things evil in themselves. This is why we do not allow a man to rule, but rational principle, because a man behaves thus in his own interests and becomes a tyrant. *The magistrate on the other hand is the guardian of justice*, and, if of justice, then of [proportional] equality also. And since he is assumed to have no more than his share, if he is just (for he does not assign to himself more of what is good in itself, unless such a share is proportional to his merits – so that it is for others that he labors, and it is for this reason that men, as we stated previously, say that justice is "another's good"), therefore a reward must be given him, and this is honor and privilege; but those for whom such things are not enough become tyrants.[17]

[4] Subject to the directions of the judge, the citizens *actually give* to each person what is due to him.

Reply to Objection 6. Just as love of God includes love of our neighbor, as stated above (Question 25, Article 1), so too the service of God includes rendering to each one his due.	Reply to Objection 6. Since love of God *includes* love of neighbor, serving God *includes* giving each person what is due to him.

The Objector views love of God and love of neighbor as mutually exclusive. Not so, says St. Thomas, because our neighbor is to be loved *for the sake* of God, *as the image* of God, and *so that he might be* in God. In fact, as the Angelic Doctor explains in II-II, Question 25, Article 1, the love of God and the love of neighbor belong to the very same species of act. Giving our neighbor what we owe to him is *part of* giving God what we owe to Him.

[17] Ibid., Book 5, Chapter 6, emphasis added.

Whether Judgment Is an Act of Justice?

TEXT	PARAPHRASE
Whether judgment is an act of justice?	Is the characteristic act of justice the act of judging?

The *act* of justice is that by which justice is *actualized* or *fulfilled.* For each virtue is a disposition or habit of performing certain kinds of acts. Consequently, with each virtue certain characteristic acts are associated. It is by means of these acts that the virtue in question is exercised, and it is by reference to them that it is understood. So what actualizes justice – what is its characteristic act? Is it judgment, as traditionally held?

I take the issue to be not whether judgment is "an" act of justice but whether it is "the" act of justice.[1] In one sense "an" is perfectly correct, for like each of the cardinal virtues, justice is a compendium of a number of subordinate virtues, for example truth and gratitude. Since each such virtue has its own characteristic act, these acts are subordinate acts of justice. However, the question posed in the present Article concerns the act of justice *as such.*

It may seem that we have already settled that question, for we saw in II-II, Question 58, Article 1, that justice is the perpetual and constant will to give each person his right. Doesn't it follow, then, that the characteristic act of justice is rendering to someone what is due to him? But wait: Before I can render someone what is due to him, I have to know *what* is due to him. So the act of giving him his right seems to presuppose a prior act of judging what his right is. Then is judgment itself the characteristic act of justice?

[1] Latin does not have definite or indefinite articles. Sometimes, demonstratives or reflexives ("that P," "P itself") are used where we would use the definite article ("the P"), and sometimes adjectives ("one P") are used where we would use the indefinite article ("a P"). However, in most cases, such as this one, whether to translate by "a" or by "the" must be understood from context.

So it would seem, yet this answer lays us open to difficulties. For example, if judging is an act of the intellect, wouldn't it be the characteristic act of an intellectual rather than a moral virtue? And isn't some kind of judgment required by every virtue, not only by judgment? On the other hand, judgment seems to be what judges do. Where then does this leave the rest of us – is no one just but the judge? To complicate matters still further, it might even be said that judgment belongs *neither* to the ordinary person *nor* to the judge, for St. Paul says that judgment, in some sense, is the act of "the spiritual man."

We see then that what might at first appear to be a fatuous question – "Is judgment the characteristic act of justice?" – turns out to be a stumper.

| *Objection 1.* [1] *It would seem that judgment is not an act of justice. The Philosopher says (Ethic. i, 3) that "everyone judges well of what he knows," so that judgment would seem to belong to the cognitive faculty.* [2] *Now the cognitive faculty is perfected by prudence. Therefore judgment belongs to prudence rather than to justice,* [3] *which is in the will, as stated above (Question 58, Article 4).* | Objection 1. Apparently judgment is not the characteristic act of justice. Aristotle remarks that each man judges well in matters that he knows; this seems to imply that judgment pertains to the power of knowing. But the power of knowing is brought into complete order by the virtue of prudence. Judgment, then, is more an act of prudence than an act of justice – especially since justice is in the will, as we have seen. |

[1] In context, Aristotle writes as follows:

Now each man judges well the things he knows, and of these he is a good judge. And so the man who has been educated in a subject is a good judge of that subject, and the man who has received an all-round education is a good judge in general. Hence a young man is not a proper hearer of lectures on political science; for he is inexperienced in the actions that occur in life, but its discussions start from these and are about these; and, further, since he tends to follow his passions, his study will be vain and unprofitable, because the end aimed at is not knowledge but action. And it makes no difference whether he is young in years or youthful in character; the defect does not depend on time, but on his living, and pursuing each successive object, as passion directs. For to such persons, as to the incontinent, knowledge brings no profit; but to those who desire and act in accordance with a rational principle knowledge about such matters will be of great benefit.[2]

[2] The Objector reasons that since the judgment is accomplished by practical reason, and the virtue which puts practical reason into complete and proper order is prudence, judgment is the characteristic act of prudence. Therefore, the traditional view, which takes it to be the characteristic act of justice, must be wrong.

---

[2] Aristotle, *Nicomachean Ethics*, Book 1, Chapter 3.

[3] Had the Objector looked a little further into what was "stated above," he might have had the materials to answer his own challenge. St. Thomas had explained in Question 58, Article 4, that justice does not *direct* the act of the cognitive power, because to be just, it is not enough to know something correctly; one must *do* something correctly. So to be just one must have the *desire* to give each what is due to him. But what is due to another person involves a *relation*, which can be grasped only by the mind. Consequently – unlike, say, the desire for food, which arises from the sensitive appetite – the desire to give each what is due to him arises from *rational appetite, that is, from the will*. This gives us a clue as to how St. Thomas responds in the Reply.

| Objection 2. [1] *Further, the Apostle says (1 Corinthians 2:15): "The spiritual man judgeth all things."* [2] *Now man is made spiritual chiefly by the virtue of charity, which "is poured forth in our hearts by the Holy Ghost Who is given to us" (Romans 5:5).* [3] *Therefore judgment belongs to charity rather than to justice.* | Objection 2. Moreover, as St. Paul declares in his first letter to the Corinthians, the spiritual man "judges all things." But as he says in his letter to the Romans, man is made spiritual primarily by the virtue of love or charity, which is "diffused in our hearts by the Holy Spirit which has been given to us." Therefore judgment is more an act of love than it is an act of justice. |

[1] St. Paul explains in 1 Corinthians 2:14–15 that the unspiritual man does not take in the gifts of the Holy Spirit, because they seem folly to him; to understand or examine them he would need spiritual discernment. By contrast, the spiritual man is able to consider and judge all these things. Regarding such a man as the exemplar of judgment, the Objector makes him the test of whether judgment is really about justice.

[2] This statement comes at the very end of St. Paul's explanation of why the followers of Christ are able to rejoice even in sufferings: "Through him we have obtained access to this grace in which we stand, and we rejoice in our hope of sharing the glory of God. More than that, we rejoice in our sufferings, knowing that suffering produces endurance, and endurance produces character, and character produces hope, and hope does not disappoint us, because God's love has been poured into our hearts through the Holy Spirit which has been given to us."[3]

[3] The Objector reasons that if the spiritual man is the only one who judges, and if what gives him the ability to judge is charity, then judgment cannot be the characteristic act of justice. So the tradition is identifying judgment with the wrong virtue.

---

[3] Romans 5:2–5 (RSV-CE).

Objection 3. [1] *Further, it belongs to every virtue to judge aright of its proper matter, because "the virtuous man is the rule and measure in everything," according to the Philosopher (Ethic. iii, 4).* [2] *Therefore judgment does not belong to justice any more than to the other moral virtues.*	Objection 3. Moreover, correct judgment is involved in the exercise of every virtue, each in its own subject matter, for as Aristotle points out, the virtuous man is the universal standard for judging how deeds should be done and the yardstick by which they should be measured. So the act of judgment is no less characteristic of other moral virtues than it is of justice.

[1] Whereas St. Paul said the spiritual man is the one who judges everything, Aristotle had said that the virtuous man is the one who judges everything: "For each state of character has its own ideas of the noble and the pleasant, and perhaps the good man differs from others most by seeing the truth in each class of things, being as it were the norm and measure of them."[4]

The way this idea is phrased here is most important, because St. Thomas says elsewhere[5] that *law is the rule and measure of everything*. In effect, the Objector is claiming that the virtuous man is the embodiment of law.

[2] If the virtuous man judges *everything*, then he judges not only concerning the subject matter of justice but also concerning the subject matter of the other virtues. Taken in this way (as the Objector takes it), there is nothing special about the connection between justice and judgment.

Objection 4. Further, judgment would seem to belong only to judges. But the act of justice is to be found in every just man. Since then judges are not the only just men, it seems that judgment is not the proper act of justice.	Objection 4. Besides, judgment seems to be the job of judges alone. Yet we observe all just persons acting justly. Since those who judge are not the only ones who are just, it seems wrong to view judgment as the characteristic act of justice.

To organize the Objector's inference a little differently: If judgment is the characteristic act of justice, then all just men judge. But only judges judge. Therefore, justice is not the characteristic act of justice unless all just men are judges, which is not the case. Therefore, judgment is not the characteristic act of justice.

To rescue the proposition that judgment is the characteristic act of justice, it would seem that we must swallow at least one of these two ideas: That all just men are judges after all, or that judges are not the only ones who judge. But if all just men are judges, what is the difference between the ones who hold public authority and the ones who do not? And if judgment is not the special work of the judges who do hold public authority, then what is? Both moves seem unpalatable. Is there another way out?

---

[4] Aristotle, *Nicomachean Ethics*, Book 3, Chapter 4.   [5] I-II, Q. 90, Art. 1.

On the contrary, It is written (Psalm 93:15[6]): "Until justice be turned into judgment."	On the other hand, consider what is said in Psalm 93 about God converting justice into judgment.

Following his common practice, St. Thomas quotes only a few words of these two verses of sacred poetry, expecting his readers to remember the rest. In context, God is reassuring the chosen people:

For the Lord will not cast off his people: neither will he forsake his own inheritance.

Until justice be turned into judgment: and they that are near it are all the upright in heart.[7]

Converting justice into judgment would seem to mean spreading justice abroad *by means* of acts of judgment – converting it from potentiality into actuality. According to the tradition, then, judgment really is the characteristic act of justice, for by judgment, justice is fulfilled.

| I answer that, [1] Judgment properly denotes the act of a judge as such. [2] Now a judge [iudex] is so called because he asserts the right [jus dicens] and right is the object of justice, as stated above (Question 57, Article 1). [3] Consequently the original meaning of the word "judgment" is a statement or decision of the just or right. [4] Now to decide rightly about virtuous deeds proceeds, properly speaking, from the virtuous habit; thus a chaste person decides rightly about matters relating to chastity. [5] Therefore judgment, which denotes a right decision about what is just, belongs properly to justice. [6] For this reason the Philosopher says (Ethic. v, 4) that "men have recourse to a judge as to one who is the personification of justice." | Here is my reply. Strictly speaking, justice is the act of a judge who is acting in his capacity as judge. We call him a judge [iudex] because he declares what is right [ius]. The right, in turn, is the object of justice, as we have said. This is why the term "judgment" was first given to a decree or determination of what is just or right.

But no matter which sphere of virtue we are speaking of, correct assessments of what is to be done flow only from a virtuous disposition; for example, only the chaste person correctly discerns what chastity requires in a given situation. This is why the characteristic act of justice is judgment, which conveys a correct assessment of what is just in a given situation; and this is why Aristotle remarks in the *Nicomachean Ethics* that men take refuge in the judge as a sort of living justice. |
|---|---|

[1] Notice that by this statement, one of the ways of escaping Objection 4 is foreclosed.

---

[6] In most contemporary translations of the Bible, this psalm is numbered 94 rather than 93.
[7] Psalm 93:14–15 (DRA). In most modern translations, this psalm is numbered 94.

[2] Suppose I have not paid a laborer his just wages, and he takes me to court. The judge declares what is right by *determining* what is due to him and *decreeing* that I shall pay it.

[3] We use the term "judgment" for all sorts of determinations. The thirsty man "judges" that one glass of water is more full than another, the temperate man "judges" that it is too early in the day to indulge in a glass of wine, the conscience-stricken man "judges" that he has done wrong, the lawmaker "judges" that the enactment of a particular general rule would serve the common good, the judge "judges" what is to be done in the particular case before him, and so on. However, St. Thomas suggests that the fundamental meaning of judgment is determination of the just by the judge; all other meanings of judgment arise from that primal one, especially including those having to do with moral judgment. He returns to this point in the Reply to Objection 1.

Such definitions are called *focal.* They are most often used when various things called by the same name lack a single common element, and yet each of the meanings of the term depends in some way on a single clear case. For example, a "healthy" diet, a "healthy" medicine, a "healthy" complexion, a "healthy" horse and a "healthy" man have no common element, yet the first is related to health in the sense that it preserves health, the second in the sense that it produces health, the third in the sense that it is a symptom of health, and the fourth in the sense that it has health.[8] In the case of judgment, however, we see that a term may have a focal meaning even when the various things called by the term things *do* have a common element. For all acts called judgments are exercises of the power to discern and define – yet discernment and definition *by a judge ruling on a case* is more fundamental to the meaning of the term than the others are, and the other meanings depend on this one.

Perhaps the best illustration of how the extended meanings of the term "judgment" depend on its focal meaning is the case of the conscience-stricken man. Conscience is like a court, and the certain judgment of conscience is like the voice of God declaring sentence. But even the thirsty man who judges which glass of water is more full may be said to call up the two glasses of water in the court of his senses and require them to present evidence.

[4] In an unchaste age such as ours, the example cuts to the quick. Not only do habitually unchaste persons fall short of sexual purity; they are unable to determine what chastity requires, and have great difficulty even understanding the motives of chaste persons. "Why don't Romeo and Juliet just sleep together and get it out of their systems?" With the other virtues it is just the same. For example, cowards aren't people who understand what fortitude requires but merely fail to do it; they don't grasp its requirements in the first place.

We must make a distinction, because earlier in the *Summa* St. Thomas has explained that judgment is rectified in two ways. He is not here denying that someone might form a correct intellectual judgment about chastity "if he has

---

[8] Aristotle, *Metaphysics*, Book 4, Chapter 2.

learned the science of morals," but a person who is actually chaste "judges of such matters by a kind of connaturality." We might say that rather than just being able to prove theorems about chastity, he understands the matter from the inside; he is *joined with* the thing he is considering.[9] So it is with every moral virtue, in particular, with justice – and as we see later, with every spiritual virtue too, in particular, with charity.

[5] In matters of chastity, only the chaste know what they are talking about; in matters of fortitude, only the courageous know what they are talking about; and in the same way, in matters of justice, only the just know what they are talking about. But in the strict sense, the term "judgment" refers not to determinations of what chastity requires or what fortitude requires, but what justice requires – and this judgment must be made by someone just.

[6] If we do not expect justice from the judge, then we might as well decide what to do by flipping a coin. We go to the judge in hope of justice – and we base our hope of justice on his actually being just.

One might protest that the virtue of the judge is irrelevant, because he is deciding according to the laws. Certainly he should decide according to the laws; later on St. Thomas makes this very clear. Even so, the application of the laws to actual circumstances, in a way which preserves justice rather than destroying it, is not a mechanical process; it requires an act of judgment, which depends on the disposition of the judge.

Reply to Objection 1. [1] *The word "judgment," from its original meaning of a right decision about what is just, has been extended to signify a right decision in any matter whether speculative or practical.* [2] *Now a right judgment in any matter requires two things.* [3] *The first is the virtue itself that pronounces judgment: and in this way, judgment is an act of reason, because it belongs to the reason to pronounce or define.* [4] *The other is the disposition of the one who judges, on which depends his aptness for judging aright.* [5] *On this way, in matters of justice, judgment proceeds from justice, even as in matters of fortitude, it proceeds from fortitude.* [6] *Accordingly judgment is an act of justice in so far as justice inclines*	Reply to Objection 1. The term "judgment," which in its primary sense means correct discernment about what is just, has been broadened to mean correct discernment about anything at all, whether concerning theory or practice.

Yet in all these matters, right judgment has two requirements. One requirement is the virtue upon which a person relies to make any sort of judgments, which are acts of reason because decreeing and determining are acts of reason. But the other is the virtue which *prompts* him to judge correctly in the particular subject matter before him. Judgments about the subject matter of justice flow from the virtue of justice, just as judgments about the subject matter of fortitude flow from the virtue of fortitude.

We conclude that judgment is an act of *justice* insofar the person judging is inclined to judge rightly, and an act of |

[9] II-II, Q. 45, Art. 2.

one to judge aright, and of prudence in so far as prudence pronounces judgment: [7] wherefore synesis which belongs to prudence is said to "judge rightly," as stated above (Question 51, Article 3).	prudence just insofar as the judgment is actually generated. This, by the way, is why synesis, even though it is an aspect of prudence [rather than justice], is said to "judge well." We discussed this point earlier.

[1] As we saw in the *respondeo*, the term "judgment" can be used in two senses. There we were using it in its original, strict sense, for judgments concerning justice. Here, though, we begin with its broad sense, judgments in general, only then turning to the specific case of justice.

[2] The wording of the next few sentences is awkward, but their point is straightforward. When St. Thomas says a right judgment in any matter "requires two things" he means that it *requires two virtues*.

[3] The first of the two required virtues is the *intellectual* virtue by which we discern and determine. Since we are speaking of practical reason, this virtue is prudence. Prudence does not cause us to judge; rather it causes us to judge well *when* we do judge.

[4] Not only do we require an intellectual virtue, prudence, so that we are *able* us to determine things correctly, we also require a moral virtue so that we *desire* to determine them correctly; otherwise prudence is not properly called into operation. The moral virtue sets the goal; prudence finds the means.

[5] Each moral virtue disposes us to seek the right end in a particular sphere of action. Fortitude makes us want to do the courageous thing; temperance, the temperate thing; justice, the just thing.

[6] We have just seen that the act of judgment depends on two virtues, not one. In the sphere of justice, these two virtues are prudence and justice. Thus, instead of asking whether judgment is an act of justice or an act of prudence, as the Objector would have us do, we should ask *in what respect* it is an act of justice, and *in what respect* it is an act of prudence. The answer is that it is an act of justice *in that we desire to judge justly*, and an act of prudence *in that we actually judge*.

[7] As we saw in our discussion of I-II, Question 58, Article 4, prudence is a complex of several subordinate virtues. *Eubolia* is the one which causes us to deliberate well; *synesis*, the one which causes us to judge particular matters well according to the common rules of thumb; and *gnome*, the one which causes us to judge according to higher, universal principles when the common rules of thumb are insufficient.

One might be tempted to say, "Well, it's all about judging, isn't it? Why split hairs?" But as St. Thomas remarks elsewhere, "different acts, which cannot be ascribed to the same cause, must correspond to different virtues. And it is evident that goodness of [deliberation] and goodness of judgment are not reducible to the same cause, for many can [deliberate well] without having good sense so as to judge well.... Hence there is need, besides *euboulia*, for another virtue, which judges well, and this is called *synesis*."[10]

Reply to Objection 2. [1] *The spiritual man, by reason of the habit of charity, has an inclination to judge aright of all things* [2] *according to the Divine rules; and it is in conformity with these that he pronounces judgment* [3] *through the gift of wisdom:* [4] *even as the just man pronounces judgment through the virtue of prudence conformably with the ruling of the law.*	Reply to Objection 2. Because he has the disposition of charity, the spiritual man is inclined to judge all matters correctly *according to God's standards.* Just as the just man renders judgments according to [ordinary] law through the virtue of prudence, so the spiritual man renders them according to Divine law through the Gift of Wisdom.

[1] As we have seen, only the chaste judge well in matters of chastity, only the courageous in matters of fortitude, and in general, only those who have the relevant virtue judge well in matters pertaining to that virtue. The same is true here, but the virtue in question is divine charity or love, which differs from the ordinary moral virtues because it is infused by divine grace rather than acquired by human effort (although of course we must cooperate with this grace). Charity transforms motives and illuminates the mind so that one is able to view things as God views them and evaluate them accordingly. According to Catholic teaching, "thus the Holy Spirit can use the humblest to enlighten the learned and those in the highest positions."[11]

[2] The spiritual man does not judge apart from law, but in the light of the higher law which comes from God.

[3] Prudence is human practical wisdom. The Wisdom of which St. Thomas speaks here, however, is *Sapientia,* one of the spiritual gifts. We may say that the Gift of Wisdom enters through the door of the virtue of charity, which is infused by the Holy Spirit. As the chaste are able to judge matters of chastity *connaturally* because they are joined with chastity, so the supernaturally wise are able to judge Divine matters *connaturally* because they are joined with that God Who is Love.

So long as does not fall from grace through unrepented mortal sin, each redeemed person receives enough Wisdom for his salvation. However, some receive a still greater share: In the first place, they contemplate and consult Divine matters more deeply and are able to convey their insights to others; in the second place, they are able to direct not only themselves but others according to God's law. In support of this point, St. Thomas refers to St. Paul's explanation of the diversity of Divine gifts, some receiving one, some another, all of them contributing to the whole.[12]

---

[10] II-II, Q. 51, Art. 3. [11] *Catechism of the Catholic Church,* Section 2038.
[12] II-II, Q. 45, Arts. 1 and 2; 1 Corinthians 12:4–31.

[4] Recalling Aristotle's description of those who are one with justice as "justice animate" or "living justice." St. Thomas applies the same term in a still higher sense to those who are one with divine truth:

Judgment belongs to truth as its standard, while it belongs to the man imbued with truth, according as he is as it were one with truth, as a kind of law and "living justice." Hence Augustine quotes the saying of 1 Corinthians 2:15: "The spiritual man judgeth all things."

He adds that the one who is most fully described by this term is Christ:

But beyond all creatures Christ's soul was more closely united with truth, and more full of truth; according to John 1:14: "We saw Him … full of grace and truth." And according to this it belongs principally to the soul of Christ to judge all things.

The upshot is that although both the just man and the spiritual man may be said to "judge all things," they are judging neither from the same perspective, by the same standard, or by means of the same resources. The just man's perspective is temporal; the spiritual man's is eternal. The just man's standard is human law; the spiritual man's is Divine law. The just man's resource is unaided reason; the spiritual man's is reason purified, broadened, and uplifted by grace.

Reply to Objection 3. [1] *The other virtues regulate man in himself, whereas justice regulates man in his dealings with others, as shown above (Question 58, Article 2).* [2] *Now man is master in things concerning himself, but not in matters relating to others.* [3] *Consequently where the other virtues are in question, there is no need for judgment other than that of a virtuous man, taking judgment in its broader sense, as explained above (ad 1). But in matters of justice, there is further need for the judgment of a superior, who is "able to reprove both, and to put his hand between both" [Job 9:33].* [4] *Hence judgment belongs more specifically to justice than to any other virtue.*	Reply to Objection 3. Other virtues put a man's interior into right order, but justice brings him into right order with respect to other persons. Even though he is master in matters concerning himself alone, he is not master in matters concerning others. This is why in the case of other virtues, no judgment is needed but that of a virtuous man (taking "judgment" in the enlarged sense which we discussed in the Reply to Objection 1) – but in the case of justice, the judgment of someone higher is needed, someone who can "weigh both our arguments and lay hands upon us both." And so judgment pertains to justice more than to other species of virtue.

[1] As we saw in I-II, Q. 65, Art. 1, all of the virtues are interconnected. Obviously, then, if my passions are disordered by intemperance or lack of fortitude, I will fail to give others what is due to them. Even so, the *direct object* of the virtue of justice is not to rectify my passions – as fortitude rectifies fear and rashness, and temperance rectifies the appetite for pleasure – but to rectify our conduct toward others:

It is proper to justice, as compared with the other virtues, to direct man in his relations with others.... On the other hand the other virtues perfect man in those matters only which befit him in relation to himself. Accordingly that which is right in the works of the other virtues ... depends on its relation to the agent only, whereas the right in a work of justice, besides its relation to the agent, is set up by its relation to others.... And so a thing is said to be just ... without taking into account the way in which it is done by the agent: whereas in the other virtues nothing is declared to be right unless it is done in a certain way by the agent. For this reason justice has its own special proper object over and above the other virtues, and this object is called the just, which is the same as "right." Hence it is evident that right is the object of justice.[13]

[2] I do not have to give an account of my temperance, fortitude, or prudence to any other human being – *unless* by intemperance, cowardice, rashness, or foolishness I deprive someone else of what is due to him. Of course this is a pretty big "unless." I would certainly be accountable to others if, say, I endangered fellow drivers by getting drunk, fellow soldiers by deserting my post, or fellow workers by exposing them to a contagious disease. Moreover, even in cases in which I do not have duties to others, I may not do exactly as I please because have duties to myself and to God. For these reasons, in other places St. Thomas softens the strong statement that we are our own masters. We return to the question of being our own masters in II-II, Question 122, Article 1.

[3] If no one else is affected by my deeds, then provided that I have virtue, my own judgment is sufficient to guide me. There is no disagreement to settle, because I do not disagree with myself. However, a third party's judgment may be needed whenever others are involved, for even if all parties want to do the right thing, they may disagree about what that thing is.

The Old Testament quotation comes from a passage in which Job is complaining because there is no one to judge between him and God. When his friend Bildad assures him that "God will not reject a blameless man," Job answers, "Truly I know that it is so: But how can a man be just before God? ... For he is not a man, as I am, that I might answer Him, that we should come to trial together. There is no umpire between us, who might lay his hand upon us both."[14]

In his commentary on the book, St. Thomas suggests that when Job complains that God is not a man that he should answer Him, he means he stands no chance of justifying himself before God, in whom no defect is to be found; when he complains that there is no umpire between them, he means that there is no one of greater wisdom than God, by whom He could be corrected; and where he complains that there is no one who could lay hands upon them both, he means that there is no one of greater power than God, by whom both parties could be directed how to act.[15]

---

[13] II-II, Q. 57, Art. 1.   [14] Job 8:20, 9:2, 32–33 (RSV-CE).
[15] Thomas Aquinas, *Commentary on the Book of Job*, trans. Brian Mullady, available online at www.dhspriory.org/thomas/SSJob.htm.

[4] The Objector had argued that judgment is required in the exercise of every virtue. St. Thomas agrees that in the broad sense of the term "judgment," this is true. However, since the intervention of a third party is necessary only in our relations with others, the virtue of justice requires judgment to a greater degree.

***Reply to Objection 4.** [1] Justice is in the sovereign as a master-virtue [Cf. 58, 6], commanding and prescribing what is just; [2] while it is in the subjects as an executive and administrative virtue. [3] Hence judgment, which denotes a decision of what is just, belongs to justice, considered as existing chiefly in one who has authority.*	**Reply to Objection 4.** In the statesman, justice functions as an architectural or supervisory virtue which issues just orders and warnings. But in ordinary citizens, it functions differently, as an executive and ministering virtue. And so judgment, which determines what is just, pertains to justice principally in the manner of someone who presides over others.[16]

[1] St. Thomas says justice functions in the foremost man as a *virtus architectonica*, an architectural virtue. Just as architects, who preside over construction, issue instructions which coordinate the efforts of diverse craftsmen so that buildings may be raised, so statesmen, who preside over the common good, issue commands which coordinate the interactions of diverse citizens so that the common good may be realized. Because of the history of the last century and a half, there is a certain tendency to read such statements in a misleadingly broad way, as though St. Thomas expected all private activities to be managed by the government from the top down. Such a view on his part is impossible, for he believes in such things as private property, the integrity of the family, and the independence of the Church and religious orders from the state. But consider: No matter how much or how little the government manages directly, it must have custody of the rules that make it possible for all individuals and forms of association to live together in justice. The rules of the marketplace must uphold contracts and prohibit force and fraud; the rules of marriage must enforce the duties of husbands and wives to each other and to their children; and so on.

Justice, in this architectural or coordinating sense, is also called "legal" justice, for the law may command acts of every virtue – but only to the degree to which the common good requires them. Thus the law requires the keeping of the marital promise, but not the keeping of a promise to be best friends forever; it requires fortitude of soldiers facing the enemy, but not of sick persons facing

---

[16] St. Thomas does not actually use the term "authority," as in the Blackfriars translation, though authority is implied. What he says is that judgment pertains to justice *secundum quod est principaliori modo in praesidente*. This phrase is difficult to render in English without taking liberties, and I have taken them.

surgery; and it requires truthfulness of witnesses in court, but not of teenagers writing in their diaries.[17]

[2] In the primary sense just described, justice is in magistrates, such as judges and lawmakers, for they *command* such acts as the ones just mentioned. But in a secondary sense, justice is in the citizens, for they *actually do* all these things (at least one must hope that they do).

[3] Since judgment is the characteristic act of justice, and in the primary sense justice is in the magistrate, then in the primary sense, so is judgment.

---

[17] See esp. I-II, Q. 96, Art. 3, and II-II, Q. 58, Art. 6.

Whether It Is Lawful to Judge?

TEXT	PARAPHRASE
Whether it is lawful to judge?	Is it permitted for any mere human being to pass judgment on another?

The term *licitum* means permitted, or allowed by the law. Human law appoints certain persons judges, but is it really right for any mere human to stand in judgment? The Objectors think that the answer should be "No"; in their view, human judgment is condemned both by natural and Divine law.

In the relativistic ambiance of our own times as well, "judgmentalism" has been judged and found wanting. Yet there is a certain difficulty with antijudgmentalism, for if no one may judge others, then how is it that we may deliver an unfavorable judgment upon those who do judge others? Could it be that we have passed judgment upon judgment too quickly – or perhaps that only certain kinds of judgment are illicit? If so, which kinds? Aquinas investigates the various senses in which human beings may and may not "judge."

Objection 1. [1] *It would seem unlawful to judge. For nothing is punished except what is unlawful.* [2] *Now those who judge are threatened with punishment, which those who judge not will escape, according to Matthew 7:1, "Judge not, and ye shall not be judged." Therefore it is unlawful to judge.*	**Objection 1.** Apparently passing judgment is *not* permitted. For only what is unlawful is punished – yet those who do judge are threatened with a punishment which is inescapable. We read this in the Gospel of Matthew, which warns "Judge not, that you may not be judged." The unlawfulness of judgment follows.

[1] For purposes of Objection 1, the standard is Divine law and punishment.
[2] Here is the context:

Judge not, that you be not judged. For with the judgment you pronounce you will be judged, and the measure you give will be the measure you get. Why do you see the speck that is in your brother's eye, but do not notice the log that is in your own eye? Or how can you say to your brother, "Let me take the speck out of your eye," when there is the log in your own eye? You hypocrite, first take the log out of your own eye, and then you will see clearly to take the speck out of your brother's eye.[1]

Focusing on the first sentence of the passage, the Objector views Christ as condemning all human judgment whatsoever.

Objection 2. [1] *Further, it is written (Romans 14:4): "Who art thou that judgest another man's servant. To his own lord he standeth or falleth."* [2] *Now God is the Lord of all. Therefore to no man is it lawful to judge.*	Objection 2. Moreover, St. Paul admonishes the Christians in Rome, "Who are you to pass judgment on the servant of another? It is before his own master that he stands or falls." Since God is the Master of everyone, no mere man may pass judgment.

[1] Some of the early Christians argued over dietary practices. Although St. Paul holds that it makes no difference whether one eats meat,[2] he says that neither those who approve nor those who disapprove should be judged by those who hold opposite views, for God has accepted both parties:

As for the man who is weak in faith, welcome him, but not for disputes over opinions. One believes he may eat anything, while the weak man eats only vegetables. Let not him who eats despise him who abstains, and let not him who abstains pass judgment on him who eats; for God has welcomed him. Who are you to pass judgment on the servant of another? It is before his own master that he stands or falls. And he will be upheld, for the Master is able to make him stand.[3]

The term "weak in faith" refers not to those who are uncertain about revelation, but to those who in their spiritual immaturity cling to taboos about unimportant things. Although they are welcome to come into the Christian fellowship, they are not welcome to insist that everyone else adopt their mistaken dietary scruples.[4] Yet others must not insist that spiritually immature persons give up their mistaken scruples either.

---

[1] Matthew 7:1–5 (RSV-CE).

[2] In some passages the issue is whether one may eat meat *that had been sacrificed to idols in pagan temples* and then sold at lower prices. For present purposes it is not necessary to decide which kind of meat St. Paul has in mind.

[3] Romans 14:1–4 (RSV-CE).

[4] This is not to say that all dietary scruples are mistaken. For example, St. Thomas holds that God forbade the Hebrew people to consume blood "that they might abhor the shedding of human blood." I-II, Q. 102, Art. 3, ad 8. We might add that even Christians, who are released from the dietary rules of the Old Law, abstain from cannibalism.

[2] The Objector draws only one thing from the Pauline passage: The principle that a servant is to be judged only by his own master. His argument seems to run like this:

1. No servant may be judged by anyone but his own master.
2. But God is the master of all.
3. Therefore no one may be judged by anyone but God.

In short, the Objector reasons that for any mere human to pass judgment on another is *insolent*, because judgment belongs to God alone.

Objection 3. [1] *Further, no man is sinless, according to I John 1:8, "If we say that we have no sin, we deceive ourselves."* [2] *Now it is unlawful for a sinner to judge, according to Romans 2:1, "Thou art inexcusable, O man, whosoever thou art, that judgest; for wherein thou judgest another, thou condemnest thyself, for thou dost the same things which thou judgest." Therefore to no man is it lawful to judge.*	Objection 3. Besides, there are no sinless human beings. The first letter of St. John makes this clear where it says, "If we say we have no sin, we deceive ourselves." May sinners pass judgment, then? No! For as St. Paul writes in his letter to the Roman Christians, "You have no excuse, O man, whoever you are, when you judge another; for in passing judgment upon him you condemn yourself, because you, the judge, are doing the very same things." So passing judgment is not permitted to any man.

[1] Whereas Objector 2 held that passing judgment is insolent, Objector 3 holds that it is hypocritical, because human judges[5] are inevitably guilty of the very things they condemn. Here is the context of the Scriptural quotation condemning hypocrisy:

If we say we have no sin, we deceive ourselves, and the truth is not in us. If we confess our sins, he is faithful and just, and will forgive our sins and cleanse us from all unrighteousness.[6]

Here St. John is contrasting two ways to seek escape from the burden of sin and guilt. If we seek escape by denying it, we are self-deceived, but if we seek escape through confessing to Christ, we are purified. The next chapter of the letter makes clear that such confession must not be mere lip-service, but an expression of true repentance for the love of God, which includes the love of our neighbors for God's sake.

[2] The Objector has established the wrong of hypocrisy; now he must try to show that *all* human judgment is hypocritical. To support his claim, he appeals to St. Paul:

Therefore you have no excuse, O man, whoever you are, when you judge another; for in passing judgment upon him you condemn yourself, because you, the judge, are doing

---

[5] Tacitly excepting Christ, who was both fully man and fully God, and entirely without sin.
[6] I John 1:8–9 (RSV-CE).

the very same things. We know that the judgment of God rightly falls upon those who do such things. Do you suppose, O man, that when you judge those who do such things and yet do them yourself, you will escape the judgment of God? Or do you presume upon the riches of his kindness and forbearance and patience? Do you not know that God's kindness is meant to lead you to repentance? But by your hard and impenitent heart you are storing up wrath for yourself on the day of wrath when God's righteous judgment will be revealed.[7]

The Objector's assumption that *everyone* is guilty of the same sins might be questioned, because Paul goes on to say,

For he will render to every man according to his works: to those who by patience in well-doing seek for glory and honor and immortality, he will give eternal life; but for those who are factious and do not obey the truth, but obey wickedness, there will be wrath and fury.[8]

On the contrary, It is written (Deuteronomy 16:18): "*Thou shalt appoint judges and magistrates in all thy gates ... that they may judge the people with just judgment.*"	**On the other hand,** We find in the Old Testament book of Deuteronomy that Moses commanded the Hebrew people to appoint judges and officers in every town who would judge the people with judgments that really were just.

By God's authority, Moses speaks to the people as follows:

You shall appoint judges and officers in all your towns which the LORD your God gives you, according to your tribes; and they shall judge the people with righteous judgment. You shall not pervert justice; you shall not show partiality; and you shall not take a bribe, for a bribe blinds the eyes of the wise and subverts the cause of the righteous. Justice, and only justice, you shall follow, that you may live and inherit the land which the LORD your God gives you.[9]

If God, through Moses, commanded the Hebrew people to appoint judges and gave instructions as to how they were to judge, then it would seem that judgment is not always illicit.

I answer that, [1] *Judgment is lawful in so far as it is an act of justice. Now it follows from what has been stated above (1, ad 1, 3) that three conditions are requisite for a judgment to be an act of justice: first, that it proceed from the inclination of justice; secondly, that it come from one who is in*	**Here is my response.** Passing judgment is permitted – but only to the degree to which it is an act of justice. Moreover, as we saw in the previous Article, three requirements must be satisfied for a judgment to be an act of justice: • It must come from the disposition to do what is just. • It must be grounded in the authority of the one who is presiding.

[7] Romans 2:1–5 (RSV-CE). [8] Romans 1:6/8 (RSV-CE).
[9] Deuteronomy 16:18–20 (RSV-CE).

authority; thirdly, that it be pronounced according to the right ruling of prudence. [2] If any one of these be lacking, the judgment will be faulty and unlawful. First, when it is contrary to the rectitude of justice, and then it is called "perverted" or "unjust": [3] secondly, when a man judges about matters wherein he has no authority, and this is called judgment "by usurpation": [4] thirdly, when the reason lacks certainty, as when a man, without any solid motive, forms a judgment on some doubtful or hidden matter, and then it is called judgment by "suspicion" or "rash" judgment.	• It must be brought forth by the sound reasoning of prudence. Unless all three conditions are fulfilled, the judgment is vicious and unlawful. Consequently, it may fall short of justice in three ways: • The judgment may deviate from the *rightness* of justice, and we call such judgment perverted or unjust. • It may be made by someone who has lacks *authority* about the matters in question, and we call such judgment usurpation. • It may be made without *reasonable certainty* – for example when the judge makes a slippery conjecture about matters that are doubtful or unknown – and we call such judgment suspect or reckless.

[1] St. Thomas says that "from what has been stated above" we find three requirements for a just judgment. Two come from II-II, Question 60, Reply to Objection 1, where we found that right judgment requires both the virtue of prudence (which brings the mind's power to make judgments to full development), and the virtue of justice (which prompts the judge to use this power correctly when a matter is set before him). Another was added in the Reply to Objection 3, where we found that because a man is not master in matters concerning other persons, the judgment of someone higher is needed, someone who can "weigh both our arguments and lay hands upon us both." Here the same three requirements are mentioned, but in a different order. The first becomes third, the second becomes first, and the third becomes second.

[2] The problem with "perverted" or "unjust" judgment is that the judge lacks a sufficient inclination to do the right thing – and so, except by accident, he doesn't.

[3] The problem with "usurped" judgment is that the judge's jurisdiction does not include the matters set before him; he has no business standing in judgment about them. The way St. Thomas puts this is to say that judgment must be *ex auctoritate praesidentis* – it must proceed from, or be grounded upon, the authority of the one who presides.

[4] The problem with suspect or reckless judgment is that the judge judges badly; though he may desire to do the right thing, he fails to do it because his reasoning is faulty. Although St. Thomas gives but a single example, any sort of faulty reasoning would come under this heading. The problem, then, lies not in the judge's appetite, but in his power of practical reason – that is to say, the root of the deficiency concerns not the moral virtue of justice, but the intellectual virtue of prudence. What St. Thomas actually says is that judgment must

be *proferatur secundum rectam rationem prudentiae* – it must be forwarded, or discovered, according to the right reason of prudence.

Reply to Objection 1. [1] *In these words our Lord forbids rash judgment which is about the inward intention, or other uncertain things,* [2] *as Augustine states (De Serm. Dom. in Monte ii, 18).* [3] *Or else* [4] *He forbids judgment about Divine things, which we ought not to judge, but simply believe, since they are above us, as Hilary declares in his commentary on Matthew 5.* [5] *Or again according to Chrysostom [Hom. xxiii*[10] *in Matth. in the Opus Imperfectum falsely ascribed to St. John of the Cross], He forbids the judgment which proceeds not from benevolence but from bitterness of heart.*	**Reply to Objection 1.** In the words the Objector is quoting, our Lord may be forbidding any of the following things. First He may be forbidding rash or reckless judgment – for example about the intention of someone's heart, or something else which is uncertain. This is St. Augustine's view. Second He may be forbidding judgment about Divine matters – since these are above us, we should not judge [what God reveals to us] but simply believe it. St. Hilary of Poitiers offers this suggestion in his *Commentary on Matthew.* Third He may be forbidding judgment which comes not from benevolence, but from bitterness of soul. This is what St. John Chrysostom thinks.

[1] Apparently St. Thomas takes the "speck" in one's brother's eye to mean not a *small* fault, but a fault *difficult to see.* Even though we humans are prone to self-deception, our own intentions are knowable to us with greater certainty than the intentions of other persons. So to ask "How can you say to your brother, 'Let me take the speck out of your eye,' when there is the log in your own eye?" is to ask, "How dare you pass judgment about the intentions of another person's heart, which you cannot discern clearly, when you are doing nothing about the intentions in your own heart, which you can discern clearly?"

Interestingly, the next sentence in the passage, "You hypocrite, first take the log out of your own eye, and then you will see clearly to take the speck out of your brother's eye," seems to suggest that those who *have* purified the intentions of their own hearts *can* discern the intentions in the hearts of other persons – which further strengthens St. Thomas's case that judgment can be licit.

[2] In the passage of which St. Thomas is thinking, St. Augustine concedes that Christ's statement that we will be judged by the same measure with which we ourselves judge may give rise to some perplexity. Surely it cannot mean that if we judge anything rashly, God will judge us rashly, or that if we judge anything unjustly, God will judge us unjustly: "By no means does God either judge rashly, or recompense to anyone with an unjust measure; but it is so expressed, inasmuch as that very same rashness wherewith you punish another must necessarily punish yourself." If we imagine that injustice always harms those who

---

[10] The Blackfriars translation gives this citation as Homily 17 rather than 23.

are rashly judged, but never harms those who judge rashly, the idea will seem strange to us. But actually, says Augustine:

> [Rash judgment] often does no harm to him who suffers the injury, but it must necessarily do harm to him who inflicts it. For what harm did the injustice of the persecutors do to the martyrs? None; but very much to the persecutors themselves. For although some of them were turned from the error of their ways, yet at the time at which they were acting as persecutors, their wickedness was blinding them. So also a rash judgment frequently does no harm to him who is the object of the rash judgment; but to him who judges rashly, the rashness itself must necessarily do harm.[11]

In short, St. Augustine thinks that Christ is condemning not all judgment but rash judgment, and that the meaning of the statement that we will be judged by the same measure with which we judge is that by the nature of things, those who judge rashly always injure themselves by doing so. This turns out to be a special case of a yet more general principle, for as he explains a bit later, "the soul dies by that very sin, whatever it may be, which it has committed."[12]

[3] By "Or else," here, and "or again," below, St. Thomas is not expressing uncertainty, but merely an additional possibility. The word he uses is *vel*, which means that the possibilities are compatible rather than mutually exclusive.

[4] St. Hilary of Poitiers suggests that when Christ prohibits passing judgment, He is referring to passing judgment upon the Divine promises – rejecting them on the basis of our own subjective opinions – in effect, passing judgment upon God Himself, as though we knew better than He does. Here is what Hilary says:

> *Do not judge, lest you be judged. For by whatever judgment you have judged, you will be judged.* God utterly rejects every element of judging, nor does he allow a place for it at all. Yet the latter part of the verse appears to be opposed to the former when it states: *By whatever judgment you have judged, you will be judged*, while it says above: *Do not judge, lest you be judged.* Is it not appropriate to accept the decision of a good judgment? Indeed, he declares that we should be judged according to the terms of our judgment and that everyone should be measured by the terms he has used to measure [another]. There will never be a righteous judgment if there is no judging at all. But ... there is nothing in the words of God that is treated lightly or in vain.... In effect, God has forbidden that his promises should be judged. Just as judgments among men are founded upon uncertainties, so we must not annul a judgment that is contrary to God on the basis of the doubt of someone's thought or opinion, and that deeply repels us, so that we may be more confident about our [own] faith. If there is sin that corresponds to our having made a wrong judgment, we are surely guilty in this instance for casting judgment upon God.[13]

---

[11] St. Augustine of Hippo, *Our Lord's Sermon on the Mount* (public domain), Book 2, Chapter 18, Section 62, available online at http://newadvent.org/fathers/1601.htm.

[12] St. Augustine says this is the meaning of Christ's statement to Peter, "all who take the sword will perish by the sword," Matthew 26:52 (RSV-CE).

[13] Hilary of Poitiers, *Commentary on Matthew*, trans. D. H. Williams (Washington, DC: Catholic University Press, 2012), Chapter 5, Section 14, p. 83.

The language at the end of the passage is a bit tortuous. When Hilary says "we must not annul a judgment that is contrary to God on the basis of the doubt of someone's thought or opinion, and that deeply repels us, so that we may be more confident about our faith," I take him to mean that we must not take the liberty of annulling a judgment of God, even one which deeply repels us, taking as our pretext someone's doubting thought or opinion that the judgment is actually contrary to God, just so that we may be more confident about our faith.[14]

[5] St. John Chrysostom suggests that the prohibition of judgment refers not to judgment in general, but to bitter or uncharitable judgment. In this life, even deserved punishment is for the amendment of the one who is doing wrong, and the same should be true of our words:

"What then!" say you: "if one commit fornication, may I not say that fornication is a bad thing, nor at all correct him that is playing the wanton?" Nay, correct him, but not as a foe, nor as an adversary exacting a penalty, but as a physician providing medicines. For neither did Christ say, "stay not him that is sinning," but "judge not"; that is, be not bitter in pronouncing sentence....

His injunction therefore in these words is as follows, that he who is chargeable with countless evil deeds, should not be a bitter censor of other men's offenses, and especially when these are trifling. He is not overthrowing reproof or correction, but forbidding men to neglect their own faults, and exult over those of other men.[15]

Notice that although Chrysostom's emphasis is on the wrong of bitterness, the wrong of hypocrisy enters into his thinking too: He says that *we who are guilty of countless sins* should not indulge in bitterness toward the sins of others. Even so, when others do sin, we should have mercy enough to humbly offer them the same correction we have so often needed ourselves.

Reply to Objection 2. *A judge is appointed as God's servant; wherefore it is written (Deuteronomy 1:16): "Judge that which is just," and further on (Deuteronomy 1:17), "because it is the judgment of God."*	Reply to Objection 2. The judge holds office as God's agent. This is why – as we find in the book of Deuteronomy – Moses commanded the appointed judges to "just righteously," "for the judgment is God's."

The Objector had argued that no human being may judge another because no human being is the master of another. St. Thomas accepts the premise but denies the conclusion, for human judges serve not by their own authority but by the authority of God. To prove the point, he cites a passage very similar to the one used in the *sed contra*. Moses is reminding the people of his instructions when their judges were appointed:

[14] I take this opportunity to express thanks to D. H. Williams, the translator with whom I corresponded about the sentence. Of course, any error of interpretation is mine alone.

[15] St. John Chrysostom, *Homilies on Matthew*, Homily 23, Section 2, available online at http://newadvent.org/fathers/2001.htm.

At that time I said to you, "I am not able alone to bear you; the LORD your God has multiplied you, and behold, you are this day as the stars of heaven for multitude...." ... So I took the heads of your tribes, wise and experienced men, and set them as heads over you, commanders of thousands, commanders of hundreds, commanders of fifties, commanders of tens, and officers, throughout your tribes. And I charged your judges at that time, "Hear the cases between your brethren, and judge righteously between a man and his brother or the alien that is with him. You shall not be partial in judgment; you shall hear the small and the great alike; you shall not be afraid of the face of man, for the judgment is God's; and the case that is too hard for you, you shall bring to me, and I will hear it."[16]

Had anyone protested that judges served as God's agents only in the divinely arranged government of the Promised Land, St. Thomas could also have quoted from the New Testament. For St. Paul holds that even the magistrates of pagan Rome, who know nothing of the true God, are God's agents to the degree that they uphold justice:

Let every person be subject to the governing authorities. For there is no authority except from God, and those that exist have been instituted by God. Therefore he who resists the authorities resists what God has appointed, and those who resist will incur judgment. For rulers are not a terror to good conduct, but to bad. Would you have no fear of him who is in authority? Then do what is good, and you will receive his approval, for he is God's servant for your good. But if you do wrong, be afraid, for he does not bear the sword in vain; he is the servant of God to execute his wrath on the wrongdoer. Therefore one must be subject, not only to avoid God's wrath but also for the sake of conscience. For the same reason you also pay taxes, for the authorities are ministers of God, attending to this very thing. Pay all of them their dues, taxes to whom taxes are due, revenue to whom revenue is due, respect to whom respect is due, honor to whom honor is due.[17]

The Pauline passage must not be taken as meaning that civil magistrates must be obeyed even when they violate natural and Divine law; for example, on an occasion when the local authorities unjustly commanded the Apostles to stop preaching about the risen Christ, St. Peter responded, "We must obey God rather than men."[18] In I-II, Question 96, Article 4, St. Thomas explores the grounds and limits of civil disobedience.[19]

Reply to Objection 3. [1] *Those who stand guilty of grievous sins should not judge those who are guilty of the*	Reply to Objection 3. As St. John Chrysostom explains in his discussion of the command to "judge not," those who

---

[16] Deuteronomy 1:9–10, 15–17 (RSV-CE).   [17] Romans 13:1–7 (RSV-CE).

[18] Acts 5:29 (RSV-CE).

[19] For discussion, see J. Budziszewski, *Commentary on Thomas Aquinas's Treatise on Law* (Cambridge: Cambridge University Press, 2014), pp. 379–393, and *Companion to the Commentary* (Cambridge: Cambridge University Press, 2014), pp. 192–197. The latter is available at online, both at the Cambridge University Press website, www.cambridge.org/us, and at the author's website, http://undergroundthomist.org.

same or lesser sins, [2] as Chrysostom [Hom. xxiii²⁰] says on the words of Matthew 7:1, "Judge not." [3] Above all does this hold when such sins are public, because there would be an occasion of scandal arising in the hearts of others. [4] If however they are not public but hidden, and there be an urgent necessity for the judge to pronounce judgment, because it is his duty, he can reprove or judge with humility and fear. [5] Hence Augustine says (De Serm. Dom. in Monte ii, 19): "If we find that we are guilty of the same sin as another man, we should groan together with him, and invite him to strive against it together with us." [6] And yet it is not through acting thus that a man condemns himself so as to deserve to be condemned once again, but when, in condemning another, he shows himself to be equally deserving of condemnation on account of another or a like sin.

are guilty of grave sin should not judge those who are guilty of the same or lesser sins. This warning acquires especially great force when the judge's sins are public, because when such a man declares judgment, a stumbling block is set up in the hearts of other people so that they too may stumble into sin. There is one exception: If the judge's sins are not public but secret, and if there is an immediate necessity for him to exercise his official duty of passing judgment, then he may convict or judge – but only with humility and fear.

Along the same lines, St. Augustine writes in his book *On Our Lord's Sermon on the Mount* that if upon reflection we find that we are guilty of the same sin as someone else, we should groan with him and invite him to join with us in struggling against it. It is not in this way that a man doubles his deserved condemnation, but rather when he condemns someone for the same sin or a similar one, showing that he deserves the very same censure.

[1] St. Thomas concedes that we should not be hypocrites, but denies that all human judgment is hypocritical. If all were guilty of the same sins, then all human judgment would be hypocritical, but in fact we are not all guilty of the same sins. The proper conclusion, then, is not that no one may judge, but that gravely guilty persons may judge only those who are guiltier still.

[2] To support the point he has just made, St. Thomas appeals to one of St. John Chrysostom's homilies on the Gospel of Matthew. Notice that Chrysostom also agrees with a point St. Augustine makes in the passage quoted earlier: Whether or not hypocritical judgments damage those who are judged, they certainly recoil upon the soul of the judge himself, for by passing such judgments he habituates himself to fierceness and inures himself to the sufferings of others:

In this place, then, as it seems at least to me, He does not simply command us not to judge any of men's sins, neither does He simply forbid the doing of such a thing, but to them that are full of innumerable ills, and are trampling upon other men for trifles....

You see, we ought not to upbraid nor trample upon them, but to admonish; not to revile, but to advise; not to assail with pride, but to correct with tenderness. For not him,

²⁰ The Blackfriars translation gives this citation as Homily 24 rather than 23.

but yourself, do you give over to extreme vengeance, by not sparing him, when it may be needful to give sentence on his offenses....

For you, who in other men's doings are so bitter, as to see even the little things; how have you become so remiss in your own, as that even the great things are hurried over by you? ...

For indeed this was a cause of men's going unto great vice, bringing in a twofold wickedness. For he, whose practice it had been to slight his own faults, great as they were, and to search bitterly into those of others, being slight and of no account, was spoiling himself two ways: first, by thinking lightly of his own faults; next, by incurring enmities and feuds with all men, and training himself every day to extreme fierceness, and want of feeling for others.[21]

[3] In English, the word "scandal" has come to mean conduct that causes a public stir. But in Latin, *scandalum* refers to something which causes others to stumble. Hypocrites commit the grave sin of causing others to stumble *morally*, because those who recognize their hypocrisy may become cynical. "There is no justice, so I may as well grab what I can, because if I don't, others will grab it from me."

[4] Suppose, on the other hand, that even though the judge is judging persons who are no guiltier than himself, his judgment does not cause scandal because his sins are not known. Suppose further that if he stands aside from passing judgment in the case at hand, a grave miscarriage of justice is threatened. Suppose still further that he judges not in bitterness of heart, or to get the better of someone, but just because it is his duty (*propter officium*) and there is no one else to do it. Finally, suppose he judges with a trembling, repentant awareness of his own hidden sins. Then he may judge – in fact, it seems that he must.

[5] St. Thomas is paraphrasing a longer statement. Here is what St. Augustine says in context:

And therefore we must piously and cautiously watch, so that when necessity shall compel us to find fault with or rebuke any one, we may reflect first whether the fault is such as we have never had, or one from which we have now become free; and if we have never had it, let us reflect that we are men, and might have had it; but if we have had it, and are now free from it, let the common infirmity touch the memory, that not hatred but pity may go before that fault-finding or administering of rebuke: so that whether it shall serve for the conversion of him on whose account we do it, or for his perversion (for the issue is uncertain), we at least from the singleness of our eye may be free from care.

If, however, on reflection, we find ourselves involved in the same fault as he is whom we were preparing to censure, let us not censure nor rebuke; but yet let us mourn deeply over the case, and let us invite him not to obey us, but to join us in a common effort.[22]

---

[21] St. John Chrysostom, *Homilies on Matthew*, Homily 23, Sections 1 and 2, http://newadvent. org/fathers/2001.htm, changing "thou" to "you" and "art" to "are."

[22] St. Augustine of Hippo, *Our Lord's Sermon on the Mount*, Book 2, Chapter 19, Section 64, http://newadvent.org/fathers/1601.htm.

An interesting feature of the passage is the saint's remark that we cannot be certain of the result of just judgment. The guilty party may take the rebuke to heart; on the other hand, he may resent it and be hardened in wrongdoing. This makes no difference to the duty of the judge, for if his judgment is just and he delivers it with humility, then he is not responsible for the failure of wrongdoers to take it in right spirit.

[6] The Objector had taken St. Paul's remark, "in passing judgment upon [the offender] you condemn yourself, because you, the judge, are doing the very same things," to mean that *in all judgment whatsoever* the judge condemns himself. St. Thomas wraps up his reply by explaining that St. Paul is referring only to hypocritical judgment. For if the judge assigns punishment P for offense Q, he is asserting that punishment P is *deserved* for offense Q, so if he himself is also guilty of Q, then he himself deserves punishment P.

Whether We Should Always Judge According to the Written Law?

TEXT	PARAPHRASE
Whether we should always judge according to the written law?	Must judgment always be rendered according to the very words of the written law?

St. Thomas's views on law and virtue are tightly connected. One connection is that law aims at *forming* virtues in the citizens – at making them good.[1] Another is that virtue and the understanding of law develop from the same seeds, in the deep structure of practical reason.[2] In this Article, we see yet a third way. Whether we should judge according to the written law concerns the very meaning of the virtue of justice, because the act of judgment is the means by which justice is actualized, and justice is in turn connected with all the rest of the virtues.[3]

Normally, we should do as the written law directs, but earlier in the *Summa* the Angelic Doctor has considered several exceptions:

1. In political communities in which the citizens have the moral capacity and legal right to make their own laws, custom may express their considered judgment as to what the common good requires. In such a case, custom has the force of written law, abolishes written law, and is the interpreter of written law.[4]
2. Citizens may disobey so-called unjust laws, because an unjust law is not a true law at all. To be sure, sometimes they might obey an unjust law not because it has true legal force, but rather because disobedience

---

[1] I-II, Q. 92, Art. 1.
[2] For virtue, see esp. I-II, Q. 58, Art. 4; Q. 62, Art. 1; and I-II, Q. 63, Arts. 1–2. For the understanding of law, compare esp. I-II, Q. 92, Art. 1, and Q. 94, Art. 1.
[3] II-II, Q. 60, Art. 1, and Q. 65, Art. 1.   [4] I-II, Q. 97, Art. 3.

would cause even greater harm to the community – either through *scandalum*, which means something which causes others to stumble morally, or *turbationem*, which means any sort of confusion, commotion, or disorder. But even so, they must disobey if obedience would require them to violate the laws of God, doing what is intrinsically wrong.[5]

3. When cases arise which the written law was not intended to cover, those who have the authority to make the law may suspend it.[6]

4. In emergencies, when such cases arise but there is no time to consult authority, the citizens themselves may set aside the words of the law and follow its intention instead.[7]

Here, we are thinking neither of lawmakers nor of ordinary citizens, but of judges. Must *they* always follow the written law? And must they do as its very words direct, or may they sometimes set aside the words and follow its intention instead?

The relevance of this query to contemporary debates about judicial activism, restraint, and discretion is too obvious to belabor. But our inquiry is not just about constitutional rules and procedures, and it is not just about judicial role definitions. Taken in its broadest sense it concerns how these matters are related to human moral character.

Objection 1. [1] *It would seem that we ought not always to judge according to the written law. For we ought always to avoid judging unjustly. But written laws sometimes contain injustice,* [2] *according to Isaiah 10:1, "Woe to them that make wicked laws, and when they write, write injustice."* [3] *Therefore we ought not always to judge according to the written law.*	Objection 1. Apparently, the answer is "No," because we should never judge unjustly, but some written laws are unjust. The prophet Isaiah made this clear when he foretold calamity to those who decree wicked laws, whose writing is nothing but injustice. So must we always judge by the written law? Obviously not.

[1] In I-II, Question 96, Article 4, "Whether human law binds a man in conscience?," St. Thomas has considered the grounds and limits of civil disobedience by ordinary citizens. Apparently the Objector believes that the same principles should apply civil disobedience by subordinate magistrates: In particular, judges.

[2] The Objector warns that one cannot be sure that the laws will always be just. Even though God had given his chosen nation a just framework of civil law, its rulers and governors enacted evil. The prophet Isaiah warns of divine retribution, for Israel will fall before the invading Assyrians:

Woe to those who decree iniquitous decrees, and the writers who keep writing oppression, to turn aside the needy from justice and to rob the poor of my people of their

---

[5] I-II, Q. 96, Art. 4.   [6] I-II, Q. 97, Art. 4.   [7] I-II, Q. 96, Art. 6.

right, that widows may be their spoil, and that they may make the fatherless their prey! What will you do on the day of punishment, in the storm which will come from afar? To whom will you flee for help, and where will you leave your wealth?[8]

The Latin term translated "wicked" in the DRA and as "iniquitous" in the RSV-CE is *iniquas*, which means literally uneven or unfair – in this case, an unevenness in the treatment of the strong and the weak. St. Thomas uses the same term later, in the Reply to Objection 2, where it forms part of a contrast between the crooked and the straight.

[3] [3] Those legal positivists who define law as the command of the sovereign[9] would say that if the command of the sovereign is unjust, then a conscientious judge has no recourse but to resign. The Objector, who recognizes a higher law, thinks the conscientious judge has another option: He may ignore the unjust law.

Notice, though, that the Objector is not just saying that the judge may depart from the written law *in this case*. He seems to be reasoning that because in this instance it would be wrong to follow the written law, therefore the principle that we must judge according to the written law should be simply set aside.

Objection 2. [1] *Further, judgment has to be formed about individual happenings.* [2] *But no written law can cover each and every individual happening,* [3] *as the Philosopher declares (Ethic. v, 10).* [4] *Therefore it seems that we are not always bound to judge according to the written law.*	Objection 2. Moreover, judgment unavoidably concerns singular facts and circumstances. But as Aristotle remarks, no written law can take in every situation that might arise. So judgment need not always adhere to the written law.

[1] The lawmaker makes laws for settling cases; the judge actually settles cases. The lawmaker composes laws on the basis of generalizations about situations that are likely to arise; the judge applies laws to the facts of the actia¹ situation before him. True, in an Anglo-American type of legal system, the

---

[8] Isaiah 10:1–3 (RSV-CE).

[9] The definition of law as the command of the sovereign descends from Thomas Hobbes and John Austin; following H. L. A. Hart, another variety of legal positivist defines law as a social convention. Neither definition supposes that the authority of human law depends on natural law. Although a legal positivist might (though few do) believe in a natural standard for evaluating law, he would not regard this standard as being true law itself, and he would consider human enactments as true law even if they violated it. Although Hobbes did use the expression "natural law," he appears to have viewed it as law only in the proleptic sense, thinking that the natural standards are not really law *until they are incorporated into human law*. Until then he holds that they are mere "theorems of prudence," using the term "prudence," moreover in a far thinner sense than it had been used in the classical tradition. See Thomas Hobbes, *Leviathan: On the Matter, Form, and Power of a Commonwealth Ecclesiastical and Civil* (1651), John Austin, *The Province of Jurisprudence Determined* (1832), and H. L. A. Hart, *The Concept of Law* (Oxford: Oxford University Press, 1961, 1994). On the Continent, legal positivism is most often associated with Hans Kelsen, especially his work *Pure Theory of Law* (1934).

judgment of a higher judge in a given case serves as a standard for the judgment of a lower judge in a relevantly similar case. Even so, if the higher judge formulates rules about dissimilar circumstances, he is overreaching.

[2] In the country of Archenland, Mr. Drakeslayer buys land from Mr. Foxcastle, but dies before paying what he owes him. Now the written law of Archenland provides that the debts of a deceased party be paid from the estate before the rest is distributed to the heirs. Upon examination of the will, however, it is found that because of the debt, Drakeslayer has left Foxcastle a legacy – another piece of land, of value even greater than the amount he owed. Because no such eventuality was foreseen by the legislators, the law makes no provision for it. Consequently, if the court rules according to the written law, Drakeslayer will be paid twice, receiving not only what is owed him under the original debt, but the legacy as well. Realizing that no law can make provision for everything that might happen, the judge does not presume to criticize the law's authors. However, because the outcome is so manifestly unfair and unreasonable, it seems that not even the lawmakers themselves, had they been in his place, would have intended that he enforce it. Consequently, following not the very words of the law but rather its presumed intention, the judge allows the legacy to wipe out the debt.

[3] The difficulty is that the one-size-fits-all principle may apply to socks, but not to laws. In the *Nicomachean Ethics*, Aristotle explains like this:

> What creates the problem is that the equitable is just, but not the legally just but a correction of legal justice. The reason is that all law is universal but about some things it is not possible to make a universal statement which shall be correct. In those cases, then, in which it is necessary to speak universally, but not possible to do so correctly, the law takes the usual case, though it is not ignorant of the possibility of error. And it is none the less correct; for the error is in the law nor in the legislator but in the nature of the thing, since the matter of practical affairs is of this kind from the start. When the law speaks universally, then, and a case arises on it which is not covered by the universal statement, then it is right, where the legislator fails us and has erred by oversimplicity, to correct the omission – to say what the legislator himself would have said had he been present, and would have put into his law if he had known. Hence the equitable is just, and better than one kind of justice – not better than absolute justice but better than the error that arises from the absoluteness of the statement. And this is the nature of the equitable, a correction of law where it is defective owing to its universality.[10]

In his *Commentary* on the passage, St. Thomas remarks that "since particulars are infinite, our mind cannot embrace them to make a law that applies to every individual case. Therefore a law must be framed in a universal way, for example, whoever commits murder will be put to death." Even though the lawmakers are clearly aware of this defect, the best they can do is fit the law to "the majority of cases," leaving it up to judges to make corrections. Equity, then, is the specific branch of justice by which this is done; it is the kind of judgment

---

[10] Aristotle, *Nicomachean Ethics*, Book 5, Chapter 10.

that the judge exercises to correct the defect which law inevitably contains just because it must be framed in universal terms.

This is the original meaning of equity, as distinguished from the more particular meanings the term has sprouted while knocking about the courts of England and other countries. My own previous example, about Messrs. Drakeslayer and Foxcastle, was adapted to make sense to Anglo-American readers, who tend to think of equity as having to do only with fairness in civil suits. St. Thomas's own illustration is much broader:

> [I]n a certain city it was decreed under penalty of death that strangers were not to climb the walls of the city for fear they would usurp the civil government. But during an enemy invasion some strangers by climbing the walls defended the city from the invaders. They do not deserve to be punished by death; it would be against the natural law to reward benefactors with punishment. Therefore in this case legal justice must be directed by natural justice.[11]

[4] As at the end of Objection 1, the Objector seems to be reasoning that because *at least in this case* it would be wrong to follow the written law, the principle that we must judge according to the written law has no force whatsoever.

Objection 3. [1] *Further, a law is written in order that the lawgiver's intention may be made clear.* [2] *But it happens sometimes that even if the lawgiver himself were present he would judge otherwise.* [3] *Therefore we ought not always to judge according to the written law.*	Objection 3. Besides, the reason laws are set down in writing is to disclose what the lawmakers intend. Sometimes, though, matters turn out so that even the lawmakers would judge differently than by the words of the law if they were there. Surely, if even lawmakers may depart from the written law, then so may judges.

[1] The Objector implicitly assumes that words are subordinate to intentions, not intentions to words. Earlier in the *Summa*, St. Thomas reminded his readers of a point which had been accepted by the tradition and was especially well put by St. Hilary of Poitiers: That the meaning of someone's statement must be gathered from what caused him to make it. This being so, we should pay attention to the causes that move lawmakers to make laws, rather than just the words that they put in them, "because things are not subject to speech, but speech to things." What Hilary meant is that the lawmaker chooses his words, and says what he says, in order to express his intention concerning real things, real states of affairs. Consequently, words are in the service of intentions, rather than the reverse. It follows that at times, when the words give insufficient guidance, in order to understand what the lawmaker meant, we may have to

---

[11] Thomas Aquinas, *Commentary on Aristotle's Nicomachean Ethics*, Book 5, Lecture 16, trans. C. J. Litzinger, rev. ed. (Notre Dame, IN: Dumb Ox Books, 1993), p. 344. Available online at www.dhspriory.org/thomas/english/Ethics.htm.

look beyond his words to their "causes," to his intentions regarding the problem about which he was legislating.[12]

In the *Commentary on St. Thomas's Treatise on Law*, I suggested the judgment in a certain nineteenth-century labor law case as an example. Congress had enacted a statute to "prohibit the importation and migration of foreigners and aliens under contract or agreement to perform labor in the United States, its Territories, and the District of Columbia." Certain categories of workers were explicitly exempted, including professional actors, singers, and lecturers, but ministers of religion did not happen to fall into one of these categories. When the Church of the Holy Trinity, a religious society duly incorporated under the laws of New York state, made a contract with an Englishman to come into the country in order to serve as its rector and pastor, US authorities took action against the church, and the church and rector sued. Writing for the Court, Associate Justice Brewer argued that a "guide to the meaning of a statute is found in the evil which it is designed to remedy." The legislative history of the statute showed that the evil which Congress had designed it to remedy was the influx of large numbers of unskilled manual contract laborers into the United States, which Congress deemed harmful to the domestic labor market. Because the importation of ministers of religion was not part of the evil that Congress was aiming to remedy, Justice Brewer concluded that Congress would not have intended that ministers be denied the same exemption that other professionals received.[13]

[2] The Objector reasons that since the standard for judgment is not the very words of the lawmaker but his intention, it follows that in any case in which the lawmaker himself would have departed from his words in the judge's shoes, the judge should do the same thing.

[3] As at the end of Objections 1 and 2, the Objector generalizes broadly, reasoning that just because in such a case it would be wrong to follow the written law, the principle "Judge according to the written law" lacks even the force of a presumption.

On the contrary, *Augustine says (De Vera Relig. xxxi): "In these earthly laws, though men judge about them when they are making them, when once they are established and passed, the judges may judge no longer of them, but according to them."*	**On the other hand,** Augustine declares in his work *On True Religion* that although men may judge temporal laws while they are making them, they may not pass judgment on them once they are established and confirmed. Once that point is reached, they may no longer judge the laws; they may only judge *by* the laws.

St. Thomas chooses St. Augustine as representative of the traditional view. The context of the quotation is Augustine's comparison of eternal with human law:

[12] I-II, Q. 96, Art. 6, *sed contra*; St. Hilary of Poitiers, *On the Trinity*, Book 4.
[13] *Church of the Holy Trinity v. United States*, 143 U.S. 457 (1892).

[The eternal] law is that according to which [God] judges all things and concerning which no man can judge. In the case of temporal laws, men have instituted them and judge by them, and when they have been instituted and confirmed, no judge may judge them but must judge according to them. He who draws up temporal laws, if he is a good and wise man, takes eternal life into account, and that no soul may judge. He determines for the time being what is to be commanded and forbidden according to the immutable rules of eternal life. Pure souls may rightly know the eternal law but may not judge it. The difference is that, for knowing, it is enough to see that a thing is so and not so. For judging, it is necessary in addition to see that a thing can be thus or not thus; as when we say it ought to be thus, or to have been thus, or to be thus in the future, as workmen do with their works.[14]

As Augustine explains, whether we are speaking of eternal law framed by God, or of temporal law framed by human legislators, subordinates do not judge the law itself, but judge other things according to the law. When the lawmaker considers whether to enact a proposal, he judges whether it would be fitting in view of all the things that might happen. But once he has judged it fitting and made it a law, subordinate public officials such as judges do not consider whether the law could be improved, or whether they themselves could have made a better one; rather they discern what the law requires in the cases that come up before them.

I answer that, [1] *As stated above (Article 1), judgment is nothing else but a decision or determination of what is just.* [2] *Now a thing becomes just in two ways: first by the very nature of the case, and this is called "natural right,"* [3] *secondly by some agreement between men, and this is called "positive right," as stated above (Question 57, Article 2).* [4] *Now laws are written for the purpose of manifesting both these rights, but in different ways. For the written law does indeed contain natural right, but it does not establish it, for the latter derives its force, not from the law but from nature:* [5] *whereas the written law both contains positive right, and establishes it by giving it force of authority.* [6] *Hence it is necessary to judge according to the written law,* [7] *else judgment would fall short either of the natural or of the positive right.*	Here is my response. We have already seen that a judgment is nothing but a decree or determination of what is just. But justice may come into being in either of two ways. One way is by the nature of the thing itself – this is called natural right. The other way is by a certain agreement among men – this is called positive right. Laws are written to clear up both kinds of right, but not in the same way. For though written law certainly preserves natural right, it does not bring it into being – its living strength comes from nature, not written law. On the other hand, written law does more than *preserve* positive right, for by bestowing on it the living strength of authority, it actually brings it into being. Consequently, judgment must follow written law, for otherwise it fails to attain either natural or positive right.

[14] Augustine, *Of True Religion*, Book 31, in J. H. S. Burleigh, ed., *Augustine: Earlier Writings* (Philadelphia: Westminster Press, 1953), pp. 254–255.

[1] Here St. Thomas restates one of the main points in the argument of II-II, Question 60, Article 1. In the strict sense, the term "judgment" refers to the act of a judge performing the duty of his office. This duty is to declare what is right, which is the object of justice. Consequently, a judgment is a decree or determination of what is just or right.

[2] Many contemporary readers find a stumbling block in the idea of justice coming into being "by the very nature of the thing." Since justice cannot be seen by the senses or weighed on a scale, they conclude that it is not in things, but only in minds, and our minds may do anything they wish. St. Thomas would say justice does lies in things – in a certain relationship of proportional equality – and that the truth of justice lies in correspondence between the judgment of the mind and the actual state of affairs. If Mr. Leon has stolen from Mr. Noel, then the judgment that Leon owes Noel restitution is *rationally appropriate* to the circumstances, and although this fact cannot be confirmed by the senses or weighed on a scale, it can certainly be measured by the instrument of a finely tuned, virtuous mind.

Sometimes my students protest "But *who is to say* what P owes Q?" St. Thomas would answer that a just judge is to say – someone who possesses the virtue of justice so that he desires the right, the virtue of prudence so that he discerns the right, and the authority of his office to declare the right."

[3] St. Thomas explains the relationship between natural and positive right with great clarity and precision in II-II, Question 57, Article 2:

[T]he "right" or the "just" is a work that is adjusted to another person according to some kind of equality. Now a thing can be adjusted to a man in two ways: first by its very nature, as when a man gives so much that he may receive equal value in return, and this is called "natural right." On another way a thing is adjusted or commensurated to another person, by agreement, or by common consent, when, to wit, a man deems himself satisfied, if he receive so much. This can be done in two ways: first by private agreement, as that which is confirmed by an agreement between private individuals; secondly, by public agreement, as when the whole community agrees that something should be deemed as though it were adjusted and commensurated to another person, or when this is decreed by the [magistrate[15]] who is placed over the people, and acts in its stead, and this is called "positive right."

Notice that positive right does not push aside or take the place of natural right; rather it pins down the details which natural right leaves unspecified. In legislation, the distinction between natural and positive right corresponds to the distinction between deriving human law from natural law by "conclusion from premises" and deriving it from natural law by "determination of

---

[15] The Latin word is *princeps* – the principal or foremost man – which the Blackfriars translation generally renders by such words as "prince" and "sovereign" (here the former). I have explained previously why I consider this rendering misleading. The term was originally used for a great man of the Roman senate. Only later, after the collapse of the republic, was it applied to the Emperors. It does not necessarily imply either lifelong, absolute, or hereditary rule.

generalities." The *locus* for the latter distinction is St. Thomas's discussion of whether every human law is derived from natural law, in I-II, Question 95, Article 2.

[4] To illustrate the point: Human law does not, say, make theft wrong by decreeing that thieves shall be punished; theft was already wrong. In such a case, human enactment merely backs up the natural law.

In the indicated sentence, as well as in the next one, the Latin word translated "force" is *robur*, a term which originally referred to oak wood, or to the firmness and strength of an oak tree. However, St. Thomas is speaking of moral force, of authority, not merely of a physical power such as the ability to decree and punish. The paraphrase "binding strength" is tempting, because a just law ties us up with bonds of duty. However, this phrase is more properly used for the expression *vim obligandi* in the Reply to Objection 1. Instead I have paraphrased *robur* as "living strength," which seems fitting because the strength of an oak is related to its life, and relationships of law and justice can exist only among living, rational beings.

[5] The bindingness of the decree that thieves shall be punished does not depend on human enactment; thieves should be punished whether lawmakers say so or not. On the other hand, the bindingness of the decree concerning *how* thieves shall be punished does depend on human enactment. Before the lawmakers have settled on a mode of punishment, any of a range of punishments might reasonably be deemed appropriate, but after they have settled on one, that is the one which must be used.

[6] St. Thomas seems to view this conclusion as establishing a strong presumption rather than an absolutely exceptionless rule, for as we see in the Replies to the Objections, he agrees that in some cases the very words of the law should not be the standard of judgment.

[7] If the judge simply refuses to enforce the human law against thievery, then his judgment falls short of both natural and positive right.[16] If he enforces the law but decrees a punishment different from the one the law sets down – for example, if the law requires restitution and imprisonment but instead he banishes the thief – then although his judgment might not fall short of natural right, it certainly falls short of positive right.

Reply to Objection 1. [1] *Just as*	Reply to Objection 1. We have seen
the written law does not give force	that written law is not the source of
to the natural right, so neither	natural right's living strength. For the
can it diminish or annul its force,	same reason, it cannot diminish that
[2] *because neither can man's will*	strength or do away with it, for nature
change nature. [3] *Hence if the written*	cannot be changed by the will of man.
law contains anything contrary to the	Consequently, anything in written law
natural right, it is unjust and has no	which is contrary to natural right is

16 The "or" in this sentence is the "inclusive or," *vel.*

binding force. [4] *For positive right has no place except where "it matters not," according to the natural right, "whether a thing be done in one way or in another"; as stated above (57, 2, ad 2).* [5] *Wherefore such documents are to be called, not laws, but rather corruptions of law, as stated above (I-II, 95, 2):* [6] *and consequently judgment should not be delivered according to them.*	unjust and lacks the power to tie us up in bonds of obligation. Indeed, positive right has a place only when natural right does not pin down the way in which something is to be done. And so we come again to a conclusion we reached earlier in the *Summa*: Unjust written enactments should be called not laws, but corruptions of law. No such thing can serve as a standard for passing judgment.

[1] As we saw in discussing the *respondeo*, theft does not become wrong merely because human law prohibits it; rather human law recognizes that the act is wrong in itself. By the same token, if something is wrong in itself, human law cannot make it right, or even make it less wrong than it is. Suppose, for example, that human lawmakers commanded or committed theft instead of prohibiting it; theft would still be unjust. Historically, such iniquitous decrees are commonplace. In 1536, Henry VIII began the dissolution of the English religious orders and the seizure of their assets merely to increase the royal revenue; later on, much of the property was sold or simply handed over to Henry's cronies. In 2005, US Supreme Court authorized much the same sort of thing when it allowed a city agency to seize the house of a widow and turn it over to a private development company, merely in the hope that the company could use it more productively. Ironically, after the woman's house was torn down, the developer abandoned the project because the developer was unable to obtain financing.[17] One may take comfort in the fact that the latter theft was smaller in scale than the former only by overlooking the fact that it established a precedent.

Writing for the Court in the 1798 case *Calder v. Bull*, Justice Samuel Chase had written:

A law that punished a citizen for an innocent action, or, in other words, for an act, which, when done, was in violation of no existing law; a law that destroys, or impairs, the lawful private contracts of citizens; a law that makes a man a Judge in his own cause; *or a law that takes property from A. and gives it to B*: It is against all reason and justice, for a people to entrust a Legislature with such powers; and, therefore, it cannot be presumed that they have done it."[18]

Such words had greater influence in a day when judges still believed in natural right.

---

[17] *Susette Kelo v. City of New London*, 545 U.S. 469 (2005).

[18] *Calder v. Bull*, 3 Dall. 386, 388 (1798), emphasis added to the italicized phrase and removed from the word "such."

[2] "Because man's will cannot change nature": Although St. Thomas believes that we cannot change the nature we possess as human beings, that is not what he means here. Rather he is saying that we cannot change nature at large: We cannot alter the constitution of the reality within which we have our being. In a way, though, human nature comes into the picture too, for our nature is a *rational* nature – one which is able to discern *what the fundamental characteristics of this reality are*. Among its characteristics is the fact that relations among persons can either fulfill proportional equality or fall short of it; they can be either just or unjust.

[3] What St. Thomas actually says is that laws contrary to natural right lack *vim obligandi*, the power to bind us, to tie us up with cords of duty. The same phrase is used in his discussion of civil disobedience, I-II, Question 96, Article 4, "Whether human law binds a man in conscience?"

[4] St. Thomas had previously established this point in II-II, Question 57, Article 2, Reply to Objection 2, where again we meet the prophet Isaiah:

> The human will can, by common agreement, make a thing to be just provided it be not, of itself, contrary to natural justice, and it is in such matters that positive right has its place .... If, however, a thing is, of itself, contrary to natural right, the human will cannot make it just, for instance by decreeing that it is lawful to steal or to commit adultery. Hence it is written (Isaiah 10:1): "Woe to them that make wicked laws."

[5] St. Augustine had explained in his dialogue *On Free Choice of the Will* that an unjust law is not truly law. Appealing to him in I-II, Question 95, Article 2, St. Thomas extends Augustine's argument, holding that an enactment is truly law only so far as it is just. Since we call laws just only when reason shows that they are right, and since the first rule of practical reason is the law of nature, it follows that a human enactment is just only so far as it is rooted in natural law. Consequently, enactments which quarrel with natural law in any way are not true laws, but only putrefied carcasses of law.

[6] If unjust laws cannot serve as a standard for judgment, then has St. Thomas taken back his previous conclusion that we *must* judge according to the law? No – *simply because a so-called unjust law is not a law*.

Notice too that St. Thomas does not say that when the so-called law is unjust, the judge may legislate from the bench. It is one thing to refuse to accept an unjust law as a guide to judgment; it is quite another substitute a rule of one's own devising. The lawmaker has no authority to enact compulsory injustice, but neither has the judge an authority to make himself a lawmaker.

Reply to Objection 2. [1] *Even as unjust laws by their very nature are, either always or for the most part, contrary to the natural right, so too laws that are rightly established, fail in some cases, when if they were observed they would be contrary*	Reply to Objection 2. Crooked laws always or almost always derive their crookedness from the fact that they are contrary to natural right. Yet even laws that are laid straight lack the character of law in those few cases in which doing as they direct would be contrary to natural right. In such

to the natural right. [2] *Wherefore in such cases judgment should be delivered, not according to the letter of the law, but according to equity which the lawgiver has in view.* [3] *Hence the jurist says [Digest. i, 3; De leg. senatusque consult. 25]: "By no reason of law, or favor of equity, is it allowable for us to interpret harshly, and render burdensome, those useful measures which have been enacted for the welfare of man."* [4] *On such cases even the lawgiver himself would decide otherwise; and if he had foreseen the case, he might have provided for it by law.*	instances, rather than following the very words of the law, judgment relies on equity – on that which the lawmaker intends. This is what the Roman legal authority Modestinus had in mind in the remark quoted in the *Digest*, where he says that "It is not allowable, under any principle of law or generous maxim of equity, that measures introduced favorably to men's interests should be extended by us through a sterner mode of interpretation, on the side of severity and against those very interests."[19] Confronted with such a case, even the lawmaker would judge other than by the words of the law. Had he anticipated the case, he might even have written the law in such a way as to cover it.

[1] Although the meaning of this statement is clear, the Latin wording suggests a contrast between the straight and the crooked, or the even and uneven, which has disappeared from the English. *Leges iniquae*, which the Blackfriars translation renders "unjust laws," refers literally to uneven laws. *Recte positae*, which the Blackfriars translation renders "rightly established," means literally "laid down straightly." To restore this understated word picture, I have freely paraphrased the respective expressions as "crooked laws" and "law that are laid straight."

[2] The lawmaker *anticipates* that law will be interpreted according to his intention, because he is perfectly aware of the defect brought about by the necessity of expressing it in universal terms.

[3] The idea is that since rulers have the duty to serve the common good, and since their enactments have the reality and authority of law only if they do serve the common good, any interpretation which twists an enactment away from the common good also deprives it of the reality and authority of law, so that no ruler has authority to do such a thing.

[4] St. Thomas's reasoning about the duty of judges under law parallels his conclusion earlier in the *Summa* about the duties of citizens under law:

Now it happens often that the observance of some point of law conduces to the common weal in the majority of instances, and yet, in some cases, is very hurtful. Since then the lawgiver cannot have in view every single case, he shapes the law according to what

---

[19] Often St. Thomas paraphrases. Since in this case he quotes Modestinus almost exactly – he merely changes *iuris ratio* to *ratio iuris* – I have adopted the wording of translator D. N. MacCormack, in Alan Watson, ed., *The Digest of Justinian*, vol. 1, rev. ed. (Philadelphia: University of Pennsylvania Press, 1998), p. 13. In the system of the *Digest* itself, the passage is Book 1, Title 3, Section 25. For clarity, I have added commas.

happens most frequently, by directing his attention to the common good. Wherefore if a case arise wherein the observance of that law would be hurtful to the general welfare, it should not be observed. For instance, suppose that in a besieged city it be an established law that the gates of the city are to be kept closed, this is good for public welfare as a general rule: but, it were to happen that the enemy are in pursuit of certain citizens, who are defenders of the city, it would be a great loss to the city, if the gates were not opened to them: and so in that case the gates ought to be opened, contrary to the letter of the law, in order to maintain the common weal, which the lawgiver had in view.[20]

In such a case the lawmaker himself would have intended the gates to be left open. So, exercising their own good sense, *the gatekeepers may leave them open*, just long enough for the defenders to get back inside. We see now that for exactly the same reason, if the public prosecutors are so foolish as to bring charges against the gatekeepers for what they have done, the judge should not find them guilty. Both the gatekeepers and the judge have violated the letter of the law, but neither the gatekeepers nor the judge have violated its intention.

At first it seems difficult to reconcile this concession with the conclusion of the *respondeo* that we must judge according to the written law. However, as suggested earlier, St. Thomas seems to view the precept "judge according to the written law" as expressing a strong presumption rather than an exceptionless rule. Moreover, he implies a distinction between following the law, and following the very words of the law. Whenever the law is just, one must follow it. However, in cases where the words of the law fall short of the lawmaker's intention, *to follow the very words of the law is to not actually to follow the law*.

One difficulty remains. In the example quoted above, St. Thomas emphasizes that the gatekeepers were right to depart from the letter of the law only because there was no time for them to ask the public authorities whether they may do so:

Nevertheless it must be noted, that if the observance of the law according to the letter does not involve any sudden risk needing instant remedy, it is not competent for everyone to expound what is useful and what is not useful to the state: those alone can do this who are in authority, and who, on account of such like cases, have the power to dispense from the laws.[21]

One might suppose that the same reservation applies to the judge as to the gatekeeper: Rather than just guessing that the lawmakers would depart from the written law in a case like the one before them, *the judge should ask them*. However, this does not follow. The lawmakers are perfectly aware of the defect the laws contain because they are expressed in general terms, and so the subordinate authority of judges allows for its correction. It belongs to the very office of the judge to interpret the intention of the lawmakers; it does not belong to the very office of the gatekeeper.

---

[20] I-II, Q. 96, Art. 6.   [21] Ibid.

Reply to Objection 3.This suffices for the Reply to the Third Objection.	Reply to Objection 3. How Objection 3 may be answered should be clear from what we have already said.

St. Thomas *agrees* with the Objector that the words of the law are in service to its intentions; he *agrees* with the Objector that even if the lawmaker himself were present, he would judge differently; and he *agrees* with the Objector that in such a case the very words of the law should not be followed. But he does *not* agree with the Objector that therefore the precept "judge according to the written law" may simply be set aside, for it is valid as a strong presumption. One might say that just as the written law must be followed equitably, with allowance for those exceptions which are compatible with the legislative intention, *so, in a figurative sense, the precept that one must judge according to the written law must also be understood equitably*, with allowance for those exceptions which are compatible with the philosophical intention.

II-II, QUESTION 60, ARTICLE 6

Whether Judgment Is Rendered Perverse by Being Usurped?

TEXT	PARAPHRASE
Whether judgment is rendered perverse by being usurped?	Is justice destroyed when a person is judged by someone who has no public authority to do so?

Usurpatio is illicit seizure – taking something that rightfully belongs to someone else. To usurp judgment is to judge a case over which one has no jurisdiction, to seize the power of judgment from the person to whom it belongs. St. Thomas defends the traditional view that the usurpation of judgment is a violation of justice – that judging without proper jurisdiction destroys justice *even if the usurper renders the correct judgment.*

Broadly speaking, the term "usurpation" may be used either for the seizure of judicial powers, or for the seizure, by a judge, of nonjudicial powers. However, in this Article St. Thomas is thinking only of the former sort of usurpation. He is not asking whether it is unjust for a judge to make the sorts of judgments which properly belong to, say, the legislature; we already know that is wrong, because the judge must render judgment according to the law. Rather he is asking whether it is unjust for someone else to make the sorts of judgments which properly belong to the judge himself. The usurper, the "someone else," might be another judge who has no jurisdiction in the case, or it might be someone who is not a judge at all.

Objection 1. [1] *It would seem that judgment is not rendered perverse by being usurped. For justice is rectitude in matters of action.* [2] *Now truth is not impaired, no matter who tells it, but it may suffer from the person who*	**Objection 1.** Apparently justice is not destroyed when a person is judged by someone who has no public authority to do so. For to do justice is do what must be done the right way. But truth does not depend on who declares it, even

ought to accept it. [3] *Therefore again justice loses nothing, no matter who declares what is just, and this is what is meant by judgment.*	though it may be denied by someone who ought to accept it. In the same way, justice does not depend on who defines the right, and defining the right is all that judgment is.

[1] Justice is doing the right thing. The Objector wishes us to notice that this definition of justice makes no reference to who does the right thing – only to the fact that the right thing is done.

[2] The truth of the statement "Snow is white" depends not on who says it but on whether it corresponds to the facts – on whether snow is white. Of course someone who ought to admit that snow is white may deny that snow is white, but this is beside the point.

[3] According to the Objector, if the truth of a true statement does not depend on who declares it, then the truth of a true statement *about what justice requires* does not depend on who declares it either. But judgment is merely declaring what justice requires.

So far the Objector has proven only that the *truth* of the judgment does not depend on who declares it. To reach the conclusion that the *justice* of the judgment does not depend on who declares it, he needs another premise which he has not stated: That every true judgment is a just judgment; that nothing but truth is necessary for the judgment to be just. In his Reply, St. Thomas will provide a reason for thinking that this silent premise is false.

Objection 2. [1] *Further, it belongs to judgment to punish sins. Now it is related to the praise of some that they punished sins without having authority over those whom they punished;* [2] *such as Moses in slaying the Egyptian (Exodus 2:12),* [3] *and Phinees the son of Eleazar in slaying Zambri the son of Salu (Numbers 25:7–14), and "it was reputed to him unto justice" (Psalm 105:31).*[1] [4] *Therefore usurpation of judgment pertains not to injustice.*	**Objection 2.** Moreover, judgment concerns the punishment of sins, but we read in Scripture that some have been praised even though they had no authority over those whose sins they punished. For example, Moses was praised for killing the Egyptian, and Phineas, son of Eleazar, was praised for killing Zimri, son of Salu. Indeed, the Psalmist says plainly that the deed of Phineas was reckoned as just. These cases show that the usurpation of judgment does not result in injustice.

[1] Judgment includes not only declaring that someone has done wrong but also exacting punishment (or at least decreeing what the punishment should be). Yet according to the Objector, Holy Scripture approves of several persons for carrying out punishment in cases in which they were not the proper judges. Holy Scripture cannot be mistaken. Therefore, if these persons really did

---

[1] The psalm in question is numbered 105 in the DRA but 106 in contemporary translations.

usurp judgment – yet what they did was right – then the traditional view that the usurpation of judgment is unjust must be wrong. Everything depends on whether these examples really show what the Objector thinks they show, so let us examine them.

[2] Although Moses he had been adopted as an infant by a daughter of the Egyptian monarch, the Pharaoh, he was a Hebrew and knew that he was a Hebrew. Now the Hebrews, who were slaves of the Egyptians, were cruelly oppressed. The Old Testament book of Exodus recounts the following incident of his young manhood, before he had become the leader of his people:

One day, when Moses had grown up, he went out to his people and looked on their burdens; and he saw an Egyptian beating a Hebrew, one of his people. He looked this way and that, and seeing no one he killed the Egyptian and hid him in the sand. When he went out the next day, behold, two Hebrews were struggling together; and he said to the man that did the wrong, "Why do you strike your fellow?" He answered, "Who made you a prince and a judge over us? Do you mean to kill me as you killed the Egyptian?" Then Moses was afraid, and thought, "Surely the thing is known." When Pharaoh heard of it, he sought to kill Moses. But Moses fled from Pharaoh, and stayed in the land of Midian[.][2]

Although the words of the passage do not say that Moses was right to kill the Egyptian, the Objector assumes, without explanation, that the act was approved – probably because Moses was later chosen by God to lead the Hebrews out of bondage.

[3] Throughout their history, the Hebrew people were often tempted to abandon the worship of God, taking up the cult of the Near Eastern fertility gods who were collectively known as *baals*.[3] Baal worship was a foul affair, involving, among other things, child sacrifice and ritual obscenity. One such period occurred sometime after the Exodus, when the Hebrews were encamped in the trans-Jordanian valley, before the crossing of the Jordan into the promised land. According to the Scriptural account, so many of the people became sexually involved with the women of the pagan Moabites, accepting initiation into the cult of the Baal of Mt. Peor, that Moses commanded the judges of Israel to execute all those who had done so. At the height of the crisis, Zimri, the son of Salu, defied the ban by openly entangling himself with a pagan woman, Cozbi, the daughter of Zur, a ruler of the Midianites, with whom the Moabites had close relations. From the way that the story is told, it seems that he was having intercourse with her publicly, in the very sight of the people who were weeping about the nation's sins in the tent of meeting and worship. Phinehas responded by impaling both Zimri and Cozbi, apparently catching them *in flagrante delicto*, with a single thrust of his spear.[4]

---

[2] Exodus 2:11–15 (RSV-CE).

[3] Generically, the word *baal* means "lord" but eventually came to be used only for the gods of the fertility cult, whose worshippers addressed them by that title.

[4] Numbers 23:1–8.

[4] The Objector views Phinehas' action as a usurpation of judgment, on grounds that he did not hold the office of a judge. Yet as the Objector points out, Scripture praises the deed explicitly. God declares to Moses, "Phinehas the son of Eleazar, son of Aaron the priest, has turned back my wrath from the people of Israel.... Behold, I give to him my covenant of peace; and it shall be to him, and to his descendants after him, the covenant of a perpetual priesthood, because he was jealous for his God, and made atonement for the people of Israel."[5] Commemorating the event, the Psalmist says Phinehas's act "has been reckoned to him as righteousness from generation to generation forever."[6] It seems to follow that usurped judgment can be just.

Objection 3. [1] *Further, spiritual power is distinct from temporal.* [2] *Now prelates having spiritual power sometimes interfere in matters concerning the secular power. Therefore usurped judgment is not unlawful.*	Objection 3. Still further, even though spiritual and temporal authority are distinct, sometimes the prelates of the Church, whose authority is spiritual, intervene in matters pertaining to secular authority. It follows that usurpation of authority is not illicit.

[1] The reason there are two levels of authority is that man has been made for a twofold end or purpose: The lower is natural happiness, which can be enjoyed in this life; the other is the supernatural happiness of the vision of God, which the blessed enjoy in the life to come. Natural happiness is incomplete, in the sense that it always leaves something to be desired. It is not that natural goods are bad, but that we were made for something more. Even so, both earthly and heavenly happiness are true ends, because both are worthwhile in themselves.

As St. Thomas explains in the *Treatise on Law*, "if man were ordained to no other end than that which is proportionate to his natural faculty, there would be no need for man to have any further direction of the part of his reason, besides the natural law and human law which is derived from it. But since man is ordained to an end of eternal happiness which is [incommensurate with] man's natural faculty, ... therefore it was necessary that, besides the natural and the human law, man should be directed to his end by a law given by God."[7]

Temporal power, then, is the authority to direct us to our this-worldly common good, according to the natural law. Normally this is the affair of the state, which administers domestic justice for the sake of the temporal common good and wages war for the sake of rightly ordered peace. But spiritual power is the authority to direct us to our supernatural common good, our heavenly peace, according to Divine law. This, which is of far greater dignity and importance, is the affair of the Church.

---

[5] Numbers 25:11–13 (RSV-CE).   [6] Psalm 106:31 (RSV-CE).

[7] II-II, Q. 91, Art. 4, substituting "incommensurate with" for "inproportionate to." One might also paraphrase "beyond the scope of."

[2] From the distinction of the two levels of authority, the Objector seems to conclude that neither is subordinate to the other: Spiritual power belongs entirely to the Church, while temporal power belongs entirely to the state. If this is true, then any interference with the judgments of the state by the authorities of the Church is a usurpation. Yet the authorities of the Church *do* sometimes interfere with the authorities of the state, presumably justly. From these premises, the Objector concludes that it is not necessarily unjust for judgment to be usurped.

Objection 4. [1] *Further, even as the judge requires authority in order to judge aright, so also does he need justice and knowledge, as shown above (1, ad 1, 3; 2).* [2] *But a judgment is not described as unjust, if he who judges lacks the habit of justice or the knowledge of the law.* [3] *Neither therefore is it always unjust to judge by usurpation, i.e. without authority.*	Objection 4. Besides, as we have seen earlier, to judge properly the judge needs not only the authority of his office, but also both the virtue and the "science" of justice. Yet judgment is not necessarily unjust merely because he lacks one of these latter two things. Neither, then, does it always become unjust merely because he renders it without the first thing – without the authority to judge.

[1] The Objector begins by reaffirming the conclusion of II-II, Question 60, Article 2: That the judgments of judges should be grounded in the authority of their office, prompted by the disposition to do justice, and brought about by sound reasoning. Here such reasoning is described as the *scientia* of justice, the understanding of how conclusions about justice flow from first principles.

[2] Yet although the Objector is willing to concede that judges *need* all three things, he does not think the absence of one of them automatically makes a judgment unjust. For actually, we do not call a judgment unjust merely because the judge is a morally careless or an ignorant man – because he lacks either the virtue or the "science" of justice. As our own adage says, even a stopped clock is right twice a day.

[3] Since we do not call the judgment unjust merely because of a deficiency in one of the other requirements, the Objector thinks it unreasonable to call it unjust merely because the judge lacks jurisdiction.

On the contrary, It is written (Romans 14:4): "Who art thou that judgest another man's servant?"	On the other hand, we read St. Paul's admonishment to the Romans to mind their own business: "Who are you to pass judgment on someone else's servant?"

Again we meet St. Paul's principle, which we previously met in II-II, Question 60, Article 2, Objection 2, that a servant is to be judged only by his own master. This time the principle is generalized to mean that justice is violated whenever the person who is judging lacks jurisdiction in the case at hand. It is easy to see why this *sed contra* does not fully settle the question before us, because the question of judicial usurpation is not even on St. Paul's mind. He is merely scolding the busybodies who insist that everyone adopt their dietary scruples (along with the reverse busybodies who insist that everyone give up their dietary scruples). Although his question "Who are you to pass judgment on someone else's servant?" clearly implies that judgment *ought not be usurped*, it does not tell us whether a usurped judgment *becomes, by this fact, unjust.* To answer this question, St. Thomas proceeds to the *respondeo*.

I answer that, [1] *Since judgment should be pronounced according to the written law, as stated above (Article 5),* [2] *he that pronounces judgment, interprets, in a way, the letter of the law, by applying it to some particular case.* [3] *Now since it belongs to the same authority to interpret and to make a law, just as a law cannot be made save by public authority, so neither can a judgment be pronounced except by public authority, which extends over those who are subject to the community.* [4] *Wherefore even as it would be unjust for one man to force another to observe a law that was not approved by public authority, so too it is unjust, if a man compels another to submit to a judgment that is pronounced by other than the public authority.*	**Here is my response.** We have already discussed the fact that because judgment must follow the written law, the judge must interpret the law by applying it to the matter at hand. But making and interpreting the law are rooted in the same public authority, without which law can be neither made nor interpreted. This authority extends to all of the community's subjects. Therefore, just as it would be unjust to make someone obey a so-called law not *made* by public authority, so it would be unjust to make someone submit to a judgment not *rendered* by public authority.

[1] As St. Thomas explained in the previous Article, written law should be followed because it "manifests" right – it puts on display the standard of justice to be followed. The law forbidding theft manifests natural right, because theft is unjust in the very nature of the case. Nothing else but prohibition would have been reasonable; no act of the legislature could have made theft just. By contrast, the law defining a category of theft and decreeing a particular penalty for it manifests positive right, because a wide range of different penalties might have been reasonable. The one the legislature decrees is just simply because it decrees it.

[2] For the judge to follow the law is to apply it to the case at hand, but no law is self-interpreting; in order to bring the law to bear, the judge must use his intelligence. Let us say the law defines theft as a class A misdemeanor if the value of the property or services stolen is at least $500 but less than $1,500, and let us say the law decrees that the punishment for a class A misdemeanor is a jail term of up to one year, a fine of up to $4,000, or both. Then the judge must determine whether what the law means by a theft has been committed; if so, then whether the value of the property or services stolen lies within the statutory bounds, and if so, then what fine or jail term within the statutory bounds is proportional to the gravity of the deed.

[3] St. Thomas had argued in I-II, Question 90, Article 3, that *because law is for the whole community*, not anyone can make a law, but only someone who by public authority is competent to do so. Here he extends that conclusion. *Because the judge has no authority to render judgment apart from the law*, not anyone can judge, but only someone who by that same public authority is competent to do so:

> A judge's sentence is like a particular law regarding some particular fact. Wherefore just as a general law should have coercive power, ... so too the sentence of a judge should have coercive power, whereby either party is compelled to comply with the judge's sentence; else the judgment would be of no effect. Now coercive power is not exercised in human affairs, save by those who hold public authority: and those who have this authority are accounted the superiors of those over whom they preside whether by ordinary or by delegated authority. Hence it is evident that no man can judge others than his subjects and this in virtue either of delegated or of ordinary authority.[8]

[4] St. Thomas had written in I-II, Question 96, Article 4, that laws made without public authority "are acts of violence rather than laws." We might paraphrase the point he makes here by saying that judgments made without public authority are acts of violence rather than judgments. For a would-be law, made by one who lacks proper legislative authority, is devoid of the character and justice of a law – and in the same way, a would-be judgment, rendered by someone who lacks proper judicial authority, is devoid of the character and justice of a judgment.

| *Reply to Objection 1.* [1] *When the truth is declared there is no obligation to accept it, and each one is free to receive it or not, as he wishes.* [2] *On the other hand judgment implies an obligation,* [3] *wherefore it is unjust for anyone to be judged by one who has no public authority.* | Reply to Objection 1. The Objector relies on an analogy between declaring truth and defining justice, but his analogy does not hold. For the mere declaration of the truth does not compel anyone to accept it; each person is free to accept or reject it, just as he pleases. Justice, by contrast, implies the bonds of compulsion. This makes it unjust to be judged by someone who lacks public authority. |

[1] St. Thomas is not denying that there is a moral duty to assent to what is known to be true. He is merely pointing out that there is no public sanction if I don't. No one threatens me with time in prison for refusing to assent to the proposition that the square of the hypotenuse is equal to the sum of the squares of the other two sides.

[2] By contrast, there is a public sanction for not obeying the judgment of the court. I am compelled to obey.

[3] But public sanction requires public authority. Therefore it is unjust to be compelled to comply with a usurped judgment, which is backed up by nothing but private presumption.

[8] II-II, Q. 67, Art. 1.

The Objector had relied on an analogy between declaring the truth and rendering a judgment, arguing that if the truth of a statement does not depend on who declares it, then the justice of a judgment does not depend on who decrees it. St. Thomas has undercut the Objection by showing that the two cases are not parallel.

Reply to Objection 2. [1] *Moses seems to have slain the Egyptian by authority received as it were, by divine inspiration; this seems to follow from Acts 7:24–25, where it is said that "striking the Egyptian … he thought that his brethren understood that God by his hand would save Israel [Vulgate: 'them'].* [2] *Or it may be replied that Moses slew the Egyptian in order to defend the man who was unjustly attacked, without himself exceeding the limits of a blameless defense. Wherefore Ambrose says (De Offic. i, 36) that "whoever does not ward off a blow from a fellow man when he can, is as much in fault as the striker"; and he quotes the example of Moses.* [3] *Again we may reply with Augustine (QQ. Exod. qu. 2) [Cf. Contra Faust. xxii, 70] that just as "the soil gives proof of its fertility by producing useless herbs before the useful seeds have grown, so this deed of Moses was sinful although it gave a sign of great fertility," in so far, to wit, as it was a sign of the power whereby he was to deliver his people.* [4] *With regard to Phinees the reply is that he did this out of zeal for God by Divine inspiration; or because though not as yet high-priest, he was nevertheless the high-priest's son, and this judgment was his concern as of the other judges, to whom this was commanded [Exodus 6:25;[9] Leviticus 20; Deuteronomy 13 and 17.[10]]*	Reply to Objection 2. We might view the incident of Moses killing the Egyptian in several ways. First, it might be said that he killed him by the authority of something like a divine inspiration – or so it seems from the seventh chapter of Acts, which states that he thought his brothers understood that God would save Israel by his hand. Then again we might say that Moses killed the Egyptian in defense of a person who was suffering injury and innocently protecting himself. Ambrose comments in his book *On Duties* that one who fails to defend his neighbor from a blow is every bit as guilty as the one who struck it, and he illustrates by mentioning Moses. Still another possibility is the one suggested by St. Augustine in his *Questions on Exodus*: Just as the earth is admired for the fertility which brings forth useless weeds, even before useful seeds germinate, so, even though what Moses did was a sin, it too signified a great fertility – it was a mark of the power by which he would liberate the people. Concerning Phineas, there are also several possibilities. We might may say that he did what he did by divine inspiration, moved by zeal for God. Or we might say that even though he was not yet the high priest, the judgment lay within his jurisdiction just because he was one of the judges who had been commanded to act in this matter.

---

[9] Corrected; Blackfriars gives the citation as Exodus 22:20.

[10] The Blackfriars translators probably have in mind Leviticus 20:1–5, Deuteronomy 13:6–17, and Deuteronomy 17:2–7. In each passage, capital punishment is decreed for participation in the cult of the baals or of associated gods such as Moloch.

[1] The Objector had claimed that Holy Scripture approved Moses' killing of the Egyptian without proper authority, therefore usurped judgment can be just. St. Thomas offers three possible solutions to the puzzle. Any one of them would be sufficient to show that the Objector is mistaken: Either Moses did have the requisite authority, or he lacked it but his act is not approved.

The first solution is that Moses was not usurping the place of an authorized judge, because, as the divinely appointed ruler of the Hebrews, he himself was an authorized judge. This suggestion is drawn from the speech of the St. Stephen before the Sanhedrin or Jewish council. Defending himself against a charge of blasphemy for preaching about Christ, the apostle presents a brief summary of salvation history. Among other things, it includes the following interpretation of the killing of the Egyptian:

When [Moses] was forty years old, it came into his heart to visit his brethren, the sons of Israel. And seeing one of them being wronged, he defended the oppressed man and avenged him by striking the Egyptian. *He supposed that his brethren understood that God was giving them deliverance by his hand, but they did not understand.* And on the following day he appeared to them as they were quarreling and would have reconciled them, saying, 'Men, you are brethren, why do you wrong each other?' But the man who was wronging his neighbor thrust him aside, saying, 'Who made you a ruler and a judge over us? Do you want to kill me as you killed the Egyptian yesterday?'[11]

St. Stephen may be suggesting that since Moses had already been chosen by God to save the Hebrew people from Egyptian oppression, his authority to render judgment was already in effect, even though he was mistaken in expecting his fellow Hebrews to understand and accept it before he had given proofs.

[2] The second solution is that Moses was not usurping judgment because he was aiding the victim of an unjust attack in self-defense. This suggestion is offered by St. Ambrose of Milan in the course of a discussion of the four cardinal virtues:

The glory of fortitude, therefore, does not rest only on the strength of one's body or of one's arms, but rather on the courage of the mind. Nor is the law of courage exercised in causing, but in driving away all harm. *He who does not keep harm off a friend, if he can, is as much in fault as he who causes it. Wherefore holy Moses gave this as a first proof of his fortitude in war.* For when he saw [a] Hebrew receiving hard treatment at the hands of an Egyptian, he defended him, and laid low the Egyptian and hid him in the sand. Solomon also says: "Deliver him that is led to death."[12]

In support of St. Ambrose's reflection we might add that according to the laws of the Egyptians themselves, failure to assist the victims of assault was a grave crime. The Greek historian Diodorus of Sicily writes in his *Library of History* that under Egyptian law,

---

[11] Acts 7:23–28 (RSV-CE), emphasis added.
[12] St. Ambrose of Milan, *On the Duties of the Clergy*, Book 1, Chapter 36, Section 179 (public domain), emphasis added, available online at http://newadvent.org/fathers/3401.htm.

[I]f anyone saw a man being murdered upon the highway in this country or suffering violence in any way and did not rescue him if at all possible, he was himself condemned to death; and even if in all honesty through lack of strength he was unable to render aid, he was at least obliged to bring charges against the brigands and prosecute their transgression of the law; and anyone who failed in this duty according to law was mandatorily sentenced to be flogged with blows and deprived of all food for three days.[13]

[3] The third solution is that although Moses did usurp authority to judge, the act was wrong; Holy Scripture records the incident not to approve his deed, but to call attention to his zeal. Rich soil which has not yet received the ministrations of the farmer gives evidence of its fertility by producing weeds; not until the farmer sows good seed does it produce useful plants. In the same way, the immature Moses gave evidence of his dedication to his people by acting rashly on their behalf; not until God had tempered his zealous spirit with hardships was he ready to lead the people with justice. This is how St. Augustine views the incident, although he gives a nod to other views too. In the work to which St. Thomas refers, *Questions on the Heptateuch*, Augustine comments only briefly, as follows:

In our book against Faustus, we have fully discussed Moses' murder of an Egyptian to defend his brothers and the lives of the Patriarchs. The question is whether we should praise the ardent spirit through which Moses sinned, as we praise the earth for its fertility, even before the seeds of useful plants germinate from it – or whether we should praise the act itself. Not that, apparently, because Moses had not yet received from God the legitimate authority which human society is set wisely in order.[14]

In the earlier work *Against Faustus*, however, St. Augustine had commented much more fully:

It might be shown that, though Moses slew the Egyptian, without being commanded by God, the action was divinely permitted, as, from the prophetic character of Moses, it

---

[13] Diodorus Siculus, *Library of History*, Book 1, trans. Edwin Murphy as *The Antiquities of Egypt* (New Brunswick, NJ: Transaction, 1990), Section 77, p. 97.

[14] I am very freely translating St. Augustine of Hippo, Questions on the Heptateuch, Book 2, Questions on Exodus, Question 2: *De facto Moysi, cum occidit Aegyptium ad defendendos fratres suos, satis disputavimus in illo opere quod de vita Patriarcharum adversus Faustum scripsimus: Utrum indoles in eo laudabilis fuerit, qua hoc peccatum admiserit, sicut solet uber terrae, etiam ante utilia semina, quadam herbarum quamvis inutilium feracitate laudari; an omnino ipsum factum iustificandum sit. Quod ideo non videtur, quia nullam adhuc legitimam potestatem gerebat, nec acceptam divinitus, nec humana societate ordinatam.* Giving a nod to the second possible solution, St. Augustine adds, "However, as Stephen said in the Acts of the Apostles, he thought his brothers would understand that God would deliver them through his testimony. In the same way – though Scripture is silent about this point – Moses seems already to have had a divine presentiment that he might boldly act." *Tamen, sicut Stephanus dicit in Actibus Apostolorum, putabat intelligere fratres suos, quod per eum Deus daret illis salutem: ut per hoc testimonium videatur Moyses iam divinitus admonitus (quod Scriptura eo loco tacet) hoc audere potuisse.*

prefigured something in the future. Now however, I do not use this argument, but view the action as having no symbolic meaning. In the light, then, of the eternal law, it was wrong for one who had no legal authority to kill the man, even though he was a bad character, besides being the aggressor. *But in minds where great virtue is to come, there is often an early crop of vices, in which we may still discern a disposition for some particular virtue, which will come when the mind is duly cultivated.* For as farmers, when they see land bringing forth huge crops, though of weeds, pronounce it good for grain; or when they see wild creepers, which have to be rooted out, still consider the land good for useful vines; and when they see a hill covered with wild olives, conclude that with culture it will produce good fruit: so the disposition of mind which led Moses to take the law into his own hands, to prevent the wrong done to his brother, living among strangers, by a wicked citizen of the country from being unrequited, was not unfit for the production of virtue, but from want of culture gave signs of its productiveness in an unjustifiable manner.[15]

St. Augustine goes on to offer two more examples of a misguided zeal which gave evidence of a spirit which might be trained and corrected by God. Saul, rebuked in a vision for persecuting Christians, became a Christian apostle, and Peter, rebuked by Christ for using a sword in the attempt to save Him from arrest, became the first universal pastor of the Church:

In both cases the trespass originated not in inveterate cruelty, but in a hasty zeal which admitted of correction. In both cases there was resentment against injury, accompanied in one case by love for a brother, and in the other by love, though still carnal, of the Lord. Here was evil to be subdued or rooted out; but the heart with such capacities needed only, like good soil, to be cultivated to make it fruitful in virtue.[16]

[4] In summarily executing Zimri and Cozbi, Phinehas too might seem to have usurped judgment, yet his act is explicitly praised. Again several possible solutions are presented. The first solution is that Phinehas was not usurping judgment because God Himself moved Phinehas to act as he did. The second is that he was not usurping judgment because, since he was next in the line of succession to be high priest after his father Eleazar, he shared in the office of judge.

We should not suppose that St. Thomas thinks that the act of Phinehas sets a precedent for the Church; he firmly repudiates the view that priests and other clerics may execute corporal punishment of wrongdoers. We must bear in mind that the law of the Old Testament was not only a moral and religious law but also a civil law: It prescribed specific temporal punishments for wrongdoing, and appointed the priests and Levites its agents. However, nothing of this sort is found in the law of the New Testament. "The ministry of clerics is concerned with better things than corporal slayings, namely with things pertaining to spiritual welfare."[17]

---

[15] St. Augustine of Hippo, *Against Faustus*, Book 22, Chapter 70, Section 70 (public domain), emphasis added; available online at http://newadvent.org/fathers/1406.htm.
[16] Ibid. "Carnal" here means "not spiritual."   [17] II-II, Q. 64, Art. 4, ad 1 and 2.

Reply to Objection 3. [1] *The secular power is subject to the spiritual, even as the body is subject to the soul.* [2] *Consequently the judgment is not usurped if the spiritual authority interferes in those temporal matters that are subject to the spiritual authority or which have been committed to the spiritual by the temporal authority.*	Reply to Objection 3. As the body is subordinate to the soul, so secular authority is subordinate to spiritual authority. And so it is not a usurpation of judgment if the spiritual authority intervenes in temporal matters, provided that either (a) the matters are of the sort which are *intrinsically* subordinate to spiritual authority, or (b) the matters have been *handed over by* the temporal to the spiritual authority.

[1] St. Thomas is not drawing an inference, but stating a premise and of-fering a comparison. He is not arguing that the body is subject to the soul, *therefore* the secular authority is subject to the spiritual. Rather he is asserting that the secular authority is subject to the spiritual, *even as* the body is subject to the soul.

Just what St. Thomas intends by this comparison is at first somewhat puz-zling. One might at first think he means that the spiritual power rules the secu-lar power *in the same way* as the soul rules the body, but this seems impossible. For how does the soul rule the body? He answers,

the body obeys the soul blindly without any contradiction, in those things in which it has a natural aptitude to be moved by the soul: whence the Philosopher says (Polit. i, 3) that the "soul rules the body with a despotic command" as the master rules his slave: wherefore the entire movement of the body is referred to the soul."[18]

In another passage, the "despotic" way that the soul rules the body is distin-guished from the "political" way in which reason rules the irascible and con-cupiscible powers:

the soul is said to rule the body by a despotic power, because the members of the body cannot in any way resist the sway of the soul, but at the soul's command both hand and foot, and whatever member is naturally moved by voluntary movement, are moved at once. But the intellect or reason is said to rule the irascible and concupiscible by a politic power: because the sensitive appetite has something of its own, by virtue whereof it can resist the commands of reason.[19]

Yet if we ask whether the spiritual authority rules the secular authority in a despotic or a political way, the answer seems to be not "a despotical way" but "a political way." For the state does not obey the Church blindly, without ever contradicting her, in such an irresistible way that whenever the state does something, we say it was done by the Church. On the contrary: Just as our ap-petites and other passions are able to defy the direction of reason, so the state is able to defy the direction of the Church.

---

[18] I-II, Q. 56, Art. 4, ad 3.   [19] I, Q. 81, Art. 3, ad 2.

For this reason it seems unreasonable to think that St. Thomas means that the spiritual authority rules the secular *in the same way* that the soul rules the body. I believe the point of the comparison is much more modest. He is merely pointing out that the spiritual power is *intrinsically superior*: Just as the rule of the soul over the body is the rule of the higher over the lower, so the rule of the spiritual over the secular is the rule of the higher over the lower. If we were to ask *why* the spiritual authority it is intrinsically superior to the secular, the answer would be that the integrity of our relationship with God is vastly more important than anything this life has to offer. It is not that the goods of this life are not real goods – they are – but that they cease to be good for us when they interfere with our greater good instead of subserving it. Now the state directs us only to our temporal well-being, but the Church directs us to our eternal well-being. Therefore, whenever spiritual matters are at stake, the state should defer to the Church – as we are about to see.

[2] The point of this obscure passage had put more clearly in St. Thomas's previous *Commentary on the Sentences of Peter Lombard*, in which he explains:

> Spiritual as well as secular power comes from the divine power. Hence secular power is subjected to spiritual power in those matters concerning which the subjection has been specified and ordained by God, i.e., in matters belonging to the salvation of the soul. Hence in these we are to obey spiritual authority more than secular authority. On the other hand, more obedience is due to secular than to spiritual power in the things that belong to the civic good. For it is said Matthew 22:21: Render unto Caesar the things that are Caesar's. A special case occurs, however, when spiritual and secular power are so joined in one person as they are in the Pope, who holds the apex of both spiritual and secular powers.[20]

So unless St. Thomas has changed his mind, the temporal matters which he describes as "subject to the spiritual authority" are the ones pertaining to salvation, and ones which he describes as "committed to the spiritual by the temporal authority" are the ones which are for some special reason *turned over* to the Church (as in the case of the papal states, where the Pope acted not only as a spiritual but as a temporal ruler).

The Objector had regarded all intervention of the Church in temporal affairs as usurpation of judgment. But if, in precisely these two cases, the intervention of the Church is *not* a usurpation, then the fact that such intervention is sometimes approved does not show that usurped judgment can be just, and the Objection fails.

---

[20] Thomas Aquinas, *Commentary on the Sentences of Peter Lombard*, II, Distinction 44, Exposition of the Text, ad 4. I am following the translation of Joseph Kenny, online at www.dhspriory. org/thomas/Sent2d44ExpTextus.htm.

Reply to Objection 4.The habits of knowledge and justice are perfections of the individual, and consequently their absence does not make a judgment to be usurped, as in the absence of public authority which gives a judgment its coercive force.	Reply to Objection 4. Judgment is usurped when it is rendered without the public authority which gives it the power to compel. But the virtues of justice and legal "science" are perfections of individual persons, not perfections of public authority. Therefore, a judgment is not a usurpation just because the judge falls short of these perfections.

The Objector had claimed that since judgment is not necessarily unjust merely because the judge is careless of justice or ignorant or its requirements, neither is it necessarily unjust merely because he renders it without authority. St. Thomas points out this argument confuses the personal qualities necessary for a good judge with the formal qualities necessary for a just judgment.

For his judgment to be just, the judge must both (1) give each person what is due to him, and (2) have public authority to judge, which includes the authority to enforce his judgments. But to be fit to hold office in the first place – that is, to be the sort of person who is *most likely* to give each person what is due to him if appointed to the job – the judge must possess both (1) the disposition to be just, and (2) the "science" of justice.

If the person who renders judgment lacks public authority to do so, then his judgment is unjust. But although it is unwise to grant public authority to someone unfit for office, the fact that he is unfit for office does not in itself deprive his judgments of public authority; therefore it does not in itself deprive them of justice.

Whether the Virtues Annexed to Justice Are Suitably Enumerated?

TEXT	PARAPHRASE
Whether the virtues annexed to justice are suitably enumerated?	Marcus Tullius Cicero has suggested that six secondary virtues are associated with justice. Is his list correct and complete?

Particular justice – justice in the sense of one virtue among others, rather than as a synonym for virtue in general – concerns giving others what is due to them. However, justice has many different aspects, and although they are all "parts" of justice, they are not all "parts" in the same sense. We may speak of its subjective parts, integral parts, or potential parts.

The subjective parts of particular justice are its species, in much the same way that hammer and wrench are species of tool.[1] It has two such species: Commutative justice regulates exchanges and interactions between individuals, and distributive justice allocates such things as honors and offices to deserving individuals in the community. The integral parts of justice are the things which must concur for a particular act of justice to be complete, in much the same way that for a gift to be completely accomplished, it must be both given and received. Two things are requisite for an act of justice to be complete: First that it gives the other person what is really due to him, and second that it avoids inflicting injury which is not due to him.

The foregoing points are fairly intuitive, and it is not difficult to follow St. Thomas's classification and subclassification of the subjective and integral parts of justice. That is why this commentary does not include any of the

---

[1] We will employ a slightly more complex definition of subjective parts when we come to the Reply to Objection 5.

Articles dealing with them. Getting the potential parts of justice right is much more difficult, and these are the topic of the present Article. Potential parts of justice are secondary virtues which are akin to or associated with justice, but which concern various secondary acts or matters so that in some way or other they fail to rise quite to its level. The precise senses in which they fall short of justice will become clear as we go along.

Before St. Thomas, the thinkers who had discussed the potential parts of justice had enumerated them in a bewildering variety of ways. In the present Article, he adopts the sixfold list of Marcus Tullius Cicero, defending it against the sevenfold list of Macrobius, the ninefold list of Pseudo-Andronicus, the fivefold list of "certain others" whom he does not name, and a single suggestion drawn from Aristotle. Had he chosen, he might also have brought in still other writers, such as Peter Abelard, William of Auxerre, or Philip the Chancellor, each of whom had suggested yet another way to classify the parts of justice.[2] Characteristically, the Angelic Doctor does not simply discard the thoughts of these all these others; whenever he comes upon a worthy insight, he works out what the writer was getting at and finds room for it – if it makes sense – in a subtler scheme to which the present Article is merely an introduction.

Two cautions must be offered before we move forward. The first concerns terminology. St. Thomas says that the potential parts of justice are "annexed" or "adjoined" to justice;[3] I have used such English terms as "linked," "associated," or "akin." However, this is not the same kind of linkage that we were looking into in I-II, 65, 1, "Whether the moral virtues are connected with each other?" There we were investigating the hypothesis that every acquired moral virtues is *mutually dependent* on every other. By contrast, here we are discussing the fact that certain lesser moral virtues *resemble* the chief moral virtues but do not possess their full power.

Second, because this Article is more complex and elliptical than most, I am taking greater than usual liberties in the paraphrase, even to the point of rearranging and adding to the text. Readers will find that the paraphrase also uses different names than the Blackfriars translation uses for many of the secondary virtues; the reasons for these changes are explained as we go along.

---

[2] Peter Abelard, in *Dialogue between a Philosopher, a Jew, and a Christian*, had classified the parts of justice as reverence, beneficence, truthfulness, and vindication; William of Auxerre, in the *Summa Aurea* ("Golden Summation"), as alms, obedience, worship, and prayer; and Philip the Chancellor, in *Summa de Bono* ("Summary of Good), as worship (owed to God), reverence (owed to religious superiors, although some might argue that the point would apply to secular superiors as well), and obedience (owed to both).

[3] In the Blackfriars translation, the expressions *virtutes iustitiae annexae* and *virtutes iustitiae adiunctas* are both translated "virtues annexed to justice."

Objection 1. [1] *It would seem that the virtues annexed to justice are unsuitably enumerated.* [2] *Tully [De Invent. ii, 53] reckons six, viz. "religion, piety, gratitude, revenge, observance, truth."* [3] *Now revenge is seemingly a species of commutative justice whereby revenge is taken for injuries inflicted, as stated above (Question 61, Article 4). Therefore it should not be reckoned among the virtues annexed to justice.*	Objection 1. Cicero lists the virtues linked to justice as • Religion [*religionem*]; • Piety [*pietatem*], in the filial sense; • Gratitude [*gratiam*]; • Vindication [*vindicationem*]; • Observance [*observantiam*]; and • Truthfulness [*veritatem*]. However, vindication is not one of the virtues *associated* with justice. Rather it is a *kind* of justice – specifically, a kind of commutative justice, which prompts punishment for injuries. So at least in this respect, the list is incorrect; vindication should have been omitted.

[1] If we are to understand what the Objector means in saying that the list is poorly drawn up, we must remember what we are supposed to be listing. The items are proposed not merely as different names for the same thing, but as different things. These different things are proposed not merely as emotions or as attitudes, but as virtues. They are not cardinal virtues, but lesser virtues associated with the cardinal virtue of justice. Finally, the manner in which they are associated with it is that they are *potential* parts of justice, not subjective or integral parts.

[2] Here is what Cicero says in *On Rhetorical Invention*, Book 2, Chapter 53:

Justice is a disposition of mind to give each his dignity while preserving the common advantage. Initially it proceeds from nature; then certain practices become widely shared because they are found to be of good purpose. Still later these things that proceed from nature and are approved by custom come to be upheld by religion and fear of the law.

Natural right is not born from opinions, but implanted in us by a kind of natural force.[4] It includes religion, piety, gratitude, vindication, observance and truthfulness. To wit: Religion is that by which men serve and worship some superior nature which they call divine. Piety, that by which they render kind service and constant reverence to kin and country. Gratitude, that by which they remember the friendship and services rendered by others, along with the will to pay them back. Vindication, that by which they defend or avenge themselves, thereby repelling force, injury, or anything likely to be harmful. Observance, that by which we hold men of surpassing dignity to be worthy of reverence and honor. Truthfulness, that by which they speak of things without changing them, just as they are, were, or will be.[5]

---

4 *Quaedam in natura vis insevit.*
5 *Iustitia est habitus animi communi utilitate conservata suam cuique tribuens dignitatem. Eius initium est ab natura profectum; deinde quaedam in consuetudinem ex utilitatis ratione venerunt; postea res et ab natura profectas et ab consuetudine probatas legum metus et religio sanxit. Naturae ius est quod non opinio genuit, sed quaedam in natura vis insevit, ut religionem, pietatem, gratiam, vindicationem, observantiam, veritatem. Religio est, quae superioris cuiusdam naturae,*

Although Cicero's explanation makes gratitude, observance, and truthfulness fairly clear, a few additional remarks about the other four may be helpful. The Blackfriars translation renders *vindicatio* as "revenge," but I think that is misleading because in contemporary English the term "revenge" is more often used for the vice of giving way to wrath. Instead, I have used the term "vindication," which better conveys the idea of the virtue which disposes us to repel injury justly. The terms "piety" and "religion" may also cause some difficulty, because St. Thomas speaks of piety in two distinct senses. In the present Article, the term refers to a virtue, linked with justice, which disposes us to reverence father, mother, kin, and country. Later on in the *Summa*, however, he uses the very same term for a gift of the Holy Spirit, which is not the same thing as a virtue; it is something God does within us to make us readier to receive the influx of His grace. The reason St. Thomas uses the term "piety" in two such different ways, one spiritual, one not, is that from a Christian point of view they bear a certain analogy: After all, the virtue of filial piety includes reverence toward our fathers, and the spiritual gift of piety moves us to regard God Himself as our Father.[6] Even so, we must remember that when St. Thomas uses the term "piety" in the present Article, he is thinking of fathers only in the earthly sense.

Now the plot thickens, for in the present Article St. Thomas does mention an entirely natural virtue, linked with justice, which disposes us to pay homage to the Divine. However, he calls it "religion," not "piety," and it is a thing of a much lower order than the spiritual gift of piety. A person who has the virtue of religion recognizes that there is such a thing as the Divine, and that whatever it is, oy deserves reverence – but without the further help of grace, his knowledge of the Divine is limited to what can be worked out by natural reason (and it may not even get that far). By contrast, the spiritual gift of piety transcends what we can do by our natural powers. We might say that the virtue of religion disposes us to reach our hands up to the infinite God, an effort which always falls short – but that the spiritual gift of piety is the work of the infinite God Himself, reaching all the way down.

[3] The Objector is not denying that vindication has something to do with justice; the problem lies in what this "something" is. We are trying to list the *potential* parts of justice, but vindication, he says, is a *subjective* part of justice. It isn't a lesser virtue associated with justice, but one of the varieties of justice itself.

---

quam divinam vocant, curam caerimoniamque affert; pietas, per quam sanguine coniunctis patriaeque benivolum officium et diligens tribuitur cultus; gratia, in qua amicitiarum et officiorum alterius memoria et remunerandi voluntas continetur; vindicatio, per quam vis aut iniuria et omnino omne, quod obfuturum est, defendendo aut ulciscendo propulsatur; observantia, per quam homines aliqua dignitate antecedentes cultu quodam et honore dignantur; veritas, per quam immutata ea quae sunt aut ante fuerunt aut futura sunt dicuntur.

[6] II-II, Q. 121, Art. 1.

Objection 2. [1] *Further,* *Macrobius (Super Somn. Scip. i, 8) reckons seven,* [2] *viz. "innocence, friendship, concord, piety, religion, affection, humanity,"* [3] *several of which are omitted by Tully. Therefore the virtues annexed to justice would seem to be insufficiently enumerated.*	Objection 2. Moreover, in his *Commentary on the Dream of Scipio,*[7] Macrobius lists seven parts of justice: • Innocence [*innocentiam*]; • Friendliness [*amicitiam*]; • Concord [*concordiam*]; • Filial piety [*pietatem*]; • Religion [*religio*]; • Goodwill [*affectum*] and • Humanity [*humanitatem*]. Since Cicero's list lacks several of the virtues included in Macrobius's, the Ciceronian list is incomplete.

[1] Macrobius had written that there are four levels of virtue, so that each of the cardinal virtues can be considered from four points of view: Political virtue, virtue which cleanses the mind, virtue of the already-cleansed mind, and exemplary virtue (virtue as it pre-exists in the mind of God Himself). The political forms of the cardinal virtues are needed even for the affairs of this life, because we are social animals:

> By these virtues the good man is first made lord of himself and then ruler of the state, and is just and prudent in his regard for human welfare, never forgetting his obligations.... By these virtues upright men devote themselves to their commonwealths, protect cities, revere parents, love their children, and cherish relatives; by these they direct the welfare of the citizens, and by these they safeguard their allies with anxious forethought and bind them with the liberality of their justice; by these "They have won remembrance among men."[8]

[2] Macrobius says the political form of the cardinal virtue of justice is safeguarding for each man what belongs to him, from which come the seven lesser virtues which he lists. Most translators, including the Blackfriars, render *affectus* by means of its English cognate "affection," which is somewhat misleading. In the context of our readings the meaning is closer to "goodwill," and this is the word used in my paraphrase.

---

7 In Marcus Tullius Cicero's dialogue *De Re Publica* ("On the Commonwealth), which was written in imitation of Plato's *Republic*, Cicero has one of his characters, Scipio Aemilianus, narrate a nighttime vision of a visit by his deceased adoptive grandfather, Scipio Africanus, who shows him the macrocosm and microcosm. This vision, called *The Dream of Scipio*, received a great deal of attention in medieval times, largely stimulated by the fifth-century *Commentary on the Dream of Scipio* written by Macrobius Ambrosius Theodosius. It is in this commentary that Macrobius offers his list of the potential parts of justice.

8 Macrobius Ambrosius Theodosius, *Commentary on the Dream of Scipio*, trans. William Harris Stahl, Book 1, Chapter 8, Sections 6 and 8 (New York: Columbia University Press, 1952, 1990), pp. 121–122. The internal quote is from Virgil, *Aeneid*, Book 6, line 664.

[3] Both lists include religion and filial piety, but only Macrobius's list includes innocence, friendliness, concord, goodwill, and humanity, and only Cicero's includes gratitude, vindication, observance, and truthfulness. The Objector does not complain about the additions, but he does complain about the omissions.

Objection 3. [1] *Further, others reckon five parts of justice, viz. "obedience" in respect of one's superiors, "discipline" with regard to inferiors, "equity" as regards equals, "fidelity" and "truthfulness" towards all;* [2] *and of these "truthfulness" alone is mentioned by Tully. Therefore he would seem to have enumerated insufficiently the virtues annexed to justice.*	**Objection 3.** Certain other writers suggest five parts of justice: • Obedience [*obedientia*] toward superiors; • Guardianship [*disciplina*] toward subordinates; • Equity [*aequitas*] toward equals, and • Fidelity and truthfulness [*fides et veritas*] toward everyone. Of these, Cicero mentions only truthfulness, omitting all the others. For this reason too his list seems incomplete.

[1] The respective ranges of the Latin word *disciplina* and the English word "discipline" are quite different. Some translators render *disciplina* as "condescension," but this term is misleading because it suggests a patronizing attitude. I have chosen "guardianship," not in the sense of the *status* of guardian, but in the sense of the *virtue* which disposes a person in a superior position to guard the well-being of his subordinates.

[2] Again the Objector protests the omissions but not the additions; his attitude seems to be that to construct a list of the potential parts of justice, one need only add together all the lists that anyone has proposed – the more, the merrier.

Objection 4. [1] *Further, the peripatetic Andronicus [De Affectibus] reckons nine parts annexed to justice* [2] *viz. "liberality, kindliness, revenge, common sense [eugnomosyne], piety, gratitude, holiness, just exchange" and "just lawgiving";* [3] *and of all these it is evident that Tully mentions none but "revenge." Therefore he would appear to have made an incomplete enumeration.*	**Objection 4.** Yet another list of the parts of justice comes down to use from Pseudo-Andronicus, who proposes these: • Liberality or generosity [*liberalitatem*]; • Kindness [*benignitatem*]; • Vindication [*vindicativam*]; • *Eugnomosyne*, good judgment about novel situations; • *Eusebeia*, good or well-offered worship; • *Eucharistia*, good or well-offered thanks; • Sanctity [*sanctitatem*]; • Good or reciprocal exchange [*bonum commutationem*]; and • Good lawmaking [*legispositivam*]. The Ciceronian list seems incomplete because the only one of these it includes is vindication.

[1] The book sometimes called *On the Emotions* and sometimes *On the Passions* is traditionally attributed to Andronicus of Rhodes, who was at one time the head of the Peripatetic school. In our time, the author is usually called Pseudo-Andronicus because the attribution is widely doubted.

[2] Here we run not only into Latin terms, but into Greek terms which are sometimes Latinized and sometimes not. I have sometimes Anglicized and sometimes not. Thus:

- *Eugnomosyne* I have rendered as "good judgment about novel situations," because as St. Thomas explains in the Reply to Objection 4, the term means "good *gnome*," *gnome* being one of the aspects of good judgment we discussed earlier in this commentary.⁹ It is tempting to follow the Blackfriars translation in calling this virtue "common sense," because in English we do sometimes call intellectual judgment "sense." On the other hand, it is a little odd that we do so, because good judgment is a virtue, which is neither common nor a sense.¹⁰ Although St. Thomas does use the expression "common sense," he uses it in a very different way, for the interior sense which is shared by all five exterior senses at once so that, for example, it can discern *white*, which pertains to sight, from *sweet*, which pertains to taste.¹¹
- *Eusebeia* pertains to the worship of the Divine. The Blackfriars translators should not have rendered the term as "piety," because in the context of this Article, St. Thomas uses the term "piety" not for reverence to God, but for reference to parents and fatherland.¹²
- *Eucharistia* has the generic meaning of well-offered thanks; for Christians it also refers to Holy Communion.
- Though I have rendered *legispositivam* by the English term "good lawmaking," the literal meaning of the Latin term is merely "lawmaking." However, since careless or unjust lawmaking is not virtuous, the goodness or justice of tis disposition is implied.

[3] Again the Objector protests the omissions. After all, the omitted virtues had been widely discussed in the ethical literature.

---

⁹ See the commentary on I-II, Q. 58, Art. 4, and II-II, Q. 60, Art. 1.

¹⁰ No doubt our bad habit of calling moral judgment a "sense," has been influenced by the Scottish moral sense theorists of the eighteenth century, some of whom really did think it was something like the bodily senses. For example, Lord Kames, wrote that *"by perception alone, without reasoning*, we acquire the knowledge of right and wrong, of what we may do, of what we ought to do, and of what we ought to abstain from." Henry Home, Lord Kames, *Principles of Equity* (1760, 1767), emphasis added. The chapter from which I am quoting is correctly numbered "VI" in the first edition, but incorrectly numbered "V" in the second.

¹¹ See I, Q. 78, Art. 4, ad 1, 2; compare I, Q. 1, Art. 3, ad 2, and I, Q. 57, Art. 2.

¹² As mentioned earlier, St. Thomas also uses the term "piety" for the spiritual *gift* of piety, which is not the same as a virtue.

Objection 5. [1] Further, Aristotle *(Ethic. v, 10) mentions epieikeia as being annexed to justice: [2] and yet seemingly it is not included in any of the foregoing enumerations. Therefore the virtues annexed to justice are insufficiently enumerated.*	Objection 5. Finally, Aristotle says in Book 5 of his *Nicomachean Ethics* that *epieikeia* is conjoined with justice, even though *none* of the lists we have mentioned include it. Surely then our enumeration falls short.

[1] Justice is pronounced according to the law, and law is expressed in general terms. But the more we descend into details, the more likely we are to find cases to which the law does not apply. In this case the judge rules not according to the very letter of the law, but according to equity, doing as the legislators themselves (supposing them to be virtuous) would have done if they were there. Here is what Aristotle says:

And this is the nature of the equitable, a correction of law where it is defective owing to its universality. In fact this is the reason why all things are not determined by law, that about some things it is impossible to lay down a law, so that a decree is needed. For when the thing is indefinite the rule also is indefinite, like the leaden rule used in making the Lesbian molding; the rule adapts itself to the shape of the stone and is not rigid, and so too the decree is adapted to the facts.[13]

In our day some judges are suspicious of equity because they think it means setting aside the intention of the legislators, while others embrace a distorted view of equity just because they *do* want to set aside the intention of the legislators. St. Thomas would disagree with both groups, since properly understood, equity means *following* the intention of the legislators in circumstances where the law would have required what they did not intend. The measuring rod used by stonemasons of the island of Lesbos was made of soft lead, not so that it could be crookedly bent any way whatsoever, but so that it could fit the actual curves of the molding.[14]

[2] The Objector is still protesting omissions, but this time he is not merely compiling other thinkers' lists; in fact he complains that Aristotle's point has been overlooked in every one of the lists.

On the contrary, – nothing!	On the other hand, – nothing!

Our commentary omits the *sed contra*. That is not a mistake; this time there is no *sed contra*. Why not? Presumably because the purpose of a *sed contra* is to restate the tradition, and in this case, the tradition was a mess; it was far from settling on a single list of the secondary virtues attached to justice. Although

---

[13] Aristotle, *Nicomachean Ethics*, Book 5, Chapter 10.
[14] For further discussion, see the discussion of I-II, Q. 96, Art. 6 in my *Commentary on St. Thomas's Treatise on Law* and in its partner volume, the online *Companion to the Commentary* (both Cambridge: Cambridge University Press, 2014).

respectful of all of his sources, St. Thomas was staking out a position in a hotly ongoing debate.

I answer that, [1] *I answer that, Two points must be observed about the virtues annexed to a principal virtue. The first is that these virtues have something in common with the principal virtue; and the second is that in some respect they fall short of the perfection of that virtue.* [2] *Accordingly since justice is of one man to another as stated above (Question 58, Article 2), all the virtues that are directed to another person may by reason of this common aspect be annexed to justice.* [3] *Now the essential character of justice consists in rendering to another his due according to equality, as stated above (Question 58, Article 11).* [4] *Wherefore in two ways may a virtue directed to another person fall short of the perfection of justice: first, by falling short of the aspect of equality; secondly, by falling short of the aspect of due.* [5] *For certain virtues there are which render another his due, but are unable to render the equal due. On the first place, whatever man renders to God is due, yet it cannot be equal, as though man rendered to God as much as he owes Him, according to Psalm 115:12,*[15] *"What shall I render to the Lord for all the things that He hath rendered to me?"* [6] *On this respect "religion" is annexed to justice since, according to Tully (De invent. ii, 53), it consists in offering service and ceremonial rites or worship to "some superior nature that men call divine."* [7] *Secondly,*	Here is my response. Concerning the subordinate virtues which are linked with a chief virtue, there are two things to consider. One is that they resemble the chief virtue; the other is that in some way they fall short of its completeness. As to the former point: Since true justice is *toward another,* all virtues which concern what one person gives or does to another have a certain resemblance to justice and can be linked with it. But as to the latter point: Since the nature of true justice is first to render the other person what is *due* to him, and second to render it in accordance with *equality,* such a virtue may either miss the mark of justice with respect to what is due, or fall short of justice with respect to what is equal. But let us consider equality first.

(I) How can a virtue fall short of justice with respect to equality? Although certain virtues linked to justice render the other person what is due to him, they are incapable of rendering *all* of what is due to him. There are three cases.

• Although whatever man gives to God is owed to God, man can never give God as much as he owes Him – a point which the Psalmist confesses by asking, "What shall I render to the LORD for all that He has rendered to me?" This is why our list of virtues linked with justice includes *religion* in Cicero's sense: The virtue which disposes us to offer ceremonial rites or reverence[16] to some superior nature which is called divine.

• No one can pay back to his parents all that he owes them, as Aristotle explains in the fourth book of his *Nicomachean Ethics.* This is why our list of virtues linked with justice includes *piety* in Cicero's sense: The virtue which disposes |

[15] This Psalm is numbered 116 in most recent translations.
[16] *Curam caeremoniamque vel cultum.*

it is not possible to make to one's parents an equal return of what one owes to them, as the Philosopher declares (Ethic. viii, 14); [8] and thus "piety" is annexed to justice, for thereby, as Tully says (De invent. ii, 53), a man "renders service and constant deference to his kindred and the well-wishers of his country." [9] Thirdly, according to the Philosopher (Ethic. iv, 3), man is unable to offer an equal meed for virtue, and thus "observance" is annexed to justice, consisting according to Tully (De invent. ii, 53) in the "deference and honor rendered to those who excel in worth." [10] A falling short of the just due may be considered in respect of a twofold due, moral or legal: wherefore the Philosopher (Ethic. viii, 13) assigns a corresponding twofold just. The legal due is that which one is bound to render by reason of a legal obligation; and this due is chiefly the concern of justice, which is the principal virtue. [11] On the other hand, the moral due is that to which one is bound in respect of the rectitude of virtue: [12] and since a due implies necessity, this kind of due has two degrees. For one due is so necessary that without it moral rectitude cannot be ensured: and this has more of the character of due. [13] Moreover this due may be considered from the point of view of the debtor, and in this way it pertains to this kind of due that a man represent himself

us to render service and constant reverence[17] to kinfolk and well-wishers of his fatherland.

• As Aristotle points out in the same book of the same work, no man can ever reward virtue enough. This is why our list of virtues linked with justice includes *observance* in Cicero's sense: The virtue which disposes us to award reverence[18] and honor to men of surpassing dignity.

(II) How can a virtue miss the mark of justice with respect to what is due? Certain virtues linked to justice render to another something that is *not, in the strictest sense, a debt.*

Then what sort of quasi-debt are we speaking of? First, notice that as Aristotle pointed out, something may be either morally or legally due – it may belong to either moral or legal justice. What is legally due is what the law demands that we render. However, what is morally due arises more generally from the demands of doing the right thing.

Considering this second kind of indebtedness more closely, we see that the idea of what is due conveys necessity – but not everything that is due conveys the same grade of necessity. Certain things which are due are of such great importance that without paying them, moral integrity cannot be preserved.[19] This grade of necessity corresponds more closely to the meaning of a debt. Before we turn to the other grade, however, yet another distinction is necessary, for the debt in question may be viewed from the perspective of either the one who owes something, or the one to whom it is owed.

---

[17] *Officium et diligens … cultus.*
[18] In II-II, Q. 102, Art. 1, where he defines observance, St. Thomas uses the term *reverentia*, although here he uses *cultu*. Since he treats the terms as synonymous, I use "reverence" throughout.
[19] *Sine eo honestas morum conservari non possit.*

to others just as he is, both in word and deed. Wherefore to justice is annexed "truth," whereby, as Tully says (De invent. ii, 53), present, past and future things are told without perversion. [14] *It may also be considered from the point of view of the person to whom it is due, by comparing the reward he receives with what he has done –* [15] *sometimes in good things; and then annexed to justice we have "gratitude" which "consists in recollecting the friendship and kindliness shown by others, and in desiring to pay them back," as Tully states (De invent. ii, 53) –* [16] *and sometimes in evil things, and then to justice is annexed "revenge," whereby, as Tully states (De invent. ii, 53), "we resist force, injury or anything obscure by taking vengeance or by self-defense."* [17] *There is another due that is necessary in the sense that it conduces to greater rectitude, although without it rectitude may be ensured. This due is the concern of "liberality," "affability" or "friendship," or the like, all of which Tully omits in the aforesaid enumeration because there is little of the nature of anything due in them.*

- Considering the debtor himself, he owes it to show himself to others as he really is, both in words and in deeds. This is why our list of virtues linked with justice includes *truthfulness* in Cicero's sense: The virtue which disposes us to speak of things without changing them,[20] just as they are, were, or will be.
- Considering the one to whom something is owed, we must compare what he receives with what he has done. One possibility is that he has done good, and this is why our list of virtues linked with justice includes *gratitude* in Cicero's sense: The virtue which disposes us to remember the friendship and services of another, with the will[21] to pay him back.
- Another possibility is that he has done evil, and this is why our list of virtues linked with justice includes *vindication* in Cicero's sense: The virtue which disposes us to repel violence, outrage, or anything which threatens disgrace, either by defending or avenging ourselves against it.

But we were saying that some things which are due are necessary to a lesser degree, because although they contribute to moral integrity, integrity is not destroyed by not rendering them. We meet this sort of indebtedness in such virtues as generosity or liberality, as well as affability or friendliness. Cicero omits these from his list because they partake so slightly in the nature of a debt.

[1] These "two points" amount to a definition: By a potential part of a cardinal virtue – by a lesser virtue which is associated with it – we mean a virtue which has something in common with the cardinal virtue, but which is some way falls short of its full power.

The sense in which such a virtue "falls short" of the cardinal virtue is easy to misunderstand. Take the potential parts of fortitude. They do not fall short of fortitude in the same sense that being only a little bit cowardly falls short of being completely courageous; being only a little bit cowardly is not a virtue at all. In what sense then do they fall short? Fortitude in the full or focal sense is

[20] *Immutata.*   [21] *Voluntas.*

defined by being able to face the *greatest* danger, which is the danger of death. But certain lesser virtues enable a person to face hardships less than death. Consider for example the disposition of character which enables us to endure the danger of failure. This disposition is not a false virtue, like being only a little bit cowardly – but though it is a real virtue, it is not the *same* virtue as endurance in the face of mortal threat; it is a lesser one linked with it. Therefore we do not call it fortitude in the full or focal sense, but one of the potential parts of fortitude.[22]

Now just as certain lesser virtues may resemble fortitude but fall short of it, so certain lesser virtues may resemble prudence, temperance, or justice but fall short of them. So it is that we are to inquire into the lesser virtues which are related to justice.

[2] Our definition of potential part requires that anything called a potential part of justice must have something in common with it; what the six items of Cicero's list have in common with justice is simply that they concern what we render to others. As St. Thomas writes previously, "since justice is directed to others, it is not about the entire matter of moral virtue, but only about external actions and things, [and only] in so far as one man is related to another through them."[23]

[3] A deed perfectly actualizes justice when it does two things. First, it gives something which is *genuinely due* to the other person; second, it gives to him *all* that is due to him, so as to bring about or restore a kind of "equality" or symmetry in the relationship. St. Thomas has already explained this point by saying "the matter of justice is an external operation in so far as either it, or the thing we use by it, is made proportionate to some other person to whom we are related by justice. Now each man's own is that which is due to him according to equality of proportion. Therefore the proper act of justice is nothing else than to render to each one his own."[24]

[4] "By falling short of the aspect of equality": This happens when, not because of moral carelessness, but by the very nature of the case, it is impossible to pay all that one owes to the other person. "By falling short of the aspect of due": This happens when what I give to the other person is not in the strictest sense "his" – even though it would be good to give it to him, he cannot claim it as a right.

[5] In Hebrew, the poet asks what he can render to the Lord for all His *benefits* to him; in the Vulgate, he asks what he can render to the Lord for all He has *rendered* to him [*quid retribuam Domino pro omnibus quae retribuit mihi*]. Although the Vulgate does not alter the literal sense of the verse, instead of two different verbs it uses the same verb twice. This repetition deepens the sense of a desire to pay back what is due – a desire which is impossible to fulfill, because no one can give God as much as he has received from Him.

---

[22] See II-II, Q. 128, Art. 1.   [23] II-II, Q. 58, Art. 8.   [24] II-II, Q. 58, Art. 11.

[6] Significantly, Cicero does not speak simply of the Divine nature, but of a nature which men *call* Divine. He is not expressing doubt about the reality of God, but humility about the mystery of who God is. According to St. Thomas, only the blessed souls in heaven see God as He is. In this life, not even the redeemed see God in His essence, but only in the light of faith – which is a true light, but a reflected one. The pagans, like Cicero, have far less even than that.

[7] God *creates* the soul, but He does so partly by making the sexual union of the parents fruitful. So just as in one sense we owe our entire lives to God, so in another sense, dependent on God's arrangements, we owe our entire lives to our parents. Not even the most devout worship sufficiently adores God, and not even the most reverent honor sufficiently venerates parents. Aristotle had written:

For friendship asks a man to do what he can, not what is proportional to the merits of the case; since that cannot always be done, e.g. in honors paid to the gods or to parents; for no one could ever return to them the equivalent of what he gets, but the man who serves them to the utmost of his power is thought to be a good man. This is why it would not seem open to a man to disown his father (though a father may disown his son); being in debt, he should repay, but there is nothing by doing which a son will have done the equivalent of what he has received, so that he is always in debt.[25]

[8] Cicero mentions not only parents but also kindred and countrymen, for we owe incalculable debts to all who have come before us. In Plato's dialogue *Crito*, Socrates extends this thought even further, calling the laws of the community our parents.

[9] Who can reckon up all that he owes to the good men and women, some known, multitudes unknown, by whom his life has been blessed? Aristotle says the man of the greatest virtue deserves the greatest honor. A well-known passage in one of the wisdom books of the Old Testament exhorts:

Let us now praise famous men, and our fathers in their generations. The Lord apportioned to them great glory, his majesty from the beginning. There were those who ruled in their kingdoms, and were men renowned for their power, giving counsel by their understanding, and proclaiming prophecies; leaders of the people in their deliberations and in understanding of learning for the people, wise in their words of instruction; those who composed musical tunes, and set forth verses in writing; rich men furnished with resources, living peaceably in their habitations – all these were honored in their generations, and were the glory of their times. There are some of them who have left a name, so that men declare their praise. And there are some who have no memorial, who have perished as though they had not lived; they have become as though they had not been born, and so have their children after them. But these were men of mercy, whose righteous deeds have not been forgotten; their prosperity will remain with their descendants, and their inheritance to their children's children.[26]

---

[25] Aristotle, *Nicomachean Ethics*, Book 8, Chapter 14.
[26] Sirach 44:1–11 (RSV-CE). This Old Testament book is also called Ecclesiasticus (not to be confused with Ecclesiastes).

It may seem that this passage is only partly about virtue, for power, music, poetry, wealth, and fame are also mentioned. Actually it is all about virtue, for these other things are to be praised only because of the good use their possessors made of them. As to fame, not even those who are said to be forgotten are truly forgotten. They are figuratively remembered in the blessings their lives have bestowed on those who have come after them and literally remembered by the imperishable mind of God.

[10] Although what is legally due is defined by the human law, which is changeable, nevertheless it is a real debt, and for this reason the virtue of justice obligates me to pay it. We are not here considering the possibility of an unjust law, because unjust laws cannot by themselves generate duties of conscience – although even in the case of an unjust law, there may arise cases in which I should pay what I am unjustly commanded pay in order to prevent even greater harm to the community, for example the harm of being a stumbling block to others because they cease to respect even just laws.[27]

[11] What is morally due is determined not by the law, but by what St. Thomas calls the *honestate* of virtue. This term refers to whatever is virtuous and upright. We might paraphrase it as "the honest and honorable," taking the honest in the double sense of telling the truth and keeping promises, and taking the honorable in the double sense of receiving honor and being worthy to receive it. Another way to say this is that there are some things we ought to do because we owe them to others, but other things we ought to do just because they are right. The latter are what is morally due.

[12] As we saw just above, legal debts are debts in the precise sense. By contrast, things that are morally due may be either more or less akin to debts. To explain, St. Thomas speaks of "grades" of moral due, corresponding to two different kinds of "necessity of end," which in English we call "usefulness" or "need." In necessity of end *per se*, a thing is necessary in the sense that without it, the end cannot be attained at all. Food, for example, is necessary *per se* for life, and oxygen is necessary *per se* for breath. But in the other kind of necessity of end, a thing is necessary or "fitting" in the sense that without it, the end cannot be attained as well. Swift conveyance, for example, is necessary in this sense for a journey, and salt is for meat.[28] The first kind of moral debt is a necessity of end in the former sense – a *per se* necessity of end – for unless we honor it, our *honestate* or moral integrity is destroyed.

[13] The kind of moral debt which integrity requires us to pay – the kind which is a *per se* necessity of end – has two aspects. One aspect is what we

---

[27] See I-II, Q. 96, Art. 4.
[28] For the five kinds of necessity, see I, Q. 82, Art. 1; compare III, Q. 1, Art. 2 and III, Q. 65, Art. 4. St. Thomas's discussion of necessity relies on Aristotle's *Metaphysics*, Book 5, Chapter 5, but he knits the different meanings together more logically. Additional discussion and examples may be found in my *Commentary on Thomas Aquinas's Treatise on Law* and its partner volume, the online *Companion to the Commentary* (both Cambridge: Cambridge University Press, 2014).

owe others *no matter what they have done*. Whether or not they have played straight with us, we owe it to them to play straight with them – whether or not they have been honest with us, we owe it to them to be truthful. As Cicero points out, truthfulness includes keeping promises, which he calls "faithfulness," "that being done which is said."[29]

Truthfulness is a real moral debt:

Since man is a social animal, one man naturally owes another whatever is necessary for the preservation of human society. Now it would be impossible for men to live together, unless they believed one another, as declaring the truth one to another. Hence the virtue of truth does, in a manner, regard something as being due.[30]

But it is a potential part of justice, rather than one of its species, because it is not a *legal* debt:

Nevertheless it falls short of the proper aspect of justice, as to the notion of debt: for this virtue does not regard legal debt, which justice considers, but rather the moral debt, in so far as, out of equity, one man owes another a manifestation of the truth. Therefore truth is a part of justice, being annexed thereto as a secondary virtue to its principal.[31]

True, certain kinds of lies and promise-breaking are punished by law, such as fraud and the violation of contract. However, there is no law which says simply "Each person has a right to be treated with truthfulness and faithfulness."

[14] The other aspect of the kind of moral debt which integrity requires us to pay is what we owe others *because of what they have done*. Good should be repaid with good; evil should be repaid with punishment.

[15] Notice that gratitude has two elements, not just one. Merely having warm or thankful feelings about what others have done for me does not make me grateful; I must also have the will to do good to them in return.

[16] The paraphrase requires explanation. Cicero had spoken of *vis* (force or violence), of *iniuria* (a Roman legal term referring not so much to injury in our sense as to moral outrage, such as rape or defamation of character), and of whatever is *obfuturum* (likely to cause harm). St. Thomas mistakenly replaces the term *obfuturum* with the term *obscurum*, which means hidden from view.[32] Later, in II-II, Q. 108, Art. 2, misquoting in the same way, but seeming to recognize that the substituted term *obscurum* is puzzling, he suggests that what Cicero meant by the term was *ignominiosum* (disgraceful). Fortunately for the friends of the two writers, Cicero's three terms, taken together, cover the same ground as St. Thomas's three terms, taken together.

[17] I may say that I "owe" my friend a postcard while I am out of town, but a postcard is not due to him in the strict sense. What I really mean when I say this is that it would be *fitting* to send the postcard. Would sending it contribute

---

[29] Marcus Tullius Cicero, *De Re Publica*, trans. C. D. Yonge, Book 4, fragment (public domain).
[30] II-II, Q. 109, Art. 3, ad 1.   [31] II-II, Q. 109, Art. 3, *corpus*.
[32] The Blackfriars translators also note this mistake.

to the exchange of good things among friends? Yes. But would failure to send it destroy such exchange? No. This is easy to misunderstand, because friends do exchange good things. However, *this particular instance* of such exchange is not obligatory. Such matters are so far removed from debts in the strict sense, which the cardinal virtue of justice concerns, that St. Thomas considers the omission of the virtues that dispose us to attend to them entirely appropriate.

| *Reply to Objection 1.* The revenge taken by authority of a public power, in accordance with a judge's sentence, belongs to commutative justice: whereas the revenge which a man takes on his own initiative, though not against the law, or which a man seeks to obtain from a judge, belongs to the virtue annexed to justice. | Reply to Objection 1. True, vindication or punishment carried out by public authority according to the sentence of the judge is an act of commutative justice, which is one of the kinds or species of justice. But if a man personally vindicates himself in a way that the law permits, or if he asks the judge to vindicate him, he has performed an act of a virtue linked to justice. It is latter sort of vindication which concerns us here. |

Consider two cases of assault with the intent to cause grave bodily harm. In the first case, a policeman intervenes before the perpetrator can succeed, and the judge, after a trial, sentences him to time in prison. In the second case, there is no one nearby to help, but the victim knocks the perpetrator unconscious in the course of successful self-defense. Although both acts seem to have something to do with commutative justice – for both inflict on the wrongdoer something he deserves – they are not the same kind of act. Why not? Because the act of the judge, *applying* the law, is an act of justice in the strict sense, which the present Article does not concern. But the act of the private person, *observing* the law, is an act of justice only in a derivative sense. The virtue which disposes him to act is one of the *lesser* virtues associated with justice, one of those which the present Article is trying to classify. So provided that we take vindication in the latter sense, Cicero was correct to include it in his list.

| *Reply to Objection 2.*
[1] *Macrobius appears to have considered the two integral parts of justice, namely, "declining from evil," to which "innocence" belongs, and "doing good," to which the six others belong.*
[2] *Of these, two would seem to regard relations between equals, namely, "friendship" in the external conduct and "concord" internally; [3] two regard our relations toward* | Reply to Objection 2. Macrobius does not seem to have been listing potential parts of justice. Rather he seems to have been subdividing the two *integral* parts of justice, which are doing good and not doing evil. Of the items on his list, *innocence* belongs to not doing evil, and the remaining six belong to doing good. Of these six:

• One pair, friendliness and concord, concern relations with equals, for friendliness is about how our treatment of them, which is external, and concord is about the agreement of our wills with theirs, which is internal. |

superiors, namely, *"piety"*
to parents, and "religion" to
God; **[4]** *while two regard our*
relations towards inferiors,
namely, "condescension," in
so far as their good pleases us,
and "humanity," whereby we
help them in their needs. **[5]** *For*
Isidore says (Etym. x) that a
man is said to be "humane,
through having a feeling of love
and pity towards men: this gives
its name to humanity whereby
we uphold one another."
　[6] *On this sense "friendship"*
is understood as directing our
external conduct towards others,
from which point of view the
Philosopher treats of it in Ethic.
iv, 6. "Friendship" may also
be taken as regarding properly
the affections, and as the
Philosopher describes it in Ethic.
viii and ix. On this sense three
things pertain to friendship,
namely, "benevolence" which
is here called "affection";
"concord," and "beneficence"
which is here called "humanity."
[7] *These three, however, are*
omitted by Tully, because, as
stated above, they have little of
the nature of a due.

- Another pair, piety and religion, concern relations with superiors, [for piety is about our relations with parents, and religion is about our relations with God];
- And a third pair, goodwill [*affectus*] and humanity, concern relations with subordinates, for because of goodwill their well-being pleases us, and because of humanity we help them in their needs. Much the same thought is expressed by Isidore of Seville, who says in his *Etymologies* that we call a man *humane* for his disposition [*affectum*] to love and compassion for other humans, and we use the term *humanity* for looking after [*tuemur*] each other.

As we have seen just above, Macrobius uses the term "friendliness" for a virtue which directs how we treat others. Aristotle uses the term in the this way in the fourth book of his *Ethics*. But as we find in the eighth and ninth books of the same work, the term "friendliness" may also be taken in another sense: Concerning not how we treat them, but how we are internally disposed toward them. Taking it in the latter sense, friendliness encompasses three things: (1) benevolence, which Macrobius calls "goodwill"; (2) concord; and (3) beneficence, which Macrobius calls "humanity." Cicero rightly disregards all three of these, because they have so little to do with what is owed to another person in the strict sense.

[1] Macrobius is not even trying to list the potential parts of justice. Rather he is listing the integral parts of justice – the things which must concur for a particular act justice to be complete. Since one cannot do justice without *both* doing good *and* avoiding evil in one's relations toward others, these are its integral parts. The first item on Macrobius's list, "innocence," simply *means* avoiding evil toward others; the other six items on his list turn out to be subdivisions of doing good toward others.

[2] At first it might seem that in saying that friendliness is about external conduct but concord is about something internal, St. Thomas must mean that friendliness concerns how we treat our equals and concord concerns how we feel about them. This is not quite right, because we are listing *virtues* linked with justice, and virtues are "habits" or dispositions. Friendliness, then, is about how we are in the habit of treating them, and concord is about how we

are in the habit of viewing them. If I have the virtue of friendliness, I habitually treat my friend as a comrade, exchanging good things with him; if I have the virtue of concord, then as St. Thomas has explained earlier in the *Summa*, my heart and his habitually "agree together in consenting to the same thing."[33]

[3] St. Thomas's point is easy to understand, though in an age like ours it may be difficult to accept. Even many adults think families ought to be "democracies" rather than parental monarchies, and I have been asked by young people why the Divine wisdom is better than "yours, mine, or my cat's."

[4] St. Thomas speaks of those who are *inferiori*. Although "inferiors" is the most obvious rendering, in contemporary English the term is slightly misleading. To us, it suggests persons inferior in human worth, but St. Thomas, who thinks even a slave is made in God's image, is thinking of persons of lesser preeminence – as foot soldiers are inferior to their officers, children are inferior to their parents, students are inferior to their teachers, clients are inferior to their patrons, workers are inferior to their bosses, and so on. For this reason, "subordinates" seems a more fitting paraphrase. It is not unjust in itself that some should have higher status; injustice may arise from the abuse of higher status.

[5] Isidore says a humane (*humanus*) man is so called because he is disposed toward love and sympathy for humans (*hominis*) through love and pity for them. Since we tend to use the expressions "love" and "pity" for passions, it is important to keep in mind that he is using the corresponding Latin terms, *amorem* and *miserationis*, to mean dispositions. In his teaching, no feeling is in itself a virtue. The virtue of humanity must therefore lie in the disposition to feel these things *correctly* so that we are moved to do the right things. As Aristotle had written, what characterizes moral virtue is having emotions "at the right times, with reference to the right objects, towards the right people, with the right motive, and in the right way."[34]

[6] Now we must back up. Above, St. Thomas said that Macrobius lists friendliness and concord among the virtues which concern doing good toward equals, and he said that the difference between them is that friendliness concerns our external treatment of them while concord concerns the internal agreement of our wills with them. But now he points out that as Aristotle understood, the term "friendship" can actually be used in *either* the external or internal sense. (Fortunately, we can make this point in Greek, in Latin, or in English!) In this case, rather than treating friendship as something external and concord as something internal, we should say that concord is *one of the aspects of* friendship in the internal sense. This raises the question: Has friendship in the internal sense any other aspects besides this one? And the answer is yes: It also includes benevolence and beneficence. On Macrobius's list, benevolence corresponds to goodwill and beneficence corresponds to humanity.

[7] The virtues of concord, benevolence or goodwill, and beneficence or humanity, taken as dispositions of will, certainly do concern doing good things toward others. But do they concern doing *those good things to others which*

---

[33] II-II, Q. 29, Art. 1.   [34] Aristotle, *Nicomachean Ethics*, Book 2, Chapter 6.

belong to them as their right – those which we owe them as a matter of justice? St. Thomas does not say that they have *nothing* to do with justice, but he says they have so little to do with it that Cicero was right to omit them from his list. The point is not that a man devoid of these virtues could still be a good man; the point is that he would not have failed in the *particular respect* which the virtue of justice concerns.

We have now accounted for all of the items Macrobius thinks important. But the fact remains that he has listed parts and subparts of the integral parts of justice – and none of them belong on *our* list, because we are trying to identify the *potential* parts of justice.

Reply to Objection 3. [1] *"Obedience" is included in observance, which Tully mentions, because both reverential honor and obedience are due to persons who excel.* [2] *"Faithfulness whereby a man's acts agree with his words" [Cicero, De Repub. iv, De Offic. i, 7], is contained in "truthfulness" as to the observance of one's promises:* [3] *yet "truthfulness" covers a wider ground, as we shall state further on (109, 1 and 3).* [4] *"Discipline" is not due as a necessary duty, because one is under no obligation to an inferior as such, although a superior may be under an obligation to watch over his inferiors,* [5] *according to Matthew 24:45, "A faithful and wise servant, whom his lord hath appointed over his family":* [6] *and for this reason it is omitted by Tully.* [7] *It may, however, be included in humanity mentioned by Macrobius;* [8] *and equity under epieikeia or under "friendship."*	Reply to Objection 3. Although Cicero does not mention obedience, he does mention observance, which includes obedience. For observance is the virtue which disposes us to render to distinguished persons the reverent honor and obedience which are owed to them. Again, although Cicero does not mention faithfulness, by which we do as we say, he does mention truthfulness, which includes faithfulness, because one of the many aspects of being truthful is keeping promises. The term "truth" is used for other things as well, but we will consider them later on. Cicero omits guardianship from his list because it is not owed as a matter of strict necessity; no one has a duty to provide for another person *just because* the other is lower in position. This is not to deny that the person who is in the higher position may have an obligation to provide those under him [for some additional reason]. Christ, for example, speaks in one place of a faithful and wise servant whose master has set him over his household [to give them their food in due season]. To be sure, guardianship can be contained under humanity, which is one of the subordinate virtues listed by Macrobius. [But as we found in the Reply to Objection 2, humanity is not a potential part of justice either. Rather it is a subdivision of one of its integral parts.] The foregoing discussion leaves only equity, which may mean either of two things. First it may mean *epieikeia*, [which we will consider in the Reply to Objection 5]. Second it may be included in friendliness, [which we have already considered in the Reply to Objection 2].

[1] Where St. Thomas speaking of distinguished persons, we should not think of persons who excel, say, in playing soccer or composing limericks, but of persons who excel in dignity – in the quality of being worthy of respect. In our day we may concede that some persons are worthy of respect – but of obedience? "Surely not," we say. Yet why is it not good to defer to the judgment of those whose judgment is superior? Actually, in our better moments we do recognize such a duty. "What do you think of this, sir?"

[2] As we saw above, truthfulness includes keeping promises. One who says "I will do P" when he has no intention of doing so is lying. If he intends to do P, but then changes his mind and does not do it, his present action retroactively falsifies his previous statement.

One may never say what one knows to be false with intent to deceive. However, truthfulness does not require saying everything which one knows to be true. The mean is "to tell the truth, when one ought, and as one ought. Excess consists in making known one's own affairs out of season, and deficiency in hiding them when one ought to make them known."[35]

[3] One of the meanings of truth is the virtue of truthfulness, but the term "truth" may be used in various other senses which are wider than the virtue of truthfulness. For all of its uses, the standard is the truth of being – the truth of *what is*, which is ultimately dependent on the First Being, who is God.[36]

- The truth of a proposition is its correspondence to what is.
- The truth of science is the correspondence of *scientific* propositions with what is (bearing in mind that St. Thomas uses the term "science" for all bodies of knowledge which can validly trace their conclusions to their premises).
- The truth of doctrine is the correspondence of *theological* propositions with what is (bearing in mind that theology is sacred science).
- The truth of life is the correspondence of one's *conduct* with what is – in the sense that it conforms to God's law, which alone can give it moral rectitude.
- The truth of justice is the correspondence of one's conduct with what is in the sense that it conforms to *legal judgments referring to other persons*. It can also mean the propositional truth of statements made in legal proceedings, such as confessing and giving evidence.

[4] For a superior to take an interest in the welfare of his subordinates is virtuous. For example, it would be a good thing to ask, "Joe, is your little girl still sick? Do you need an extra day off?" But this would not be an act of justice in the strict sense of the term; the workers may have many rights, such as fair treatment, but the mere fact that the boss is in a superior position does not give his subordinates a *right* that he look after them in general. To be sure, someone in a superior position *may* have a duty to provide for his subordinates; for example, as a father I owe care and protection to my children, and this really

---

[35] II-II, Q. 109, Art. 1, ad 3.
[36] For the following uses of the term "truth," see II-II, Q. 109, esp. Arts. 1–3.

is their right. Yet in such a case, the duty of care does not arise simply from the fact that my status is higher than theirs; it arises from other considerations, in this case the teleology of the family.

[5] These words about a faithful and wise servant come from to the following parable:

> Therefore you also must be ready; for the Son of man is coming at an hour you do not expect. Who then is the faithful and wise servant, whom his master has set over his household, to give them their food at the proper time? Blessed is that servant whom his master when he comes will find so doing. Truly, I say to you, he will set him over all his possessions.[37]

The point of the comparison is that just as the steward in the parable must be faithful and ready for his master's return, so Christ's followers in the world must be faithful and ready for His return. Although St. Thomas is well aware of this fact, his own purpose in alluding to the passage is merely to provide an illustration of his point about the duty of caring for others. The steward in the parable owes it to the members of the household to care for them not because of his rank, but because his master has specifically assigned him the duty.

[6] The antecedent of the phrase "this reason" may be unclear. It refers not to the fact that a superior *may* for special reasons have a duty to care for subordinates, but to the fact that he does not have a duty to care for subordinates *just because* they are subordinate.

[7] Although care for subordinates *merely because they are subordinates* is not in the strict sense an act of justice – because it is not owed to them as a right for this reason alone – nevertheless it may be viewed as an act of the virtue which Macrobius calls "humanity." But we have already seen, in the Reply to Objection 2, that humanity need not be added to our list because even though it is virtuous, it has "little of the nature of a due."

[8] Only one item remains from the list of the unnamed "other writers": Equity. The term equity [*aequitas*] is often used as synonym for *epieikeia*, so *epieikeia* may be what these writers had in mind. St. Thomas will discuss whether *epieikeia* is a potential part of justice in the Reply to Objection 5.

But St. Thomas suggests that the term "equity" may also refer to an aspect of friendliness. How might that be so? As we find out in a passage later in the *Summa*, the answer is that "friends rejoice and grieve for the same things," leading to clemency which "judges it equitable that a person be no further punished."[38] We might put the matter this way: Equity in the sense of *epieikeia* refers to what seems reasonable in the absence of a legal rule; but equity as an aspect of friendliness refers to what seems reasonable *to friends* in the absence of a legal rule. But suppose the unnamed "other writers" really were thinking of equity as an aspect of friendliness. Does this fact give us a reason to put equity on the list of lesser virtues linked with justice? No, for as we saw before,

---

[37] Matthew 24:44–47 (RSV-CE).   [38] II-II, Q. 157, Art. 4, ad 3.

in the Reply to Objection 2, at best friendliness may be viewed as an *integral*, not a potential, part of justice.

Reply to Objection 4. [1] *This enumeration contains some belonging to true justice.* [2] *To particular justice belongs "justice of exchange," which he describes as "the habit of observing equality in commutations."* [3] *To legal justice, as regards things to be observed by all, he ascribes "legislative justice," which he describes as "the science of political commutations relating to the community."* [4] *As regards things which have to be done in particular cases beside the general laws, he mentions "common sense" or "good judgment," which is our guide in such like matters, as stated above (Question 51, Article 4) in the treatise on prudence:* [5] *wherefore he says that it is a "voluntary justification," because by his own free will man observes what is just according to his judgment and not according to the written law.* [6] *These two are ascribed to prudence as their director, and to justice as their executor.* [7] *Eusebeia*[39] *means "good worship" and consequently is the same as religion,* [8] *wherefore he says that it is the science of "the service of God" (he speaks after the manner of Socrates who said that 'all the virtues are*	Reply to Objection 4. Some of the dispositions in Pseudo-Andronicus's list really do concern true justice in some way. But let us consider them one by one.

Good exchange, or reciprocity, belongs to particular justice. Pseudo-Andronicus describes it as the disposition to preserve equality in exchanges. [But this makes it a kind of particular justice, not a virtue linked to justice.]

Good lawmaking belongs not to particular but to legal justice, which concerns duties prescribed by law which everyone must fulfill for the sake of the common good. He describes it as the "science" not of economic but of political "exchanges" or interrelationships [*commutationum politicarum*] among the community.

In the *Treatise on Prudence*, earlier in this *Summa*, we discussed the virtue of gnome. What Pseudo-Andronicus calls *eugnomosyne* – good *gnome* – is the same thing. This is the virtue which guides our judgment concerning things to be done in special cases not covered by the ordinary laws. Pseudo-Andronicus says it concerns "voluntary justification" – "justification" in the sense that a man does what seems just, and "voluntary" in the sense that he determines what is just by his own judgment rather than by written law.

We may view both good lawmaking and *eugnomosyne* as parts of either prudence or [legal] justice, for they belong to prudence insofar as it directs them, but to justice insofar as it carries them out. [However, we are listing the parts of particular justice, not of legal justice – of justice as one virtue among others, not of justice as a synonym for the acts of virtue in general, as commanded by law for the common good.]

Eusebia means something like "good reverence," so it is the same virtue as religion. |

---

[39] The translators place the word "piety" in square brackets after the word *eusebia*, but this is incorrect: As St. Thomas makes clear in very next line, he associates *eusebia* not with the virtue of piety, but with the virtue of religion.

sciences' [Aristotle, Ethic. vi, 13]): [9] and "holiness" comes to the same, as we shall state further on (81, 8). [10] Eucharistia (gratitude) means "good thanksgiving," and is mentioned, as well as revenge, by Tully. [11] Kindliness seems to be the same as affection, mentioned by Macrobius: wherefore Isidore says (Etym. x) that "a kind man is one who is ready of his own accord to do good, and is of gentle speech": and Andronicus too says that "kindliness is a habit of voluntary beneficence." [12] "Liberality" would seem to pertain to "humanity."

Pseudo-Andronicus calls it as the "science" of serving God; here he is following Socrates, who viewed all virtues as "sciences" or forms of knowledge.

Sanctity, the next item on his list, comes to much the same thing, as we see a little later in this work.

Eucharistia means good thanks, that is, gratitude, which is already on Cicero's list.

So is vindication, as the Objector acknowledges.

We have already discussed kindness in connection with Macrobius's list, for it seems to be the same as goodwill. In support of our claim that they are the same thing we might also mention Isidore, who says the kind man is willingly prepared to do good and is soft of speech, and Andronicus, who says kindness is the disposition of voluntarily doing good.

Finally, liberality seems to pertain to humanity, [which we have also discussed.]

[1] Although St. Thomas concedes that some of the items on this list are parts of true justice, he goes on to show that not all of them are parts in the relevant sense, and those which are, are not really missing from Cicero's list.

[2] We are not speaking here of commutation in the sense of commuting a punishment (making it less), but in the sense of trade or exchange. Equality in commutation means equality in exchange, which means equal value given and received.

[3] The expression "political commutations" is rather obscure. Certainly politics concerns exchanges in a certain sense; for example, a citizen may offer wise counsel in the assembly, and in return he may receive honors or public office. However, rendering honors or offices to the wise would normally be called distributive rather than commutative justice. I think that in this case the term "commutations" is being used simply for the interactions among citizens in general, the regulation of which is the object of law.

[4] As explained previously, *eugnomosyne* is not "common sense." However, the phrase "good judgment" conveys the meaning well, provided that we bear in mind that we are not speaking of good judgment in general, but of the aspect of good judgment which guides us in situations which the laws do not cover. St. Thomas explains that *eugnomosyne* means *bona gnome*, "good gnome," alluding to his previous discussions of the virtue of *gnome*:

Now it happens sometimes that something has to be done which is not covered by the common rules of actions, for instance in the case of the enemy of one's country, when it would be wrong to give him back his deposit, or in other similar cases. Hence it is necessary to judge of such matters according to higher principles than the common laws, according to which *synesis* judges: and corresponding to such higher principles it is necessary to have a higher virtue of judgment, which is called *gnome*, and which denotes a certain discrimination in judgment.[40]

[5] St. Thomas is speaking of justification in the sense of *making* something just, *showing* that it is just, or *doing* what is just. In English, the term can also be used for making the unjust *appear* to be just: "He justified the murder by claiming that it was an accident." However, that is not the meaning here.

[6] "These two" being *eugnomosyne*, good judgment about novel situations, and *legispositivam*, good lawmaking. Insofar as these dispositions require the right use of practical reason, they may be viewed as parts of prudence; insofar as they require the right action toward another person, they may be viewed as parts of justice.

[7] The translators place the word "piety," here omitted, in square brackets after the word *eusebia*, but this is not correct: As St. Thomas makes clear in very next line, he associates *eusebia* not with the virtue of piety, but with the virtue of religion.

[8] Socrates is famous for having apparently held the view that virtue is a kind of knowledge[41] – an opinion which seems to obliterate the distinction between moral and intellectual virtue so that sin appears to be no more than intellectual error. St. Thomas is not endorsing the Socratic view; he is merely trying to explain why Pseudo-Andronicus phrased his definition of *eusebeia* in the somewhat odd way he did.

[9] St. Thomas says (Question 81, Article 8, Reply to Objection 1) that although the virtues of sanctity and religion may be identified, sanctity has "a certain generality." It not only disposes us to worship God but transforms our motives so that every other good thing we do, we do for God's sake.

[10] This is the meaning of *eucharistia* as a name for a virtue. Christians use the term in a derived sense, speaking of Holy Communion as the Eucharist, or as the Eucharistic feast, because it is the feast of gratitude for the truly present Body and Blood of Jesus Christ.

[11] The translation of *affectu* as "affection" rather than as "goodwill" misses the point here, because the kind man is not a man who likes everyone. It is because of how his *will* is disposed that he is ready to do good *voluntarily* (Pseudo-Andronicus) and *of his own accord* (Isidore). But we have already

---

[40] II-II, Q. 51, Art. 4, substituting for the Blackfriars paraphrases the Greek words which St. Thomas actually uses.

[41] "Socrates, then, thought the virtues were rules or rational principles (for he thought they were, all of them, forms of scientific knowledge), while we think they *involve* a rational principle." Aristotle, *Nicomachean Ethics*, Book 6, Chapter 13, emphasis added. Not all scholars agree with Aristotle's interpretation of Socrates' view.

considered whether goodwill needs to be added to Cicero's list of the potential parts of justice, and we have found that it does not.

[12] Just as we have already discussed goodwill, we have already discussed liberality.

Reply to Objection 5. Epieikeia is annexed, not to particular but to legal justice, and apparently is the same as that which goes by the name of eugnomosyne [common sense].	Reply to Objection 5. We have been speaking of the virtues linked to particular justice. The virtue of *epieikeia* does not belong on our list because it is an adjunct of legal justice. It seems to be the same as the virtue called *eugnomosyne*.

Unlike particular justice, which gives others what is due to them, general justice is a synonym for virtue in general. *Legal* justice is St. Thomas's term for those acts of general justice which are prescribed by law for the common good. But as we saw earlier, *eipieikeia* is the virtue which enables us to judge what to do in cases which the law does not cover; as he explains in II-II, Question 120, Article 2, it is a higher rule of human acts by which legal justice is directed. This makes it, he says, a part of *legal* justice – of general justice, insofar as it is upheld by the law. But in this Article we have been classifying the parts of *particular* justice, so it does not belong on our list.

The terminology of the Reply to Objection 5 is slightly confusing. St. Thomas has used several words, apparently interchangeably, to describe the association of particular justice with its potential parts: Sometimes he says "annexed," sometimes he says "adjoined." Here he uses one of the same words to say that *epieikeia* is linked not with particular but with legal justice: *Epieikeia non adiungitur* [adjoined] *iustitiae particulari, sed legali.* From the phrasing, one might get the impression that *epieikeia* is a *potential* part of legal justice. However, any such impression must be unintended, because St. Thomas argues later on that it must be a *subjective* part of legal justice.

If we ask exactly how *epieikeia* is a subjective part of legal justice, we find that the "hammer and wrench are potential parts of tool" illustration which we used above does not quite cover it. St. Thomas says in I-II, Question 120, Article 2 that a subjective part of a whole is something which does not comprise all of the whole but does possess its essence. This can happen in two ways. One is the way horse and ox are parts of animal – although animal can be predicated of both of them, neither comprises the whole of animal. The other is the way substance and accident are parts of being – although being can be predicated of both of them, one stands in relation to the other as prior to posterior, or perhaps higher to lower. *Epieikeia* is a subjective part of justice in the latter sense, because it is not *less* than the whole of legal justice; rather it *directs* legal justice.

Whether the Precepts of the Decalogue Are Precepts of Justice?

TEXT	PARAPHRASE
Whether the precepts of the decalogue are precepts of justice?	Traditionally, the rules set forth in the Ten Commandments have been viewed as concerned above all with justice. Is this view correct?

In this Article even more than in others, we see how firmly St. Thomas connects virtues with precepts, dispositions of character with authoritative rules: The notion of some people that "virtue ethics" is a way of doing ethics without rules would strike him as very strange, for the acts to which the virtues dispose us are things which we *ought to do.*

Some background is necessary to follow the discussion. A vast change takes place in Divine law after the coming of Christ, especially because now man is offered not only direction about what to do, but also, through grace, the power to do it. However, not all of the Old Testament law ceases to be binding. The present Article concerns the Ten Commandments, which continue in force because they would have been authoritative by reason alone apart from Revelation. Just what kind of precepts are they?

Commands of Old Testament law may be divided into three categories: Moral, ceremonial, and judicial. The moral precepts, which include the precepts of the Decalogue, are precepts of natural law, commanding acts of virtue and forbidding acts contrary to virtue. They are "conclusions" of reason in the same sense that theorems are "conclusions" of axioms. There is a certain difficulty here, for sometimes St. Thomas states that reason alone is needed to see that they are right, but sometimes he states that in addition to reason we need Divine instruction; at one point, he offers the paradoxical remark that the rightness of loving God and neighbor is "self-evident to human reason, *either through nature or through faith.*"[1] The solution to this puzzle seems to lie in the fact that that although natural reason perceives something of the invisible things of God, "In many respects faith perceives the invisible things of God *in a higher way* than natural reason does." Consequently, "It is necessary for man to accept by faith not only things which are above reason, *but also those which can be known by reason.*"[2] We might say that among other things, faith enables us to recognize and assent to moral truths that are obvious in themselves but not necessarily obvious *to us*. So it is that we need Divine instruction about certain matters concerning our moral duty to God, not because natural reason is utterly unable to see what is right – in which case these matters really would lie outside natural law – but because natural reason needs corrective lenses. Or perhaps because it needs the reminder, "Stop turning your face aside – *look there.*"

Ceremonial and judicial precepts differ from moral precepts because their authority rests not just on reason, which shows what must be done, but also on further decisions, which could have gone differently, specifying the details of how it is to be done. Rules of this sort – rules that "fill in the blanks" when more than one way of doing so might be reasonable – are called not conclusions but "determinations" of reason. As St. Thomas has explained earlier in the *Summa*, and as he further explains below, the ceremonial precepts are determinations concerning how man is to conduct himself toward God, but the judicial precepts are determinations concerning how man is to conduct himself toward other human beings.[3]

In this Article, we are concerned not so much with whether the precepts of the Decalogue have *anything to do* with justice, as whether justice is their main concern. The moral precepts of Divine Law in general address each one of the virtues; do the Ten Commandments *specialize* in justice, as the tradition had held that they do?

Objection 1. [1] *It seems that the precepts of the decalogue are not precepts of justice.* [2] *For the intention of a lawgiver is "to make the citizens virtuous in respect of every virtue,"* *as stated in Ethic. ii, 1. Wherefore, according to Ethic. v, 1, "the law prescribes about all acts of all virtues."* [3] *Now the precepts of the decalogue are the first principles of the*	**Objection 1.** The rules of the Decalogue do not seem to be *chiefly* precepts of justice. As Aristotle points out, legislators aim at cultivating all of the virtues among the citizens, and the law issues commands concerning each of them. These points should certainly apply to the rules of the Decalogue, which are the foundational principles of the entire Divine law. Therefore,

---

[1] To see the difficulty, compare I-II, Q. 100, Art. 1; ibid., Art. 3; and Q. 104, Art. 1. For the quotation, see I-II, Q. 100, Art. 3, ad 1; compare Art. 4, ad 1. For discussion, see the *Commentary on Thomas Aquinas's Treatise on Law* (Cambridge: Cambridge University Press, 2014).

[2] II-II, Q. 2, Art. 3, ad 3; II-II, Q. 2, Art. 4; emphasis added.

[3] I-II, Q. 94, Art. 4, and Q. 101, Art. 1. In the present Article, see also below, ad 2.

| whole Divine Law. [4] Therefore the precepts of the decalogue do not pertain to justice alone. | the rules of the Decalogue concern not only justice, but other virtues as well. |

[1] The Objector does not deny that the precepts of the Decalogue address justice; rather he holds that they have no greater concern with justice than with any other virtue. This is not explicit until the last line: "Therefore the precepts of the Decalogue do not pertain *to justice alone*" (*ad solam iustitiam*).

[2] St. Thomas agrees with Aristotle that the tendency of law is to *make men good* – that is what it is for, and that is what it does. However, he certainly does not think human law makes men good completely, unfailingly, unproblematically, or without further qualification. If the lawmakers are just, then human law tends to make men good simply; otherwise it tends to habituate them only to the acts which are good for the continuation of a particular form of rule. Even at its best, human law habituates men only with respect to the acquired virtues, because the formation of the infused virtues, which are motivated by the love of God, requires the special help of grace. Moreover, although human law commands acts of every *kind* of acquired virtue, it does not direct every *act* of acquired virtue; for example, it may forbid driving on the public street while intoxicated, but it does not forbid reading a book in one's house while intoxicated, because although both cases concern temperance, the common good is implicated only in the former. For these and other reasons, the Aristotelian view that law makes men good is much more fully true of Divine law, of which Aristotle knew nothing, than of human law.[4]

[3] Each of the many detailed precepts of Divine law is derived from the general principles of the Decalogue, though some by "conclusion" and other by "determination," as explained above.

[4] The argument works like this:

1. Law aims at cultivating all the virtues.
2. This statement is pre-eminently true of Divine law.
3. Therefore it is pre-eminently true of the precepts of the Decalogue, which are the foundational principles of Divine law.
4. Therefore the precepts of the Decalogue aim at cultivating all the virtues, not just the special virtue of justice in the sense of giving to each what is due to him.

| Objection 2. [1] Further, it would seem that to justice belong especially the judicial precepts, [2] which are condivided with the moral precepts, as stated above (I-II, 99, 4). | Objection 2. Moreover, justice seems to be chiefly about the judicial precepts of the Divine law. But we have distinguished judicial from |

---

[4] Concerning whether law makes men good, see I-II, Q. 92, Art. 1; concerning the limitations of human law in comparison with Divine, see I-II, Q. 91, Art. 4.

[3] *But the precepts of the decalogue are moral precepts, as stated above (I-II, 100, 3). Therefore the precepts of the decalogue are not precepts of justice.*	moral precepts, and the rules of the Decalogue are moral precepts. It follows that the rules of the Decalogue are not precepts of justice.

[1] The Objector is relying on St. Thomas's explanation earlier in the *Summa* that "just as the determination of the universal principle about Divine worship is effected by the ceremonial precepts, so the determination of the general precepts of that justice which is to be observed among men is effected by the judicial precepts."[5] More particularly, judicial precepts direct the conduct of (1) rulers toward those whom they rule, (2) citizens toward other citizens, (3) citizens toward "strangers" or noncitizens, and (4) members of the household toward one another.[6]

[2] To say that the moral and judicial precepts are condivided is simply to say that they are of different kinds, that they fall into different categories.

[3] The argument works like this:

1. The moral and judicial precepts are distinct.
2. Directing men in matters of justice is the concern of the judicial precepts.
3. Therefore it is not the concern of the moral precepts.
4. But the Ten Commandments are moral precepts.
5. Therefore it is not the concern of the Ten Commandments.

Objection 3. [1] *Further, the Law contains chiefly precepts about acts of justice regarding the common good, for instance about public officers and the like.* [2] *But there is no mention of these in the precepts of the decalogue. Therefore it seems that the precepts of the decalogue do not properly belong to justice.*	*Objection 3.* Still further, most laws command acts of justice for the sake of the common good – for example in relation to such things as public officials. But the precepts of the Decalogue do not even mention such things. So again, it seems that these rules are not especially concerned with justice.

[1] A good many of the judicial precepts concern the form of government, the qualifications of persons who are to fill offices of authority, how they are to be chosen, and how they are to behave. Taken together, these rules may be viewed as Old Testament constitutional law. Though their details are not universally binding, they do have universal interest, for according to St. Thomas, they are not mere whims, but have a rational basis.

[2] The Objector's argument may be viewed as proposing a kind of test:

1. Precepts of justice are concerned above all with the common good.
2. Conspicuous among such precepts are rules for the regulation of public officials.

---

[5] I-II, Q. 99, Art. 4.   [6] I-II, Q. 104, Art. 4.

3. Therefore, if it is really true that the Decalogue is concerned *chiefly* with justice, we should expect it to contain rules for the regulation of public officials.
4. But this is not the case: The Ten Commandments say nothing about the form of government, the qualifications or choice of persons who are to fill offices of authority, or how they are to behave.
5. Therefore, the Decalogue is not concerned chiefly with justice.

Objection 4. [1] *Further, the precepts of the decalogue are divided into two tables, corresponding to the love of God and the love of our neighbor,* [2] *both of which regard the virtue of charity.* [3] *Therefore the precepts of the decalogue belong to charity rather than to justice.*	Objection 4. Besides, both of the two tablets of the Decalogue concern the virtue of charity, for the First Tablet concerns love of God, and the second concerns love of neighbor. It follows that the rules of the Decalogue are not precepts of justice, but precepts of charity.

[1] The book of Exodus records that when God was finished speaking with Moses on Mt. Sinai, he gave him "the two tables of the testimony, tables of stone, written with the finger of God."[7] According to the tradition followed by St. Thomas, the First Table contains the precepts about not placing other gods above God or making and serving carved images of gods, not speaking of God in empty ways, and observing the Sabbath day of rest and worship of God – duties which arise from love of God Himself. In turn, the Second Table contains the precepts about honoring father and mother, not murdering, not committing adultery, not stealing, not bearing false witness, not coveting one's neighbor's spouse, and not coveting his house, servants, or possessions – duties which arise from love of our neighbors, who are made in God's image.[8]

[2] From earliest times it has been recognized that love is the root of the whole Law. A good précis of all that follows from the First Table is the *sch'ma*, found in the book of Deuteronomy and still recited twice daily by observant Jews:

Hear, O Israel: The Lord our God is one Lord; and you shall love the Lord your God with all your heart, and with all your soul, and with all your might.[9]

---

[7] Exodus 31:18 (RSV-CE).

[8] A point that often causes needless confusion is that although the Bible sets forth the Ten Commandments in two different places, Deuteronomy 5:6–21 and Exodus 20:2–17, it does not specify any particular way of dividing them into ten. Like most Catholics, St. Thomas enumerates them in the manner of St. Augustine; others, including most Protestants, follow a different enumeration, found in Philo, Josephus, and Origen, which splits the First Commandment into two but combines the last two Commandments into one. Thus, for example, St. Thomas calls the precept against murder the Fifth Commandment, but some call it the Sixth.

[9] Deuteronomy 6:4–5; compare Deuteronomy 11:1, 30:6 and Joshua 22:5.

The implications of the Second Table are put in a nutshell in the book of Leviticus:

You shall not hate your brother in your heart, but you shall reason with your neighbor, lest you bear sin because of him. You shall not take vengeance or bear any grudge against the sons of your own people, but you shall love your neighbor as yourself: I am the Lord.[10]

The New Testament brings both resumes together in what has come to be called the Summary of the Law:

And one of them, a lawyer, asked [Jesus] a question, to test him. "Teacher, which is the great commandment in the law?" And he said to him, "You shall love the Lord your God with all your heart, and with all your soul, and with all your mind. This is the great and first commandment. And a second is like it, You shall love your neighbor as yourself. On these two commandments depend all the law and the prophets."[11]

The point of these teachings is not that if one loves God and neighbor, then one may disobey the Ten Commandments, but that the reason for obeying the Ten Commandments is that they spell out the meaning of the love of God and neighbor. This may seem obvious, but in a world in which people say that a little bit of adultery may refresh a marriage, or that socially mandated theft will make the world more fair, or that the murder of unwanted children will ensure that every surviving child is wanted, it needs to be stated.

[3] The Objector reasons that since the root of the Decalogue is love or charity, it cannot be said to be concerned chiefly with justice. He does not consider the possibility that it may concern love in one sense but justice in another.

On the contrary, [1] *Seemingly justice is the sole virtue whereby we are directed to another.* [2] *Now we are directed to another by all the precepts of the decalogue, as is evident if one consider each of them. Therefore all the precepts of the decalogue pertain to justice.*	On the other hand, justice seems to be the only virtue which regulates our acts toward others. Yet one can see by considering the rules of the Decalogue one at a time that each one of them does this. So the rules of the Decalogue are rules of justice after all.

[1] The meaning of the *sed contra* is that justice is the only *acquired* virtue which directs us to others; it is not considering the infused virtues, otherwise it would also have to list charity (which the hypothetical opponent makes the basis of Objection 4).

Now acts of any acquired virtue may certainly concern others *incidentally*. For example, it would be an act of fortitude to dash into the path of an oncoming truck to push a child out of the way, an act of temperance to bear hunger in order to have enough food to give others, and an act of prudence to enact a law for the common good. But among the acquired virtues, only justice directs us

---

[10] Leviticus 19:17–18; compare Romans 13:8–10; Galatians 5:14; and James 2:8.
[11] Matthew 22:35–40; compare Mark 12:28–34; see also Luke 10:25–28 as amplified by 29–37.

to others *essentially* – only justice is *defined* by the observance of our duties to them. Some acts of the other acquired virtues concern others, but in this sense all acts of justice concern others.

[2] Justice is about rendering to others what we owe to them. What the *sed contra* points out is that the Commandments of the First Table concern not just what to do concerning God but what we *owe* to God, and the Commandments of the Second Table concerns not just what to do concerning our neighbors but what we *owe* to our neighbors. Traditionally, each of these precepts is understood as a metonym – a placeholder, so to speak, for a large number of more detailed commandments. For example, although taken literally, the Third Commandment commands only Sabbath day observance, taken metonymically, it commands *all* service owed to God in thoughts; in the same way, although taken literally, the Sixth Commandment forbids only adultery, taken metonymically it represents *all* that we owe to our spouses, our procreative partners.

St. Thomas works all this out in I-II, Question 100, Article 5. Thus:

- The First Commandment directs us to render to God the fidelity that we owe Him in deeds: "I am the Lord your God, who brought you out of the land of Egypt, out of the house of bondage. You shall have no other gods before me. You shall not make for yourself a graven image, or any likeness of anything that is in heaven above, or that is on the earth beneath, or that is in the water under the earth; you shall not bow down to them or serve them; for I the Lord your God am a jealous God, visiting the iniquity of the fathers upon the children to the third and fourth generation of those who hate me, but showing steadfast love to thousands of those who love me and keep my commandments."[12]
- The Second Commandment directs us to render to Him the reverence that we owe Him in words: "You shall not take the name of the Lord your God in vain: for the Lord will not hold him guiltless who takes his name in vain."
- The Third Commandment directs us to render to Him the service that we owe Him in thoughts: "Observe the Sabbath day, to keep it holy, as the Lord your God commanded you. Six days you shall labor, and do all your work; but the seventh day is a Sabbath to the Lord your God; in it you shall not do any work, you, or your son, or your daughter, or your manservant, or your maidservant, or your ox, or your ass, or any of your cattle, or the sojourner who is within your gates, that your manservant and your maidservant may rest as well as you. You shall remember that you were a servant in the land of Egypt, and the Lord your God brought you out thence with a mighty hand and an outstretched arm; therefore the Lord your God commanded you to keep the Sabbath day."

Turning now to the precepts concerning neighbors:

- The Fourth Commandment concerns what we owe to our neighbors *in particular*, in that it directs us to render the payment of our actual debts to

---

[12] Here, and below, I am following the wording of Deuteronomy 5:6–21 (RSV-CE).

them: "Honor your father and your mother, as the Lord your God commanded you; that your days may be prolonged, and that it may go well with you, in the land which the Lord your God gives you."

The remaining six Commandments concern what we owe to our neighbors *in general*. Thus:

- The Fifth Commandment directs us not to harm our neighbors by deed with respect to their existence: "You shall not kill."
- The Sixth Commandment directs us not to harm them by deed with respect to unity for the propagation of offspring: "Neither shall you commit adultery."
- The Seventh Commandment directs us not to harm them by deed with respect to their possessions: "Neither shall you steal."
- The Eighth Commandment directs us not to harm them by word: "Neither shall you bear false witness against your neighbor."
- The Ninth Commandment directs us not to harm them by thought through the lust of the flesh: "Neither shall you covet your neighbor's wife."
- Finally, the Tenth Commandment directs us not to harm them by thought through what St. John calls the lust of the eyes:[13] "and you shall not desire your neighbor's house, his field, or his manservant, or his maidservant, his ox, or his ass, or anything that is your neighbor's."

I answer that, [1] *The precepts of the decalogue are the first principles of the Law:* [2] *and the natural reason assents to them at once, as to principles that are most evident.* [3] *Now it is altogether evident that the notion of duty, which is essential to a precept, appears in justice, which is of one towards another.* [4] *Because in those matters that relate to himself it would seem at a glance that man is master of himself, and that he may do as he likes: whereas in matters that refer to another it appears manifestly that a man is under obligation to render to another that which is his due.* [5] *Hence the precepts of the decalogue must needs pertain to justice.* [6] *Wherefore* [7] *the first*	**Here is my response.** The rules of the Decalogue are the foundational principles of law. Natural reason assents to them right away; they are the most obvious of all starting points. Plainly, though, the idea of duty, so crucial to any rule, is linked with justice, which concerns our acts toward others. Why? Because concerning himself, it seems to a man (though only at first glance) that he is his own master and may do whatever he wishes, but concerning others, he clearly recognizes that he has a duty to give them what he owes them. Fittingly, then, the precepts of the Decalogue do address justice: • The first three concern acts of religion, the greatest potential part of justice;

[13] "Do not love the world or the things in the world. If anyone loves the world, love for the Father is not in him. For all that is in the world, the lust of the flesh and the lust of the eyes and the pride of life, is not of the Father but is of the world. And the world passes away, and the lust of it; but he who does the will of God abides forever." 1 John 2:15–17 (RSV-CE).

three precepts are about acts of religion, which is the chief part of justice; [8] *the fourth precept is about acts of piety, which is the second part of justice;* [9] *and the six remaining are about justice commonly so called, which is observed among equals.*	• The fourth concerns filial piety, which is the next most important potential part of justice; and • The other six concern justice in the everyday sense of the term, which concerns our relations with our equals.

[1] The first principles of law are their seeds or starting points – the kernels from which the more detailed rules are derived, whether by conclusion or determination. St. Thomas does not say merely that the precepts of the Decalogue are the first principles of *Divine* law, but that they are the first principles of *law* – from them flow not only the laws of the Jewish people in Old Testament times, but the true and just laws of all people in all times. This would be impossible if they were promulgated only to the community of faith, by direct, verbal Revelation. However, they are principles of natural law, promulgated to the entire human race, "by the very fact that God instilled it into man's mind so as to be known by him naturally."[14]

The notion of natural moral knowledge unsettles some Christians, who on the basis of the Reformation motto *sola scriptura*, "Scripture alone," think it unbiblical to believe that nonbelievers have any sure knowledge of right and wrong apart from the sacred Scriptures. Remarkably, the sacred Scriptures claim just the opposite, for in them God appeals to pre-existing moral knowledge. For example, in commending His commandments to the Hebrews, He asks, "And what great nation is there, that has statutes and ordinances so righteous as all this law which I set before you this day?"[15] Had He not already inscribed this same law on the deep structure of the practical intellect, there would have been no point to the question; they would have been unable to answer it. We may therefore paraphrase God's query, "Do you not see that this body of laws I am setting before you is a more perfect expression of what I have already made known by other means?"

It may at first seem puzzling that although in the sentence under examination St. Thomas calls the precepts of the Decalogue the first principles of law, he says earlier in the *Summa* that the first precept of law is that "good is to be done and pursued, and evil is to be avoided."[16] There is no inconsistency, because the precept "Good is to be done and pursued, and evil is to be avoided" is not an empty formality; in St. Thomas's view it virtually contains all of the precepts of the Decalogue, in the same way that the acorn virtually contains the oak.[17] The precept to do and pursue good and avoid evil is so plain to the mind that to command it in words would be superfluous, perhaps even ridiculous:

---

[14] I-II, Q. 90, Art. 4, ad 1.   [15] Deuteronomy 4:8 (RSV-CE).   [16] I-II, Q. 94, Art. 2.
[17] "For the first general principles are contained in them, as principles in their proximate conclusions." I-II, Q. 100, Art. 3.

What else but good *would* one pursue? Even one who does evil *thinks* it is good.[18] But the Decalogue reminds us *what it is* to do and pursue good and to avoid evil.

[2] It might be supposed that although the precepts of the Decalogue are right for everyone, they are not known to everyone. According to St. Thomas, the very opposite is true: Not only are they known to everyone, but they are known plainly and right away.[19] Someone might be honestly confused about whether withholding the car keys of a man who is too drunk to drive is theft, but someone who says "How do I know that theft is wrong?" is not really ignorant about the wrong of theft; he is prevaricating.

Although the difference between genuine ignorance and willful self-deception is one of the most important implications of St. Thomas's theory of moral knowledge, it is also one of the most neglected – even among many Thomists. Endless confusion has been caused by the mistranslation of St. Thomas's remark in I-II, Question 94, Article 4, that "Thus formerly, *latrocinium*, although it is expressly contrary to the natural law, was not considered wrong among the Germans, as Julius Caesar relates." The term *latrocinium* is often incorrectly rendered "theft," which if correct would imply that the Decalogical precept against stealing is *not* actually known to all by natural reason – that it is not one of the first principles of law, but merely one of its remote implications. Actually, *latrocinium* is a Roman legal term which refers not to theft in general, but to banditry, or plundering – a particular kind of robbery, or taking by force, which St. Thomas distinguishes from theft, or taking by stealth, as did Roman law. The ancient Germans knew very well that banditry in general is wrong, for as reported by St. Thomas's source, Julius Caesar's commentaries on the Gallic Wars, they punished it severely.[20] St. Thomas is apparently referring to raiding against other tribes, which they refused to view as banditry.[21] This sort of evasion is not unique to the Germans; it has been going on since the Fall.

[18] Among the precepts omitted from the Decalogue are "first general principles, for they need no further promulgation after being once imprinted on the natural reason to which they are self-evident; as, for instance, that one should do evil to no man, and other similar principles." Ibid.

[19] Compare I-II, Q. 94, Art. 4: "the natural law, as to general principles, is the same for all, both as to rectitude and as to knowledge."

[20] In the sixth book of Julius Caesar's commentaries on the Gallic Wars, he remarks that the Germans considered such crimes as *furtum*, theft, and *latrocinium*, banditry, so detestable that on those occasions when they burned victims to propitiate their gods, they preferred to burn perpetrators of these crimes: "They consider that the oblation of such as have been taken in *furto*, or in *latrocinio*, or any other offence, is more acceptable to the immortal gods; but when a supply of that class is wanting, they have recourse to the oblation of even the innocent." Julius Caesar, *The War in Gaul*, Book 6, Chapter 16, W. A. MacDevitt, trans., "De Bellico Gallico" and Other Commentaries of Caius Julius Caesar, available at http://classics.mit.edu/Caesar/gallic. html (public domain). (For *furto* and *latrocinio*, MacDevitt has "theft" and "robbery.") Though Julius does not mention the more routine Germanic penalties for theft, such as compensation, these double the proof that they knew theft was wrong.

[21] This issue deserves more discussion, which I provide in the online *Companion to the Commentary*, the partner volume to my *Commentary on Thomas Aquinas's Treatise on Law*.

- Street thug: "Sure, I lifted the guy's wallet. But it wasn't, like, *stealing* or nothing. He was so drunk he didn't even know."
- Embezzling accountant: "Yes, I did transfer money from the corporation's account to my own. But I've done nothing criminal. What's a few thousand dollars to a company that makes tens of millions?"
- German tribesman: "I know I shouldn't rob my neighbor. But those guys in the other tribe – *they* ain't neighbors. They live way over in the other valley."

[3] The word which St. Thomas uses, *debiti*, has both the more general meaning of *that which ought to happen* and the more particular meaning of *that which is owed*. Every precept whatsoever conveys the idea of something which ought to happen. Precepts of justice convey this idea with special force, because the thing that ought to happen is owed to someone.

[4] The expression "at first glance" (*primo aspectui*) is central to the meaning here, for St. Thomas does not mean that in matters concerning himself man *really may* do whatever he pleases – but only that *this seems at first* to be the case. In reality, even where no one else is concerned, I may *not* do just as I please; I have duties not only to others but also to myself. The difficulty is that although it is perfectly obvious to me how I can owe something to you, I may find it obscure how I can owe anything to myself. It isn't that I don't know that I should love myself, for this is obvious to me. The problem is that I may fail to grasp that true self-love requires not doing as I please, but aiming at God in all things. The same point is made more clearly, and with the same expression about the "first glance," in an earlier passage in which St. Thomas gives two possible reasons why the Decalogue does not include any precepts about loving oneself:

Now there was need for man to receive a precept about loving God and his neighbor, because in this respect the natural law had become obscured on account of sin: but not about the duty of loving oneself, because in this respect the natural law retained its vigor: or again, because love of oneself is contained in the love of God and of one's neighbor: since true self-love consists in directing oneself to God. And for this reason the decalogue includes those precepts only which refer to our neighbor and to God.

... Now a precept implies the notion of duty. But it is easy for a man, especially for a believer, to understand that, of necessity, he owes certain duties to God and to his neighbor. But that, in matters which regard himself and not another, man has, of necessity, certain duties to himself, is not so evident: for, at the first glance, it seems that everyone is free in matters that concern himself.[22]

We see then that the Fall has put us in a strange condition: Although the fact that I should love myself is more obvious to me than the fact that I should love others, the fact that I can love myself only by loving God and my neighbor may not be obvious to me at all.

[22] I-II, Q. 100, Art. 5, ad 1.

[5] St. Thomas's reasoning here is highly elliptical, and the "hence" seems to come much too soon. Let us unpack the argument. With respect to the acts of justice, the situation is like this: Although I am quite aware of the general outlines of what I owe to God and neighbor, I may not be well disposed to render it to them. Therefore, it is necessary for the Decalogue to confront me with these duties, as though to answer my temptations by saying "You know better than that":

The notion of duty is not so patent in the other virtues as it is in justice. Hence the precepts about the acts of the other virtues are not so well known to the people as are the precepts about acts of justice. Wherefore the acts of justice especially come under the precepts of the decalogue, which are the primary elements of the Law.[23]

But I may be rather fuzzy about duties which do not concern what I owe to God and neighbor. Consequently, in those cases the great need is not to confront me with what I know already, but to instruct me in detail about what I do not understand very well. Therefore, most such duties are left out of the Decalogue and promulgated to me by other means:

[T]he precepts which prohibit disorders of a man with regard to himself, reach the people through the instruction of men who are versed in such matters; and, consequently, they are not contained in the decalogue.[24]

[6] "Wherefore" (*unde*) signifies a transition. We have just seen *why* the Decalogue focuses the acts of justice rather than on the acts of the other duties. Now we are about to see *how* it addresses them – which precepts command which acts of justice.

[7] As we saw in the discussion of the *sed contra*, the first three Commandments concern the fidelity we owe God in deeds, the reverence we owe Him in words, and the service we owe Him in thoughts. However, a pitfall lies in wait for the unwary reader in the statement that the acts of religion are the "chief part" of justice. The meaning of the word "chief" is clear enough: Our debt to God is infinitely greater than our debt to any other being. However, we may easily misunderstand the word "part" because of our tendency to forget the distinction among the subjective, integral, and potential parts of justice. Our tendency is to read the sentence as though religion were its chief *subjective* part – its most important species. This is incorrect, for as we saw in II-II, Question 80, Article 1, religion is a *potential* part of justice. It is not a species of justice, because in the strict sense it is not justice at all; rather it is a subordinate virtue associated with justice. Why is it not justice in the strict sense? Because to do justice to God in the strict sense would be to repay all we owe to Him, and this is impossible. Even if I love God with all my heart, with all my soul, and with all my might, I have rendered him infinitely less than He has given. Not only do my heart, soul, and might come from God, but my very power to offer these things back to God comes from God.

[23] I-II, Q. 100, Art. 3, ad 3.   [24] I-II, Q. 100, Art. 5, ad 1.

[8] As in Question 80, the term "piety" is used here in the filial rather than the religious sense: The Fourth Commandment is to honor one's father and mother. Yet in a certain way, the filial and religious senses are related. The parents are God's representatives to a child – a fact of such importance that some writers have listed the commandment to honor them in the First Table rather than the Second. Moreover, God is the Father of all, the one "for whom all paternity in heaven and earth is named."[25] Even the pagans to whom St. Paul spoke in Athens recognized that in some sense "we are indeed His offspring."[26]

[9] Justice is about rendering to others what we owe them, but justice in the most common sense of the term concerns rendering to equals what we owe them. We are certainly not equal to God, who is superior to us in every way. Nor are we equal to our fathers and mothers, the kings and queens of their family commonwealths, the natural rulers, guides, and protectors of their children. However, each of the other Commandments – against murder, adultery, theft, bearing false witness, coveting one's neighbor's wife, and coveting his resources and advantages – does pertain to our relations with our equals.

| *Reply to Objection 1. The intention of the law is to make all men virtuous, but in a certain order, namely, by first of all giving them precepts about those things where the notion of duty is most manifest, as stated above.* | Reply to Objection 1. Yes, law does aim at making men virtuous – but not all at once. For as we have explained, it begins with rules about matters in which it is especially obvious that something is to be done toward another. |

The pedagogy of Divine law aims at cultivating all of the virtues, not only justice. But like all sound pedagogy, it proceeds from the more known to the less known; it begins with the duties we all understand, even if we do not always follow them. Duty is clearest to us in matters in which something is owed to another, so that is where the Decalogue begins.

The pedagogy of human law is more limited, but arrives at much the same place, because although it aims to cultivate all of the virtues, it directs only those *acts* of each virtue which concern the common good. Consequently, whereas Divine law *begins*, in the Decalogue, with precepts about justice, human law is made up *entirely* of precepts about justice:

Now human law is ordained for one kind of community, and the Divine law for another kind. Because human law is ordained for the civil community, implying mutual duties of man and his fellows: and men are ordained to one another by outward acts, whereby men live in communion with one another. This life in common of man with man pertains to justice, whose proper function consists in directing the human community. Wherefore human law makes precepts only about acts of justice; and if it commands acts of other virtues, this is only in so far as they assume the nature of justice.[27]

[25] Ephesians 3:15 (DRA).   [26] Acts 17:28 (RSV-CE).   [27] I-II, Q. 98, Art. 2.

Reply to Objection 2. [1]*The judicial precepts are determinations of the moral precepts, in so far as these are directed to one's neighbor,* [2] *just as the ceremonial precepts are determinations of the moral precepts in so far as these are directed to God.* [3] *Hence neither precepts are contained in the decalogue:* [4] *and yet they are determinations of the precepts of the decalogue, and therefore pertain to justice.*	Reply to Objection 2. Even though we place judicial precepts in a different classification than moral precepts, they are related to moral precepts, for they *apply* moral precepts in order to specify certain details of our conduct toward our neighbors. In much the same way, ceremonial precepts apply moral precepts in order to specify certain details of our conduct toward God. This is why neither judicial nor ceremonial precepts are included in the Decalogue itself. Yet since the judicial precept do specify details of our conduct toward our neighbors, they do concern justice.

[1] The Objector had argued that if the chief concern of the Decalogue had been justice, then the Decalogue would have listed judicial precepts, not moral precepts. St. Thomas points out that this is mistaken, because the judicial precepts are *derived from* the moral precepts. As we saw above, there are two modes of derivation: Conclusion, which draws inferences from premises (as when we see that because murder should be forbidden, therefore poisoning should be forbidden), and determination, which specifies some detail which needs to be filled in (as when we specify that because people must be kept safe on the road, therefore everyone should drive on the right). The judicial precepts, which direct our acts toward our neighbors – of rulers toward the ruled, citizens toward other citizens, citizens toward "strangers," and members of the household toward one another – are derived from the moral precepts in the latter way. As St. Thomas explains, "The act of justice, in general, belongs to the moral precepts; but its determination to some special kind of act belongs to the judicial precepts."[28] Thus, many details about the judicial precepts might have been different with no injury to the universal moral principles which motivate them. For example, the rules of evidence might have required a different number of witnesses to a crime.

[2] The judicial precepts "have something in common with the moral precepts, in that they are derived from reason," for a universal principle evident to reason underlies them, "and something in common with the ceremonial precepts, in that they are determinations of general precepts,"[29] for something has to be added to them to specify *the precise manner* in which what reason requires shall be done. For example, reason tells us that there should be outward signs of our reverence toward God, but something has to be added to specify what signs shall be made.

[3] With but two exceptions, the Decalogue contains only the first principles of the law, knowable by reason alone, not those things derived from it

[28] I-II, Q. 99, Art. 4, ad 3.   [29] I-II, Q. 99, Art. 4, ad 2.

either by conclusion or determination. For this reason, it omits the judicial and ceremonial precepts.

A word might be added about the two exceptions. These are found in the First and Third Commandments, for the former specifies not only that God is to be reverenced above all, but also forbids graven images, and the latter specifies not only that times and places be set aside for rest and the worship of God, but that the Sabbath, in particular, be set apart. St. Thomas points out that *just because* these two Commandments are the only ones to include determinations, they are also the only ones which include any explanation; in the case of the other Commandments, no explanation was needed.[30] Because the Sabbath day observance is a determination, by Divine permission it can also be changed. Thus, under the New Covenant, the Lord's day is substituted for the Sabbath, since the Resurrection took place on the first day of the week.[31]

[4] The Objector had reasoned that justice lies in the judicial precepts *rather than* in the moral precepts of the Decalogue. St. Thomas corrects him by explaining that justice lies in the judicial precepts *because of their derivation from* the precepts of the Decalogue, which already concern justice.

Reply to Objection 3. [1] *Things that concern the common good must needs be administered in different ways according to the difference of men.* [2] *Hence they were to be given a place not among the precepts of the decalogue, but among the judicial precepts.*	Reply to Objection 3. Depending on the differences among the kinds of persons with whom they deal, various matters concerning the common good must be handled in various ways. For this reason, such details are set forth not among the precepts of the Decalogue itself, but among the judicial precepts.

[1] One might suppose that merely because the common good is "common" or shared by all, it must be administered in the same way toward all. A moment's reflection shows this supposition to be false. For example, we do not allow small children to operate construction equipment or drink whisky; though such rules are for the good of all, they obviously treat children differently than adults. The Objector is thinking of public officials rather than children, but

---

[30] I-II, Q. 100, Art. 7, ad 2. The gist of the explanation for the prohibition of graven images is that they would have tempted the people to worship created things instead of the Creator. St. Thomas suggests in II-II, Q. 122, Art. 2, ad 2, that the prohibition of graven images complements the prohibition of having strange gods before God, because thereby the worship of false deities is prohibited in both of its two forms – with images and without them. Interestingly, images which were part of the worship of the God rather than in competition with it were omitted from the prohibition, for we find that two golden images of cherubim were affixed to the mercy seat which covered the Ark of the Covenant. (Exodus 25:16–26). In explanation of the Sabbath observance, Exodus 20:11 comments that God rested after the six days of creation; Deuteronomy 5:15 (RSV-CE) offers the complementary explanation that "You shall remember that you were a servant in the land of Egypt, and the Lord your God brought you out thence."

[31] St. Thomas discusses this substitution in II-II, Q. 122, Art. 4, ad 4.

different kinds of public officials must also be treated differently, for the arrangements fitting for a king will differ from those fitting for a judge, and the arrangements most fitting for a judge will differ from those fitting for a public dogcatcher. Prudent judgment provides some guidance concerning such details, yet there will always remain a great many details which might reasonably be arranged in more than one way, and must simply be pinned down.

[2] Since the detailed arrangement of matters concerning the common good depends not just on universally valid precepts, but also on further decisions which could have gone differently – since they are not first principles, but determinations of first principles – they are expounded not in the Decalogue, but among the judicial precepts.

Reply to Objection 4. [1] *The precepts of the decalogue pertain to charity as their end,* [2] *according to* 1 *Timothy* 1:5, *"The end of the commandment is charity":* [3] *but they belong to justice, inasmuch as they refer immediately to acts of justice.*	Reply to Objection 4. As St. Paul wrote in his letter to Timothy, charity is what the precepts of the Decalogue ultimately seek to further. About that, the Objector is right. However, the means by which they do so are to command acts of justice, so they are precepts of justice.

[1] Everything in the Decalogue is ultimately about love – the love of God, or the love of neighbor for the sake of God. God is not pleased by the mere outward observance of the Commandments, without the inner motive of charity.

[2] More fully, the passage from which St. Thomas is quoting reads as follows:

Now the end of the commandment is charity, from a pure heart, and a good conscience, and an unfeigned faith. From which things some, going astray, are turned aside unto vain babbling: Desiring to be teachers of the law, understanding neither the things they say, nor whereof they affirm.[32]

St. Paul is making the point is that love is the whole purpose of Divine law; if we have no love, we do not even grasp what its precepts are for.

It may seem strange that St. Paul uses the term "commandment" for all of the Commandments together. However, we employ the same rhetorical device when we say "law," meaning all laws, or "language," meaning all languages. These are instances of *enallage*, the figure of speech in which one grammatical form is deliberately substituted for another – in this case, singular for plural.[33]

---

[32] 1 Timothy 1:5–7 (DRA).

[33] Enallage is not as well known in English as in inflected languages like Greek and Latin, in which the grammatical possibilities are richer. Yet even with us it is used to achieve particular effects, for example when Shakespeare frames a parallelism of form by having Macbeth say of Duncan, "Whiles I threat, he lives; / *Words* to the heat of deeds too cold breath *gives*" (*Macbeth*, Act 2, Scene 1, lines 60–61). I borrow this example from Bernard Dupriez, *A Dictionary of Literary Devices*, trans. Albert W. Halsall (Toronto: University of Toronto Press, 1991), p. 154.

[3] Although the *purpose* of the Decalogue is the love of God and neighbor, its precepts do not explicitly command "Love God and neighbor." Rather they command us to do certain things toward them, and not to do certain other things toward them, in the light of what they are owed. Precisely in this sense, they are precepts of justice.

Index

CPSIA information can be obtained
at www.ICGtesting.com
Printed in the USA
LVOW07*2111190617

538628LV00005B/116/P